1994

Maternity and Gender Policies

This important collection is the first to analyse the influence of women's movements on the emergence of Europe's welfare states and the limits of that influence. It reveals how these organizations influenced and promoted new welfare policies, particularly in relation to the needs of women and children. It not only examines these developments in the different countries, but explores state attitudes towards gender before and after the rise of the dictatorships in Germany, Italy and Spain, in comparison to democracies in Britain, France, Sweden and Norway.

These studies go further than revealing how European women sought to obtain more rights. By exploring how they sought to make effective use of them, they show that this widespread struggle for mothers' welfare was not a diversion from feminist goals, but intrinsic to the transformation to the gender-based distribution of resources and power in society. In emphasizing the role of women's history within a political, rather than a social context, the research throws new light on feminism, especially in the inter-war period, and makes a significant contribution to contemporary women's studies.

Maternity and Gender Policies

Women and the Rise of the European
Welfare States, 1880s–1950s

Edited by Gisela Bock and Pat Thane

London and New York

First published 1991
First published in paperback 1994
by Routledge
11 New Fetter Lane, London EC4P 4EE

Simultaneously published in the USA and Canada
by Routledge
a division of Routledge, Chapman and Hall, Inc.
29 West 35th Street, New York, NY 10001

Typeset in 10/12 pt Garamond by
Selectmove Ltd, London
Printed in Great Britain by
T J Press (Padstow) Ltd, Padstow, Cornwall

British Library Cataloguing in Publication Data
Maternity and gender policies: women and the rise of the European welfare states,
1880s-1950s.
1. Europe. Welfare services. Role of women's movements, history
I. Title II. Bock, Gisela – III. Thane, Pat 361.61094.

Library of Congress Cataloging in Publication Data
Maternity and gender policies: women and the rise of the European welfare states,
1880s-1950s / edited by Gisela Bock and Pat Thane.
p. cm.
Includes bibliographical references and index.
1. Family policy–Europe–History. 2. Motherhood–Government policy–Europe–
History. 3. Feminism–Europe–History. 4. Welfare state–History.
I. Bock, Gisela. II. Thane, Pat
ISBN 0415 04774 9

For Klara the mother and Mary Elizabeth the grandmother

Contents

Tables and Figures

Contributors

Ida Blom is professor at the University of Bergen (Norway), Department of History. Her research focuses on women and reproduction, life-cycle studies and women and politics. Her books include *Synd eller sund fornuft? Barnebegrensning i Norge c. 1890 – c. 1930* (1980, Sin or common sense? Family limitation in Norway, 1890s–1930s) and '*Den haarde Dyst': Fødsler og fødselshjelp gjenom 150 år* (1988, 'The hard fight': births and birthhelp through 150 years). She has published numerous articles in Norwegian and international journals on various aspects of women's history. She is president of the International Federation for Research in Women's History.

Gisela Bock is professor of social, women's and gender history at the University of Bielefeld (Federal Republic of Germany), and external professor at the European University Institute (Florence), where she was professor of European history from 1985 to 1989 and directed the project that led to this volume. Her publications include *Thomas Campanella* (1974), *Zwangssterilisation im Nationalsozialismus: Studien zur Rassenpolitik und Frauenpolitik* (1986), *Il Corpo delle donne: immagini e realtà storiche* (1988), *Storia, storia delle donne e storia di genere* (1988), 'Women's history and gender history', in *Gender and History* (1989).

Annarita Buttafuoco teaches contemporary history at the Università di Siena in Arezzo (Italy). In 1975 she founded *Dwf. donna woman femme*, the first Italian journal on women's studies, and was its editor up to 1985. Her publications on the history of prostitution, of poor women and of the women's movements in Italy in the nineteenth and twentieth centuries include the books *Le mariuccine* (1985) and *Cronache femminili. Temi e momenti della stampa emancipazionista in Italia dall'unità al fascismo* (1988). She is currently writing on women in the French Revolution and in the Italian Jacobine Republics.

Anne Cova is a Ph.D. candidate at the European University Institute (Florence) and the Ecole des Hautes Etudes en Sciences Sociales (Paris). She is doing research on the subject 'Women's rights and the protection of maternity in France, 1890s–1939', and has published several articles on the French women's movement and the history of child and maternity welfare.

Hilde Ibsen has been research fellow at the University of Oslo since 1990. She has written her thesis on the poor law system in the capital: 'Fattigvesenet i Oslo gjennom krise og reform, 1920–1940' (1988, Poor relief in Oslo between crisis and reform), and published a book about a Norwegian organization for fighting cancer: *Med kunnskap mot kraft* (1980, Knowledge against cancer). Presently she is working on industrial welfare in Norway in the twentieth century.

Jane Lewis is reader in social administration at the London School of Economics. She is the author of *The Politics of Motherhood* (1980), *Women in England, 1870–1950* (1984), *Daughters who Care* (1988), and will be publishing two books in 1991, *Feminism and Social Action since 1860* and, with David Clark and David Morgan, *Whom God Hath Joined Together: The Work of Marriage Guidance, 1920–1990*.

Mary Nash is professor of contemporary history in the Department of Contemporary History, University of Barcelona, and director of the Centre d'Investigació Histórica de la Dona, which she founded there in 1982. Her publications include *Mujeres libres: España 1936–1939* (1976, translated into French 1977, into German 1979), *Mujer y movimiento obrero en España, 1931–1939* (1981), *Mujer, familia y trabajo en España, 1875–1936* (1983), *Mes enllá del silenci. Historia de les dones a Catalunya* (1988), *Las mujeres en la Guerra Civil* (1989), *Les dones fan història* (1990), and numerous articles on women's and social history in Spanish, Catalan, English and Italian.

Karen Offen (Ph.D., Stanford University) is a historian and independent scholar, affiliated to the Institute for Research on Women and Gender, Stanford University (USA). She has co-edited two documentary collections: *Victorian Women: A Documentary Account of Women's Lives in Nineteenth-Century England, France, and the United States* (1981) and *Women, the Family, and Freedom: The Debate in Documents, 1750–1950* (2 vols., 1983) and is presently completing a book on the woman question in modern France. Her most recent publications focus on the comparative history of feminism and the historiography of women and the French Revolution. She is secretary-treasurer of the International Federation for Research in Women's History and will serve as 1991–3 president of the Western Association of Women Historians (USA).

Ann-Sofie Ohlander is associate professor at the University of Uppsala (Sweden), Department of History. Her English-language publications include *More Children of Better Quality? Aspects of Swedish Population Policy in the 1930s* (1980, under the name of Kälvemark), 'Swedish reaction against emigration', in H. Runblom and H. Norman (eds), *From Sweden to America* (1976), 'Illegitimacy and marriage in three Swedish parishes in the nineteenth century', in P. Laslett *et al.* (eds), *Bastardy and its Comparative History* (1980), 'Suicide in Sweden', in *Death: the Public and Private Spheres* (1986). She conducts the Women's History Seminar at Uppsala University and is currently working on the official view of the father–child relationship in the Swedish law on parental leave of 1973.

Chiara Saraceno is professor of family sociology at the University of Turin, Faculty of Political Science. Her main publications include *Età e il corso della vita* (1986), *Pluralità e mutamento: Riflessioni sull'identità al femminile* (1987), *Sociologia della famiglia* (1988), 'La famiglia operaia sotto il fascismo', in *Annali della Fondazione Giangiacomo Feltrinelli* (1979/80), 'La struttura di genere della cittadinanza', in *Democrazia e diritto* (1989).

Anne-Lise Seip has been professor of modern history at the University of Oslo since 1985. She started in the field of political history and the history of ideas, and is now working on the history of social policy and the welfare state. She has published numerous articles as well as books, among them *Vitenskap og virkelighet* (1974, Science and reality), and *Sosialhjelpstaten blir til. Norsk sosialpolitik 1740–1920* (1984, The rise of the welfare state: Norwegian social policy).

Irene Stoehr Berlin, is an independent scholar in sociology and history. Her main publications are *Emanzipation zum Staat? Der allgemeine Deutsche Frauenverein/Deutscher Staatsbürgerinnen-Verband, 1893–1933* (1990), 'Organisierte Mütterlichkeit: Zur Politik der deutschen Frauenbewegung um 1900', in Karin Hausen, *Frauen suchen ihre Geschichte* (1983). She is co-founder of the journal *Frauen und Schule: Zeitschrift für Lehrerinnen und Gelehrte, Mütter und Töchter.* Her research interests include women's history in the nineteenth and twentieth centuries, particularly the women's movement, female conservatism, the history of sexuality.

Pat Thane is reader in social history, University of London, and teaches at Goldsmiths' College, University of London. Her publications include: *The Origins of British Social Policy* (1978); *The Foundations of the Welfare State* (1982); and, most recently, 'The women of the British Labour Party and feminism, 1906–45' in H.L. Smith (ed.), *British Feminism in the Twentieth Century* (1990); 'Government and society in England and Wales, 1750–1914', ch.1., vol. 3, in F.M.L. Thompson (ed.), *The Cambridge Social History of Britain, 1750–1950*; 'The debate on the declining birth-rate: the "menace" of an ageing population in Britain, 1920s–1950s', *Continuity and Change*, 1990, vol. 5, no. 2.

Acknowledgements

We are grateful to many people who have made this book possible. We want to thank all of them, and particularly those who have been directly involved. The European University Institute in Florence, where the project 'Maternity, visions of gender and the rise of the western welfare states' was located in the History Department, sponsored and generously financed the project over three years; it provided the beautiful Villa Schifanoia for our conference in spring 1988 and subsidized this publication. Most importantly the spirit of that centre for intellectual exchange on matters of central importance to European history and culture has informed both the project and this volume.

Unfortunately it was not possible to include the contributions of all those who participated in the project. Bonnie G. Smith enriched the project with her transnational research on lower-class women's autobiographies and on middle-class women's studies of female poverty from the late nineteenth century ('On writing women's work', Working Paper HEC no. 91/7 of the European University Institute, Florence 1991). For various reasons we confined the framework to Europe, but we benefited from Elisabetta Vezzosi's work within the project on maternity policies in the United States from 1900–1935; her work has been published in *Storia Nordamericana* (1988). At our conference, Angela Taeger presented her research on changes in French family policy from nineteenth-century child abandonment to twentieth-century maternity policy, which has been published in *Francia* (1989); and Stefania Bartoloni made a valuable contribution on fascist maternity policies. Elisabeth Elgan and Jan Gröndahl dealt with specific aspects of the Swedish case; their contributions have been published in *Mother, Father and Child: Swedish Social Policy in the Early Twentieth Century*, editors Marie C. Nelson and John Rogers, Uppsala 1990. Karin Hausen presented lectures at the European University Institute on widows and the meaning of unemployment insurance to women in Weimar Germany, and Françoise Thébaud on the history of motherhood and child allowances in France. Frank Prochaska shared with us his knowledge of the religious motives of women philanthropists and of the mothers' meetings movement in Britain; this work has been published in *Historical Research* (October 1987) and *History* (October 1989).

Bruno Waanroij assisted with research on various countries when the project was at an early stage and Jutta Bischoff and Wiebke Kolbe helped at the final stages. Some of the first drafts of the translations (from Italian, German and French) were produced by Iain Fraser, the multilingual translator at the European University Institute, and Allan Grieco. William N. Dodd, a scholar in British literary history, was kind enough to give his time to translating one of the Italian contributions. Cornelia Usborne helped with a last-minute translation emergency. Lucy Thane has assisted cheerfully in re-reading and re-typing final revisions of the translations, supporting lovingly one of the editors, as did Volker Hunecke for the other editor. We dedicate the book to the mother of one editor and the grandmother of the other, taking up, in a different sense, the old formula which so often hides rather than highlights the contributions of scholars' wives to scholarship: 'Without them this book would not have been completed.'

Editors' introduction

This volume seeks to explore comparatively and transnationally, across seven countries of western Europe, some aspects of the relationship between the parallel development of welfare states and of women's movements between the 1880s and 1950s and the visions of gender which both of these processes embodied and helped to construct. At the centre of this exploration is the issue of maternity in some of its crucial aspects: as a life experience of women, as it appeared in the views and policies of the women's movements of that time and as an object of the policies of the rising European welfare states. Much recent writing about the history of women, of the women's movement and about welfare states has stressed the degree to which modern welfare reforms are about women.[1] Social policies of official or unofficial agencies are often, though not invariably, shaped by assumptions about gender relations, in particular about the gender divisions of labour, of power and of social responsibility, with their primary assumption of each adult woman's dependency upon a male earner.

The essays in this volume deal, to varying degrees, with three major groups of women whose history was shaped by the emergence of state welfare actions. These are, firstly, the women who lived in poverty, and particularly the mothers among them. Throughout the period under consideration here, and for long before, though poverty has not, of course, been exclusively a feminine condition, women have had a higher propensity than men to suffer deprivation. Their poverty often resulted from specifically female conditions, above all because economies have not been so structured as to enable them to support themselves and very often children at an adequate level, even though the death, desertion, sickness or unemployment of men so often forced them to seek to do so. The second group are those who were organized in, or affiliated with, the women's movements in all western countries. Around the beginning of the period covered here, these movements turned their attention to motherhood and the lot of mothers, particularly those in poverty,[2] but also to those mothers who were not actually poor but were dependent and at risk of poverty precisely because of this dependency on a man's work and income. Thirdly, there are the women who to a significant extent administered welfare provisions and policies, whether voluntary or paid, trained or untrained. Welfare states have opened new careers to women, though they have usually been more prominent at the lower and more localized administrative and policymaking levels. In certain respects such careers – as social workers for example – have reinforced the gender division of labour because they have been defined, often by women themselves, as primarily female and within the caring sphere. On the other hand, these women, together with the broader women's movement, created innovative welfare approaches – such as health visiting in Britain – that prepared the way for future social policies at large, for women's role in them and for a new vision of the relationship between the public and the private sphere.[3]

The welfare policies concerned and the ideas and ideals of gender relations underlying them have not been explored for all European countries or their precise relationship to legislation and its implementation analysed. And we know still less about how the women's movements of the past century, whether or not or in whatever ways they defined themselves as 'feminist' – a term that was coined, and became popular, at the beginning of this period[4] – have related to, been influenced by and sought to influence these processes. Hence this is a rewarding field for comparative study because it is possible to take a clearly defined focus: the women's movements which existed in all Western European countries, their perspectives on maternity and their relationship to state policies directly concerning motherhood. This is limited enough to facilitate comparison, yet of sufficient centrality to the broader topic – women and the welfare state – to be capable of yielding significant generalizations.

Studying the similarities and differences among individual nations raises a number of methodological difficulties which have surprisingly rarely been explicitly addressed.[5] Not only are there the objective difficulties of comparing complex national experiences, but historians of different countries come from differing historiographical experiences in terms of asking and answering different questions; both women's history and welfare history are at different levels and have different trajectories of development in the different countries. Fortunately, comparative approaches are widely practised in the research on the welfare states; but unfortunately, this research usually presents itself as gender-neutral, thus leaving out women and the issues that concern them.[6] For Britain there is a large number of studies of welfare state developments for our period, whereas for Germany such research is usually limited to the 1880s–1920s and leaves out National Socialism for which – in view of its inhuman features – the concept of the 'welfare' state has seemed to be inadequate; however, new approaches now also place this German experience into an international context.[7] Until recently, for Italy and Spain, the concept has hardly been used,[8] while, of course, it is central for the Scandinavian states.

In women's and gender history, comparative research is much less developed; this is obviously due to its having been neglected for so long. Different questions have been raised in different national contexts; for example, much more research has been done on Britain than on other countries in respect of working-class women's situation. In Germany, women's history initially focused more on domestic work than elsewhere. Currently, the balance is being redressed as work on women's and gender history everywhere expands, and this process is facilitated by frequent contact between scholars working in different countries and fields, of which this volume represents one example. The relationship of women's movements to the state, relatively neglected everywhere until recently, is now widely attracting interest and fruitful work.

Yet another problem for comparative history is that even the seemingly limited issues on which this book focuses still encompass many internal differences. In particular the women's movements present not only striking transnational similarities, but also strong internal heterogeneity. These essays stress the variety of strands and the vigour of debate within feminism everywhere. They stand as a warning against too simple chronological or other categorization of women's movements, e.g. the widespread assumption of a clear political and chronological divide – placed at different points in time in different countries – between the women's movements that predominantly promoted individualism and 'equal rights' and those that promoted a supposedly less vigorous 'maternalist' or 'relational', 'welfare' or 'social' feminism.[9] As with the history of women generally, it can often be better understood on a local or regional level than on a national one. On the level of policy, the essays reveal within each country significant regional and local differences in the introduction and implementation of reforms. The problem is to trace similarities and differences within and between nations in ways which are sensitive to, but not swamped by, the nuance of detail; to inform and to seek to offer useful generalization whilst remaining sensitive to complexity and detail, avoiding abstractions so broad as to offer elegance rather than insight.

Of course, this volume is no more than one step to such a vision of comparative history. We seek to stress the richness of women's history, its openness to new questions and new approaches and its relationship to social, economic, political and intellectual history. We wish to inform readers about different experiences in the past but also about different interpretations of similar experiences between contemporaries and historians; and to allow the reader to draw alternative conclusions about national experiences, transnational trends and comparisons, whilst offering conclusions of our own.

THE RELATIONSHIP BETWEEN RESEARCH ON WELFARE STATES AND ON WOMEN'S AND GENDER HISTORY

The reforms by which the development of welfare states is usually studied and which are compared with each other normally relate to a limited range of 'social problems': sickness, disablement, old age, unemployment, labour protection and the introduction of progressive income taxes. This literature deals at best marginally with policies to do with motherhood, fatherhood, childbearing and childraising. The conclusion cannot be avoided that the reforms normally highlighted are oriented mainly towards men and towards the alleviation of problems of members of the male labour force. In fact, in some countries – particularly in those where the early welfare policies were based on social insurance arrangements – they originally concerned only those who were active in the labour market and, since the majority of these were men, 'focussed on the male laborer rather than on women and children, the main beneficiaries of previous poor relief.'[10] At their introduction they were everywhere conceived as assisting the male who could no longer assist himself and his wife by his paid employment. Such measures of social insurance have been seen as the key feature differentiating modern welfare states from older programmes of poor laws or public assistance.

Yet this focus has underestimated or obscured the degree to which both social insurance and other welfare schemes were related, directly or indirectly, to women and particularly to mothers. In most European countries, including the classic welfare states of Britain, Germany and the Scandinavian countries, early and particularly later welfare reforms had an important meaning for, and impact on, mothers and maternity. Their indirect impact was to reinforce women's dependency on husbands who benefited from the welfare measures, and hence also to reinforce the gender gap in terms of income and (relative) poverty. On the other hand, certain welfare provisions which are rarely mentioned in work on the emergence of the welfare states were aimed directly at women and contributed to relieving some aspects of female misery and poverty, particularly those related to maternity. In some countries, such measures emerged as an appendix to mostly male-oriented reforms; in other countries, such as Italy and the United States, the very first steps towards a modern welfare state focused on women. Under the German health insurance law of 1883, female factory workers could obtain modest benefits for three weeks of maternity leave after the birth of a child (which implied that childbirth was considered to be a 'sickness'), but the benefits were minimal, optional and rarely paid, and only in 1924 were maternity benefits extended to non-employed wives of insured husbands. The British National Insurance Act of 1911 included cash maternity benefits for insured women and for the wives of insured men, and the Maternity and Child Welfare Act of 1918 encouraged the further development of local maternity clinics and services. In Italy, the Maternity Insurance Act of 1910 was the first effective national welfare provision, and so was the Sheppard-Towner Maternity and Infancy Act of 1921 in the United States. In France, too, several laws of 1913 on maternity benefits, on support to needy families with many children and on child allowances to civil servants preceded by far the introduction of a comprehensive national insurance scheme in 1928. In Norway, the Sickness Insurance Act of 1909 introduced cash maternity benefits for insured women as well as for the wives of insured men, and the Child Welfare Act of 1915 granted small maternity allowances, paid out of taxes, to poor single mothers, whereas in Sweden maternity benefits were introduced only in the framework of the National Social Insurance Act in 1931. In the Netherlands, a 1913 law on compulsory sickness insurance provided for maternity benefits, and in Denmark, such benefits were included in a voluntary insurance scheme of 1915.[11] Payments during maternity leave for women employed in the formal labour market were generally modest, and the provisions often differentiated between different fields of employment. Sometimes they were coupled with state services and assistance in childbirth and to pregnant and breastfeeding women, sometimes they were for employed women only, or married women only, and they generally incorporated some element of formal or informal discrimination against the unmarried mother.

Whereas these measures, which were introduced in the period before and during the First World War, aimed only at specific groups of mothers (mostly the needy and the employed), the period between the wars and shortly after the Second World War brought about innovations which had been hardly conceivable for most of the nineteenth century: state child allowances and a range of further maternal welfare provisions. State child allowances were introduced – with great differences in chronology and form – in most European countries: the *allocations familiales* in France in 1932, *Kinderbeihilfen* in Germany in 1935, *assegni familiari* in Italy in 1936, the *subsidio familiar* in Spain in 1938, family allowances in 1945 in Britain, *barnetrygd* in Norway in 1946, *allmänna baruhidrag* in Sweden in 1947, *børntilskund* in Denmark in 1952. Their form varied: for example in Britain they were universal from 1945, in Sweden from 1947, in Denmark not before 1969. The Netherlands had universal family allowances from 1939, Ireland from 1944. Upon their introduction, child allowances were rarely paid for the first child of the family. It is notable that a child allowance system was introduced in almost all European countries, but that they were absent in the comparable industrial societies of the United States and Japan; though universal family allowances were introduced in the former British colonies of Australia in 1941, New Zealand in 1946 (it was, after France in 1913, the first country to introduce a means-tested scheme in 1926) and in Canada in 1944.[12] At about the same period, income tax relief in respect of wife and children for heads of households, usually husbands and fathers, was introduced in most countries by stages: in Britain from 1911, France from 1917, Italy from 1926 and Germany in 1934 and 1939. This feature of state family policy has not been adequately researched, least of all in terms of gender.

The excessively limited focus of so many studies of European welfare states has indeed misled some into underestimating the importance and extent of maternal welfare provisions in Europe and to believing that before the Second World War welfare policies provided almost exclusively for male needs. To redress this imbalance, as this volume seeks to do, does not mean maintaining that such provisions considerably reduced the gender gap in poverty and income – they were usually too modest to achieve this end – but it may provide deeper insights into the changing structure of, and motives for, state welfare, into the history of women's lives and into the images of gender underlying men's as well as women's attitudes and policies. Indeed, the traditional research focus has led to an underestimation of women's contribution to the construction of welfare states. The study of the social and political forces which demanded, brought about, influenced or introduced welfare state reforms has focused mainly upon the labour movement, religious or lay philanthropic groups, left, progressive, liberal or conservative parties, prominent politicians and bureaucrats. The 'first-wave' women's movement, which was active throughout Europe from the early or mid-nineteenth century and which will be considered in this volume for the period from the 1890s, appears to have played no role in the history of welfare states.[13]

Yet in many respects and many places, as these essays show, it was precisely that movement that helped to bring about or influenced the introduction of maternity benefits, family allowances and other maternity- and family-centred policies. This was the case whether or not women had the vote. Annarita Buttafuoco shows how the demands of the Italian women's movement brought about the *cassa di maternità* in 1910 without female suffrage. Women's vote at the federal level and their other political activities strongly shaped the US Sheppard-Towner Maternity and Infancy Act of 1921, and it was considered to be a victory of the 'maternalist' strand of the American women's movement. No British women had the vote in national elections though one million of them were entitled to it for local elections when locally based child and maternal infant welfare services were introduced in the 1900s and maternity benefits in 1911, largely due to organized women's pressure; when it turned out that the benefits were being paid to fathers, they pressed strongly for payment directly to the mothers, and succeeded in 1913. Women were thus struggling not only for political rights, but also for social rights. Indeed, it was the experience of voluntary work among the very poor, and particularly among poor women, which led some women to demand the vote. They argued that male-dominated states had signally failed to remedy terrible social problems, which only states had the resources to do, and only with respect to the state could women achieve the right to access to such resources, a right which differed from mere hand-outs and from relief which depended upon the fluctuations of private philanthropy. Women's suffrage, citizenship and political influence were needed to remedy women's poverty. Hence from the earliest stage there were close links between the women's demand for political rights and for state welfare, which was understood as their social right.

The complex history of Eleanor Rathbone and British family allowances has been very extensively researched and commented upon, as shown in the contributions by Jane Lewis and Pat Thane, which add important further aspects, insights and interpretations to this history. The other essays in this volume demonstrate the strength of similar work which is emerging in other countries. They need to be seen against the background of a historiography of women which, in the course of its considerable expansion over the past two decades, has dealt less with the subject of this volume than with the history of female suffrage, of women's employment, contraception, abortion and issues of sexuality. The existence of women as mothers, their housework, experience of motherhood, maternalism as a perspective on certain cultural, moral and intellectual processes are of course dealt with in women's history because they are an inescapable part of women's historical experience. However, this has been an area in which interpretation has had the stamp of present-day ideas strongly projected onto the past. Today, stressing motherhood as an important feature of many women's lives is often seen as 'traditional', 'conservative' or even 'reactionary', by contrast with actually or allegedly more modern activities of women, and the main paths to women's liberation are seen as running through contraception, abortion and engagement in extra-domestic work. The situation of women is often analysed in terms of the sexual division of labour and true feminism is often seen as necessarily aiming for its abolition, as escape from motherhood and as the abolition of gender roles. This was not usually the earlier women's movements' view of liberation. Therefore some of the essays in this book – particularly those dealing with the earlier part of the time period covered – seek to reconstruct those women's voices when they speak on gender relations, motherhood, feminism and women's rights and not to measure them by present-day models and theories but by their own values and those of their own time.

A widespread though not uncontested view was expressed by Hubertine Auclert, apparently the first woman in Europe to describe herself as a 'feminist' with pride. In 1885 she challenged the leaders of the French Republic to declare whether the French state was to be a 'minotaur' state or a 'motherly' state: would it 'devour the blood and resources of its citizens through taxation and war' or would it 'nurture its citizenry offering security and work to the healthy, assistance to children, old people, the sick and disabled'? She believed that the role of women as citizens was to build up this nurturing attitude, extending to politics, to the whole of society, the capacities for caring required from women. The aim was to use the distinctive qualities and experiences of women to enrich and improve society, but equally importantly, to use these qualities as a basis for the empowerment of women and for a change in the gender division of power. The qualities conventionally associated with women should be accorded equal worth with those associated with men. Another French feminist, Léonie Rouzade, responded to the conventional claim that it was the male capacity to bear arms which justified their superior citizenship status with the comment: 'If one gets rights for killing men, one should get more rights for having created humanity.'[14]

This was an influential view within the European women's movements, as many of the essays in this volume demonstrate. It should be stressed that women who adopted this perspective did not argue that all women should have children, nor did they argue that all women must exclusively take on a nurturing role, in politics or elsewhere, or that this was the role that women should play for all time. Rather they argued that, as society then was, women had a tendency and were assigned and accepted the responsibility to be more caring, for whatever reason, that this was a desirable human trait, insufficiently influential in public policy, and that its influence should increase if society was to progress. Equally important for most of them was that women should be free to develop whatever aptitudes they possessed, be free to control their own lives in the present and future, and that it should be a goal of state policy to facilitate this. From this perspective, the liberation of women would be achieved not through their assimilation to and equalization with men, not in 'sameness', but in 'difference'. The traditional equation of female difference with inferiority was rejected, in favour of a vision that saw the sexes as complementary, equal in value and sometimes saw the female sex as superior to the male. In France, such notions were summarized in the slogan 'equality in difference'. The issues of motherhood, of women's domestic work, of improving the situation of mothers, of freeing them from poverty and dependency played an important role in this vision, and motherhood was seen as part of what made up the 'difference' of the female sex. Not only was the equation of such difference with inferiority rejected, but so also was its equation with 'biology', and 'motherhood is a social function' was another important slogan among radical and moderate women, in countries that were otherwise as diverse as France, Germany, Italy and Norway. The slogan expressed the claim for economic rewards, social recognition and political rights to be awarded to those who performed, with their hard labour, this 'function'; the more radical feminists everywhere demanded payment by the state of women's work as mothers, sometimes under the title 'motherhood endowment', sometimes under that of the 'mothers' wage', thereby challenging the sexual division between paid and unpaid labour. Ida Blom shows how the international dissemination of this view was sustained by direct and personal contacts among women across national boundaries. 'Motherhood is a social function' applied to bodily motherhood, but also, as Irene Stoehr shows for Germany, to a vision of 'social' or 'spiritual motherhood', understood as the caring activities of women who did not necessarily have children of their own, in extra-domestic professions such as social work and health care.

These essays contribute to exploring what was defined as feminism and its goals in the past in the contexts in which they were formulated. The discourse of feminism at no time inhabited intellectual and political worlds insulated from those around it, but was part of them, though obviously, like other strands of intellectual or political discourse, it had its distinctive preoccupations. This is also true for the gradual decline of this feminist discourse from the late 1920s and for its outright suppression in some countries. In part it was associated with a decline in the wider debate about citizenship, the search for and structures of democratic participation which was active and prominent throughout Europe in the period from the later nineteenth century, when demands by men and women for extended political and social rights rose to a peak unprecedented in modern history. In Germany, Italy and Spain these were abruptly silenced. Elsewhere, amid the crises of the 1930s and 40s attention turned rather towards mechanisms for central planning, to an enhanced role for the state itself to solve the problems of economic crisis and war. In the 1960s, few feminists of the 'second wave' took up the earlier heritage. As family size fell, childbearing was increasingly concentrated into a shorter period of early adulthood and fewer women had children, maternalist feminism seems to have lost its appeal. In comparison to the early twentieth century, employment conditions had improved considerably – even for women, and not least due to the pressure of women – and state welfare outside the traditional wage structure had brought them little autonomy. No wonder, then, that liberation, justice and equality now seemed to be more attainable if pursued through affirmative action in favour of extra-domestic work and private pressure on men to share parenthood, than through a maternal vision of the female sex and public recognition of maternity which had contributed so much to the shaping of the European welfare states.

COMPARATIVE AND TRANSNATIONAL DIMENSIONS: SOME GENERALIZATIONS AND HYPOTHESES

Women's movements and their ideas were, of course, far from being exclusive influences on social policies which particularly concerned women, nor were these policies exclusively directed at women. Rather, they should be seen as a complex mixture of policies that aimed at influencing procreation, combating poverty in general, determining wages and more generally shaping the situation of women. Anne-Lise Seip and Hilde Ibsen show, for the Norwegian case, how such diverse policies and interests shaped the emergence of state welfare over a long period, and how interest shifted from a mother-centred approach to one which focused on children. Clearly a major difficulty is to assess the influence of the women's movements in relation to that of other forces. Unquestionably the policies with which this volume deals are to a large degree transnational: they emerged in all the countries included here, and they emerged largely out of discourses in which concern about the quantity and quality of the population and the responsibilities of mothers in relation to this were prominent. The decline of the birth-rate was a matter of concern throughout Europe from the later nineteenth century, though earliest and most acutely in France, where it started soonest.

One of the initial responses was to seek to reduce the infant mortality rate, which was everywhere very high and everywhere, though at varying paces, declined significantly from the turn of the century. The role of maternity policies in achieving this is unclear, though it is likely to be only part of the explanation, along with the effects of public health measures, improved sanitation, improved living standards and the spread of knowledge about nutrition, health and hygiene. For women living in the very poor conditions which prevailed in most major cities, and for example in Italy also in the countryside, quite small accretions of such knowledge could make the difference between the survival or not of their infant, or their own health being ruined or not following pregnancy and childbirth. Such collections of letters from working women as those published by the British Women's Co-operative Guild in 1915, the German Textile Workers' Union in 1930 and mothers' letters to the feminists who administrated the US Children's Bureau contain many affirmations by women of how beneficial it was to learn about the importance, for example, of avoiding unnecessary heavy labour during pregnancy, such as whitewashing a room or cleaning windows.[15] Such information no doubt played a part in the decline in infant mortality. It also promoted awareness that motherhood could be less painful and distressing, that stronger children could be reared by fitter mothers who had greater control over the whole process of motherhood – that there was the possibility of 'conscious' or 'voluntary' or 'free' motherhood, as it was variously called by feminists of that time – and thus contributed further to the decline of the average number of children per family.

The concern with the falling birth-rate further increased in response to the population losses due to the First World War and then to the acceleration of the birth-rate decline almost everywhere in the inter-war years. By 1933, the birth-rate had arrived at an international nadir in Sweden (13.7 births per 1,000 population), Austria (14.3), England and Wales (14.4), Norway and Germany (14.7).[16] This led to varying degrees of panic and to pronatalist policies pursued with varying levels of rigour, extreme in Francoist Spain, mild in Britain and Scandinavia. Pronatalism was very strong in France, not only among politicians and panic-ridden organized male pronatalists, but also in traditional popular culture and, as Anne Cova and Karen Offen show, among feminists who either believed in it or used it as a rhetoric and tactic for demanding mothers' rights. Here, a combination of the efforts of male pronatalists, secular and Catholic feminists brought about considerable improvements for mothers; Ann-Sofie Ohlander shows that also in Sweden pronatalist ideas could promote reforms that were beneficial for mothers. But pronatalist policies nowhere produced a reversal of the trend in the birth-rate, which seems to have been responsive more to long-term changes than to direct government policy (see Appendix, Table 0.3). Nor did pronatalist policies, as is often maintained, lead women 'back' to 'home and hearth'. According to official statistics and apparently with the exception of Italy, women's extra-domestic employment did not decline and the employment rate even of married women appears to have risen in a number of countries, although during the world economic crisis of the 1930s there was much polemic against it, in all the countries included in the volume (see Appendix, Tables 0.1 and 0.2.)

Even though the feminist discourse of the time, in so far as it focused on maternity and the improvement of the lot of mothers, was a transnational phenomenon, it incorporated important variations in the different countries, particularly when it came to concrete proposals and policies. Whereas in Norway, Sweden, Britain and France feminists continued throughout the inter-war period to demand universal maternity or child allowances for all mothers for the period of childraising, regardless of their occupational status and actual poverty level, this seems not to have been the case in Italy, Germany and Spain. In Italy and Germany, some feminists had at times, particularly around the turn of the century, advocated some kind of child allowances for all mothers; but the Italian and German women's movements soon focused their attention on obtaining or raising maternity benefits for employed mothers (and the wives of employed men) to be paid during several weeks of maternity leave around the time of parturition, and particularly for the mothers of the working classes. For these demands – but not for those concerning all mothers – the women's movements won the support of the respective labour movements with which they, or some of them, were affiliated or co-operated. In all three countries, the initiative for family allowances to be paid also to families with non-employed mothers and over the whole period of childraising, appears to have come from the state, not from women.

Demographic anxiety was accompanied and reinforced by concern not just about the quantity of populations, but also about its 'quality', about the physical 'unfitness' of the mass of those who survived infancy. This anxiety was in part a product of intensified international competition from the later nineteenth century; it seemed that nations needed fit work-forces, fit armies and fit mothers to rear them if they were to compete effectively in an increasingly internationalized market, for imperial domination and in war. Thus demographic issues became closely linked with national sentiment and discussed in terms of the 'national stock', the size and 'quality' of the 'race'. Whilst this terminology spread rapidly, it must be stressed that it had different meanings in different contexts and that use of the term 'race' did not always imply racism, i.e. discrimination on grounds of 'inferior' ethnic or eugenic value. As Chiara Saraceno's and Mary Nash's essays on Italy and Spain show, it often meant little other than 'society', 'community' or 'nation'. In most countries, it could assume narrowly nationalistic overtones, such as when British welfare politicians warned of a British population decline which, compared to India's population expansion, would endanger Britain's 'status in the world', 'genius for colonization' and 'love of political freedom'. It could also assume European or rather eurocentric overtones and refer to western 'superiority', such as in the statement that 'All would agree that a decline to half its present size would make it very difficult for this country and other western powers to maintain their position and their present state of civilization. If the downward trend of the population were to become, as is threatened, a downward plunge, western culture and western ideals would go at the same time.'[17]

In National Socialist Germany, the widespread slogan 'not only quantity, but quality' of births led to a policy which was internationally unique; it may be seen as a political realization of Hubertine Auclert's nightmare vision of a 'minotaur' state of which she would not even have dreamt (the minotaur was a monster that killed and devoured women and men equally). As Gisela Bock shows, 'quality' was not just to be attained by reducing infant mortality and promoting infant care, but by preventing the 'unfit' and 'inferior' from being born, i.e. by eugenic antinatalism. The National Socialist policy of compulsory and mass sterilization began in 1933 and was one of the trajectories that led to the massacres of those considered to be eugenically and ethnically 'inferior', in particular Jewish men and women. Whereas only in Germany sterilization policy became a fully-fledged state policy and only there led to massacre, the underlying ideas were not limited to National Socialism. Eugenics or race hygiene was an international movement in the industrialized and predominantly protestant parts of the western world (i.e. not in Italy, Spain and France). Before the onset of the Nazi regime, considerable sections of the progressive currents everywhere had also taken up eugenic ideas, and small minorities in the women's movements – particularly some of the radical birth-controllers – accepted at times the eugenic and antinatalist advocacy of compulsory sterilization of the deprived and deviant; they did so sometimes in order publicly to legitimate their demands for abortion and contraception in the framework of an increasingly respectable discourse. Sterilization laws with provisions similar to the National Socialist law of 1933 were enacted in Denmark in 1929, in Sweden and Norway in 1934 and between 1907 and 1939 in 30 of the 48 states of the United States, though not at federal level. But their actual policies were comparatively mild. The number of those sterilized on eugenic grounds in National Socialist Germany was ten times that in the United States between 1907 and 1945; the number of compulsory sterilizations in Denmark, Sweden and Norway was minimal in comparison to Germany.

In other respects, National Socialism was less unique and was similar to the other European dictatorships which, taken together, strikingly differed from the countries with liberal-democratic parliamentary institutions and policies. In France, Britain, Norway and Sweden, state child allowances were payable from the time of their introduction or soon after to the mothers. In Fascist Italy, Francoist Spain and National Socialist Germany, the child allowances were paid to the fathers. Some of the essays in this volume suggest that this difference may be due to the fact that in countries with functioning parliaments women have exerted – despite their overall underrepresentation – more influence than in dictatorships where women were not able to influence political decision-making. The three dictatorships practised a thorough-going cult of masculinity, striving to reinforce male authority in the family, to compensate male workers for paternity and to develop a new vision of paternity as it was pronounced by Mussolini in a famous speech of 1927: 'He who is not a father, is not a man!'[18]

Another notable contrast is that in the democratic United States the first-wave women's movement was initially able to bring about services and financial support for needy mothers and children similar to those introduced in European liberal democracies before the mid-1930s, but they did not develop further, particularly after the repeal in 1928 of the Sheppard-Towner Act. There the historical process has not led to the implementation of policies universal in Europe (in particular maternity benefits and child allowances) despite earlier attempts to do so. By the mid-1960s the United States was the only developed country with no universal family support system. 'Welfare' retained the association long discarded in Europe with discriminatory handouts to the poor, and from the 1960s 'welfare' was rediscovered as a women's issue, that of the 'welfare mothers'. On the other hand, the United States did develop a system of tax exemptions for parents, the direct beneficiaries of which were mainly fathers, and which excluded or hardly benefited the poorest, who were beneath or only a little above the tax threshold. In comparison with the United States, there appears to be an intra-European level of similarity, whereas developments in Australia, Canada and New Zealand corresponded more to the European pattern than to that of the United States.

In much of Europe the introduction of family allowances around the time of the Second World War was closely related to bargaining among workers, employers and the state over wage levels. At a time when all European states were to some degree seeking to manage their economies and to establish full employment whilst avoiding inflation, family allowances provided a means of boosting income and domestic demand whilst holding back wage rises. Women had played an important part in placing and keeping family allowances on the political agenda, but lacked the power to bring about their implementation. In liberal democracies, they were, however, able to wield some influence over the final shape of legislation, in particular in ensuring that allowances were paid directly to women.

CONCLUSIONS

The European women's movements of this period formulated visions which gave a positive value to maternity and theorized that the sexes had, in the world of that time, some different characteristics and were active generally within different spheres. They did not formulate these differences in terms of 'biology', but in social and cultural terms, and they proposed that these differences be recognized and valued socially and culturally for the benefit of women as well as of society at large. Nor did they usually view them as more or less eternal or unchanging, but as the existing situation from which any programme for change had realistically to start.

The praise and valorization of maternity as female experience and of the female contribution to society was usually linked to a critique of the actual conditions and institutions of motherhood in a world which was increasingly dominated by competition and the 'struggle for life' both within and between the nations. Often, this approach led to a wider-ranging critique of the gender division of power. The feminist vision of motherhood was not simply the acceptance of a 'traditional' female role, but a call for reform – from some even for revolution – in the situation of mothers, of women and of society at large. Rather than having motherhood imposed upon them, they sought to keep it within women's own control and to improve its conditions; as Annarita Buttafuoco puts it for the Italian case, they were asserting not just the duties, but the rights of mothers.

The women's movements advocated equal rights or, more broadly, women's equality, but they also worked for the improvement of women's situation in those fields in which women were 'different', worked differently, lived differently from men, i.e. particularly in respect of marriage, the family, motherhood. Here the problem was not only to affirm the 'right to be equal' but also the 'right to be different' without therefore being considered inferior and being discriminated against. This vision of change in gender relations was expressed sometimes as a version of 'equality' in the sense of 'equal worth', sometimes as 'equality in difference', sometimes as insistence more on 'difference' than on 'equality', sometimes as the right to 'protection', sometimes – for instance in the French case presented by Anne Cova – as the demand for women to have 'the right to have rights'.[19] These concepts may be interpreted as attempts to formulate different versions of an equilibrium between women's 'equality' and their 'liberty', as a search for equality on terms which had not been formulated by men. As the German feminist Käthe Schirmacher put it in 1905: 'We live in a "man's world", created by man in the first place for himself ... For him equal value lay only in sameness; only assimilation could count for him as equality.' A female version of equality should give women freedom without their having, unless they chose, to give up features of life which many women valued; and to bring into being structures which made such choices possible. Despite all the differences between the women's movements of the first and second waves, there is a line of continuity in the search for the difficult conceptual, cultural, political and social balance between the 'right to be equal' and the 'right to be different' as an important feature of gender relations.

As to the relation between these visions of gender and the rise of the European welfare states, it seems useful to recall the words of Vera Brittain, a feminist since her youth in the years around World War I, who argued in 1953 that the 'woman's question' had been transformed into the substance of the welfare state: 'In it women have become ends in themselves and not merely means to the ends of men. . . . The Welfare State has been both cause and consequence of the second great change by which women have moved within thirty years from rivalry with men to a new recognition of their unique value as women.'[20] Today, probably few feminists would share this positive judgment on the welfare state. Nonetheless, the essays in this volume suggest several hypotheses which both support and question this view. Both women's impact and the shape of state policies have differed considerably in different European countries. The authoritarian welfare states, the dictatorships of the inter-war period, pursued policies that contrasted sharply with previous feminist maternalism, both in their common focus on paternity and in the uniquely National Socialist features of race policy which put a definite, consistent and deadly limit to state welfare. On the other hand, the democratic welfare states everywhere would look very different if their development had not coincided with the growth of women's movements and women's acquisition of citizenship rights – political as well as social rights. By working with and within other political and intellectual currents of the time as well as by insisting upon their own and unique contributions to society at large, they ensured that women's needs were incorporated into policymaking. They did not achieve all their short-term policy goals, still less their claim for full recognition of the economic, social and political dignity of motherhood, but they were able to raise and bring firmly into public discourse some of the important issues which are still with us and which are waiting to be solved through the further development of democratic structures in all of Europe which must respect the equal rights of women and men as well as the right to legitimate difference.

APPENDIX TO INTRODUCTION

At this period, the official statistics of all European countries seriously underestimated the work which women performed for payment inside and outside the household (with payment or without, such as was often the case in agriculture), and they underestimated it more than in the case of men. The extent of this underestimation may vary in different countries, but because of its very nature it cannot be calculated or compared between countries. After this period, the situation changes, but possibly less than one might assume; it

Table 0.1 Women as percentage of the economically active population according to official statistics in France, Britain and Germany, 1881–1961

France		Britain		Germany	
1881:	32.2			1882:	24.0
1891:	31.4	1891:	31.0	1895:	25.0
1901:	34.6			1907:	30.4
1911:	36.9	1911:	29.5		
1921:	39.6	1921:	29.5	1925:	35.6
1931:	36.6	1931:	29.8	1933:	34.2
1946:	37.9			1939:	36.1
1954:	34.0	1951:	30.8	1950:	31.3
1961:	33.4			1960:	33.4

Sources: for France, P. Bairoch, 'The Working Population & its Structure', in T. Deldycke, H. Gelders, J-M Limbor, *et al.* (eds), *International Historical Statistics* vol. 1, Brussels, Free University of Brussels, 1968.

For Britain, B.R. Mitchell, *Abstract* of *British Historical Statistics*, Cambridge University Press, 1962, pp. 60–1.

For Germany, Walter Müller, Angelika Willms, Johann Handl, *Strukturwandel der Frauenarbeit 1880–1980*, Frankfurt a.M./New York, 1983, pp. 34–5.

depends on the extent of unregistered ('black') labour, e.g. child-minding. The differences in different countries are also due to the differing weight of the agricultural sector in which usually a high percentage of women is employed. Furthermore, the statistical methods and categories of the official statistics and censuses have changed over time and have done so differently in different countries.[21] Because of all these problems, we have not attempted, in these comparative tables, to render the figures seriously comparable – this would require a project of its own – or to make calculations for all of the countries discussed in this volume. The figures are therefore only, and at best, illustrative of possible trends.

Table 0.2 Employed women as percentage of all women of employment age (France and Britain: 15 years and over; Germany: 15/16–60 years)

France		Britain		Germany	
1886:	40	1881:	39	1882:	37.5
		1891:	40	1895:	37.4
1901:	48	1901:	36	1907:	45.9
1911:	51	1911:	37		
1921:	54	1921:	35	1925:	48.9
1931:	47	1931:	35	1933:	48.0
1946:	47			1939:	49.8
		1951:	35	1950:	44.4
1962:	36			1961:	48.9

Sources: S. Pedersen, 'Social Policy and the Reconstruction of the Family in Britain and France, 1900–1945', PhD dissertation, Harvard University, 1989, p. 580; Müller *et al.*, p.35.

Table 0.3 Births per thousand population in seven European Countries, 1880–1950

Year	England and Wales	Germany		France	Italy	Spain	Norway	Sweden
1880	34.2	37.6		24.6	33.9	35.5	30.9	29.4
1890	30.2	35.7		21.8	35.8	34.4	30.4	28.0
1900	28.7	35.6		21.3	33.0	33.9	29.7	27.0
1910	25.1	29.8		19.6	33.3	32.7	25.8	24.7
1920	25.5	25.9		21.4	32.2	29.5	26.1	23.6
1930	16.3	17.6		18.0	26.7	28.3	17.0	15.4
1933	14.4	14.7		16.2	23.8	27.7	14.7	13.7
1935	14.7	18.9		15.3	23.4	25.7	14.3	13.8
1940	14.1	20.1		13.6	23.5	24.4	16.1	15.1
1943	16.2	16		15.7	19.9	22.9	18.9	19.3
1945	15.9	n.a.		16.2	18.3	23.1	20.0	20.4
		West	East					
1950	15.8	16.2	16.5	20.5	19.6	20.1	19.1	16.5

Source: B.R. Mitchell, *European Historical Statistics* (Abridged edition) London, Macmillan, 1978, pp. 21–36.

NOTES

1 J. Dale and P. Foster (eds), *Feminists and State Welfare*, London, Routledge and Kegan Paul, 1986; A. S. Sassoon (ed.), *Women and the State: The Shifting Boundaries of Public and Private*, Boston, Unwin Hyman, 1987; Jane Lewis (ed.), *Women's Welfare, Women's Rights*, London, Croom Helm, 1983; J. Goodnow and C. Pateman (eds), *Women, Social Science and Public Policy*, Sydney, Allen & Unwin, 1985; Carole Pateman, 'The patriarchal welfare state', in Amy Gutman (ed.), *Democracy and the Welfare State*, Princeton University Press, 1988, pp. 231–60; S. Michel, S. Koven, 'Womanly Duties: Maternalist Policies and the Origins of Welfare States in France, Germany, Great Britain, and the United States', *American Historical Review*, 1930, vol. 95, pp. 1076–1108.

2 Bonnie G. Smith, 'On writing women's work', Working Paper HEC no. 91/7 of the European University Institute, Florence, 1991.

3 For the United States see P. Baker, 'The domestication of politics: women and American political society, 1780–1920', *American Historical Review*, 1984, vol. 89, pp. 620–47.

4 K. Offen, 'On the French origins of the words "feminism" and "feminist"', *Feminist Issues*, 1988, vol. 8, no. 2, pp. 45–51.

5 Exceptions are G. M. Fredrickson, 'Comparative history', in M. Kammen (ed.), *The Past Before Us: Contemporary Historical Writing in the United States*, Ithaca, Cornell University Press, 1980, pp. 457–73; Pietro Rossi (ed.), *La storia comparata. Approcci e prospettive*, Milan, Mondadori, 1990.

6 P. Flora and A. J. Heidenheimer (eds), *The Development of Welfare States in Europe and America*, New Brunswick–London, Transaction, 1981; P. Flora (ed.), *Growth to Limits. The Western European Welfare States Since World War II*, 4 vols (European University Institute Series C, 16), Berlin, De Gruyter, 1986–87; Wolfgang J. Mommsen (ed.), *The Emergence of the Welfare State in Britain and Germany, 1850–1950*, London, Croom Helm, 1981. For a comparative approach that does not leave out women see P. Thane, *The Foundations of the Welfare State*, London, Longman, 1982.

7 G. A. Ritter, *Der Sozialstaat. Entstehung und Entwicklung im internationalen Vergleich*, Munich, Oldenbourg, 1989.

8 But see e.g. I. Colozzi, 'L'evoluzione del sistema italiano di "Welfare State"', in G. Rossi and P. Donati (eds), *Welfare State: Problemi e alternative*, Milan, Angeli, 1982.

9 For discussion of the diverse strands of 'first wave' feminism see esp. K. Offen, 'Defining feminism: a comparative historical approach', *Signs*, 1988, vol. 14, pp. 119–57; O. Banks, *Faces of Feminism*, Oxford, Martin Robertson, 1981; Naomi Black, *Social Feminism*, Ithaca, Cornell University Press, 1989; J. S. Lemons, *The Woman Citizen: Social Feminism in the 1920s*, Urbana, University of Illinois Press, 1973.

10 Flora and Heidenheimer, *The Development of Welfare States*, p. 27. For a similar conclusion, but from the perspective of poor relief in earlier times, see V. Hunecke, 'Überlegungen zur Geschichte der Armut im vorindustriellen Europa', *Geschichte und Gesellschaft*, 1983, vol. 9, p. 511.

11 For an overview see H. J. Harris, *Maternity Benefit Systems in Certain Foreign Countries* (US Department of Labor, Children's Bureau), Washington, Government Printing Office, 1919. For the Sheppard-Towner Maternity and Infancy Act: Lemons, *The Woman Citizen*; M. M. Ladd-Taylor, 'Mother-

work: ideology, public policy, and the mothers' movement, 1890–1930', Ph.D. dissertation, Yale University, 1986; E. Vezzosi, 'From Roosevelt to Roosevelt: women's welfare and maternity policies in the United States, 1909–1939', *Storia nordamericana*, 1988, vol. 5, pp. 95–114; L. G. Moore, 'Mothers' Pensions: The Origins of the Relationship Between Women and the Welfare State', Ph.D. dissertation, University of Massachusetts, 1986; J. B. Chepaitis, 'The first federal social welfare measure: the Sheppard-Towner Maternity and Infancy Act, 1921–1932', Ph.D. dissertation, Georgetown University, 1968.

12 P. R. Kaim-Caudle, *Comparative Social Policy and Social Security. A Ten Country Study*, London, Martin Robertson, 1973; Flora (ed.), *Growth to Limits*; C. T. Adams and K. T. Winston, *Mothers at Work: Public Policies in the United States, Sweden, and China*, London, Longman, 1980; S. B. Kamerman and A. J. Kahn, *Child Care, Family Benefits and Working Parents: A Study in Comparative Policy*, New York, Columbia University Press, 1981.

13 For example H. L. Wilensky, 'Leftism, Catholicism, and democratic corporatism: the role of political parties in recent welfare state development', in Flora and Heidenheimer, *The Development of Welfare States*, pp. 345–82.

14 H. Auclert, 'Programme électoral des femmes', *La Citoyenne* (Aug. 1885), cited in E. Taüeb (ed.), *Hubertine Auclert: La Citoyenne, 1848–1914*, Paris, Syros, 1982, p. 41; L. Rouzade, *Développement du programme de la Société 'L'Union des Femmes'*, Paris, 1880, p. 24; both cited in K. Offen, 'Minotaur or mother? The gendering of the state in early Third Republic France', mimeographed proceedings of the conference on 'Gender and the origins of the welfare state', Harvard University 1987; see S. Koven and S. Michel, 'Gender and the origins of the welfare state', *Radical History Review*, 1989, vol. 43, pp. 112–19.

15 M. Llewelyn Davies (ed.), *Maternity. Letters from Working Women* (1915), repr. London, Virago, 1978; *Mein Arbeitstag – mein Wochenende. 150 Berichte von Textilarbeiterinnen*, ed. Deutscher Textilarbeiterverband/Arbeiterinnensekretariat (1930), new edn by A. Lüdtke, Ergebnisse Verlag, 1991; M. Ladd-Taylor (ed.), *Raising a Baby the Government Way: Mothers' Letters to the Children's Bureau, 1915–1932*, New Brunswick, Rutgers University Press, 1986; for similar letters in Norway see Blom's article in this volume, note 32; in Italy: A. Buttafuoco, *Le Mariuccine*, Milan, Angeli, 1985. For a transnational analysis of such working-class and poor women's autobiographical documents in many countries see Smith (note 2 above).

16 B. R. Mitchell, *European Historical Statistics*, London, Macmillan, 1975, pp. 114–20. See the graphs in the articles by Blom on Norway, Offen on France, Nash on Spain. For an international overview on the reactions to the falling birth-rate, the best and most detailed is still D. V. Glass, *Population Policies and Movements in Europe* (1940), repr. London, Frank Cass, 1967.

17 Quotes from R. M. Titmuss, *Poverty and Population*, London, Macmillan, 1938, p. 53; C. Blacker and D. V. Glass, *The Future of Our Population*, London, The Population Investigation Committee, 1937, p. 165; P. Thane, 'The debate on the declining birth-rate in Britain: the "menace" of an ageing population, 1920s–1950s', *Continuity and Change*, 1990, vol. 5, pp. 283–305.

18 B. Mussolini, preface to R. Korherr, *Regresso delle nascite, morte dei popoli*, Rome, 1928, p. 23.

19 The importance of the 'right to have rights' has also been explored (though not in relation to the sexes) by H. Arendt, *Origins of Totalitarianism*, New York, Harcourt Brace Jovanovich, 1968, ch. 9. For some versions of the 'right to be different' see G. Bock, 'Challenging dichotomies: perspectives on women's history', in K. Offen, R. Pierson, J. Rendall (eds), *Writing Women's History*, on

behalf of the International Federation for Research in Women's History, London and Bloomington, Macmillan and Indiana University Press, 1991.

20 V. Brittain, *Lady Into Woman. A History of Women from Victoria to Elizabeth II*, London, Dakers, 1953, p. 224.

21 For the difficulties of using census material on women's occupations see, e.g., Müller *et al.*, op. cit., pp. 18–23; R. Wecker, 'Frauenlohnarbeit – Statistik und Wirklichkeit in der Schweiz an der Wende zum 20. Jahrhundert', special issue of *Schweizerische Zeitschrift für Geschichte*, 1984, vol. 34, pp. 346–56; D. Deacon, 'Political arithmetic: the 19th-century Australian census and the construction of the dependent woman', *Signs*, 1985, vol. 11, pp. 27–47; E. Higgs, 'Women, occupations and work in the 19th century censuses', *History Workshop*, 1987, vol. 23, pp. 59–80.

Chapter 1

Voluntary motherhood 1900–1930: theories and politics of a Norwegian feminist in an international perspective

Ida Blom

A spectre is haunting Europe: the spectre of a birth-strike. All the powers of old Europe have entered into a holy alliance to exorcize this spectre . . .

The expanding birth-strike, that has already started in the upper classes, is the vice that will force state authorities to give in to our claims.

These words are cited from an article written in 1913 by a German Social Democratic politician, Ludwig Quessel, and from a speech given by a Norwegian wife, mother and feminist, Katti Anker Møller (1868–1945) two years later.[1] They may represent the conflicting concerns of a large number of authoritative public figures, mostly men, and of millions of women all over Europe and the United States.

It would, however, be false to pretend that most women shared the ideas put forward by Katti Anker Møller in this quotation, and that the fear of the spirit of birth-strike was common to all male politicians and other officials. What the quotations do indicate is the unrest felt by most of 'responsible society' – men *and* women – from observing the sharply declining curves of birth-rates in most western European countries during the last quarter of the nineteenth century and well into the twentieth. By 1913 the reduction in working-class fertility had only just started to follow that of the middle class, and little change had so far been observed in fertility patterns in agrarian districts. The Malthusian fear of over-population was replaced by the neo-Malthusian and eugenist fear of seeing the multiplication of the 'poorest and least fit classes' at the expense of the 'the more prudent middle classes'.[2] Were an increasing number of women really going on strike as far as producing babies was concerned? And if so, what should be done about it?

Many answers were then – and still are – given to such questions. Among the host of replies, this chapter will focus on those of one woman who was central to the Norwegian feminist movement at the beginning of this century. My concern is to follow the channels of communication of ideas and inspiration to action across national frontiers at a period when the welfare state was at best a dream in the minds of some people and when worries

Table 1.1 Live births per thousand married women aged 15/20 years – 45/50 years, Norway 1891–1930

	1891	1900	1910	1920	1930
Towns	268	297	203	180	106
Country	264	304	234	235	166
Total	265	302	225	218	148

Sources: Norwegian Official Statistics, Census 1891, Tredje Række, No. 229, table 16. Census 1900, Annet hefte, table 3. Census 1910, Femte hefte, table 2. Census 1920, Tredje hefte, table 1. Census 1930, IX,70, table 8 give the number of married women in relevant age groups.
Norwegian Official Statistics, Folkemængdens Bevægelser 1891, table 7. Folkemængdens Bevægelser 1900, Fjerde Række, No. 64, table 7. Folkemængdens Bevægelser 1910, VI, table 14. Folkemængdens Bevegelser 1920, VII, 92, table 3. Folkemengdens Bevegelser 1930, Tredje hefte, table 1 give number of children born alive within marriage.

over birth-rates and over the emancipation of women put the concept of motherhood on the political agenda. I want to get behind the labelling of groups as feminists, socialists, Malthusians, etc., by analysing the theories and politics of one central individual, trace her connections at the international level and her friends and enemies in the national political field.

By studying responses to the theories and practical political actions of one individual, I hope to offer insight also into the reactions of different organizations and different political parties to the question of voluntary motherhood. Drawing on other sources I will try to judge how near or how far the ideas of this individual were from those of anonymous mothers. By placing her theories and politics in an international setting we shall see that she embodied ideas and strategies similar to those found in other European countries at about the same time. I shall argue that there was a lively contact across national borders between women and men of similar minds. Ideas inspired by such contacts were instrumental in formulating policies, but the reception these ideas got in the different national settings shaped the character of actions taken. Finally, this study may contribute to our understanding of

Table 1.2 Live births per thousand married women 20–49 years of age, Kristiania/Oslo 1890–1930

Parishes	1890	1900	1910	1920	1930
Centre	215	210	132	133	71
West end	223	221	142	118	67
North–east end	250	291	201	154	73
South–east end	257	273	197	166	74
Total	238	254	171	144	71

Sources: Statistiske meddelelser ang. Kristiania, 1891.
Statistisk årbok ang. Kristiania, 1900, 1910, 1911, 1920 og 1931.

what it took to be heard within a democratic political framework such as that existing in Norway at the time.

The first part of the paper will describe the theories of Katti Anker Møller as to what maternity should mean to women and the politics through which she chose to implement her theories. The second part asks what motivated her actions and which strategies she followed. The third part analyses her international contacts and reactions to her theories and policies at the national level. The concluding section attempts to characterize her with respect to central ideologies about motherhood.

THEORIES AND POLITICS OF A NORWEGIAN FEMINIST

'We love motherhood, we want to promote motherhood, but it should be voluntary and the responsibility should all be ours.'[3] This was the essence of Katti Anker Møller's theories of women's relationship with maternity. Endless numbers of speeches, articles and letters mostly between 1901 and 1924 show how such theories developed out of her initial concern for unmarried mothers.

Her theories about motherhood rested on two pillars: first, motherhood should be voluntary, and therefore women needed free access to contraception and abortion. Secondly, motherhood should be given equal status to a profession, presupposing formal schooling in all necessary knowledge about pregnancy, childbirth and child care. The state should be responsible for the economic independence of mothers, making it possible for mothers and children to subsist without the direct support of the husband/father.

In two lengthy and highly controversial articles and lectures in 1915 and 1918, she finally put forward a complete theory on maternity.[4] She built on nineteenth-century ideals of the separate spheres, but she constructed a world of female self-confidence and power on the concept of voluntary and responsible motherhood. She persistently argued for abolishing the differences between unmarried and married mothers. The state should take over economic responsibility for all mothers, paying them for the work they were doing when producing and raising children. A monthly state-financed salary from the very beginning of pregnancy, sufficient to keep mother and child healthy, should continue until the school system took over some of the responsibility for the child. The state should provide the mother with the same amount of money for every child born, making the bearing of children a viable source of income. Starting with needy mothers, this system should eventually reach all mothers, independent of the economic status of husbands. The important condition should be that mothers themselves took care of their children and did not pay others to do so. When such a principle had been accepted, Møller expected women to ask for even higher pay for producing a child, rendering this activity the best-paid of all women's work.

All measures needed to regulate and create the ideal conditions of maternity should be decided on and taken care of by women – from production and distribution of contraceptives and decisions about abortion via education in all aspects of child rearing and family planning, to assistance during normal deliveries. Møller made exceptions for complicated deliveries, and agreed with physicians that these deliveries were best assisted in hospitals.

Katti Anker Møller never confronted the problem of reconciling motherhood and paid work outside the home. She seemed to have seen motherhood as women's main profession, and only mentioned other work when she talked of poor mothers who had no other option but to contribute to the family economy.

Møller seemed to believe that what she called 'the emancipation of motherhood' would also strongly influence the development of society at large. A child would be a costly product, too costly to squander in wars. She cited the well-known Norwegian author, Bjørnstjerne Bjørnson, an intimate friend of her parents: 'When the women come, they will come with peace, because they come from the children's cots'.[5]

Her active involvement in politics started in 1900, claiming state assistance for unmarried mothers. She initiated the organization of two homes for unmarried mothers between 1902 and 1906, and she closely followed later developments in this field.

In close co-operation with her brother-in-law, Johan Castberg – a Member of Parliament between 1900 and 1926, Minister of Justice in 1908–10, and Minister of Commerce and Social Affairs in 1912–13 – she was instrumental in beginning and continuing a fourteen-year struggle for laws assuring children born out of wedlock paternal inheritance rights and the right to their fathers' family name. She provoked public discussion through her articles and toured the country lecturing on the importance of assisting unmarried mothers. She commented extensively to Johan Castberg on the propositions which were put to Parliament.

The laws were passed in 1915, and came to be known by the name of Johan Castberg, since he had propelled the propositions through Parliament. In the fierce battle for and against inheritance and patronymic rights, it was almost forgotten that the laws also provided a certain measure of economic assistance to needy – mostly unmarried – mothers in the months surrounding delivery, the first such help outside the poor relief system and entirely financed by public means. Municipal authorities, having the responsibility to carry out these measures, did, however, neglect them to a great extent, except for the bigger towns. In Bergen, the second largest town in Norway, around three-quarters of unmarried mothers were given this support by the mid-1920s; before 1940 all of them received it. But, although municipal authorities stressed the medical and moral importance of helping the mother nurse her child, economic support was kept at the lowest legally acceptable level. Care was taken to impress upon unmarried mothers their duty to support themselves and their children financially. Regulations concerning behaviour in the municipal home for unmarried mothers reminded these mothers that 'No mother should waste her time sitting with her child in the lap'. Idle profusion of loving care for the infant was seen as the prerogative of the married mother, who was not expected to depend on public assistance.[6]

The next step in Møller's policies was to widen economic support to include married mothers. Economic assistance during the time of pregnancy and especially during the weeks surrounding delivery was to be supplemented by free assistance from midwives. The Law on Health Insurance of 1909 included mainly unmarried mothers, but in 1915 wives of insured husbands were given the same support. In the same way as when she was fighting for better conditions for unmarried mothers, she campaigned from 1911 to 1914 for this broadening of insurance policies, this time in co-operation with the Norwegian National Council of Women (NNCW, the Norwegian branch of the International Council of Women, ICW). She instigated a resolution to the government from this organization in 1913, which was extensively cited in the government proposal to the *Storting* (Parliament) the same year. A variety of local women's organizations of all political shades also sent resolutions supporting the proposal. This support was referred to as important during the debate in the *Storting*, but an opponent of women's suffrage warned against attributing any importance to what he called 'the hysterical part of Norwegian women'. When in 1915 the law was enacted, the magazine of the Norwegian Association for Women's Rights greeted it as a direct result of votes for women, which had been adopted in 1913. Again Møller co-operated with her brother-in-law, Johan Castberg, sending him accounts of German and English legislation in the field.

Her vision was, however, assistance to all mothers, paid through general taxation, not on an insurance basis, partly paid by the insured themselves.[7] The municipal 'mothers' pension' carried through in Oslo in 1919, therefore, was more in line with her ideas. Though no direct evidence has been found to support it, her close co-operation with the women of the Labour Party and the public discussions raised by her lectures and articles, make it seem likely that she was involved in paving the way for the Oslo mothers' pension. Some of her ideas came to be accepted by the Labour Party, when in 1923 the party set up a committee to discuss a 'mother's wage'. At the time, Møller was very busy organizing the first maternity clinic in the country, though her sister, Ella Anker, was a member of the Labour Party committee.[8]

The idea of motherhood as a profession also meant providing women with education in the field. Starting at school level, Katti Anker Møller wanted to see education in all the aspects of mothering built into a fully-fledged system, ending at university level. Her contribution lay in having information and a text-book prepared for this purpose and using her influence to have the theme incorporated in the curricula of existing schools of home economics.

But she was disappointed to find that almost all such books were written by male doctors. She disliked their admonishing patriarchal tendencies, the critical attitude to mothers, and what she found to be misleading concepts of women as preferring a leisurely existence to that of responsible and hard-working mothers. She maintained that women generally did want children, and that economic problems were common reasons why mothers were unable to nurse their new-born children for long enough. Another reason in her opinion, was the fact that husbands urged another pregnancy on wives quickly after birth.

There is local and national evidence that she was not alone in reacting negatively to the doctors' criticism of mothers' way of looking after children. Energetic attempts at persuading mothers to change traditions of nursing their babies by spreading systematic information on new methods were disregarded by mothers and had little or no effect on the numbers of mothers nursing their children and on infant mortality. In 1940 fewer mothers breast-fed than in 1911.[9]

Finally, the other important plank of her theory was that motherhood should be voluntary. This meant free information on contraception as part of women's education. In 1907 she started taking measures to have this taught in schools and getting a book written on female health, including advice on contraception. Soon similar attempts were made by women in the Labour Party. The chapter on contraception was, however, taken out of the manuscript in 1916, because of opposition from the NNCW who sponsored the book.[10] But in 1924, in the face of strong opposition, the fight for free information on contraception led to the first Norwegian maternity clinic. It was located in Oslo, but served women from all over the country.

Contraception was an important help in ensuring voluntary motherhood. If this failed, abortion was the final measure. In 1913 and 1915 Møller reacted strongly against court decisions punishing women who had had or helped assist in abortions. In 1915 she coined the now well-known phrase: 'The base for all freedom is the right to decide over our own bodies and over what they contain. The opposite is slavery'. Having achieved the vote – gradually between 1901 and 1913 – women were in her opinion no longer disposed to accept enforced motherhood. She was the first to point to the inconsistency of arguments claiming abortion effected by trained doctors to be legitimate, but condemning abortions undertaken by midwives and other women.[11] She wanted to decriminalize abortion and was especially critical of punishments of women involved in terminating a pregnancy.

In spite of prolonged struggles in the 1930s and again in the 1950s, this programme did not become reality until the abortion law of 1978 was enacted. The abortion campaign involved Katti Anker Møller's daughter and her granddaughter.[12]

To promote healthy deliveries under female guidance Møller worked to improve the education of midwives and was instrumental in the process which started in 1916 of establishing local maternity homes, especially in the towns. For mothers who could not afford the necessary outfit and the assistance of a midwife in their homes, she advocated local maternity homes, run by midwives and assuring a comfortable and homely atmosphere.[13] But the maternity homes successfully established in Oslo and other cities from 1916 before long developed into maternity clinics under the supervision of male doctors and with a close resemblance to hospital wards.

Møller advocated painless deliveries, but maintained that complicated deliveries should take place in hospitals. She never opposed the process of shifting an increasing proportion of births from women's own homes to hospitals and never expressly voiced the wish to see more female obstetricians or gynaecologists. She seems to have taken for granted that even in hospitals most help would be given by midwives. But her policy of working as far as possible in co-operation with the medical profession may have resulted in somewhat inconsistent ideas at this point.

Born and raised within the liberal intelligentsia, married into a liberal agrarian family of some means, how did this woman come to take up such ideas and to contribute as much as she did to putting such views into practice? What was her relationship to the feminist movement and other contemporary movements active in the same fields? From whom did she find inspiration and support? And what strategies did she use when trying to implement her visions?

MOTIVATION AND STRATEGY

It seems fair to maintain that her initial involvement sprang from personal experience in her youth and during her early years of marriage. Later she developed wide and lively contacts with people of the same mind, especially in Germany and Great Britain.

The fourth child of parents who ran a liberal Lutheran school for adolescents, Katti Anker Møller soon had six more sisters and brothers. She was very close to her mother, and suffered at seeing her struggling through pregnancies and childbirths. The eighth child, a handicapped boy, was taken over by the grandparents, the ninth, a girl, died of pneumonia at the age of 12 months, and the tenth, also a girl, was given away to childless friends of her parents. All this testifies to the grave burden ten children imposed on the mother. It explains the impact on Katti when, at the age of 15, her mother told her that she now, belatedly, understood that women did not have to bear so many children, and that using means to avoid pregnancies was not a sin, but a right. Katti herself, although marrying at the age of 20, had only three children.

As a wife she became responsible for running a landed estate, employing 10–11 domestic servants and with close contact with neighbouring families of farmers, farmhands, and crofters. She was deeply impressed by the lives of the crofters' wives, their hard work and many children, and even more by the tragic fates of some of the unmarried mothers she met in and out of her own household. In 1901, when women were granted a limited franchise at municipal elections, she was already engaged in discussions in the journal *Nylænde*, a journal close to the Norwegian Association for Women's Rights. For Møller the vote meant a strong obligation to change what she felt was wrong in society.[14]

A few years later – in 1903–4 – she was involved in organizing the NNCW. The Labour Party's Women's Organization wanted her on the board. As they later decided not to join the NNCW, Møller nevertheless tried for some years to promote her radical ideas from within its board, but withdrew when such a strategy proved impossible. In spite of many disappointments, she continued to try to spread her ideas both through this influential and respected organization and through the women's organizations within the Liberal Party. Her heart – and possibly also her actual membership – was, however, with the women of the Labour Party, with whom she developed close co-operation from the beginning of the century through work for unmarried mothers.[15]

Arousing public opinion through articles and lectures and in 1916–17 through an exhibition on maternity homes that toured the major towns, she made efforts to influence public politics. At the same time she used all the informal channels of influence open to one of her social position, approaching ministers and well-known medical men, and even the Queen, to get support. Her relationship with organizations as different as the Norwegian branch of the ICW and the Labour Party's Women's Association is an example of how she managed to rally a very wide range of supporters.

She also found connections and important inspiration abroad.

INTERNATIONAL NETWORKS

Scandinavian ties were very pronounced in Katti Anker Møller's family and social environment. It is no surprise therefore that she read the pamphlets on contraception by the Swedish socialist Hinke Berggreen. For some time in 1912–13 Møller co-operated with Frida Steenshof who at the time headed the organization *Svensk Förening för Moderskydd och Sexualreform* (Swedish Association for Protection of Mothers and Sexual Reform), later the *Sällskapet för Humanitär Barnalstring* (Society for Humanitarian Child Care).[16] Considering how close her ideas were to those of Ellen Key, put forward in 1900 and 1904, it is surprising that there seems to be no sign of connection between the two women. They may have had differing views on central strategies, such as abortion. It is even more surprising that as far as sources can tell Møller also had no contact with Elise Ottesen Jensen, a socialist woman of Norwegian extraction who played a significant role in Swedish struggles for family planning and who in 1959 became president of the International Planned Parenthood Federation. Differences in age may be part of the explanation, but should not have prevented contact.[17] Nor should anti-Swedish feelings occasioned by the abrogation of the political union between the two countries in 1905, seeing that Ellen Key supported a peaceful agreement on the question, and that Møller had other close Swedish friends.[18]

It is interesting to notice that Møller seems to have had no connections in France, in spite of the fact that she spent some time there in her youth and mastered the language very well. Her ideas resembled closely those of Nelly Roussel and of Madeleine Vernet and the group surrounding her, a fact that indicates parallel national feminist responses to similar social and population changes.[19]

But her ties first to Germany, then Great Britain played an important role. In 1904 she spoke on unmarried mothers at the conference of the ICW in Berlin.[20] She met Charlotte Perkins Gilman and was very impressed by her. She also met other American and British feminists, and the German Marie Stritt, who was among the group leading the *Bund für Mutterschutz* in 1905. From at least 1912 she took Helene Stöcker's journal *Die neue Generation* (up to 1908 it had the title *Zeitschrift für Mutterschutz und Sexualreform*), where she found some of the same views as those she was herself defending.[21]

Her writings and speeches have certain similarities with the thoughts of Helene Stöcker, though she did not agree with Stöcker's commitment to gender reconciliation. Her reasoning around solutions to the problems for unmarried mothers, her attitude to abortion and to family planning, as well as her very moderate eugenic tendencies, seem to harmonize with the German *Bund für Mutterschutz und Sexualreform* (League for the Protection of Mothers and Sexual Reform). Her opinion on marriage was in line also with that of Marie Stritt, who was on the board of the *Bund* and also President of the *Bund Deutscher Frauenvereine* (1899–1910). Møller wanted marriage to be a union of two equal partners and advocated the idea that it was not the religious ceremonies, but the coming of a child that constituted the start of marriage. She preferred to do away with clerical marriages and for women to stop abandoning their maiden surname when they married.[22]

If German and a few Swedish connections played an important role in the starting phase of Katti Anker Møller's work, the most important inspiration was later to come from Great Britain. In 1912 she assisted at the First International Eugenics Congress in London, and was repelled by the members' way of reasoning. But she met – and was attracted to – the leaders of the Malthusian League for their interest in alleviating poverty by family planning. She took their journal for many years, and her correspondence shows that she was approached in August and November 1912 by the Dutch Dr Johannes Rütger and the British Dr Drysdale of the Malthusian League with a view to establishing a Norwegian branch. The following year she became a member of the *Internationale Vereinigung für Mutterschutz und Sexualreform* and corresponded extensively with Frida Steenhof on the possibility of some Norwegian organization. She planned to call it *Kundskap og Ansvar* (Knowledge and Responsibility), but gave up in the face of opposition created by her opinions on contraception and abortion.[23]

She sympathised with the suffragettes, and although there is no sign of personal connection with that movement, the thoughts of Eleanor Rathbone, President of the National Union of Societies for Equal Citizenship and of Mary Stocks, executive member of the same organization, were in important respects close to Møller's. Family allowances and free access to contraception became part of the programme of NUSEC in 1925. But Rathbone's opinion on unmarried mothers ran directly counter to Møller's work. There is reason to believe that Katti Anker Møller furnished the Norwegian law commission working on the drafting of the Law on Health Insurance of 1915 with information on the outcome of the protest of British women against having maternity benefit paid to the husband, and the success of their protests in 1913.[24]

As from 1914 she exchanged letters with Margaret Llewelyn Davies, of the Women's Co-operative Guild, who in 1919 sent her Marie Stopes' books. By then, however, Møller had already started out on a very similar road of action to the one taken by Marie Stopes.[25]

In 1918 she tried to convince the Women's Organization of the Liberal Party that they should support her idea of a mothers' clinic, giving information on and practical assistance in contraception. In March 1919 they strongly rejected her plan. Even her approach to the Labour Party's Women's Organization had no immediate effect, although the party had paid for her lectures of 1915 and 1918 to be printed and distributed. She then translated into Norwegian Stopes' pamphlet 'A Letter to Working Mothers on How to Have Healthy Children and Avoid Weakening Pregnancies', omitting Stopes' rejection of abortion. The pamphlet was published by the Labour Party, and although it was sold cheaply the profit provided the initial funding for the mothers' clinic.

In 1922 Møller went to London to study the functioning of Marie Stopes' clinics. Like Stopes she co-operated closely with doctors and medical authorities whenever it was possible to find supporters in those quarters. Even when the Medical Faculty rejected her idea that it should take responsibility for the diffusion of her translation of Stopes' brochure, she found verbal support from the majority of the medical professors. They admitted that economic and health reasons as well as in some instances eugenic reasons might legitimize the use of contraception. Katti Anker Møller repeatedly referred to these arguments to win support for her further actions.

The Oslo mothers' clinic opened in 1924 and was a success. It was started as a shareholding company with Møller as the chief shareholder, led by a board consisting of women representing the Social Democratic Party, the

Norwegian Communist Party and the Labour Party and with the full support of the local branch of the Labour Party. Even the venomous campaign resulting from the splits in the Labour Party in 1921 and 1923 did not succeed in stopping co-operation between women who were members of the three parties, as far as the mothers' clinic was concerned. In 1926 the Oslo branch of the Labour Party took over the majority of the shares in the clinic. From 1930 the Oslo municipal council, and from 1934 also the neighbouring Aker municipal council, decided to support the clinic, and from 1931 so did the Oslo Health Insurance Office.

By 1937 similar clinics were established in thirteen other towns and were under preparation in another six localities. All except one were started by the women in the Labour Party, the Social Democratic Party and the Communist Party and gave advice on contraception. The only exception was the one in Bergen. Dominated as it was by conservative women of the *Husmorforbundet* (The Housewives' Association) it mostly concerned itself with advice to mothers on child care and only gave advice on contraception at the instigation of doctors. This clinic resembled the much more numerous clinics built up by the *Norske Kvinners Sanitetsforening* (Norwegian Women's Public Health Association), founded in 1896 and soon becoming one of the largest women's associations with many local groups. At these clinics assistance and advice was given on breast-feeding and other infant-care problems, but not on contraception.[26] In 1939, however, the clinics built up by Møller and the socialist women obtained the same financial support from government as the clinics run by the Norwegian Women's Public Health Association.

NATIONAL REACTIONS

There is no doubt that socialist ideas made a deep impact on Katti Anker Møller. As we have seen, she co-operated closely with women central to the Labour Party's Women's Organization, and she may even have been a party member.[27] Like the Labour Party she preferred public assistance to needy mothers financed through taxation, not through the insurance system. Her phrasing was clearly inspired by socialist theories. She referred to Marx and Bebel, asserting that they would have agreed with her had they known her thoughts about the 'emancipation of motherhood'. She claimed that state responsibility for production as such should be paralleled by state responsibility for the production of children, i.e. making the state responsible for the economic maintenance of mothers and children. She talked about the 'birth-strike' and 'mothers' fight for better wages'; she likened maternity to production, induced women to 'produce sparingly so as to make their product, the babies, more expensive' and thus bring up wages. This way of expressing herself was especially clear in the years between 1915 and 1918, and was met with fierce criticism, even from socialist women, for neglecting the vocation of motherhood and the feelings binding mother, child and father in a union of love.[28]

However, she did not advocate collective child care, and her socialism was more in line with the radical liberal approach, also found in her brother-in-law Johan Castberg, the leader of the small party *Arbeiderdemokratene* (The Workers' Democratic Party).

Some of the socialist women found co-operation with Møller problematic. Her constant attack on working-class husbands and pronounced feminist views made them protest that her activity would split the working class along gender lines, when co-operation was needed to revolutionize society.

Many middle-class women – and men – were friendly and supportive of her move to establish municipal maternity homes and broaden the education of girls for motherhood. But the same people were horrified by most of her other policies. Even the women's organization within the Liberal Party – despite the fact that in 1918 they adopted part of her idea of wages for mothers, to be limited to needy mothers – was otherwise very reluctant to support her, and mostly avoided doing so. She met strong opposition to her activities to combat criminalization of abortions and to spread knowledge on contraception from important persons like the well-known writer Sigrid Undset, who was awarded the literary Nobel prize in 1928, and from influential organizations like the NNCW, as well as the numerous and influential *Sedelighets/Moralvernforeningene* (Organizations for the Promotion of Sexual Respectability and Morality). These latter organizations were members of the NNCW and had an important influence upon the politics adopted there. Leading positions in both of these organizations were at times filled by the same women, some of whom also headed the Norwegian Housewives' Association, another strong opponent of Katti Anker Møller's, in the inter-war years growing to become one of the biggest organizations for Norwegian women. Together and separately these three organizations did their utmost to prevent advertising and information on contraception, and supported legal action taken in 1927 to strangle the activity of the Oslo Mothers' Clinic. They did not succeed.[29]

In 1919, although they co-operated in Møller's work to provide municipal maternity homes, the NNCW refused to allow her to give her talk on 'Wages for Mothers' at their annual meeting and turned down all proposals from her. But in 1920 she gave a speech on the subject at the ICW meeting, held in Oslo. The principle of wages for mothers was accepted after a long and lively debate, but with the restriction, not contained in Møller's proposal, that it only should apply to needy mothers. One of the radical liberal papers reminded its readers of the refusal of support from the Women's Organization of the Liberal Party two years earlier and qualified the acceptance by the ICW as a 'splendid reward' for Møller, 'being supported by a world conference'. Her brother-in-law congratulated her on her 'conspicuous international victory'.[30]

It can be no surprise that the clergy protested at her views. There was little to indicate acceptance of contraception on the part of the Norwegian clergy before 1940. Among doctors the head of the Bergen Maternity Hospital and other influential obstetricians warned strongly against Møller's ideas. So did the majority of the Medical Faculty at Oslo University – at the time the only Norwegian university. But younger and more liberal doctors, and especially the socialist doctors, during the inter-war years came to accept contraception, primarily as a means to reduce the growing number of illegal abortions, but also as a help to strengthen family economy and improve the health of children and mothers. Eugenic and population arguments figured in the broad discussion of these problems, sparked off by the opening of the Oslo Mothers' Clinic in 1924, and in the 1930s by demands for liberalization of the criminal code on abortion. Some of the defenders of voluntary motherhood even argued that contraception was important as a pre-condition for women's emancipation.[31]

VOLUNTARY MOTHERHOOD – THE FINAL AIM OF FEMINISM OR PART OF EUGENIC AND MALTHUSIAN POLITICS?

An analysis of women's reasons for family planning between 1900 and 1930 has shown that east-end as well as west-end mothers in Oslo – although in extremely different settings – admitted anxiety as to the economic problems of the family, worries over the health of the children born, as well as over the health of the mother as prominent reasons for limiting the number of births. A collection of over 4,000 letters to the Oslo Mothers' Clinic in the 1920s confirms that these reasons also prevailed outside the capital.[32] Only a minority of the west-end women mentioned as a reason for limiting the number of their children the wish to pursue other activities than those flowing from maternity. For east-end women work outside the home was seen as a burdensome necessity. Katti Anker Møller's arguments, stressing the importance of mothering, were therefore well in keeping with the thoughts of many mothers. So was her failure to discuss women's professional work or, for that matter, political or other engagements outside the home and family. But we may doubt whether her very radical idea of mothers' wages, financed by the state, was acceptable to more than a few.

The very importance Møller gave to women's work as mothers, the fact that she limited her interest in women's professional work to midwives, and mostly talked about their participation in organizations or party politics as a means of influencing conditions of motherhood, made her an ambiguous figure to some of the equal rights feminists. The discussion in the 1930s about child allowances shows that at least the leader of the Norwegian Association for Women's Rights, Margarete Bonnevie, harboured the idea that such remuneration for child care might be used to procure help from maids or nurses to take care of children so that mothers who wanted to pursue their personal professional careers or political activities might be free to do so. Women in the Labour Party, however, maintained that child allowances should permit mothers to stop working outside their homes and to take better care of their children.[33]

Møller's visions were phrased in the language of socialist feminism. They did, however, build on the nineteenth-century idea of a women's world separate from that of men, transforming this idea into a base for women's self-reliance, independence and power in society. Her vision in that respect forecast some of the content of the modern women's liberation movement, as it did also in stressing the important precondition that women should themselves decide on everything pertaining to motherhood.

For all the socialist and feminist content of Katti Anker Møller's visions and policies, she also harboured elements of Malthusian and eugenic ideas. Stressing all the time that the important aim was to help poor and worn-out mothers to have fewer children, and that fewer children would benefit the family budget, she went some way towards seeing family planning as the cure for poverty. However, she never argued that this policy would stop the procreation of the least valuable part of the population, as did the eugenists, in Norway and elsewhere, and her vision of wages for mothers was not in line with Malthusian ideas.

Better quality in care of the new-born child was an important part of Katti Anker Møller's reason for promoting family planning. But the reasoning was at most a very mild and positive version of eugenic arguments, hardly to be distinguished from the arguments behind a liberal social policy. When prominent socialists like Martin Tranmæl in the 1930s voiced eugenic ideas, defending contraception as a means to prevent 'the feeble-minded' and 'weaklings' from having children, Katti Anker Møller was silent. Arguments and measures to be found in the German National Socialist state were heard in the Norwegian debate. The socialist doctor Karl Evang, with a prominent position in the state bureaucracy, accepted the Norwegian law on sterilization in 1934, with minor critical remarks. 'The idea of limiting the number of people with low-quality genes is a very rational thought, always accepted within socialism. In the socialist planned society this will be a natural part of preventive health policies', he maintained. The decisive differences between the Norwegian and National Socialist German policies were that Norwegian scientists and politicians did not consider 'low-quality genes' more prominent in one part of the population than in others, and that such ideas had no influence upon serious practical action. It might also be mentioned that nothing like the French pronatalist policies during the inter-war period was implemented in Norway.[34]

Møller's politics were far from even the Norwegian version of eugenic thinking. She persistently aimed at assisting mothers for their own sake, not as a means of influencing population developments. Stressing women's responsibility for and possibilities of wielding political power through the vote as well as through their reproductive capacities, she represented those feminists who saw the world as a big home and perceived women's political activities as an extension of their maternal function outwards from family to society.[35] She embodied in one person what Karen Offen has seen as opposing positions within the feminist movement – 'relational' feminism as well as individual feminism.[36] Women's rights as political individuals were to her important as means towards a better world for mothers. Like a good liberal feminist she never tired of stressing the importance of information and schooling in educating better mothers. But she wanted education to follow the wishes of the mothers more than the ideas of medical men and she saw education as the core of self-reliance and independence. In that respect she continued the policy of the nineteenth-century feminists working for better educational opportunities for women, opportunities that proved in the long run also to benefit them outside the realm of maternity. Finally, with her open socialist sympathies she embraced often opposing strands within the feminist movement.

Her theories and political actions make it problematic to put her clearly in one or other of the generally accepted groups of feminists – or of other political groups for that matter. A woman from the upper middle class with a strong socialist preference, a 'relational feminist' advocating individual political rights, a Malthusian wanting the state to take economic responsibility for all mothers: she is a warning against categorizing individuals too easily within one group or the other.

Her politics and strategies are also a reminder of the unorthodox creative inventiveness needed by people engaged in political activity outside and between political parties and other organizations. We get a glimpse of the process of grassroots political activity as well as of networking between individuals in influential posts in political decision-making. It seems clear that being listened to and succeeding within the political structure of Norwegian democracy in the first decades of the twentieth century took not only an immense amount of networking within often mutually opposing organizations, but also solid connections within the corridors of power. Women's vote was a source of support, but would never on its own have yielded such results.

It should not be forgotten that the pioneers fighting for voluntary motherhood also needed a good deal of tenacity and courage. Already in 1921 at the age of 53 Møller, speaking of her political activity, wrote to one of her sisters: 'I shall do no more. I am much too tired deep inside. I only now realize the effort it takes'. But shortly afterwards she started the demanding work that led to the first mothers' clinic three years later. In 1935 when she had ceased to take part in public discussions, she said: 'In my daily surroundings out of sheer consideration and tact nobody ever mentions a word about my work. It seems to be a silent agreement not to touch on such a disagreeable subject. It must be lovingly forgotten. This is why it has always been so painful to live in the circles to which we are usually limited'.[37]

CONCLUSION

An analysis of the theories and practical politics of the leading figure of the Norwegian women's fight for voluntary motherhood between 1900 and 1930 shows parallel developments with western European countries. The socially uneven reduction of fertility sparked off lively discussions, and some practical measures to transform motherhood everywhere became an important part of the political agenda. Differences of opinion in this field corresponded roughly – but not without exceptions – to overall socio-economic and political differences between conservative groups and radical, often socialist groups. The negative attitude to voluntary motherhood within the first group was indicative also of a negative view of women as individuals with interests sometimes different from those of husbands and children, a view that was also quite strong within the eugenist camp. This is not to say that all radicals and socialists were friends of voluntary motherhood and of women's emancipation. Even the Women's Association of the Labour Party advocated barring married women from jobs outside the home in the 1920s and early 1930s.[38] Indeed, the majority of politically active people as well as of anonymous mothers appear to have accepted the close bonds between women, children and the family. These bonds were not seriously questioned before the rise of the modern women's movement in the 1970s.

Women's political activity on questions pertaining to voluntary motherhood was lively, even in countries such as France, where they had no right to vote. They played an important role in the opposing camps in these matters through organizations of their own as well as through participation in organizations open to both women and men, through lectures, articles and books, and not least by extensive and skilful lobbying in the corridors of power. They formed and used a wide international network, sharing ideas and providing inspiration. If the limitation of births was not a conscious political action – no strike – it nevertheless caused serious worries among political and other authorities. Supported by many voices explaining the whys and hows of family planning and working to legitimate this action, the fall in fertility contributed to making the private political and propelled women to the forefront in public decision-making. If the vision of motherhood put forward by the *Bund für Mutterschutz*, by Eleanor Rathbone, by Marie Stopes, by Ellen Key and by Katti Anker Møller was a break with part of nineteenth-century equal rights feminism, this vision was nevertheless an important step in the formation of a consciousness of self-esteem and self-reliance, of the construction of a basis for women's active political participation in the twentieth century.

NOTES

1 Quoted and translated from A. Bergmann, 'Frauen, Männer, Sexualität und Geburtenkontrolle. Die Gebärstreikdebatte der SPD im Jahre 1913', in K. Hausen (ed.), *Frauen suchen ihre Geschichte*, Munich, Beck, 1983, pp. 81–108. The quotation is an adaptation of the first sentence of Marx's Communist Manifesto. The second quotation is from T. Mohr, *Katti Anker Møller – en banebryter*, Oslo, Tiden, 1968, p. 127. This book contains *in extenso* a number of Katti Anker Møller's most important speeches and articles, as well as ample quotations from her correspondence. The author, Tove Mohr, was Møller's daughter. As a physician she continued much of her mother's work and was active in the struggle against penalties for abortion in the 1930s.

2 Quoted from a pamphlet introducing the Neo-Malthusian League at the First International Eugenics Conference, London, 1912. Katti Anker Møller Archives (KAMA), University Library, Oslo. Map XIA.

3 T. Mohr, *Katti Anker*, p. 130.

4 Printed in ibid., pp. 102–30 and 149–69.

5 ibid., p. 169.

6 A-L. Seip, *Socialhjelpstaten blir til. Norsk sosialpolitikk 1740–1920* (The emerging of the social help state. Norwegian social politics 1740–1920), Oslo, Gyldendal, 1984, pp. 193–8; I. Blom, '"Ingen mor maa til tidsfordriv sitte med sit barn paa fanget". Konflikt mellom forsørgeransvar og omsorgsansvar blant ugifte mødre i Bergen 1916–1940' (The conflict between economic responsibility and child care among unmarried mothers in Bergen 1916–1940), in P. Fuglum and J. Simensen, *Historie nedenfra. Festskrift til Edvard Bull*, Oslo, Universitetsforlag, 1984, pp. 25–43.

7 T. Mohr, *Katti Anker*, pp. 95–6; I. Blom, 'Barselkvinnen mellom befolknings-politikk, sosialpolitikk og kvinnepolitikk fra 1880-årene til 1940' (Mothers between population politics, social politics and women's politics from the 1880s to the 1940s), *Historisk Tidsskrift*, 1982, vol. 2, pp. 141–61.

8 See Seip and Ibsen's contribution to this volume.

9 I. Blom, '"Smaa barn som prøveklut for alskens gammeldags husråd . . .?" Konflikter om ammerutiner i Bergen 1910–1940' (Conflicts over breast-feeding routines in Bergen 1910–1940), in I. Norrlid et al. (eds), *Över gränser. Festskrift till Birgitta Odén*, Lund, Historiska institutionen, Lunds universitet, 1987, pp. 41–64; K. Liestøl, M. Rosenberg and L. Waløe, 'Breast-feeding practice in Norway 1860–1984', *Journal of Biosocial Science*, 1988, vol. 20, pp. 45–88, using other sources, also find a reduction of breast-feeding from around 80 per cent of Norwegian mothers in 1920 to 20–30 per cent in 1960.

10 M. Tokheim, 'Norske Kvinners Nasjonalråd (Norwegian Women's National Council) 1904–1916', in I. Blom and G. Hagemann (eds), *Kvinner selv . . . Sju bidrag til norsk kvinnehistorie*, Oslo, Aschehoug, 1977, 2nd edn 1980, pp. 122–50; I. Blom, *Synd eller Sund fornuft? Barnebegrensning i Norge c. 1890 – c. 1930* (Sin or common sense? Limiting family size in Norway, 1890s–1930s), Bergen, Universitetsforlaget, 1980, p. 198.

11 T. Mohr, *Katti Anker*, p. 120.

12 I. Blom, *Synd eller sund*, pp. 223–51.

13 T. Mohr, *Katti Anker*, pp. 135–47; I. Blom, *'Den haarde Dyst'. Fødsler og fødselshjelp i Norge gjennom 150 år*, (Deliveries and birth help in Norway through the past 150 years), Oslo, Cappelen, 1988.

14 T. Mohr, *Katti Anker*, pp. 9–57; I. Blom, '"Really excellent men do not grow on trees . . .". Breadwinning and structures of authority in Norwegian bourgeois marriages around the turn of the century', in Norwegian National Research

Council (ed.), *Bürgertum und Bürokratie im 19. Jahrhundert. Technologie, Innovation, Technologietransfer.* Bericht über das 2. deutsch–norwegische Historikertreffen in Bonn, Mai 1987, Oslo, 1987, pp. 69–86.

15 M. Tokheim, 'Norske Kvinners' pp. 131–3; I. Blom, *Synd eller sund*, p. 198; I. Blom, 'Smaa barn'; T. Mohr, *Katti Anker*, p. 86.

16 Letters to Møller from Steenhof in Jan., Feb. and Oct. 1913, Jan. and March 1915, KAMA, UiO, Ms 4.2416:II. The otherwise radical feminist, Åse Grude Koht, with whom Møller co-operated for some time within the NNCW was reluctant in these matters. Berggreen and Friedhof shared the same radical approach to women's suffrage, but more moderate social democrats shaped the politics of the party. Even if Friedhof and Key had many ideas in common, Friedhof criticized Key's polarization of femininity and masculinity and maintained an androgynous ideal giving women the possibility of motherhood as well as of economic independence through paid work outside the home. See C. Carlsson, *Kvinnosyn och kvinnopolitik. En studie av svensk socialdemokrati 1880–1910*, Lund, Arkiv förlag, 1986, pp. 202, 204, 243, 257–9, 265–6, 270.

17 Elise Ottesen Jensen was born in 1886; Ellen Key lived from 1849 to 1926. See C. Register, 'Motherhood at center: Ellen Key's social vision', *Women's Studies International Forum*, 1982, vol. 5, pp. 599–610.

18 I. Blom, *Synd eller sund*, p. 197.

19 T. Mohr, *Katti Anker*, pp. 26–7; K. Offen, 'The theory and practice of feminism in nineteenth-century Europe', in R. Bridenthal, C. Koonz and S. Stuard (eds), *Becoming Visible. Women in European History*, 2nd edn, Boston, Houghton Mifflin, 1987, pp. 359–60; see also Offen's and Cova's contributions to this volume.

20 T. Mohr, *Katti Anker*, p. 69. KAMA, UBO Ms 4–2416, XIB contains handwritten reports as well as a manuscript from the ICW meeting in Berlin 1904.

21 T. Mohr, *Katti Anker*, pp. 69 and 195; I. Stoehr, 'Organisierte Mütterlichkeit. Zur Politik der deutschen Frauenbewegung um 1900', in K. Hausen (ed.), *Frauen suchen*, pp. 221–49. On Helene Stöcker, see P. Rantsch, *Helene Stöcker zwischen Pazifismus und Revolution*, Berlin (DDR), Morgen, 1984; K. Offen, 'The theory', in *Becoming Visible*.

22 A. Hackett, 'Helene Stöcker: left-wing intellectual and sex reformer', in R. Bridenthal, A. Grossmann and M. Kaplan (eds), *When Biology Became Destiny. Women in Weimar and Nazi Germany*, New York, Monthly Review Press, 1984 pp. 109–30; I. Blom, 'Really excellent men'; T. Mohr, *Katti Anker*, pp. 166–7.

23 KAMA, UBO Ms 4–2416, XIA: Letter from Marie Hübner and from IVMS; MS 4–2416, IVB: Letters to and from Frida Steenhof and Alette Schreiner 1913 and 1915. It is indicative of the way Møller worked that she co-operated in other matters with Alette Schreiner who was instrumental in torpedoing her attempt at establishing this organization.

24 J. Lewis, *The Politics of Motherhood*, London, Croom Helm, 1980, pp. 165–90 and 198–9, and her and Offen's contributions to this volume.

25 For full information on the following subject see I. Blom, *Synd eller sund*, pp. 204–12.

26 E. Strømberg, *The Role of Women's Organizations in Norway*, Oslo, Likestillingsrådet, 1980; S. Bringslid, 'Norske Kvinners Sanitetsforening, Stifting og aktivitet 1896–1905', unpublished thesis, Department of History, Bergen, 1985; I. Blom, 'Women in organizations in modern Norwegian history', in *Report from the International Symposium on the Research on Women's Organizations*, Stockholm, Frederikka-Bremer-Förbundet, 1978, pp. 84–101.

27 In 1904 she wrote that, being met with opposition within the NNCW, 'I addressed the Socialist women and took membership there'. Mohr, *Katti Anker*,

p. 86. No other sources indicate that she was actually a member of the Social Democratic Party.

28 Blom, *Synd eller sund*, pp. 202–3.

29 Mohr, *Katti Anker*, pp. 174–86; Blom, *Synd eller sund*, pp. 191–5.

30 *Dagbladet*, 18 September 1920; Mohr, *Katti Anker*, pp. 186–8, 190–1; letters in KAMA, UBO. MS 4–2416, XIA.

31 I. Bull, 'Norske legers holdning til spørsmålet om barnebegrensning' (Attitudes among Norwegian doctors as to family planning), *Norsk Historisk Tidskrift*, 1977, vol. 4, pp. 398–432; Blom, *Synd eller sund*, pp. 214–22.

32 Blom, *Synd eller sund*, pp. 64–154.

33 Blom, 'Barselkvinnen', at this point partly built on the unpublished thesis by I.K. Thorstad, 'Barnetrygdspørsmålet i Norge i mellomkrigstiden', Oslo, 1980.

34 N. Roll-Hansen, 'Den norske debatten om rasehygiene' (The Norwegian debate over eugenics), in *Historisk Tidskrift* 1980, vol. 3, pp. 259–83; A.-S. Kälvemark, *More Children of Better Quality? Aspects on Swedish Population Policy in the 1930s*, Uppsala, Almquist & Wiksell, 1980; G. Bock, *Zwangssterilisation im Nationalsozialismus. Studien zur Rassenpolitik und Frauenpolitik*, Opladen, Westdeutscher Verlag, 1986, and her and Offen's contributions to this volume; Blom, *Synd eller sund*, pp. 208–9.

35 O. Banks, *Faces of Feminism*, Oxford, Robertson, 1981; F.K. Prochaska, *Women and Philanthropy in 19th Century England*, Oxford, Clarendon, 1980, and 'A mother's country: mothers' meetings and family welfare in Britain, 1850–1950', Working Paper of the European University Institute, No.87/292, Florence, 1987.

36 Offen, 'The theory', and 'Defining feminism: a comparative historical approach', *Signs*, 1988, vol. 14, pp. 119–57.

37 Mohr, *Katti Anker*, pp. 222–3.

38 E. Lønnå, 'LO, DNA og striden om gifte kvinner i arbeidslivet' (Trade unions, the Labour Party and the fight over married women's work), in Blom and Hagemann, *Kvinner selv*, pp. 151–76.

Chapter 2

Family welfare, which policy? Norway's road to child allowances

Anne-Lise Seip and Hilde Ibsen

THE END: THE WELFARE STATE

In 1946 the Norwegian Parliament, 'Stortinget', decided by a unanimous vote to give allowances to every family with more than one child. Single parents were to receive payment from the first child. There was no debate, since this was considered by the Speaker to be more 'dignified'.[1]

The introduction of child allowances was the first social reform after the war. One important feature was new in Norwegian social policy: it was universal. The target group was not limited to a particular social class either as regards income or as regards contributions to a social insurance scheme tied to the labour market. The allowance was given to all children and families as of right. This innovation has led to the reform being regarded as the first welfare state measure in Norway.

This unanimity was taken as evidence of a new political climate after the war. But the reform was a product of old struggles. Many groups had been involved, with differing ideologies and aims. The debate had lasted for more than thirty years. At last a compromise was reached, in which everyone got something, but few got exactly what they had fought for.

In this chapter, we shall see how a problem considered to be of a private nature, the cost of taking care of one's children, came to be defined as a political question and forced on to the agenda of political parties. Various pressure groups demanded a public policy. New considerations became important along the road, and influences from abroad made themselves felt. An analysis of the reform will show that it had many and various roots.

This complicated background compels us to enquire into the motives behind the reform. Which purposes should it serve? Which group was the winner in the political contest? Norway was just one among many countries which established family allowances after the Second World War. In particular England passed similar legislation in 1945, Sweden in 1947. The making of the English law is the most thoroughly studied. The campaigns pursued by the different pressure groups for a policy aimed at bettering the conditions of the family had a minor influence, if any, upon those who prepared and passed the bill. Family allowances were granted 'for reasons of economic control', that is as a measure of economic policy, not of social policy.[2] Do we find the same ambiguity in the motives behind the Norwegian reform?

The analysis of a single reform can illuminate the general process leading up to the welfare state. Ashford argues that the politicians and civil servants who prepared the piecemeal legislation which eventually constituted a 'welfare state' never conceived of the idea of such a state.[3] The concept did not exist, although separate ideas did. The welfare state is a result of many pragmatic solutions to problems, not the realization of one idea or conception. The proposition is irrefutable. Still, in search of the origins of some particular welfare measure, it often happens that we can see formulated goals and strategies which aim directly at solutions that we today define as typical of the welfare state. Let us, therefore, pursue elements of 'planning' and the continuity of ideas as energetically as we trace contingencies and transformation in the process.

Let us go back to the beginning. Which problems triggered off the process?

THE PROBLEM OF MAINTENANCE

In the years around the First World War the economic problem connected with maintaining and caring for children was defined in two different ways. It was seen as a wage problem for those with families to support. The civil servants, who had their salaries granted by Parliament, complained that families with children could not make ends meet. Parliament therefore set up a committee in 1913.[4] It was to consider whether wages should rise in proportion to the number of children. This claim for a family wage is the first source of family allowances.

But the maintenance of children was also part of the poverty problem and thus a question of social policy. Single mothers – unmarried, widowed, divorced and separated – were too poor to bring up their children. At the time of birth they were entitled to a small maternity benefit according to the provisions of the Child Welfare Act of 1915, which established the important principle of society's obligation to take care of unmarried mothers and their children, especially around the time of their birth.[5] But afterwards? And what about poor married women, who very seldom came into consideration for benefits? Didn't they need help, so that they could stay at home with their children? When the problem was presented in this way, it was related to care. Economic aid to the mother should enable her to take care of the child herself. Here we are at the second source of pressure for family allowances. The economy of motherhood was put on the agenda.

The struggle for a mother's wage was fought on two fronts. The first was the demand for a pension for single mothers. The second was a claim for a mother's wage, either for poor mothers, or for all mothers, as compensation for the work of being a mother.[6] This second line of reasoning points towards family allowances. We shall pursue this argument further later in this chapter.

But the two lines of reasoning are intertwined. In particular it was the debate about the desperate situation of single mothers which started the discussion about the needs of the children, and also living conditions in the family. Let us, therefore, first look at the introduction of the first mothers' pension scheme in Norway, a scheme which was adopted in the capital in 1919.

MOTHERS' PENSIONS FOR SINGLE MOTHERS: AN EXPERIMENT IN THE CAPITAL

The mothers' pension scheme in Oslo was initiated first and foremost by women members of the labour movement, and was carried by means of a Labour majority on the City Council. It thus reflects the preferences of the Left concerning both target group and policy: pension to low-income groups financed out of taxes. The debate over the pension scheme highlights the ideals of the Labour Party in 1919, ideals which imperfectly anticipate the establishment of a welfare state. They also illuminate political features typical of the social legislation of the time.

The claim for pensions was raised by the Labour Party's Women's Associations. In the poorer industrial districts, single mothers had to work all day to keep themselves and their children alive.

> The day is long and hard, but in the evening and on Sundays they can be together with their children. Wage levels do not, however, permit children to enjoy the full company of their mothers. In addition to ordinary work, mothers must also carry out their duties in the home

wrote one Women's Association member, who asserted that 'a mother never had an hour to herself'.

The proposal was limited to pensions for widows: 'We implore the committee to free these widows from poor relief, and thus enable them to keep their reputation as good citizens'. The case on behalf of the widows also had its background in considerations of citizenship.[7] Until 1919 poor relief led to the loss of the vote. Women were fully enfranchised in 1913.

The question of mothers' pensions was investigated by a committee established by the City Council. The members proceeded at once to more radical measures, proposing to include all single mothers in the plan. The most likely reason for this was that the committee saw the whole pension question in the light of the wish to do away with as much of the poor law system as possible. Half of the single mothers in the capital were reported to be receiving poor relief.[8] The greater boldness of the male members of the committee in comparison with the Labour women must be evaluated in the context of the possibility of backing up the argument on behalf of a wider target group by referring to the poverty problem of mothers.

But political differences appeared. The most radical members wanted to include all poor single mothers in a pension scheme. The Conservatives went in for a narrow target group, the Liberals a somewhat wider one. Behind the disagreement were different views on two questions: on who were to be reckoned as 'deserving' and how important that criterion should be, and on the proper limits to state responsibility.

Widows were considered to be 'deserving'. They had an established home to take care of. But the Conservatives would not include unmarried mothers, since they were judged unfit to make a good home for their children. 'Even if the unmarried mother gets 2–3–4 children, there will be no question of making a real home, and she will never become a real mother for her child.'[9] The group was thus singled out on moral criteria, disguised as a realistic appraisal of their situation and of what could be expected of them.

The non-socialist politicians also feared the consequences of letting the state take on responsibility belonging to fathers, thus encouraging them to neglect their duty. They admitted that alimony was insufficient, difficult to collect, and that mothers divorced or separated from their husbands often had to resort to poor relief, since the Norwegian state, unlike Denmark,[10] could not afford to advance the money. Nevertheless, it was considered more important to restrict public responsibility. For the Conservatives this was also an argument used for excluding separated and divorced mothers from the scheme, since they had, in principle, a provider.[11] Here the Liberals went with the Labour Party, placing this group on an equal footing with widows.

The Labour representatives, however, got the reform they wanted: a pension for all single mothers with small children, as of right, and paid out of taxes. This was a radical measure. But the strong element of control in the pension scheme betrays the moralistic attitudes at that time, as well as the need for economy in the scheme. To protect the municipality from being invaded by pregnant single women, the time of residence necessary in order to become a beneficiary was fifteen years. To protect the taxpayer against misuse of the scheme, a system of control of clients was established. Five women inspectors were to supervise the mothers. This was a new device in the municipality. 'Bad mothers' would lose their children as well as their pensions. There were no soft feelings towards working-class clients on this point. The inspectors, however, also took care of mothers and children during periods of illness.

An interesting final point worth mentioning is the amount of the payment. It was not sufficient to cover the whole cost of living. Mothers were supposed to supplement their pensions with some earnings, unless they were disabled. One reason was, of course, the cost of the pension scheme. But it was also argued that the mothers themselves would prefer to work outside the home:

Particularly a mother with only one or two children will find it difficult to use all her work capacity in the home and will not be content . . . unless she can contribute somewhat to the upkeep of herself and her children.[12]

This became a point of discussion when the Oslo model was proposed in other places. In 1937, one municipality argued that the pension ought to enable the mother to stay at home and devote all her time to her children. Ten years later, the Oslo model was defended both with reference to mothers who wished to participate in the labour force, and to the interests of society in a period of a tight labour market.[13] Attitudes to the role of mothers changed in accordance with economic conditions.

Many welfare state measures started as local initiatives, and found their way onto the statute book much later. The pension scheme introduced in the capital was not meant to end there, and was adopted explicitly for that purpose. It was seen by Labour representatives as a spearhead. The municipality had only started what the state ought to take over: the municipalities 'ought to be at the forefront and show the right course to the state . . . who has the main responsibility, . . . the municipalities must . . . force the state'.[14] In 1919 the County Council sent a deputation to Parliament asking the state to solve the mothers' pension question. Municipalities could not do this single-handed in the long run.[15] Local initiative was here seen as a strategy in what we call 'welfare state building'.

A goal had been reached. A pension scheme for all poor single mothers had been established. But this was only one of the goals and part of a wider aim. In the debate it was stressed by members of all parties that the real target group was the children. The more radical members spoke of the state recognizing its responsibility for children as being in its own interest: 'children are a resource, which it is in the interest of the state to guard', and even a Conservative representative admitted that the state would profit from having 'well-behaved children'.[16] Others were less explicit, but wanted something done to secure better conditions for all children. The Labour Party women followed this line of thought when they also proposed a pension for single fathers. A proposal for a state pension for children of single parents had already been presented in Parliament by the Labour Party in 1914. This preoccupation with the child was typical of the period, and the capital had its child care reorganized on a large scale during these years.[17] In the continuing discussion about the economy of motherhood it pointed towards new perspectives.

THE INTER-WAR YEARS: GROPING FOR PRINCIPLES

In the years to follow, the debate on the economy of motherhood took new turns. Interest shifted from mother-centred measures to family-centred measures. Thus the question of the economy of single mothers, even fathers, was separated from the question of a mothers' wage and the economy of the family. Women had a wider aim than getting a pension for single mothers. The target group was widened. The main concern was for poor families. Next, families with many children were by definition considered to be 'disinherited' and to have low-income or high-expenditure problems. The road was paved for universal measures.

A wider range of measures was taken into consideration. Three main roads were marked out: (1) mothers' wages or child allowances either paid out of taxes or by insurance, (2) wage reform giving supplementary wages, a family wage, to breadwinners, or (3) support in kind for families. The models would lead in different directions and have different effects in the economic system. But it was not always necessary to choose one of them. The models could be combined, and, as we shall see, this was what came about. The different goals and models reflected different economic and political preferences and ideologies. The ways in which they were combined reflect an ideological consensus or flexibility, which made the welfare state compromises after the Second World War possible.

A MOTHERS' WAGE

The idea that all mothers, or at least all needy mothers, should have a 'wage', and an allowance for the upkeep of their children, was launched by one of the pioneers of the Labour Party Women's Movement, Katti Anker Møller, in 1918.[18] But nothing much happened before the Labour Party set up a committee to discuss a 'mothers' wage' in 1923.[19] The question of economic assistance was now put in a new way. It was no longer a question of a temporary pension for those who had no provider. What was to be discussed was the economy of the poor family.

The committee was staffed by members who in the years to come were prominent in the discussion of this problem, and also in the formation of social policy in the Labour Party as a whole. One of the men, Inge Debes, was later the chairman of the committee set up by the Labour government in the thirties to revise and expand the Norwegian social insurance system. One of the women, Sigrid Syvertsen, was later to represent Labour on the Commission of 1934 which prepared a bill for family allowances. We would, therefore, expect to be able to trace the ideas of the thirties back to this committee of the twenties. But it is not so easy. The committee never developed a consistent view of the problem and the remedies to be sought.

Some principles, though, seemed to weigh heavily with Labour. One was that an allowance should be paid to the mothers. This would be a recognition of their work in line with any other paid occupation: 'We are used to the fact that a woman's work in the home is not appreciated. But we surely agree that *this* work is just as valuable as that of any man.' The other principle was that a mothers' wage should be independent of the position of the fathers in the labour market. This was important in years of mass unemployment, strikes and lock-outs. The standard of living of the families would be kept up and the children protected, whatever happened to the breadwinner. Thus a mothers' wage should be seen as a tool 'in the service of the working class'.[20]

Consideration of working-class interests probably also influenced the methods of finance. To tie family allowances to the wage system, as was the rule in many European countries, must have been considered risky.[21] But it was not easy to find an alternative model. In the scheme presented in 1925 to the National Conference of Labour Women, the financing was modelled on the Norwegian health insurance, with contributions from the state, the county and the employer. Contribution by the insured individual was omitted. This social insurance model was not retained. In later discussions the question of financing was left open or it was vaguely said that allowances should be paid for by the state.

Some kind of social insurance seemed to be preferred by the Labour Party Women's Movement. Ella Anker, a member of Labour's committee on mothers' wages and the sister of Katti Anker Møller, was deeply impressed by the French system of caisses familiales, and proposed a solution in this direction. She maintained that the wages of the working class did not 'take into consideration the needs of the family'.[22] It should be noted here that the women in the labour movement always gave strong support to the continuance of family supplements to the salaries of public employees when these salaries were discussed in Parliament, even if this was not their favourite system or a measure benefiting their own social class.[23]

Family supplements as part of the wage system could not, however, be accepted by the trade unions. When asked in 1935, the secretariat answered that family allowances must be administered by the state, not negotiated as part of wage agreements. This view was held by trade unions in many countries.[24] One of Labour's leading young economists, Ole Colbjørnsen, pleaded, however, for a family wage in one of the most influential writings on socialist economics in Norway in the thirties, A Norwegian Three Years' Plan.[25] The choice between different principles was thus not clear-cut. But as a main tendency we can say that the preference of most members of the Labour Party was for financing allowances out of taxes.

There were other disagreements. Different opinions on the population question made their impact. Some wanted to give allowances on a rising scale, maintaining that the older children needed more than the younger. Others wanted to follow the opposite principle. In the twenties the labour movement feared over-population, and it was considered unwise to stimulate population growth. Karl Kautsky was referred to as an authority.[26] In the thirties, the population crisis provided an opportunity for social policy initiatives. A falling birth-rate gave rise to arguments for a new policy to protect the family. But pronatalist arguments were never strong in the labour movement. Quality, not quantity, was stressed.

At the beginning of the thirties, the Labour Party model, as far as it was elaborated, comprised cash allowances financed out of taxes. In 1930 the reform was put on the party's agenda. The mothers' wage was now called child allowance. But one thing was clear: cash, if provision were made, should be paid to the mother.

Should all mothers, or only poor mothers, benefit? The issue was kept vague. But there are statements pointing in the direction of universal allowances. By financing them out of taxes, all mothers could be included: 'The state must support the service to society which is performed by the families as regards childrearing'.[27]

WAGE REFORM

The suggestion that society should in one way or other come to the rescue of the family was raised at about the same time as the idea of a mothers' pension or a mothers' wage. One way to deal with the problem was through the tax system. This solution was implemented, but it was never considered to be sufficient.[28] Another way was through the wage system. In 1913 Parliament had set up a committee to consider whether family supplements could be incorporated in the wage system for public employees.[29] It came to nothing, but during the First World War such a system was established to compensate for rising prices. It was not abandoned in the inter-war years, and interest in the question was kept alive, with frequent debates in Parliament in connection with revisions of salaries. In 1927 it was decided to give a temporary family supplement to public employees whose wages were reduced. It was argued that mothers and children would suffer from the wage cuts. Besides, mothers deserved the 'encouragement' of the measure: 'What was society today without the many homes in which Mother toils out of immeasurable goodness and never-ending loyalty, binding the children to the strong and secure idea of the home, putting every penny that Father brings home to good use, being economical in a way that many a Chancellor of the Exchequer would envy.'[30] The following year the municipality of Oslo set up a committee to look into the problems affecting the employees in the capital, who faced wage reductions.[31]

Wage reform, a system for which there were practical models abroad, seemed to be favoured by the non-socialist women's organizations. But they did not agree among themselves. The Norwegian National Council of Women set up a committee in 1925 to discuss the economy of the family. The committee was to consider wage reform first in the public sector, then in industry and lastly they were to discuss whether it was possible to devise a system which could include the self-employed.[32] The Council discussed the problems, but opinion was divided, and a resolution was never carried. Much of the interest in the question was kept alive by individual pioneers, notably Mrs Helga Eide Parr, who had worked for this reform since 1910. The claim was that the wage fund was unjustly distributed between single wage-earners and fathers of families. A wage reform would further redistribution, and that would be no more than reasonable: 'What we demand is justice. Justice for our children, justice for our husbands, justice for ourselves, the ones who carry the future of the race under our hearts.'[33]

A wage reform was, however, not so simple and self-evident a reform as some claimed. There were several objections. We have mentioned the fear of the trade union movement of pressure on wages: the supporters of families would get a slight rise in wages, while the rest would have theirs reduced, with an overall reduction as a consequence. This was not a preposterous thought, since some of the adherents of wage reform argued that wages already were stipulated to be at least sufficient for a small family, and that single persons thus took out of the wage fund more than their due. The problem was discussed by labour organizations and officials taking part in the procedure for fixing wages. Most agreed that wages were meant to be sufficient to support more than one person.[34] Another argument against the family wage was that it violated the principle of equal pay for equal work, which was important to many groups. A practical objection against wage reform was that it only benefited wage-earners. An arrangement for the self-employed would necessitate some sort of social insurance, involving the state. For some, this would ruin the idea of the reform. It was also unnecessary. The self-employed in agriculture would benefit indirectly, it was maintained, through the rise in purchasing power among wage-earners.[35]

Regardless of whether they favoured mothers' wages or child allowances, as the reform was more often called after 1930, or whether they wanted wage reform, the women's pressure groups wanted *women* to benefit from reform. But in what way? Here a division developed between women which did not follow party lines, but revealed different attitudes to the role of women and their work. The majority thought that wages for mothers should make it possible for women to stay at home. It was remuneration for their work there. This work was to be put on an equal footing with paid work: to 'give birth and to nourish the new generation, the entire work of a mother, can . . . be fully compared to work in agriculture, industry and commerce',[36] Katti Anker Møller maintained, and others joined in. Socialist and non-socialist women shared the same values. The wish to support mothers and their work at home was a common cause.

But some adhered to other ideals. The feminist middle-class movement for women's rights fought for equal pay in the labour market. The fact that higher wages for men could be justified because they were supposed to support a family was a strong argument for wage reform, giving equal pay to all single persons with the same job. This view was maintained most consistently by Margarete Bonnevie, who was to join the Commission on Child Allowances in 1934, where she constituted a minority of one. A wage reform should, in her opinion, enable women to join the work-force and pay for a skilled worker, male or female, in the home, her own domestic work being as a rule 'amateurish' anyhow. Mothers' wages she saw as a fascist idea, and the French and Belgian system she found paternalistic.

> Instead of tying and binding women which will be the result of giving 'mothers' wages', family supplements should be given in such a way that they liberate women and give them the opportunity to participate as valuable members of society.[37]

Thus, while some wanted to enable mothers to stay at home, some wanted to enable mothers to go out of the home.

The mothers' wage or wage reform were in the twenties debated among the rank and file. But the problem was complicated, and both women's organizations and political parties wanted to refer the question to a government commission. They pressed to get the reform onto the political agenda and, at the beginning of the thirties, both Labour and the Liberals put it on their election programmes.[38] After a bombardment of requests, including the claim that 'an experienced mother' should be elected,[39] the government set up a commission in 1934. Here the main views were to be seriously discussed.

THE COMMISSION ON CHILD ALLOWANCES OF 1934

The Commission delivered its report in 1937. With the exception of the minority, Margarete Bonnevie, the members were probably influenced by the work done by the important Social Insurance Committee set up by the new Labour government in 1935. The majority recommended universal allowances paid to the mothers in families with more than one child,[40] financed out of the taxes. The majority, consisting of members from different political parties and civil servants, thus came up with a proposal very much in accordance with the old established ideas of the Labour Party women.

Wage reform was, however, recommended in the minority report. This meant a restricted target group. The minority also favoured income-related allowances. Income redistribution and social change were not to be connected with a wage reform. The Commission on Child Allowances thus presented the politicians once more with the two main alternatives of the 1920s.

A POLICY FOR THE FAMILY: A TOOL
FOR A PLANNED ECONOMY?

The years between the appointment of the Commission on Child Allowances and the publication of its recommendations, were crucial to Norwegian policy. A minority Labour government took office in 1935, seeking support first from the Agrarian Party, later often from the Liberal Party. In the field of economic policy, the government struggled to fulfil its election promise to 'put the nation to work'. In the field of social policy the government promised to overhaul and expand the social insurance system. But new methods to solve the problems of the day were sought by young economists. To these problems, unemployment and poverty, was added a third problem, that of the population question. The debate on economic and social policy in the late thirties discussed the falling birth-rate, its causes and remedies.

The Commission on Child Allowances had evaded the population question. Its proposals were not supported by pronatalist arguments. On the contrary, five members proposed to allocate allowances on a scale which fell with rising family size. There was no reason to fear that allowances would lead to over-population among the poorest section of society, and besides 'there is not in our society any social class whose number should give rise to anxiety'.[41] Social hygiene was also a topic in the Norwegian debate. The full discussion of the population problem was left to a later commission on population, as in Denmark, Sweden and Britain, but this was never carried out in Norway.[42]

But the population crisis stimulated discussion about the economy of the family in all countries. One of the most important contributions came in Sweden in a book by Alva and Gunnar Myrdal, *Crisis in the Population Question*, published in 1934. Here they outlined a new policy, a policy for the family. Conditions must be improved in order to make it easier to have children. The authors documented the fact that housing and nutrition were inadequate for large sections of the population, both rural and urban. Families with children were worse off. It was time society did something to alleviate their burden. This could be done in several ways. The economist Gunnar Myrdal proposed not to give cash to poor families. Instead he argued in favour of the superiority of services in kind: school meals, free health service and day-care centres, and subsidized food. By giving support in kind, society could direct consumption and stimulate production. Social policy could be integrated into a planned economy. Wage reform was rejected as a 'technical trick'.

Not everybody felt that the policy advocated by the Myrdals was so beneficent for children. The idea that the state should take more direct responsibility for the upbringing of children was not in accordance with the ideology of the twenties concerning the role of the mother nor with the importance attached to the family by most people. The two authors were very outspoken in their denunciation of the authoritarian bourgeois family.

Nevertheless, the book became important in the debate in Norway. It was translated in 1936, and adapted to give a picture of social problems in Norway. Young, radical economists took up the idea of connecting social policy with a modern planned economy. They expounded their ideas in a fierce attack on the recommendations of the Commission on Child Allowances.[43]

The question of services in kind was not a new one. Women's organizations of all political shades had demanded more child-care services in the twenties.

There was rising interest in state provision of these services. Political parties put services in kind on their electoral programmes in this period. The question was discussed in the newspapers. In England this policy was discussed and favoured by Labour at an early stage.[44] But it was not until the debate on child allowances in the thirties that services in kind came to be proposed on a large scale as an integrated part of a consistent policy, and solely as a remedy for poor families.

The arguments for services in kind can be summed up in three points. First, the real need for services in kind: the standard of nutrition and housing was low, as had been shown by recent surveys.[45] To allocate resources to meet these needs would yield the greatest advantage. Second, resources were scarce. Payment in cash would eat up the budget, making it impossible to establish services in kind. Third, services in kind could more easily be allocated where the need was more obvious, in the poorer part of the population. This was a departure from the principle of universality introduced by the Commission.

Behind these arguments we find a vision of social policy as a part of a planned economy. The consumption pattern should be altered and brought into line with what was considered 'rational'. What was rational was to be prescribed by the scientific community, especially physicians, experts on nutrition, on housing and so on. To leave the consumption pattern to free choice was suboptimal; the housewives had not enough knowledge to make 'rational use of income'.[46]

Social policy was thus meant to serve production directly, and notably the market for agricultural products. Economic policy ought to be conducted as a 'co-operation between experts with knowledge of social policy, economics, medicine and agriculture'. Special reference was made to the works of Myrdal, and to committees set up by the League of Nations. Thus the hope for a better economy for poor mothers concluded with a vision of a brave new world, ruled by science and, presumably, socialism.

DILEMMAS IN SOCIAL POLICY

The policy of services in kind was controversial. The debate throws light on some crucial dilemmas which confronted groups and political parties on their way towards the welfare state. Some of the most fervent wishes of the Labour Party women could not be met through services in kind, especially the wish to make mothers the recipients of benefit. Labour women, therefore, split. Some supported the new line, which was propagated by the women's secretariat, and by the editor of the Labour Party women's journal. She had also edited the Myrdal book. But some fought for payment in cash to the mother.[47] To give everything in kind would demonstrate that society had no confidence in the mothers. It would also degrade the working class, since it would establish a system which closely resembled poor relief. Poor relief in kind (food requisitions) was a common and hated system in the inter-war period. Milk and food were, however, also distributed outside the poor relief system.[48]

Many groups joined the debate. A number of women's organizations became supporters of the new line. But other groups raised objections, pointing especially to the difficulties in distributing services in kind in rural areas, and the injustice of setting up institutions in the towns while families with many children mainly lived in the countryside. Would school meals help children in the rural areas who went to school only some months in the year? Pressure groups in the rural areas were mobilized against a policy intended to serve agricultural interests. It soon became evident that one of the big farmers' organizations was also sceptical.[49]

But although services in kind were rejected as a sole remedy, it was never denied that they were an important part of any policy to improve the circumstances of mothers and children. The Commission on Child Allowances had pointed to services in kind as a supplement to cash benefits. The minority even proposed that it should be obligatory for the municipalities to provide day-care centres. Those who favoured benefits in cash emphasized that these would improve the standard of living for children as well as living standards in general. If need be, cash could be handed out together with a nutrition plan which mothers should be obliged to follow.[50] It was argued that a rise in purchasing power would result in better food for families and better sales of agricultural products. Services in kind alone would not help solve the crisis in agriculture.

THE FINAL CHOICE

The question of family allowances was not put on the agenda in Parliament before the Second World War. When this was done in 1945/46, the world had changed. Regulation of consumption was by now a well-known phenomenon. Politics had been radicalized, Labour and the Communists were in the majority in Parliament. The young economists who took part in the debate in the thirties held influential positions; one was permanent secretary to the Minister of Social Affairs. One would have thought that this was the moment to bring in the most radical ideas of the thirties: income-tested benefits with redistributive effects, preferably given in kind.

This was not to be the outcome. Child allowances were introduced as a universal cash benefit. But the unanimous vote for this solution was obtained only after half a year of much confusion. The government presented two bills, and a third proposal was put forward by the Agrarian Party. There was still uncertainty about principles. The conflict reveals well-known pressure-group interests. The Norwegian debate was influenced partly by positions taken up in the thirties, partly by new insights developed during the war. The Norwegian government, as well as the young economists, had stayed in London during the war, through the period of German occupation. They were well acquainted with the proposals in the Beveridge report for universal child allowances. The British Labour Party had submitted to pressure and had, in spite of opposition from the trade union movement, supported the scheme.[51] The Norwegian trade union movement wrote during the war a political planning document, *Norway in the Future*, in which benefits in cash were supported, but those in kind were not rejected. The two strategies were said to be compatible.[52] The Beveridge principle was established in the Income Security Recommendation of the International Labour Organization (ILO) in Philadelphia in 1944. It was stressed that allowances should be given universally and as of right. The economic argument was that the income flow to families would maintain purchasing power and thereby secure employment.

The first government bill proposed insurance-based allowances for those who contributed to health insurance. That meant that the self-employed were left out. This was the model that had been suggested by the chairman of the Commission in 1934, but dropped. Why was it taken up again now?

Child allowances had been established in January 1945, some months before the war ended.[53] This law gave allowances to families who were included in the Sickness Insurance Scheme. It was probably a measure designed to gain the regime some popularity, and also to compensate for inflation, since wages were not regulated during the war. Laws passed during the German occupation of Norway (1940–45) were, however, abolished after the war. The new bill was thus modelled on a scheme that had already functioned for some time. It was meant to be a first step towards a more comprehensive insurance system. But the problem of how to include the self-employed was left for the future.

The bill had an unmistakably pre-war quality: an insurance paid by employers and a narrow target group limited to wage-earners below a certain income. It met opposition. The Agrarian Party pointed out that the scheme did not further equality. A large part of the poorest section of society, notably the fishermen, was excluded. The party wanted to include all classes, if not all income-groups. It also requested that services in kind should be considered. A proposal was submitted to Parliament.[54]

As for services in kind, the government had already committed itself to a very extensive subsidizing of food prices. The aim was to keep down prices, as well as wages, and thus 'stabilize' the economy. But even if price subsidies had a beneficial effect on food expenditure in families with children, the redistributive effect was slight, as the whole population benefited.

The economists advanced new proposals, this time a compromise between cash and kind. It was suggested that the general subsidies should be taken away, and the money instead used to finance allowances to all families with children under sixteen years. As part of the package, subsidies should be granted on milk and butter to families with children. The Minister of Finance supported this as 'a rational population policy'.[55] It sounded like an echo of the thirties.

Women in the labour movement were willing to accept the compromise to a certain extent. They now preferred subsidies on food, but would agree to a combination of cash and subsidies. What they would not accept was redistribution by means of subsidies. Here they followed the trade union movement. Subsidies on food were considered to be part of the wage bargain, and should not be tampered with.[56] The government then moved in a new direction. In a new bill it proposed allowances in cash to all families, starting with the second child but starting with the first child in the case of single parents. Services in kind were not included.

What were the arguments for this solution? What kind of profile did the government and, evidently, Members of Parliament, want to give to this piece of social policy? First, there was the wish for universality. In the new proposal all classes and all income-groups were included. Child allowances should increase redistribution between families and the rest of the population, and alleviate the burden on breadwinners. The war had paved the way for universal allowances. All children had suffered, and all needed help: 'The strain of the war has made it more necessary than ever to secure that children can grow up in as favorable conditions as possible.' Redistribution between different income-groups should be taken care of in other areas of economic policy. Universality would also guarantee that allowances were given in a manner that did not remind anyone of poor relief. This argument weighed heavily with the left. It was also used to rule out means-tested services in kind, such as food rebates.[57]

Lastly, it was argued that a universal allowance would cut the costs of administration considerably. It would not be more expensive to give it to everybody than to establish an administrative system to take care of a means-tested scheme. Besides, effectiveness and rationalization were important items on the political agenda after the war.[58]

The allowances were to be financed out of taxes. The insurance principle was brushed aside. This principle had traditionally been most favoured by the parties on the Right. They no longer supported it. Financing out of taxes was the solution to the problem of including the self-employed in the scheme.[59] In short, what was wanted was a modernized policy, giving universal allowances as of right. In the Norwegian welfare state, the notion of class was to be erased from social policy. This was a breach of principles that were important to many of the Left before the war.

Services in kind were not included in the scheme. Representatives from several parties wished, however, to introduce them piecemeal. And the responsibility of the state to provide better housing, standardized production of clothes, school meals, day-care centres and all the rest, was stressed by the government.[60] Here we can discern, at least on the part of the government, the ideas of a planned economy stemming from the thirties. The vision of a society in which the state took responsibility for the living conditions of families had not faded. What had faded was the vision of integrating social policy with economic policy: 'to tie social policy to the policy of production', as it was put in the thirties.[61] Subsidies were used as a general instrument in economic policy, not as a tool for social policy. Probably this made them more acceptable to all political parties.

Child allowances were established. But for what purpose? Whose economy was to gain: the economy of mothers, the economy of the family or the economy in general?

The mother had receded into the background. Interest had been focused on the child. Even if the interest of the one could not be separated from that of the other, it is obvious that the ideology of motherhood which was so strong in the twenties did not legitimate the new measure. It was not mother-centred, but child-centred or family-centred. But the allowance was to be paid to mothers, as a 'recognition on the part of society of mothers' work in child-rearing'.[62] The allowances could not under any circumstances be seen as a 'mothers' wage'. It was too small. Child allowance was not sufficient as a source of income; it was a supplement to existing income. While all families got the family allowance, for which, it is true, women of all political shades had worked, the poorest mothers had to wait for additional benefit. More municipalities now took it upon themselves to establish mothers' pensions. In 1950 municipalities covering about half of the population had pensions for widows and single mothers.[63] But geographical inequalities persisted. Only the richer municipalities could afford the arrangement, which was almost non-existent in the northern part of the country. The state did not introduce measures on a national scale until 1957 and 1964. In 1957 children without supporting parents were insured. The law was based on a new principle: the payment was directly tied to the child. This law had a close connection with another law passed in 1958. The state arranged for the payment of alimony in advance in cases where the father did not fulfil his obligation. In 1964, widows and single mothers, married or unmarried, became entitled to payment as of right. The law was introduced following strong pressure from several women's organizations. Only then can we say that the plan to make local reform a spearhead for a national arrangement had succeeded in this area of policy.

Nevertheless, many mothers regarded child allowances as a real 'mothers' wage'. This was demonstrated when the Treasury around 1970 planned to modernize the system, and convert the allowance into a tax rebate. The proposal met with strong opposition, and had to be dropped. This demonstrates clearly how poor many mothers still felt, at least in terms of cash at their disposal, in the growth economy of the welfare state.

The proposal for wage reform seemed to have been put on the shelf. The trade union movement never accepted it. But was not even child allowance a tool in the attempt to stabilize wages and prices? It was:

Since it is the aim of the government to stabilize prices and wages, it will be very difficult for supporters of families to augment their income, and child allowances will in the present situation be a means to lessen the economic pressure on families with children.[64]

More light is shed on this kind of motive in the recommendations of the Committee on Wages which was set up in 1951. Prices were by this time getting out of control. The government, together with the organizations of employers and wage-earners, decided to have a look at the incomes policy. The idea of a wage graduated according to number of children was again brought forward. Again the trade unions rejected the system. The argument now was the same as was earlier used by the self-employed. Such a system could not be universal. Universalism was wanted by everybody and recommended by the ILO.

The sources do not permit us to say that the main consideration of Norwegian politicians when child allowances were introduced was to stabilize prices. But it had considerable weight, and was an extra argument for a reform which many wanted for quite different reasons.

The ideological roots of the welfare measures after 1945 aimed at mothers, children and families were diversified. All possible models from the inter-war period were re-examined. No grand design was worked out, but ideas from the past were picked up and served as elements in the construction of the welfare state. By this process of ideological exchange and compromise, a rather high degree of consensus was reached in this area of policy. But consensus and good will do not necessarily solve economic problems. As for single mothers, they still belong to the poorest sections of society.[65] The family with small children is still a problem group in the welfare state economy. Services in kind are inadequate. Child allowances still serve as a tool of economic policy. To provide for and give care to children is still a problem in the welfare state.

NOTES

1 Smitt Ingebretsen (Conservative Party), *Stortingsforhandlinger* (*SF*), 1945–6, vol. 8, p. 563 (*SF* is Proceedings of Parliament).
2 J. Macnicol, *The Movement for Family Allowances, 1918–45*, London, Heinemann, 1980, p. 217.
3 D. E. Ashford, *The Emergence of the Welfare States*, Oxford, Blackwell, 1986, p. 3.
4 *SF*, 1913, vol. 7, p. 901. Rinde (Liberal) asked the committee to consider whether wages should rise with the number of children. See also I. Thorstad, 'Child allowances in the inter-war period', thesis, University of Oslo, 1980, p. 28.
5 A. L. Seip, *Sosialhjelpstaten blir til. Norsk sosialpolitikk 1740–1920*, Oslo, Jyldendal, 1984, p. 193; I. Blom, 'Ingen mor maa til tidsfordriv sitte med sitt barn paa fanget. Konflikt mellom forsørgeransvar og omsorgsansvar blant

ugifte mødre i Bergen 1916–1940', in P. Fuglum and J. Simensen (eds.), *Historie nedenfra. Festskrift til Edvard Bull på 70-årsdagen*, Oslo, Universitetsforlag, 1984, pp. 25–44.

6 P. E. Pettersen, *Pensjon, penger og politikk*, Oslo, Universitetsforlag 1987.

7 *Kvinden* (periodical of the Labour Women's Association), 1919, no. 8, p. 58 ('The poor relief system, which puts up barriers to full citizenship, is not the right institution to take care of poor widows'). *Aktstykker Kristiania Kommune*, 1919–20, proceedings no. 30, p. 1 (Proceedings of Kristiania Municipal Council). In Denmark widows with children got a pension from the state in 1913. See S. A. Hansen and I. Henriksen, *'Sociale brydninger 1914–1939. Dansk social historie*, Copenhagen, Jyldendal, 1980, vol. 6, p. 89.

8 *Aktstykker* 1919–20, no. 30; see also A. Hatland, *Oslotrygen – fra nasjonal modell til lokal fortidslevning*, Oslo, Institutt for sosialforskning, 1987, p. 10.

9 *Aktstykker*. 1919–20, no. 30, p. 14.

10 S. A. Hansen and I. Henriksen, *Sociale brydninger*, p. 89.

11 *Aktstykker*, 1919–20, no. 30, p. 12.

12 ibid., p. 14.

13 *Aktstykker*, 1948–49, no. 105, p. 33.

14 *Aktstykker*, 1919–20, no. 30, p. 139. See also pp. 127, 136 and 142.

15 The National Council of Norwegian Women and groups in the Liberal Women's Movement sent proposals to Parliament for a law guaranteeing pensions to poor widows with children. See Child Allowances Bill 1937 with explanatory preamble, in *SF*, 1945–6, Supplement.

16 *Aktstykker*, 1919–20, no. 30 pp. 136–139.

17 *SF*, 1920, Bill 18, p. 3. A.L. Seip, 'Who cares? Child, family and social policy in twentieth-century Norway', *Scandinavian Journal of History*, no. 4, 1987, pp.331–43.

18 *For Hjem og Samfund* (periodical of the housewives' organization), 1919, pp. 58–66. See also Blom's article in this volume. The proposal met opposition.

19 DNAs Landskvinnekonferanse, Protokoll 1925, p. 35 (protocol of the Labour Party Women's Conference).

20 ibid., p. 36.

21 Child Allowances Bill 1937, Appendix 1, p. 100.

22 *Arbeiderbladet* (newspaper of the Labour Party), 23 March 1932. Anker wrote frequently on the different European systems of family wage in *Arbeiderkvinnen* (The Labour woman, previously *Kvinden*) from 1927 onwards. See *Arbeiderkvinnen*, no. 11, 1927, p. 83; 1927, no. 12, p. 98; 1928, no. 1, p. 2; 1928, no. 3, p. 26.

23 *Arbeiderkvinnen*, 1928, no. 1, p. 2; 1929, no. 6, p. 94.

24 Child Allowances Bill 1937, Appendix 3; J. Macnicol, op. cit., p. 160.

25 O. Colbjørnsen and A. Sømme, *En norsk 3-Årsplan. Veien frem til en socialistisk planøkonomi i Norge*, Oslo, Det norske arbeiderpartis forlag, 1933, p. 35.

26 *Arbeiderkvinnen*, 1929, no. 9, p. 136; no. 10, p. 145.

27 ibid., 1930, no. 2, p. 19.

28 Helga Eide Parr in *Socialt Arbeid* (periodical of the Norwegian Association for Social Work), 1939, no. 7, p. 295. The Committee on Wages of 1951 tried to estimate the value of deduction in taxes for families with children, but found that this was impossible because of the variations in taxation rules among the municipalities. The committee claimed that the burden of taxation was relieved after 1945 due to new social and economic conditions, but there was a long way to go before the tax relief corresponded to family responsibilities. *Tilråding fra Lønnssystemutvalget* (Proposal from the committee on the wage system), p. 6 and Appendix no. 4, p. 27.

29 Child Allowances Bill 1937, p. 10.
30 *SF*, 1927, vol. 7, p. 254. The question was also discussed in 1919 in a bill presented to Parliament, *SF*, 1919, vol. 2, Bill 217, Appendix I. Appendix to *SF*, 1927, vol. 2, Bill 75, report from the wage committee of 6 July 1926, p. 124. The committee agreed not to propose child allowances tied to the wage system. The argument was based on the principle of equal pay for equal work: *SF*, 1929, vol. 1, Bill 1, chapter 1003; ibid., 1930, vol. 1, Bill 1, chapter 1003; ibid., vol. 7, 1931, 1920–1930. During the debate the MPs raised a discussion of principle related to incorporating child allowances in the wage system. One of the Labour Party members proposed the setting up of a committee with five members, with at least one housewife, to consider the question of child allowances. The proposal was rejected. The wage system which was established for employees in public administration was, however, maintained.
31 *Aktstykker*, 1927–8, no. 151, p. 327.
32 Norwegian National Council of Women (ed.), *Utredning av prinsippene for familielønn* (the principles for a family wage), Oslo, Haakon Arnesens, 1929.
33 *Nylænde* (periodical of the Norwegian Association of Feminists), 1921 p. 252.
34 Child Allowances Bill 1937, Appendix 3, p. 145. G. Wiesener, 'Barnetrygd', in *Socialt Arbeid*, 1935, no. 8, p. 314. *Den Høiere Skole* (periodical for secondary school teachers), 1935, no. 2, p. 50. *Befalsbladet* (periodical for army officers), 1935, no. 32, p. 249.
35 Child Allowances Bill 1937, pp. 75, 87.
36 K.A. Møller, 'Mødrehjælp' (Mother's help), *Kvindernes Enhetsfront* (United Front of Women), 1925, no. 1, p. 1.
37 Child Allowances Bill, pp. 77, 38. For France see Offen's chapter in this volume.
38 Election programme for the Labour Party 1930 and 1936. Election programme for the Liberal Party 1933 and 1936. Election programme for the Nationalist Socialist Party 1936.
39 Child Allowances Bill 1937, p. 11.
40 Two members, Mrs Stray (Liberal) and Mrs Syvertsen (Labour), wanted to give allowances starting with the first child.
41 Child Allowances Bill 1937, p. 38.
42 A.L. Seip, 'The influence of science on social policy in Norway in the 1930s', paper presented to the conference on 'The welfare state in transition', Solstrand Fjord Hotel, Bergen 1989; A.S. Kälvemark (Ohlander), *More Children of Better Quality? Aspects of Swedish Population Policy in the 1930s*, Uppsala, Almquist & Wiksell, 1980; S.A. Hansen and I. Henriksen, *Sociale brydninger*; K. Höjer, *Svensk Socialpolitisk Historia*, Stockholm, Norstedt, 1952.
43 See esp. A. Skaug and K. Getz Wold in *Socialt Arbeid*, 1938, no. 8; 1, 4 and 5, 1939 and 1940, vol. 4. As for the outcome of the proposals for services in kind in Sweden see A.S. Kälvemark, *More Children*.
44 J. Macnicol, *Family Allowances*, p. 147.
45 *Socialistisk medicinsk tidsskrift* (Socialist journal of medicine), 1935, p. 1 (nutrition); E.Storsteen, 'Boligforholdene i Norge', in *Social Håndbok for Norge*, published by Norsk Forening for Socialt Arbeid, Oslo, 1937 (housing); A. and G. Myrdal, *Krise i befolkningsspørsmålet*, Oslo, Tiden, 1937, ch. 5.
46 The need to educate women both as mothers and as housewives had been a theme since the turn of the century. See Kari Martinsen, 'Legers interesse for svangerskapet – en del av den perinatale omsorg. Tidsrommet ca. 1890–1940', *Historisk Tidsskrift*, 1987, no. 3. See also Blom's chapter in this volume.
47 *Socialt Arbeid*, 1939, no. 5, p. 187. Ella Anker, 'Child allowances in cash', *Socialt Arbeid*, 1940, no. 4, pp. 145–52.

48 'Beretning om Oslo Kommune 1911–47', p. 577 (Report on the municipality of Oslo); Child Allowances Bill 1937, p. 99.
49 Norges Bondelag (a farmers' organization) voted for the majority proposal. G. Wiesene, 'Child allowances, collective measures and benefits in cash', *Socialt Arbeid* 1940, no. 7, p. 236. Wiesener claimed that several organizations which had commented on the proposal wanted services in kind.
50 Tidens Tegn, 1 February 1939. Anker wanted to make special control schemes for milk and butter.
51 J. Harris, *William Beveridge*, Oxford, Oxford University Press, 1977, pp. 412–15. J. Macnicol, *Family Allowances*, p. 187.
52 *Framtidens Norge*, 1944, p. 85.
53 O. Melsom, *Nasjonal samling og fagorganisasjonene*, vol. III, Oslo, Institutt for norsk okkupasjons-historie, 1977, p. 195.
54 *SF*, 1945–6, vol. 5, document no. 4.
55 *Arbeiderbladet*, 11 May 1946.
56 A. Lionaes in *Arbeiderkvinnen*, 1946, no. 5, p. 2. See also Gunnar Braathen, *Arbeiderbladet*, 23 May 1946.
57 *SF*, 1945–6, vol. 8, pp. 560, 562, and ibid., Bill 127, p. 4.
58 T. Bergh and H. Pharo (eds), *Vekst og Velstand. Norsk politisk historie 1945–1965*, Oslo, Universitetsforlag, 1981.
59 The preference of the Conservatives for universalism increased. See P.E. Pettersen, *Pensjon*.
60 *SF*, 1945–6, vol. 8, p. 561, and ibid., vol. 3, Bill 127, p. 5.
61 *Socialt Arbeid*, 1939, no. 5, p. 188.
62 *SF*, 1945–6, vol. 8, pp. 83, 563.
63 *Statistiske Meldinger* (Statistical report) 151, table 5.
64 *SF*, 1945–6, vol. 3, Bill 127, p. 4.
65 S. Stjernø, *Den Moderne fattigdommen* (Poverty in modern Norway), Oslo, Universitetsforlag, 1985.

Chapter 3

The invisible child? The struggle for a Social Democratic family policy in Sweden, 1900–1960s

Ann-Sofie Ohlander

In 1900 a new labour protection law was passed in Sweden. One of the clauses concerned women who had recently given birth to a child. It constituted the first step in the introduction of family policies into Swedish law. According to this clause 'A woman who has given birth to a child shall not undertake any industrial work during the four weeks following the child's birth unless a doctor testifies that she can resume work earlier without damage to her health'.[1]

The law had been passed to ensure for mother and child a necessary period of rest and also to allow the mother to breast-feed. However, the law did not provide for any payments to be made during this enforced period of vacation. In consequence, the new maternity leave contrasted with the need of the mother and child for financial support. The law tacitly relied on the presence of a husband's wage to ensure the necessary income. However, in practice, there were many women who were the sole providers for the family, and in those families where both husband and wife worked, the wife's salary was often essential to ensure the necessary minimum income. It was to take as much as thirty years for necessary changes to be made in this area. The clause in Swedish labour law on compulsory maternity leave continued to be applied and the time period was even increased to six weeks in 1912. But a maternity insurance law providing mothers with financial support during that period was not passed until 1931.

The history of maternity insurance is not only of interest as an important issue in family policy, it also helps to illustrate a fundamental problem of Swedish and Social Democratic policy with respect to the family. A law which calls for an unpaid maternity leave expresses a mechanism of social control which constantly surfaces when family policy questions are evoked. At the turn of the century it was felt that one way to reduce infant mortality was to ensure that the mother could care for her child and could breast-feed. This was the main reason for passing the above-mentioned law. But there was also a widespread contemporary opinion which condemned women as being morally responsible for child mortality. Women, it was felt, needed to be informed and directed as to the best way to breast-feed their children and to care for them hygienically. However, it was not taken into consideration –

either among those who held this view or in the above-mentioned law – that many women had insoluble problems in their endeavour to combine the tasks of financially supporting their children and of caring for them. Mothers were considered both responsible and dependent. They were held responsible for the well-being of their children but at the same time they were discriminated against, both financially and by the law, in such a way that it became difficult to assume the responsibility expected of them.

Women were thus exposed to deeply contradictory social expectations and definitions. In their private lives they were forced to deal with a fundamental social conflict which they had to resolve in one way or another. In the last instance this conflict had its origin in a denial of the social character of parenthood, child care and child raising, in a denial of reproduction as the very basis for the continued existence of a society. The conflict which is particularly evident in the case of mothers is one between being powerless and being held responsible precisely for that over which they had no power. This conflict between powerlessness and responsibility can only be resolved when it is externalized by the women who have to live with it and when it is rendered visible as a fundamentally social phenomenon. One of the characteristics of such a conflict, however, is that it often remains unexpressed. It is therefore often difficult to locate it in its historical context or to verify it in historical source material.

The conflict between parenthood and financial constraints, which was particularly acute amongst women/mothers, is fundamental for any analysis of Swedish and Social Democratic family policy in the twentieth century. This conflict not only divided different political parties, but it also caused divisions within parties such as the Social Democratic Party. To put it simply, it may be said that this conflict was expressed in a struggle of women above all, which aimed at bringing out into the open this repressed dimension of social reality, and thus politicizing it.

THE CONCEPT OF FAMILY POLICY

'Family policy' is a term that is so widely used and accepted that it might surprise the reader that this term, in its present-day meaning, is relatively new to the Swedish language. According to the Swedish Language Institute, it first appeared in this modern meaning in an article published in the *Morgonbladet* in 1948.[2] Previously, two other terms had been used in a similar context: 'maternity policy', which was widespread from the beginning of the century, and 'population policy', which came to prevail during the 1930s. The latter term was abandoned once it became known what it had meant in National Socialist Germany. When in the post-war years the term 'family policy' began to be used, it also denoted the will to acknowledge that not only women/mothers were to be seen as being responsible for the care of children and the family, but also men/fathers. It was not until the 1950s that the term was used in a public and political context. In 1965 it appeared in the title of the 'Family Policy Committee', which was instituted by the Social Democratic government with State Councillor Ulla Lindström as its president. The first Social Democratic Party programme which used the term was the municipal programme of 1964, which recommended an 'active municipal family policy'.[3]

Chapter 2 of the suggestions made by the Family Policy Committee dealt with 'society's support for families with children'. The sub-sections of this chapter mentioned all of the basic elements that were to constitute such support: child allowances, housing allowances, education grants, advance payments, marriage loans, tax rebates, services such as kindergartens and day-care centres, and specific protective laws to be drawn up by the youth offices.[4] The document can thus be seen as a definition of the scope of family policies. One must add to these all of the measures connected to giving birth to children, in particular those concerning pregnancy, childbirth and maternity leave, as well as those defining the number of working hours required from parents of newly born children. For the following historical analysis, I will use this definition of the scope of family policy. However, for such an analysis it is important to recall the fact that the Swedish family underwent a great deal of change both in terms of the law and in practice during the nineteenth century.

THE SWEDISH FAMILY AND HISTORICAL CHANGE

In the eighteenth century marriage was the normal way of life for the great majority of the Swedish population. At that time the average life expectancy stood at 35 years; rates of widowhood and re-marriage were high for men and women. In the nineteenth century the number of single people began to increase and numbers of men and women went through life without marrying. Amongst the women born in the 1870s, one out of four were never married.[5] In the course of the twentieth century the marriage rate began to climb while the age at marriage was decreasing steadily. To be married again became the normal life pattern. In the 1960s there was a marked increase in the number of unmarried couples living together, a development which may be viewed as a kind of privatization of marriage. It was no longer necessary to have society legitimate the existence of a family and, as a consequence, society seemed to lose interest in controlling the process of family creation.

Divorce was fairly rare in nineteenth-century Sweden and the laws concerning it were very restrictive. Nonetheless, the number of divorces increased towards the end of the century and the increase further accelerated as a result of a more liberal divorce law which was put into effect in 1915. The increase in numbers of divorces has continued ever since, reaching its highest level in the wake of the further liberalization of divorce laws in the 1970s.

In the nineteenth century families tended to have a great number of children, but many of them died before completing the first year of life. Even as late as 1900 one-fifth of the children born died in their first year. In the years after the turn of the century the child mortality drastically declined so that by the 1930s Sweden had one of the lowest rates in the world. Towards the end of the nineteenth century a new and important development began to make itself felt: family planning. At the turn of the century families had, on average, four children but by the 1930s this figure had sunk to no more than two children per family and sometimes even fewer. Today most Swedish families have one or two children.

Family planning, however, met a great deal of resistance, above all from the more conservative sections of society. One of the results of this resistance was that in 1910 a law was introduced which prohibited the dissemination of information about and the sale of contraceptives. It remained in force until 1938. Until the same year, the legislation against abortion was very severe and a real liberalization occurred only in 1974.

Children born out of wedlock and their mothers faced a difficult life. Until late in the twentieth century, they were penalized in manifold ways by society and the community. The mortality rate of children born out of wedlock was very much higher than that of children born to married couples. Their situation and that of their mothers improved considerably when in 1905 the children were entitled to inherit from their mothers, and when in 1917 the state supported the claims of mothers for support from the fathers of their children and when in the same year youth offices were instituted to look after the interests of single mothers and their children. Widows with children, too, bore sole responsibility for their families, as well as wives whose husbands were unable to work, for whatever reason, or had deserted their families. At the turn of the century a Stockholm survey estimated that about a third of women were solely responsible for their children. The proportion was bound to be much higher among the lower classes.

Marriage and family patterns were not the same throughout the population. Amongst the poorer, unpropertied groups, both in towns as well as in the country, pre-marital cohabitation had been a common practice since the nineteenth century; nor was it unusual to be pregnant or have children before marriage. The authorities tried hard to encourage more orthodox practices, but usually with little success. There was a striking contrast in this respect between an upper- and middle-class norm of behaviour in which marriage formation and pre-marital relations were strongly controlled within the social group, and a working-class norm which was little influenced by the views of the dominant social groups and middle-class conventions. These differences in family patterns continued until the 1930s, and they may have expressed a certain nonconformity, perhaps even a protest of the lower classes against official and conventional upper-class life patterns.[6]

EARLY SOCIAL DEMOCRATIC FAMILY POLICY

There were only very few items in the earliest Social Democratic Party programmes which could be considered to belong to the realm of family policy as it is known today. One of these, point 12 of the 1900 municipal programme, concerned the 'installation of city and school canteens for dispensing good and healthy food at the lowest possible price; starting a free meals programme for school children whose parents wish to sign up'. This issue was brought up again in 1901 and in the programme of 1905, which went still further in calling for holiday camps for weak and sickly city children. According to the 1908 programme, family welfare policy was to be developed further to include a medical service in schools, free medical attention, and the organizing of sports, games and physical exercise.

However, all of these issues continued to be limited in scope and did not relate to family policy in its more precise meaning. It was only the 1911 programme which finally called for more substantial changes: 'In order to protect and care for women and the new generation the following measures are to be taken. Maternity homes and rest homes are to be set up for the use of women before and after birth. A town authority is to be created for the protection of the rights of women and children. Women are to be enabled, with the help of a subsidy if they wish, to breast-feed their own children. Medical attention is obligatory for all children during their early years of life. Towns are to ensure the health conditions of children by providing milk subsidies and day-care centres with free meals for underfed children. Camps in the country for weak children. A strengthening of the powers of the Youth Office.'

This can be considered a complete programme since it tackled the problem of birth, breast-feeding, medical care and the difficult situation of foster children, not dealt with by the previous programmes, but which were central elements of family policy. However, only women were mentioned in connection with children, and the programme showed a patriarchal slant in such expressions as 'protection and care for women'. In other words, the programme was more of a maternity policy than a family policy.

Where must one look for the pre-history of the programme quoted above? An important source is certainly a proposition put forward at the Malmö Social Democratic headquarters during the 1905 party conference. The proposition had been drafted by the women's discussion club of the local party group and demanded measures to help pregnant women who were single, abandoned and poor. During the debate that followed at the party conference Emma Danielsson and Anna Sterky stressed the fact that a man who abandoned a woman carrying his child could be compared to a strike-breaker who had turned on his mates. With such arguments they were able to ensure the support of a man, F.V. Thorssen.[7]

In this case, it was women who took the initiative. Indeed, most of the maternity policies were developed by Social Democratic women's groups, whereas those issues played little part in other party contexts. The Social Democratic women's conference of 1907 discussed four separate proposals, three of which were explicitly concerned with the problems of single mothers and their children. The doctor Alma Sundquist, who was also active in fighting prostitution, delivered the opening speech and proposed comprehensive measures to improve the financial and legal situation of such mothers.[8]

Social Democratic women thus focused exactly on the issue where the conflict between mothers' twofold task – their responsibility for the financial support of the child and their responsibility for child care – is most obvious, i.e. the case of the single mother. Their proposals were drawn up without any moralizing undertone except in condemning fathers who had abandoned their families. The social and legal state of single women and their children was still marked by injustice and prejudice. Thus, for example, in Gävle in 1910 widows with young children were treated far better by the poor relief system than unmarried mothers and their children. In the latter case children were often forcibly separated from their mothers.[9]

The position adopted by the Social Democratic women concerning unmarried mothers also had another motive: a radical conception of what marriage should be. What was ultimately being sought was the possibility of maternity without engaging in marriage.[10] This was to be made possible in two different ways. The first was to make the father assume his responsibility, and the second was to call for state intervention. The Social Democratic women's conference of 1907 adopted a resolution which claimed for women the right (which fathers had) to bear witness under oath in paternity suits. The resolution also called for the state to pay out a sum for the upbringing of children proportional to the needs of both parents, and finally, that both mother and child be given relief by the state, not from the poor relief funds, if the father did not honour his financial responsibilities. Some participants went even further. Ruth Gustafsson, later one of the first Social Democratic women to sit in Parliament, pleaded for what she called 'free marriage'. Her article, published in *Morgonbris* 1908, proposed 'conscious marriage' in order to circumvent the demeaning marriage laws which put women under the tutelage of their husbands. Married women did not acquire legal rights independently of their husbands until 1920. However, it is quite difficult to know to what extent this radical view of marriage was shared by Social Democratic women in general.[11]

Maternity insurance was also discussed at the 1907 Social Democratic women's conference. Fruitless efforts were made to invite a male speaker. Ruth Gustafsson spoke on the subject and mentioned in a more general way that 'We must not encourage any kind of charity. Our task here is to advance rights and reforms that will enable our children to live a happy and healthy life'. If the suffrage bill then pending were to be enacted women would be enabled to participate in the local decision-making committees and to work on such issues.[12] The maternity benefits proposal was accepted by the conference without any debate.

The women's Social Democratic conference may have influenced the fact that the question of maternity insurance came up in Parliament in 1908. Edvard Wavrinsky's parliamentary proposal was, however, criticized in *Morgonbris* for being too limited. The anonymous author of the article pointed out that financial independence was the basic necessity for the liberation of both women and men and that society as a whole should help to make it possible. Furthermore, the author of the article called for a generalized maternity insurance scheme independent of marital status, profession or class, which should be paid until the child was old enough to take care of itself. Thus, according to the author, childbearing, child care and upbringing had to be considered work in the same way as extra-domestic employment.[13]

The article expressed a radical opinion, exposing and politicizing the conflict between financial support and the task of caring which is central to any understanding of the historical development of family policies. The point of view expressed in this article was also much more advanced than that of the Parliamentary Committee, since the latter suggested in 1911 only a very limited proposal for a maternity insurance. This proposal was voted in by Parliament in 1912, but it was immediately repealed on the grounds that it was not constitutional. It was not until 1931 that such a law was voted in and put into effect.[14]

Mothers' and women's desire for independence and the financial responsibility of fathers were recurring themes in the political work done by Social Democratic women. In 1910 the Social Democratic women's group of Norrköping presented a proposal to the second international women's congress which strongly insisted that all labour parties should demonstrate their solidarity with women and 'condemn as traitors all men who abandoned women who bear their children'. The proposal was never discussed during the congress and an article in the *Socialdemokraten* labelled it a failure.[15]

The greatest conflict with men of the party appeared when the problem of single and unmarried mothers was invoked. Social Democratic women also appear to have been much more radical in their views on marriage and motherhood than the middle-class women's movements. However, these women had a hard time convincing men who belonged to their own party, even though there were occasional exceptions.[16]

The demands of the Social Democratic women for financial support and greater justice for single mothers resurfaced in the women's congresses of 1908, 1911 and 1914.[17] In 1908, for example, the congress examined the 'foster-child industry' and suggested that in order to struggle against it women should be granted the possibility to take care of their own children. The congress particularly stressed that single mothers should have an allowance for their children, to be paid by a maternity insurance fund. Fathers of children born out of wedlock were to be held responsible for them, and homes and day nurseries should be built for single women and their children.[18] The report on the congress period of 1914–19 proudly reminded readers of the new laws of 1917 which had improved the legal position of unmarried mothers and their children, as well as of the more liberal marriage laws voted in 1915.[19] Social Democratic politicians, both men and women, continued to press for a maternity insurance scheme but had no success until 1931, when such a measure was finally voted in by a Liberal government. As early as 1914 Erik Palmstierna and Gustaf Steffen had drawn up similar proposals for a maternity insurance bill which was to be presented in both chambers of the Swedish Parliament.[20] Although they both requested special measures for aid to mothers and new-born children, the bills were not passed. Kerstin Hesselgren (voted in with Social Democratic and Liberal votes) and Agda Östlund (Social Democrat) presented a maternity relief bill in Parliament in 1924. Kerstin Hesselgren was to become the head of the Maternity Benefits Commission which was set up in 1926, and whose work finally brought about the 1931 law. Yet another example was the proposal presented to Parliament in 1928 by the Social Democrat Signe Vessman.[21]

The first women in Parliament showed much concern with the maternity problem. However, although they had the Social Democratic women's group behind them on this issue, the Social Democratic Party as a whole did not seem to be any more concerned about this problem than it had previously been. In 1928 the municipal programme was revised. The earlier point VI became point VII, being shortened in the process: 'Obligatory medical attention for infants. Courses in child care. Maternity counselling offices, homes for unmarried mothers with newly born children, summer camps and day nurseries will be set up. Financial relief for needy mothers during nursing period.'

The debates of the Social Democratic parliamentary group distinguished themselves by their lack of interest in maternity and family policy problems. Social insurance was generally dealt with in 1926, and it was defined as accident, sickness and unemployment insurance. Gustaf Möller opened a meeting of the Social Democratic parliamentary group in 1928 with a talk on 'social insurance questions, that is unemployment insurance, health insurance and flat rate old age pensions'. Thus, the issue of unemployment was taken very seriously whereas maternity policies were mentioned only in the minutes of a meeting in 1930, in the course of which a proposal for maternity insurance coincided more or less with the proposal put forward by the committee.[22]

Some attention should be paid to the importance the party gave to the problem of unemployment in the 1920s and 1930s as opposed to the problems of maternity in general and of women and children in particular. It thus becomes apparent that the Social Democrats engaged above all in male-oriented politics, and that the women were neither able to outnumber men in their party nor to wield influence in areas they felt to be important.

The family policy as formulated in the 1928 party programme remained in the municipal programme for a long time without any changes. It was not until 1944 that point 13 was added to the main party programme. This point called for 'help in establishing a family and creating a home for it. Society guarantees spacious and good apartments at acceptable costs for families with children. Measures are to be taken to support domestic work, the care and upbringing of children. Social measures for reducing the burden of child care must be introduced.' It must be pointed out that this programme came somewhat late, since the 1930s had already witnessed a breakthrough in Social Democratic family policy. This, however, was not so much concerned with maternity issues as such as with population policy.

FAMILY POLICY AS POPULATION POLICY

Population issues appeared in the Swedish political arena around the turn of the century. However, they were hardly taken up by the Social Democratic Party. This situation was completely changed by Alva and Gunnar Myrdal. The way in which they reshaped the previous maternity policies was novel and caused a certain amount of bewilderment and even irritation amongst those who had supported the Social Democratic position. However, it won acceptance from politicians like Gustaf Möller, Minister for Social Affairs, who felt that pronatalist arguments could be used to win over middle-class parties in the battle for urgent social reforms.[23]

Social Democratic women felt overtaken by the new situation created by the publication of Alva and Gunnar Myrdal's book *Kris i Befolkningsfrågan* (Crisis in the population question). The book suddenly gave a new legitimacy as well as a new appearance to old and specific women's questions. This can be illustrated if we look at the abortion controversy. In 1935 a bill drawn up by a committee designed by the Minister of Justice introduced the concept of social reasons for abortion. The bill was greeted with satisfaction by the Social Democratic Women's Association, but when the bill was made public it met a storm of protest. The pronatalist ideas of the Myrdals were put forward as arguments against the bill. The historian of the Social Democratic women's movement wrote that 'those who had been the most eager in fighting for the humanizing of the abortion law (which Social Democratic women always did), seemed now to have less of a sense of responsibility when it came to the number of children born'.[24]

In 1938 a new abortion law was introduced. It did not mention any social reasons justifying abortion. This was a direct consequence of the refusal of the 1935 Population Commission to accept abortion on social grounds. Such a liberalization of the abortion law would have increased the number of abortions and would have affected the goals set by the pronatalist population policy for the birth-rate.[25]

The 1935 Population Commission also suggested other measures. Most of the proposals in the experts' main report as well as in the eighteen sub-reports of the commission were rejected, though others were adopted. For example, in 1937 marriage loans were introduced. These were meant to encourage earlier marriages, longer periods of fertility in wedlock and, as a consequence, an increase in births. The aims of the 1937 law for maternity relief were to influence population growth in terms of both quantity and quality. Relief funds were paid out to young mothers who were particularly needy. The money that had to be paid out reached such levels that the allocated funds were exhausted several times over. Quite obviously, poverty among Swedish mothers had previously escaped the politicians' notice. At the same time, the Swedish government put into effect a modest benefits programme, the 'motherhood penny', aimed at practically all women who became mothers. Furthermore, in 1935 it was decided to build so-called 'child-abundant houses' for families with many children and in serious economic difficulties. An important law was passed in 1938 which forbade employers to fire women on the basis that they were pregnant. In the same year the 1910 law forbidding the sale of contraceptives was repealed – free choice in having children was the principle that stood behind this law.[26] The pronatalist motives on which the great breakthrough in family policy measures in the 1930s was based continued to direct the policy of the 1940s and particularly that of the Population Committee established in 1941. The most striking achievement of this committee was the introduction of universal child allowances by a law of 1947 which came into effect in 1948.[27]

Pronatalist policies see the individual as the means, not as the end. This is the reason why such policies are fraught with problems in any democratic society. Many people, although belonging to the Social Democratic movement, did not agree with the pronatalist ideas of the Myrdals. Some, like Gustaf Möller, saw pronatalism as a tactical means of pushing through social reforms. The same tactical motivation for accepting pronatalist policies can also be found, at much the same time, in the Norwegian Labour Party.[28]

What was the impact of this pronatalist vision on the women and children who were its objects? I have already mentioned the negative reaction of the Social Democratic Women's Association to the 'quantity of births question' as applied to the abortion law. Another negative effect was that the maternity insurance of 1931 was absorbed into the maternity relief scheme of 1937. The consequence was that women who worked outside the home during their maternity leave did not receive any benefits.[29] The policies did, however, also entail concrete improvements for mothers and their children. That a married woman could not be fired because she was pregnant was an important step forward. Very important also was the fact that maternity relief money, the 'maternity penny', and later the universal child allowances were paid out to the mother. This gave women a real, though limited, influence on the financial situation of the family.[30] In a 1939 conference on maternity relief it was pointed out that married women who managed money were an entirely new phenomenon, especially in rural areas.[31]

The issue of money being paid out rather than being deducted from income taxes continued to be an important one for Social Democratic women. A comment on the 1954 report of the Family Committee to the Ministry of Social Affairs pointed out that 'an opinion poll conducted by us has underscored the social and psychological importance of paying benefits directly to the mother. A standard increase by means of any kind of tax rebate for families with children will not be felt to be the same thing as a sum paid out for taking care of children'.[32]

The care for children continued to be seen as the responsibility of women while men/fathers were not expected to take on any responsibilities. Financial support paid out to women was therefore the only logical step. The problem of women's sole responsibility for children, combined with their financial incapacity, had remained unchanged since the turn of the century.

The mixed feelings of the Social Democratic women about the population policy objectives of the 1930s and 1940s surfaced again. The Social Democratic Women's Association conducted an inquiry amongst its members in conjunction with the establishment of the Population Committee in 1941.[33] One of the many questions asked was whether the population question required a 'changed outlook on life' and a new view on children and the family.

Amongst the local groups answering this question thirteen gave a positive answer while 135 gave a negative one. The latter answers were often motivated by the belief that the populationist view was not democratic, and they showed a deep-seated criticism of pronatalist policies. 'No dictatorship, no children on command!' was one of the responses. Others were: 'We cannot agree that people should bear children in order to fulfil their duty towards society', 'The new way of life mentioned in the question is unacceptable for all of us Social Democratic women. . . . Society must not become a goal in itself, its citizens must be able to live in a dignified and human way. . . . We would like to point out that the individual is the prime concern and society only a secondary consideration'. One group wrote: 'We feel that women should be able to decide by themselves whether they want to have children or not. They should have other tasks and interests in society besides acting as child producing machines.' And another insisted: 'An attitude to life which disregards the well-being of people and which focuses instead on fulfilling a debt to society cannot be accepted by Social Democratic women. We must decide by ourselves whether we want children and how many we want.'

Social Democratic women were thus very consciously defending democratic values, more so perhaps than many of their male party companions. They continued to do so after the 1950s, when family policy – particularly the Family Commission established by Ulla Lindström in 1962 – focused on the task to 'analyze the various problems connected with the social services for families with children'.[34] From the 1970s, the goal of maternity benefit and child allowances was replaced by the call for a parenthood insurance. This change expressed that the conflicts around reproduction and the responsibility for it were no longer considered to concern only women, but also men. The Social Democratic Party programme of 1975 included the demand for 'equal rights and equal responsibility for men and women in family, employment and society'.[35] This call for equal rights of women and men in the family is based on a new attention for the continuity and the core of human society, namely reproduction.

Beyond the practice of such equality of rights, in family and employment, there is possibly a further insight to be gained: i.e. that a society which refuses to take account of its own essential core problem necessarily bears a profound conflict within itself. It risks becoming a society in which those who are both its weakest and most important members – the children – are forced to bear the future burden of this conflict. In the course of the entire history of the Social Democratic Party, the Social Democratic Women's Association and its predecessors have continuously attempted to bring this conflict into the open, to render it visible and to politicize it, and usually they met little response within the party as a whole. Will it be their future task to influence, with a greater impact, the Social Democratic family policy and thereby also a new vision of social equilibrium and justice in an extremely important area of society?

NOTES

1　SFS (Svensk författningssamling – Swedish legislative records), 1900, no. 75.
2　Report in a letter of the Swedish Language Institute, Stockholm.
3　Sveriges Socialdemokratiska Arbetareparti (SAP) Programme, 22nd Party Conference, 1964, p. 19.
4　Statens offentliga utredningar (SOU, Swedish government reports), 1972, no. 34, pp. 52ff.
5　S. Carlsson, *Fröknar, mamseller, jungfrur och pigor. Ogifta kvinnor i det svenska ståndssamhället*, Studia Historica Upsaliensia 90, Acta Universitatis Upsaliensis, Uppsala, 1977; A.-S. Kälvemark (Ohlander), 'Kommer familjen att överleva? Historiska aspekter på äktenskap och familj i det svenska samhället', in H. Norman (ed.), *Den utsatta familjen. Liv, arbete och samlevnad i olika nordiska miljöer under de senaste tvåhundra åren*, Kristianstadt, LTs förlag, 1983.
6　A.-S. Kälvemark (Ohlander), *More Children of Better Quality? Aspects of Swedish Population Policy in the 1930s*, Uppsala, Almquist & Wiksell, 1980, p. 137.
7　C. Carlsson, *Kvinnosyn och kvinnopolitik. En studie av svensk socialdemokrati 1880–1910* (The image and politics of women. A study of Swedish Social Democracy 1880–1910), Lund, Arkiv avhandlingsserie, 1986, vol. 25, pp. 266ff.
8　ibid., pp. 266, 270.
9　J. Gröndahl, 'Single mothers and poor relief in a Swedish industrial town (Gävle) at the beginning of the twentieth century', in M. C. Nelson and J. Rogers (eds), *Mother, Father and Child. Swedish Social Policy in the Early Twentieth Century*, Reports from the Family History Group, Uppsala University, Department of History, 1990, no. 10, pp. 31–50.
10　C. Carlsson, *Kvinnosyn och kvinnopolitik*, p. 266.
11　ibid., p. 286.
12　Transactions of the First Social Democratic Women's Conference of Sweden, 1908, p. 59.
13　Quoted in C. Carlsson, *Kvinnosyn och kvinnopolitik*, p. 268.
14　SFS, 1912, no. 339; SOU, 1929, no. 28, p. 23; SFS, 1931, no. 281.

15 Y. Hirdman, 'Den Socialistiska hemmafrun. Den socialdemokratiska kvinno-rörelsen och hemarbetet 1890–1939' (The socialist housewife. The Social Democratic women's movement and housework 1890–1939), in B. Åkerman *et al.* (eds), *Vi kan, vi behövs. Kvinnorna går samman i egna föreningar* (We can, we are needed. Women form their own associations), Stockholm, Akademilitteratur, 1983, pp. 24ff.; C. Carlsson, *Kvinnosyn och kvinnapolitik*, p. 269.

16 C. Carlsson, *Kvinnosyn och kvinnapolitik*, p. 276.

17 H. Flood, *Den socialdemokratiska kvinnorörelsen i Sverige* (The Social Democratic Women's Movement in Sweden), Stockholm, Tidens förlag, 1960, p. 108 and *passim.*

18 ibid., p. 109.

19 ibid., p. 126.

20 MFK (proposal in the first chamber of the Parliament), 1914, no. 80, and MAK (proposal in the second chamber of the Parliament), 1914, no. 168.

21 MFK 1924, no. 202, and MAK 1924, no. 327; SOU 1929: 28.

22 Protocol of the Social Democratic parliamentary group (Labour Movement Archives, Stockholm).

23 A.-K. Hatje, *Bevolkningsfrågan och välfärden. Debatten om familjepolitik och nativitetsökning under 1930- och 1940-talen* (The population question and prosperity. The debate about family policy and the rise of the birth-rate in the 1930s and 1940s), Stockholm, Allmäna förlaget, 1974, p. 31.

24 H. Flood, *Den Socialdemokratiska kvinnorörelsen*, p. 193.

25 A.-S. Kälvemark (Ohlander), *More Children*, p. 86.

26 ibid., pp. 55ff.

27 A.-K. Hatje, *Bevolkningsfrågan och välfarden*, p. 102; see also Å. Elmér, *Från Fattigsverige till välfärdsstaten. Sociala förhållanden och socialpolitik i Sverige under nittonhundratalet* (From the Sweden of the poor to the welfare state. Social conditions and social policy in Sweden in the twentieth century), Lund, Aldus, 1975, p. 102.

28 K. H. Nielsen, 'Det norske Arbeiderparti og befolkningsspørmålet i mellom-krigstida' (The Norwegian Labour Party and the population question in the inter-war years), *Norsk Historisk Tidskrift*, 1979, pp. 287–304.

29 L. Drangel, *Folkpartiet och jämställdhetsfrågan: Liberal ideologi och politik 1934–1984* (The people's party and the question of equality: Liberal ideology and politics 1934–1984), Falköping, A. B. Folk & Samhälle, 1984.

30 H. Hernes, 'Die zweigeteilte Sozialpolitik: eine Polemik' (Divided social policy: a polemic), in K. Hausen, H. Nowotny (eds), *Wie männlich ist die Wissenschaft?* (How male is science?), Frankfurt a.M., Suhrkamp, 1986, pp. 163–75.

31 A.-S. Kälvemark (Ohlander), *More Children*, p. 95 and *passim.*

32 Swedish Social Democratic Women's Association, Report 1956, p. 35.

33 Swedish Social Democratic Women's Association, Report 1941, p. 42.

34 Statens offentliga utredningar (Swedish government reports), 1961, vol. 38, and 1964, vol. 36, p. 2. For details of the development up to the present time see A.-S. Ohlander, 'Das vergessene Kind? Der Streit um die sozialdemokratische Familienpolitik', in M.C. Nelson and J. Rogers (eds), *Mother, Father and Child*, pp. 22–7.

35 Programme of the SAP, 1975, and its changes at the SAP conference of 1984.

Chapter 4

Models of equality for women: the case of state support for children in twentieth-century Britain

Jane Lewis

The campaign for family allowances and its pre-World War I variant, mothers' endowment, was initiated and led by feminists, and state payments in respect of children have remained an important issue for feminists throughout the twentieth century. This is because provision for children raises two fundamental issues pertaining to the gender division in modern industrial societies: first, that of the division of resources within the family, and second, the relationship between wages and work and the support of and care for dependent family members. The classic surveys of poverty in the late nineteenth century by Charles Booth (in London) and Benjamin Seebohm Rowntree (in York), and in the late twentieth century of a national sample by Peter Townsend, all failed to examine carefully the way in which resources were divided after they entered the family.[1] Throughout the twentieth century this concern has been the prerogative of feminists, concerned about the relative poverty of both wives and children. Eleanor Rathbone, who formed the Family Endowment Society in order to campaign for family allowances in 1917, and who was in Parliament as an Independent MP to oversee the passage of the Family Allowances Act in 1945, pointed out that the male wage should provide a reward for individual effort and should not necessarily also have to meet the needs of a wife and unspecified number of children. She also emphasized that women's work as wives and mothers was not rewarded and that a disproportionate amount of child poverty resulted from these two factors. In her initial formulation, family allowances were intended to provide an allowance for children and a wage for mothers.[2]

This chapter seeks first to locate the debate over family allowances in the context of (i) the assumptions of social investigators and policymakers about family relationships and about the proper role of the state in relation to the family, and (ii) the social reality of women's position in the family and the meaning women gave to it. It may be argued that the feminist case for family allowances, which emerged in the years before World War I and which was formalized chiefly by Rathbone in the early 1920s, accurately reflected the aspirations of early twentieth-century women and challenged both the structure of the wage and the direction of state policy in respect of social security provision. The claim to family allowances was based on motherhood and 'difference', which Rathbone saw as an explicit break with the pre-war mainstream feminist movement's preoccupation with the vote, a claim based on equality, although not infrequently also justified by the importance of securing representation for the views of mothers. But the argument for family allowances was profoundly radical in terms of its idea that allowances would both value women's unpaid domestic work and promote women's equal pay in the labour market; once provision for dependants became a charge on the state rather than on the wage, the case for a family wage for men disappeared.[3] However, from the mid-1920s, the feminist case for allowances became submerged (the idea of providing a wage for mothers was abandoned completely in 1924),[4] and the proposal became the focus of a wide variety of political groups who believed that family allowances would achieve widely differing social goals, from population growth to a better 'quality' population, and the vertical redistribution of wealth. This part of the story is accorded less space here because it has already been told in some detail. The historian of family allowances has concluded that no single group can be credited with the passage of the family allowances legislation. Rather, government was converted to the necessity of introducing allowances in order to hold down wages during a period of war-time inflation.[5] Reflecting the strength of this motive behind their introduction, family allowances were never sufficient to cover the costs of a child, nor was there any intention that they should be seen as a means of valuing women's work. In 1977 allowances and child tax credits were merged into a payment called child benefit, which, like its predecessor, was (after considerable parliamentary debate) paid directly to the mother.

The question of how to pay and care for children still provides one of the most challenging questions feminists can put to economists.[6] It has also proved a divisive question for feminists, because it begs what has been called the impossible choice between 'equality' and 'difference'.[7] The final part of the chapter suggests that while the feminist campaign transcended the equality/difference dichotomy in that it sought to make a claim based on motherhood that would also help to secure equal pay for women in the labour market, it did not challenge the gender division of work, paid and unpaid. Eleanor Rathbone wanted women to be rewarded for their work as mothers. However, there was no question in her mind but that the idea that the care of young children was properly women's work, and, like nineteenth-century feminists, she continued to believe that women had to make a choice between marriage and motherhood, and paid employment. In its final form, the policy of family allowances sought to mediate unequal outcomes in terms of the division of resources within the family, without seeking to change the structures which gave rise to the inequality in the first place.

When the idea of family allowances was first mooted, in the years before the First World War, such an idea of state intervention was radical and the acceptance of the gender division of labour in and outside the home reflected the reality of women's position and the hardship that would be imposed on working-class women if they had to undertake full-time work as well as undergo frequent pregnancy and do hard household labour. The position of late twentieth-century women is very different. Family size has become considerably smaller and household labour easier, and the proportion of married women working outside the home has increased sixfold since World War II. The increase in paid employment since the war has been predominantly in the service sector and has been intimately connected to the growth of the welfare state. Working hours have shortened and the vast majority of married women with dependent children entering the labour market since the 1950s have worked part-time. Child benefit (and the campaign to increase its value) has continued to represent a valid response to the problem of the unequal division of resources within the family, especially because it is paid to women. However, it does not address inequalities in the division of paid and unpaid work and indeed may be argued to encourage the assumption that caring for children is 'women's work'. In addition, the value of the allowance has been allowed substantially to erode during the 1950s and 1960s, and again from the late 1970s. In the circumstances of the late twentieth century therefore, the power of such a policy to effect substantial change in the position of women is severely reduced.

THE EARLY DEBATE: STATE ASSUMPTIONS AND WOMEN'S POSITION

During the late nineteenth and early twentieth centuries, the ideology of 'separate spheres', with men taking their place in the public world and women remaining in the private sphere of the family was firmly supported by Victorian social and medical science[8] and informed social policymaking. It was the position of middle-class women that most closely conformed to prescribed behaviour. Prior to World War I neither single nor married women of the middle class engaged in paid labour, with the result that marriage was, as the feminist Cicely Hamilton bitterly remarked in 1909, their only 'trade'.[9] A majority of working-class women, both single and married, had in contrast always engaged in paid employment, although the regional variations were considerable. For example, in textile districts equal numbers of women worked alongside men, while in mining districts little or no paid work for women was available. In the case of married women, their paid labour was often casual, consisting of a day's charring or hawking fruit as and when the dictates of the family economy demanded it. Significant numbers of married women were also engaged in 'homework', particularly in London, and particularly in the tailoring trade and in box making. Not surprisingly such work tended to escape the attentions of the census enumerators. However, women's contribution to the family economy was crucial: 1/6d so earned could feed a family of three for two days in the years before World War I.[10]

Irrespective of the different behaviour of women in different social classes, policymakers legislated on matters affecting primarily poor families as if the ideology of separate spheres was actually reflected in the behaviour of all women. The 'ought' regarding women's role in society was thus conflated with the 'is'. Most middle-class social investigators and philanthropists were in no doubt but that the fundamentals of the male breadwinner family model, whereby men earned a 'family' wage and kept their dependent wives and children at home, was crucial to the well-being of society as a whole. In large part this was because such a model was believed to secure male work incentives. Helen Bosanquet, a leading member of the Charity Organisation Society, the most influential voluntary organization concerned with the relief of poverty between 1870 and 1910, remarked that the male breadwinner family model was the 'only known way of ensuring with any approach to success that one generation will exert itself in the interests and for the sake of another.'[11] The working-class wife's job was seen to be that of household manager and was deemed to be crucial in determining a family's level of comfort. The work of the Charity Organisation Society was geared to carrying out social casework with poor families, such that husbands and wives would be encouraged and enabled to fulfil their appointed tasks.[12]

Social investigators were quick to stress the important role played by working-class mothers. In 1893, Henry Higgs stressed that the quality of the working wife's housekeeping was crucial and 'could throw the balance of comfort in favour of one workman whose wages are much below those of another'.[13] Helen Bosanquet believed the working-class wife and mother's role to be pivotal.[14] It was she who somehow made the money go round and was, in the final event, prepared to sacrifice herself for the children. The passing of the 1870 Married Women's Property Act allowed women to keep control of their own earnings and was strongly influenced by arguments that mothers were more likely than fathers to see to it that their children were fed and their school pence paid. Policymakers were prepared to give sympathetic consideration to the 'needs of motherhood'. But they failed to recognize the situation of working-class mothers, most of whom were not fully supported by a family wage and were not likely to be full-time wives and mothers. After all, both Booth and Rowntree's surveys of London and York in the late nineteenth century showed almost a third of the population falling below a subsistence poverty line. In these families there was no chance of women and children being supported by a male wage. Even in skilled working-class families, sickness, accident or unemployment on the part of the male breadwinner could easily plunge a family into poverty. The letters of the respectable members of the Women's Cooperative Guild about maternity (published in 1915) are full of cases in which such misfortune forced the wife to work, washing or sewing, up to the eve of childbirth.[15] Social policies directed towards adult women were concerned primarily to further their welfare as mothers, but were designed to do so primarily through educational means rather than by providing transfers in the form of cash. Thus the years before World War I saw a rapid increase in the numbers of child welfare clinics and health visitors employed by local authorities.

In assuming that the husband would and should maintain, policymakers neglected the real needs of mothers. Thus the social policies affecting women that were developed by the Liberal government of the years 1906–14, particularly national health and unemployment insurance, embodied similar ideas about the responsibilities of men and women in the family. The legislation had two main characteristics: it treated adult women as the dependants of men and sought to further their primary role as wives and mothers. The first was not always compatible with the second. Despite the outcry about high levels of infant mortality, wives and children were not included under national health insurance legislation passed in 1911. The cost of covering 'dependants' would have been enormous, but as the debate over the provision of school meals for children (legislated in 1906) had shown, there was also grave concern about the state assuming the father's obligation to maintain.[16] The 10 per cent of married women who worked in insurable trades were covered under both national health and unemployment insurance (also introduced in 1911) in their own right. But their position under national insurance was never secure. Early national health insurance records showed them to be experiencing a much higher than expected rate of sickness, which led to charges of 'malingering' and a cut in their benefits in 1915.[17] In all probability their higher sickness rates were genuine; married women who worked full-time added paid labour to arduous domestic work and child care.[18] Nor were married women the only group to experience high sickness rates. Miners did likewise, but it was not suggested that they suffer penalty. Married women were singled out as scroungers and malingerers under both health insurance and unemployment insurance because the schemes operated through the labour market and they were perceived as wives and mothers first and as waged workers a poor second. In the case of unemployment insurance, the rules were tightened significantly during the inter-war years in accordance with this perception. The 1931 Anomalies Act required married women to prove that they had not abandoned insurable employment and could 'reasonably expect' to secure it in their districts. Effectively this meant that it was assumed that any woman leaving a job did so voluntarily (in order to return to her proper place at home) and just over one-third of all claims by women for unemployment benefit were refused under the Act.[19] Once in the home, women's welfare became the concern of their husbands. This kind of thinking assumed that men received a 'family wage' adequate to keep a wife and children.

If we turn to the views of working-class women themselves, we find that in large measure they shared the ideal of the male breadwinner family model which bulked so large in the imagination of policymakers, but unlike the policymakers, women were only too aware that they did not have the wherewithal to carry out the work of full-time wife and motherhood effectively. They were in no danger of confusing the 'ought' with the 'is'. The acceptance of the ideal of a male breadwinner and wife and child dependants by a large number of working women can only be understood in the context of early twentieth-century working-class marriage, which has been shown to have consisted of a complex system of reciprocal obligations.[20] At its best it may be understood as a system of economic and emotional mutual support. Neither romantic love nor sexual intimacy were central to working-class husbands and wives, but rather each fulfilled financial obligations and performed services and activities that were sex-specific. This does not mean that affection was necessarily lacking, but at the core of the working-class marriage bargain was an element of 'solid calculation'.[21] Women took responsibility for home and children. They expected to act, as social investigators felt they should, as the 'chancellors of the domestic exchequer'. In return they expected their husbands to provide and tended to judge husbands by the amount and regularity of the wage they brought home. Research into the extent and causes of domestic violence in the late nineteenth century suggests that wives were tolerant of both verbal and physical abuse if they judged themselves to have neglected their housekeeping duties in some way.[22] By the same token, men might be 'nagged' into handing over a larger portion of their wages.

Women's subscription to the ideal male breadwinner family model made sense given their material context. Early twentieth-century housework involved hard physical labour, water might be fetched from a communal tap five floors below, clothes had to be pounded in a dolly tub and cooking often had to be done on an open fire in an already overcrowded living room. In addition working women underwent frequent pregnancy. Women interviewed in an oral history of the north-west reported that they felt sorry for any married woman who was forced to do a full-time paid job as well as look after home and family.[23] This view was reflected in the writings of the (usually middle-class) women who comprised the executive bodies of working women's organizations. For example, Margaret MacDonald, wife of the future Labour Prime Minister, supported the idea of a family wage on behalf of the Women's Labour League in the belief that this would give working-class wives more leisure and more time for self-development. She added, in a manner more reminiscent of the moralizing of middle-class social investigators than of the women they represented, that this would allow working-class wives to become better companions to their husbands during the evenings spent sitting by the hearth.[24] Women trade unionists also felt that the withdrawal of female labour would benefit male wages and have the additional advantage that working-class homes would be better ordered and managed. In 1894, Gertrude Tuckwell, secretary and later president of the Women's Trade Union League, advocated 'the gradual extension of labour protection to the point where mothers will be prohibited from working until their children have reached an age at which they can care for themselves'.[25]

Thus broad support for a family wage came from female as well as from male workers, employers, and the state. It is not part of the project of this chapter to comment at length on the basis for such a shared ideal;[26] however, accepted ideas as to women's place and capacities, in other words a shared understanding of what constituted femininity and masculinity, certainly underpinned acceptance of the family wage and the gender division of labour that accompanied it. Above and beyond that, the interests of those supporting the family wage ideal differed profoundly. As we have seen, social investigators and policymakers were most concerned to promote male work incentives. In the case of male workers it may be suggested that they had a vested interest in securing the unpaid services of wives as well as in furthering the welfare of their families by claiming a family wage. Late nineteenth-century government committees of inquiry into the conditions of labour heard copious evidence from male trade unionists as to the evils of competition from female labour and the neglect of households that resulted when married women worked.[27] Working women were concerned above all to make their work manageable. They accepted the primacy of their role as wives and above all as mothers and were seeking both the time and the financial resources to do a good job. At significant points, then, their demands for social reform differed significantly from those of both policymakers and working-class men.

WOMEN'S CLAIMS 1910–1924

The leaders of organizations such as the Women's Labour League (WLL), the Women's Industrial Council (WIC), the Women's Cooperative Guild (WCG) and the Fabian Women's Group (FWG) sought above all material support for working-class women to make their position as wives and mothers more tenable. In the Women's Corner of the *Cooperative News*, the debate over the economic position of married women opened with a consideration of whether they could or should be independent. It was argued that childbearing was a social function, deserving of state support. One correspondent asked: 'Because a man sells his labour while the mother applies hers directly in the home, why should he claim to be the breadwinner?'[28] The FWG and the WIC saw immediately that a measure like national insurance, while grounded in assumptions relating to appropriate gender roles within the male breadwinner family model, offered little to women, and indeed 'merely intensified the regrettable tendency to consider the work of a wife and mother in her home of no money value'.[29] Women's organizations did not conflate the family wage ideal with the actual circumstances of working-class women and they were not likely to give support to policies that did so. Working women's representatives were on the whole content to leave women's position in the labour market to be dealt with by the trade union movement, but felt that the state should step in to help wives and mothers, so many of whose husbands did not earn a family wage. Not only should the state provide education and information, but also better maternity services and cash support. Thus, while accepting the gender division of labour, women's demands ran counter to policymakers' concerns to do nothing to undermine the assumption that men provided for their families.

In the years before World War I, women's groups and individual women social reformers differed in terms of what they felt the best form of state intervention to provide cash support for mothers should be. The FWG conducted an investigation into the circumstances of a small group of women and their families in a poor area of South London and stressed both the way in which the struggle to make ends meet sapped the health and strength of the wives, and that the state should act as a guardian to children, providing maintenance.[30] As a group they proved one of the strongest early advocates of 'mothers' endowment'. However, a suffragist and settlement worker, Anna Martin, took a rather different view.[31] Martin was above all conscious of the burden imposed on mothers as a result of both the responsibilities they bore for care of home and children and their lack of ready access to financial resources. She felt that many of the state measures taken to improve maternal and child welfare only made matters worse. For example, the 1907 Act requiring the medical inspection of school children, which nevertheless failed to make adequate provision for the treatment of any problems that might be discovered, amounted, she believed, to an injunction to mothers 'to make bricks without straw'.[32] Mothers were told what was wrong with their children without being provided with the means to do something about it, with the result that the burden of managing the household economy and making ends meet was actually increased.

Anna Martin also reported that the working-class women living in houses around the settlement in which she worked were not pleased by the government's decision in 1906 to allow local authorities to provide school meals for needy children:

> The women have a vague dread of being superseded and dethroned. Each of them knows perfectly well that the strength of her position lies in the physical dependence of husband and children upon her and she is suspicious of anything that would tend to undermine this. The feeling that she is the indispensable centre of her small world is indeed the joy and consolation of her life.[33]

The wives she knew objected to state provision of school meals on the grounds that it would both undermine their role and authority within the family, and their husbands' obligation to provide. In thinking the latter, the views of at least this small group of working-class women, reported second-hand by Martin, would seem to have had more in common with policymakers who worried about any measure that threatened male work incentives than with the male labour movement leaders who campaigned hard for the school meals legislation. Martin's solution to the problems of working-class wives was for the state to legislate them a portion of their husbands' wages. She thus implicitly attributed more blame to working-class men's failure to share income equally than to the inability of men to earn a family wage.

The truth of this is hard to establish. It may be suggested that trade union men's first preference was for a higher – family – wage, which was in line with that of their wives, but that they campaigned for school meals because they seemed more immediately attainable.[34] Certainly, recent historical research has tended to stress the mutual interdependency of working-class husbands and wives;[35] however, contemporary research into the division of money within families has revealed that women and children tend to receive a distinctly unequal share.[36] There is no reason to suppose that this was untrue of the early twentieth century; after all, Rowntree saw fit to comment on the fact that few wives appeared to know what their husbands earned and the FWG documented the way in which husbands would usually reserve a greater or lesser amount from their wages for their own use, although in some communities it was not uncommon for men to 'tip up' their wages and hand across their pay packets unopened.[37] Martin's proposals were echoed by other feminists during the 1910s, but in face of evidence as to the number of men who did not earn a family wage the FWG idea that the state should take more financial responsibility for motherhood attracted more widespread support. It also served to sidestep the issue of where to apportion blame for married women's economic insecurity. Mrs Pember Reeves, who took charge of the FWG's South London investigation, felt that 'the woman who shrinks from the feeling that her wifehood is a means of livelihood will proudly acknowledge that her motherhood is a service to the state'.[38] However, by no means all men in the labour movement approved of the idea. In 1909, Ramsay MacDonald, leader of the Labour Party, declared mothers' endowment to be 'an insane burst of individualism, under socialism mothers' and children's right to maintenance would be honoured by the family and not by the state'.[39] In other words, he saw the campaign for the state endowment of motherhood and for female autonomy as a threat to the integrity of the family and to men's claim for a family wage, and as an attack on one of the basic underpinnings of late nineteenth- and early twentieth-century respectable working-class masculinity, viz. that a man should 'keep' a wife and child.

During World War I, government took up the idea of mothers' endowment in relation to the position of widows. Some American states already paid allowances to widows and in 1917 the British Local Government Board reported on the US experience. It found that it was a cheaper method of providing for widows with children than taking children into institutional care, but government officials felt that the principles behind such legislation were far from clear: if the allowances were to be restricted to widows, then the theory must be that they were compensation for loss of husbands' earnings, which meant that all women with incapacitated husbands were eligible; if the allowances were to be paid to widows as mothers, then all mothers were eligible. Either way, government feared the extent of demand for such a benefit. It also remained suspicious of any measure that failed adequately to distinguish between the deserving and the undeserving: 'Ten shillings is not transmuted into eighteen by calling it a pension, nor is a shiftless mother converted into a model of care and forethought by a grant of money. The gain which comes from any new principle will depend largely on how its adoption is translated into administrative practice.'[40] If the state were to step in effectively to take the place of a male breadwinner, it was believed that it should reserve to itself the traditional expectations of a husband as to chaste behaviour and sound domestic management on the part of the female recipient of benefit. However, ensuring this would prove too great a burden of inspection and widows were left, until 1925, to the mercy of the Poor Law.

However, the war-time experience provided another incentive to women's campaign for family allowances. Eleanor Rathbone, who had already studied the position of widows in Liverpool in 1913, was impressed during the war by the workings of separation allowances.[41] These were contingent on men's military participation rather than benefits awarded to mothers *per se*, and their administration was accompanied by intrusive house-to-house investigations to ensure sobriety and good conduct.[42] Nevertheless, the policy contributed to the rise in living standards which resulted in an improvement in the health of school children (measured in terms of heights and weights),[43] and although no record was kept of the physical well-being of the mothers, there were grounds to suppose that better food and freedom from financial worries had beneficial effects on mind and body.

In 1919, Rathbone became president of the National Union of Women's Suffrage Societies (NUWSS), the largest women's suffrage organization, and her taking up of the campaign for family allowances signalled a significant reformulation of the organized feminist movement's conception of equality for women. Under her leadership, the NUWSS (or, as it became later in 1919 after the vote was granted, the National Union of Societies for Equal Citizenship, NUSEC) moved towards claiming what Rathbone referred to as a 'real equality for women'. By this she meant that 'the whole structure and movement of society [should] reflect in proportionate degree their [women's] experiences, their needs and their aspirations'.[44] It was argued that feminists should work for reforms which reflected the reality of women's interests, rather than those which aimed to make them equal to men on men's terms. Women should be able to choose the mode of employment which suited them best, whether in the home or outside it, and should receive fair recompense for it. Family allowances would provide the means of paying women a wage for their work in the home as well as giving a cash allowance for each child. Rathbone and other executive members of the NUSEC were concerned above all to end the economic dependence of married women and children, which they felt reduced them to the status of 'male luxuries'.[45] Furthermore, if women and children achieved economic independence, the chief impediment to equal pay for women working outside the home would disappear. Men would no longer be able to claim a family wage on the grounds that they had a family to support. In practice, the Family Endownment Committee set up by Rathbone in 1917 asked for a weekly allowance of 12/6d for the mother, 5/- for the first child and 3/6d for subsequent children.

In taking up the cause of mothers, the inter-war organized feminist movement was deliberately allying itself with the long-standing concerns of women in the labour movement, although, in Rathbone's formulation, the demand for family allowances also ran the risk of antagonising male trade unionists, in particular because it threatened wage bargaining on the basis of men's demand for a family wage. Eleanor Rathbone condemned what she viewed as the selfishness of middle-class women, who, having got 'all they wanted for themselves out of the women's movement when it gave them the vote, the right to stand for Parliament and the local authorities, and to enter the learned professions' sat back.[46] A significant number of leading feminists, Millicent Garrett Fawcett among them, could not accept Rathbone's new vision of equality. In particular, Fawcett objected to the way in which the priority Rathbone accorded women's 'natural' role as mothers led her to accept the claim of employers and other labour market analysts (such as Sidney Webb) that women workers were inherently less productive than men.[47] Adhering to a nineteenth-century classical liberal view of rights for women, Fawcett believed that women should confine themselves to campaigning for strict equality with men, although she was quite prepared to use arguments that relied on difference and to contend that 'the womanly and domestic side [should] weigh more and count for more'.[48] She agreed with policymakers that family allowances would probably destroy parental responsibility for children and undermine male work incentives. Fawcett also opposed Rathbone's analysis of women's inferior pay as being the result of the family wage system, arguing rather that it was the result of women being crowded into a very few occupations. Thus for Fawcett the answer was for women to seek a fair field of competition with men and to insist that their work be accepted or rejected on its merits. While Rathbone demanded reform centring on the (private) family position of women, Fawcett demanded reform centring on the (public) labour market position of women. Neither addressed the problem of the gender division of work which supported inequality in both spheres.

Rathbone's brand of what she called 'new feminism' relied more on making claims based on difference than had that of nineteenth-century feminists. But just as Fawcett was willing to appeal on the basis of motherhood, so many new feminists remained in sympathy with equalitarian aims; Vera Brittain, for example, combined active campaigning for baby clubs (aimed at middle-class mothers) with membership of the Six Point Group, which continued the fight for 'a fair field and no favour'. The lines between equality and difference have never been as clear as some commentators have assumed.[49]

Thus the campaign for family allowances grew out of women's observations of working women's actual experience of family in the pre-war years and from a conscious reformulation of what equality meant for women in the immediate post-war years. Rathbone was asking fundamental questions about the position of women in relation to the wage and the division of resources within the family, but her analysis did not extend to the gender division of work. If nineteenth-century equalitarian feminists like Fawcett claimed equality for women defined on men's terms, Rathbone was content to settle for a species of 'separatism' and ask that 'women's work' be valued: 'Women are the natural custodians of childhood. That at least is part of the traditional role assigned to us by men and one that we have never repudiated'.[50] Her concerns about men were twofold: first that, as young adult workers, they got used to a significant amount of disposable income, which resulted in the status of mother and child becoming that of male luxuries. Second, she was anxious to demonstrate that family allowances would not undermine male work incentives. Nowhere did she discuss the possible benefits of men taking a more active role in the unpaid work of the home. Thus while the post-war campaign for family allowances was not in sympathy with the idea of a family wage, sufficient to support children as well as women, it did not go so far as to question the gender division of labour that supported it. Nor indeed did Rathbone feel that the relationship between marriage and motherhood should be called into question: the Family Endowment Committee and later the Family Endowment Society did not support the idea of paying family allowances to unmarried mothers.[51]

THE FAMILY ALLOWANCES CAMPAIGN DURING THE INTER-WAR YEARS

In 1917, the Family Endowment Committee comprised seven members, four feminists from the NUSEC and three socialists. Membership expanded rapidly and in 1925 the Council became the Family Endowment Society (FES) with William Beveridge elected president and Rathbone vice-president. By this time, the feminist voice had become both outnumbered (by fifteen to five) and submerged beneath numerous other groups who supported the principle of family allowances for very different reasons, and who advocated a variety of schemes for its implementation. Rathbone was unconcerned about this development, believing that mobilizing commitment to the principle of family allowances was the most important role for the Family Endowment Society. Her own writing soon emphasized the problem of child poverty, about which most members of the society were concerned, rather than the economic independence of mothers. The Society became sensitive to any suggestions, such as that by Beveridge, the Director of the London School of Economics, in 1927, that the campaign for family allowances was infected by 'the taint of feminism'.[52] In this instance an FES member was quick to point out that Beveridge was in favour of allowances and that he was not a feminist. Rathbone's major work on family allowances, *The Disinherited Family*, published in 1924, showed that the average family of five on which all previous calculations as to family poverty had been based was atypical. Only 8.8 per cent of families had three children. Unmarried workers accounted for 27 per cent of families, 24.7 per cent consisted of a married couple with no child under fourteen, 16.6 per cent had one child, 13 per cent two, and 9.9 per cent more than three. Furthermore, 40.4 per cent of the child population was to be found in the 9.9 per cent of families with more than three children, which were also likely to be the poorest families. All subsequent social surveys of the 1930s made a point of showing not only the percentage of families falling below the poverty line, but also the percentage of children, which was always greater. During the 1930s, the highly charged debate about the relationship between mass unemployment and nutrition levels was joined by activists in the campaign for family allowances, who formed the Children's Minimum Council and argued for a range of reforms from the raising of unemployment benefit rates to free milk for school children and nursing mothers and rent rebates as well as family allowances.[53]

While the humanitarian concern about child poverty was perhaps the strongest motivation within the movement for family allowances, another vocal source of support came from the Eugenics Society, which hoped family allowances would prove a solution to the population question. In the 1920s, eugenicists argued that if allowances were given only to the able it would be possible to create a 'true aristocracy'.[54] Rathbone herself was not averse to such arguments and saw merit in allowing the state to have its hand on the 'tiller of maternity' by varying the amount payable to each child and so manipulating the birth-rate to favour 'quality' rather than 'quantity'.[55] One proposal from the Eugenics Society advocated payment of allowances only to families which had risen above 'the mean social level,' defined as those with an income of £500 or more.[56] Socialists stood in direct opposition to this, advocating allowances for the poor to be financed out of taxation. Conservatives remained suspicious of the effect family allowances might have on the father's obligation to maintain until in 1937 the Report of the Unemployment Assistance Board showed that 6 per cent of male wage-earners were better off drawing unemployment benefits than when they were working. For the most part, these cases were ones 'in which the applicant has a low wage rate and a large family'.[57] After 1937, Conservative opinion swung towards family allowances as a means of maintaining work incentives for men with large families and low wages.

Firms and institutions began experiments paying family allowances during the inter-war years. For example, under Beveridge's directorship, the LSE paid allowances in an effort to raise the birth-rate among academic staff. By 1939, twenty firms, including Pilkingtons, Tootals and Cadburys, had adopted some system of allowances. L.J. Cadbury stated categorically that family allowances were 'a method of wage payment'.[58] Indeed male trade unionists were correct in their early suspicions as to the way in which the relationship between family allowances and wages would be exploited by both government and employers. The Family Endowment Society (FES) had sought to persuade the Royal Commission on the Coal Industry of the wisdom of paying family allowances to miners and thereby securing a living wage for those with large families.[59] In her enthusiasm for the ease with which a scheme for family allowances might be implemented among a specialized workforce, where the danger of workers with dependants flooding in and single men leaving would be minimized, Rathbone failed to stress the importance of keeping the issue of allowances separate from wage negotiations. The Royal Commission accepted the logic of the arguments put forward in the FES's Memorandum, but justified their recommendation on the grounds that the allowances could be used as part of, or as a substitute for, wages. Recognition by the Commission took the question of allowances out of the theoretical stage, but not surprisingly the suggestion that allowances be introduced in an industry where employers were attempting to reduce wages alienated the trade union movement. The idea of family allowances as a part of, or substitute for, wages was taken up again in World War II and was the single most important factor prompting the passage of the Family Allowances Act.[60] A memorandum submitted to the Treasury in 1938 assumed that it would not be possible to maintain wage rates at their pre-war level of purchasing power.[61] In 1940, the House of Lords seized eagerly on allowances as means of breaking 'the vicious spiral of wages and prices'[62] and introduced two motions in 1941 and 1942 in support of a state system of family allowances.

When family allowances were introduced in 1945, they were paid only in respect of children after the first and at five shillings a week per child, a much lower rate than the eight shillings recommended by Beveridge in his 1942 Report on Social Insurance and Allied Services.[63] It was maintained that all benefit rates, family allowances included, were set according to an objectively determined level of minimum subsistence. However, in the case of insurance benefits, the rates could not be allowed to exceed the lowest wage levels. While the cost of maintaining a child (at 1938 prices) was reckoned to be seven shillings, the family allowance was set deliberately and substantially lower, making it harder for lobbyists to press for increases in line with the cost of living.[64] Such a sum was not sufficient to provide a solution to the problem of child poverty, or an incentive to parenthood; it was condemned in *The Times* as showing a 'soup kitchen mentality'.[65] Nor did it secure the economic independence of mothers and children. Only one small part of the original feminist proposal for allowances was achieved. The original Family Allowances Bill proposed to pay the allowance to the father. Rathbone warned that 'sex grievance' would play a large part in the next election if the clause were not changed. Her protests, together with those of women's groups, were successful and allowances were paid directly to women.

MODELS OF EQUALITY

Since 1945, two major issues have persisted in regard to the payment of family allowances, first whether they should be paid to the father rather than to the mother, and second and more broadly, how the purpose of family allowances should be defined and whether allowances should be paid selectively rather than to all families. Rathbone's position on the first issue was clear. She believed allowances should be paid to the mother, who took primary responsibility for her children's welfare, in order to reduce her economic dependence on her husband. This issue has been raised on two specific occasions since 1945. In 1977 the Labour government faltered in its resolve to merge family allowances and child tax credits into the new child benefit because of the transfer that would take place from male 'wallet' to female 'purse'.[66] Male trade unionists were not keen to see men's tax advantage in respect to child tax credits disappear. More recently, the Thatcher government's 1984-5 review of social security floated the idea of abolishing child benefit entirely and proposed to pay a new benefit for low-waged families, family credit, through the male pay packet rather than through the Post Office where it is usually collected by women.[67] The justifications for these changes have not been dissimilar from those underlying Ramsay MacDonald's objections to family allowances before World War I, viz. that there was no reason to suppose that working men would not provide for their wives and children.

In respect to the second issue of universality versus selectivity, from 1924 onwards the leading edge of the Family Endowment Society's argument was the need to reduce child poverty, but Rathbone was not inclined to target allowances selectively so that they went only to poor families, not least because she was as concerned about gender as class inequalities. Others, like Beveridge, supported the principle of universality chiefly out of a desire to avoid means testing. Today it has been suggested that the purposes of child support payments may be threefold: to secure greater vertical equity (that is to do something about child poverty); to secure greater horizontal equity (that is to support families with children); and to secure greater intra-family equity (to give mothers more financial resources as against fathers). It is possible to argue for greater selectivity as a means of advancing the first of the objectives, although the statistical evidence does not support it.[68] Nevertheless, policy development has been and will be dependent on which objective is given priority. In the final event, because the introduction of family allowances owed most to the pragmatic desire to hold down wages, they have never achieved the objectives of any lobby group; indeed their value has been substantially eroded during the 1950s and early 1960s and again since the mid-1970s.

From the point of view of achieving greater equality for women, policies that address the issue of how to care for and support children have as much power to break what Breugel has called the 'vicious circle'[69] of inequality women find themselves in as they did when Rathbone first pointed out the implications of attaching a value to unpaid work, both for the division of resources within the family and for women's struggle for equal pay. Because women relate to a more complicated set of structures than do men, including reproduction as well as production, on the assumption of heterosexual coupling and very little collective child care (the position in post-war Britain), women become trapped in certain segregated roles in both the labour market and the home. The assumption that those who bear children will also rear them results in an unequal division of domestic and caring work which must in turn be linked to (even if it is by no means the only cause of) women's unequal position in the labour market and economic dependency on men.

In its original formulation at the end of World War I, a policy for family allowances was intended only to attach value to women's unpaid work (much in the same way as the 1970s campaign for wages for housework) and thereby to decrease women's economic dependency on men and to increase the chance of women receiving equal pay in the labour market. There was no intention of increasing women's leverage on the paid labour market; on the contrary, married women's primary role as wives and mothers was accepted. Nor was there any intention of achieving a more equal division of paid and unpaid work. While post-World War I feminists recognized that nineteenth-century 'fair field and no favour' feminism had sought equality on men's terms, their own attempt to redress the balance and achieve a 'real equality' for women was also sought on men's terms in that it addressed no challenge to the gender division of work (especially unpaid work), whose terms were dictated by men. Both feminists and the child poverty lobby group were concerned to use family allowances as a means of redressing the balance of inequality. In the classic manner of liberal welfare reforms from the period of the Liberal government of 1906–14 to the present, the measure was inspired by concern to compensate and correct outcomes – to modify market forces in determining who gets what – without attention being paid to the effects of such a policy in sustaining the unequal division of work. This may be explained in part by the way in which women in the early twentieth century seemingly shared the ideal of a family wage and had no great wish to increase their burdens by engaging in regular paid employment, although from women's point of view it was obviously problematic that the objective of redistribution in favour of children was given priority over intra-familial redistribution during the inter-war period.

Since World War II the material circumstances of adult women have changed dramatically. The labour participation rate of married women has increased from a relatively steady 10 per cent between 1911 and 1931 to 62 per cent in 1980, some 40 per cent of whom work part-time, although census figures are a notoriously unreliable guide to the actual extent of women's paid employment. This together with the decrease in the number of years spent in pregnancy and nursing (from fifteen in the 1890s to four in the post-war years), means that women's concerns are very different from the beginning of the early twentieth century and from the late 1960s have focused far more on their position in the labour market, the demand for equal pay and child care. The family wage has become no more of a reality and increasingly also a contested ideal. In this context, support for an increased rate of child benefit still has an important role to play in securing greater equality for women, but only if it is made part of a package designed to secure changes in the structures to which women relate such that a genuine equality of opportunity is created. Measures to correct inequality of outcome and attempts to achieve equality of opportunity by legislating only to provide individual redress of grievance have proved inadequate. Child benefits remain important because they are paid to women and thereby provide a sure source of income for women, who, even though they are likely to be earning, are also likely to be in low-paid, part-time jobs. But equal opportunities fully to share paid and unpaid work and leisure must rest on a broader package of policies (the most obvious being parental leaves) designed to get men to share unpaid work of household chores and caring and also human service work in the labour market, whether in old people's homes or day-care centres. Historical examination of the conceptualization of equality for women helps us to see that genuine equality of opportunity can only be achieved by more of a focus on gender, rather than on women, and more attention not just to the relationship between benefits and welfare as conceptualized by Rathbone, but between the gender distribution of benefits, work and welfare.

NOTES

1 C. Booth, *London Life and Labour*, London, Williams & Norgate, 1889; B. Seebohm Rowntree, *Poverty: A Study of Town Life*, London, Macmillan, 1913; and Peter Townsend, *Poverty in the UK*, Harmondsworth, Penguin, 1979.
2 K.D. Courtney *et al.*, *Equal Pay and the Family*, London, Headley Bros, 1918.
3 H. Land, 'Eleanor Rathbone and the economics of the family', in H. Smith (ed.), *British Feminism in the Twentieth Century*, Cheltenham, Edward Elgar, 1990, has stressed the importance of the way in which family allowances demanded a rethinking and a restructuring of the wage.
4 E. Rathbone, *The Disinherited Family*, London, Edward Arnold, 1924, pp. 296–7. Rathbone concluded that allowances should only be paid in respect of children and that the minimum wage for men should be sufficient to maintain husband and wife. S. Pedersen, 'The failure of feminism in the making of the British welfare state', *Radical History Review*, Winter 1989, vol. 43, pp. 86–110, has traced the way in which the post-war feminist vision of guaranteed economic independence for mothers evaporated by the mid-1920s.
5 J. Macnicol, *The Movement for Family Allowances*, London, Heinemann, 1980.
6 A. Coote, 'The AES (Alternative Economic Strategy): a new starting point', *New Socialist*, Nov./Dec. 1981, pp 4–7.
7 J. Scott, *Gender and the Politics of History*, New York, Columbia University Press, 1988, p. 172.
8 E. Fee, 'Science and the woman problem: historical perspectives', in M.S. Teitlebaum (ed.), *Sex Differences: Social and Biological Perspectives*, Garden City, Doubleday, 1976.
9 C. Hamilton, *Marriage as a Trade*, London, Chapman & Hall, 1909.
10 E. Roberts, *A Woman's Place*, Oxford, Blackwell, 1984.
11 H. Bosanquet, *The Family*, London, Macmillan, 1906.
12 The standard history of the Charity Organisation Society is that of C. Loch Mowat, *The Charity Organisation Society, 1869–1913*, London, Methuen, 1961. An important revisionist interpretation has been offered by A. W. Vincent, 'The Poor Law Reports of 1909 and the social theory of the COS', *Victorian Studies*, Spring 1984, vol. 27, pp. 33–63, and A. W. Vincent and R. Plant, *Philosophy, Politics and Citizenship*, Oxford, Blackwell, 1984.
13 H. Higgs, 'Workmen's budgets', *Journal of the Royal Statistical Society*, 1893, vol. 56, pp. 255–85.
14 H. Bosanquet, *Family*, p. 279.
15 M. Llewelyn Davies, *Maternity: Letters from Working Women*, London, G. Bell, 1915.
16 Cited by P. Thane, 'The working class and state "welfare" in Britain, 1880–1914', *Historical Journal*, 1984, vol. 27, pp. 877–900.
17 J. Lewis, *The Politics of Motherhood*, London, Croom Helm, 1980, p. 44.
18 Parliamentary Papers (PP), 1914, Cd. 7687, 'Report of the Departmental Committee on Sickness Benefit Claims under the National Health Insurance Act', and PP, 1931–2, Cmd. 3978, 'Report by the Government Actuary on an examination of the sickness and disability experience of a group of approved societies in the period 1921–27', trace the sickness experience of women.
19 A. Deacon, *In Search of the Scrounger*, Occasional Papers in Social Administration, no. 60, London, G. Bell, 1976.
20 E. Ross, '"Fierce questions and taunts": married life in working class London 1870–1914', *Feminist Studies*, 1982, vol. 8, pp. 575–602.
21 J. Burnett, *Destiny Obscure. Autobiographies of Childhood, Education and Family from the 1820s to the 1920s*, London, Allen Lane, 1982, p. 258.

22 N. Tomes, '"A torrent of abuse": crimes of violence between working class men and women in London, 1840–1875', *Journal of Social History*, 1978, vol. 11 pp. 328–45; P. Ayers and J. Lambertz, 'Marriage relations, money and domestic violence in working class Liverpool, 1919–39', in J. Lewis (ed.), *Labour and Love*, Oxford, Blackwell, 1986.

23 E. Roberts, *A Woman's Place*, pp. 136–8.

24 Mrs J.R. MacDonald et al., *Wage Earning Mothers*, London, Fabian Women's Group, n.d.

25 G. Tuckwell, *The State and its Children*, London, Methuen, 1894, p. 161.

26 This is explored further in my 'The working class wife and mother and state intervention, 1870–1918', in Lewis (ed.), *Labour and Love*.

27 For example, PP 1888, Cmd. 165, 'The Third Report of the Select Committee of the House of Lords on the Sweating System, Minutes of Evidence', Q. 18010; and PP, 1984, C. 7063, 'Report of the Royal Commission on Labour, Minutes of Evidence', Q. 447.

28 'Shall married women be dependants?', *Co-operative News*, 2 Nov. 1912, pp. 1375–6, and letter from 'Wife and Mother', 16 Nov. 1912, p. 1436.

29 Women's Industrial Council, *Memo on the National Insurance Bill as it Affects Women*, 1911, British Library of Political and Economic Science.

30 M.S. Pember Reeves, *Round about a Pound a Week*, London, G. Bell, 1913.

31 A. Martin, *Married Working Women*, London, National Union of Women's Suffrage Societies, 1911.

32 ibid., pp. 36–7. More medical inspection of children was taking place by 1914. See D. Hurst, 'The Growth of Treatment through the School Medical Service, 1908–18', *Medical History*, 1989, vol. 33, pp. 318–42. But as C. Webster, 'Healthy or hungry thirties?', *History Workshop Journal*, Spring 1982, no.13, pp. 110–129 has shown, during the inter-war years there were huge disparities in the results of medical checks for evidence of malnutrition in school children.

33 ibid., pp. 29–30.

34 P. Thane, 'The working class,' pp. 884–6, though she does not use the concept of the 'family wage.'

35 See especially E. Ross, '"Fierce questions"' and E. Roberts, *A Woman's Place*.

36 J. Pahl, *Money and Marriage*, London, Macmillan, 1989.

37 M.S. Pember Reeves, *Round about a Pound a Week*, p. 155; and Lady F. Bell, *At the Works: A Study of a Manufacturing Town*, London, Thomas Nelson, 1911 (first edn 1907), p. 79.

38 Mrs Pember Reeves, 'Introductory lecture: wifehood and motherhood', in Mrs Bernard Shaw (ed.), *Summary of Eighty Papers and Discussions upon the Disabilities of Mothers and Workers*, London, Fabian Women's Group, 1910, p. 5.

39 Quoted by H. Land, 'The family wage,' *Feminist Review*, 1980, vol. 6, p. 70.

40 Local Government Board, *Mothers' Pensions in the USA*, London, Her Majesty's Stationery Office, 1918, pp. iii and 14.

41 E. Rathbone, 'The remuneration of women's services', *Economic Journal*, March 1917, vol. 27, pp. 55–68.

42 S. Pedersen, 'Social policy and the reconstruction of the family in Britain and France, 1900–1945', Ph. D. dissertation, Harvard University, 1989, pp. 86 ff.

43 J.M. Winter, 'Aspects of the impact of the First World War on infant mortality in Britain', *Journal of European Economic History*, 1982 vol. 11, pp. 713–38 concludes that a rise in income was responsible for the improvement in children's health.

44 *Women's Leader*, 17 July 1925, p. 145.

45 E. Rathbone, *The Ethics and Economics of Family Endowment*, London, Epworth

Press, 1927; and M. Stocks, *The Case for Family Endowment*, London, Labour Publishing Co., 1927, p. 10.

46 E. Rathbone, *Milestones: Presidential Addresses at the Annual Council Meetings of the NUSEC*, London, National Union of Societies for Equal Citizenship, 1929, p. 8.

47 E. Rathbone, 'The remuneration of women's services', and M.G. Fawcett, 'Equal pay for equal work', *Economic Journal*, March 1918, vol. 28, pp. 1–6. Sidney Webb's influential analysis of women's wages was also published in the *Economic Journal*. 'The alleged differences in the wages paid to men and to women for similar work', *Economic Journal*, December 1891, vol. 1, pp. 635–62.

48 Mrs Henry Fawcett, *Home and Politics*, London, Women's Printing Society, 1894, p .3.

49 Scott, *Gender and the Politics of History*, ch. 9, has written about the swings between the concepts of equality and difference, using the example of American women historians, while Karen Offen has stressed the importance of difference in understanding European feminism: 'Defining feminism: a comparative historical approach', *Signs*, Autumn 1988, vol 14. However, Harold Smith has stressed that there was no clear divide between equality' and 'difference' feminists during the 1920s in Britain: 'British feminism in the 1920s', in H. Smith (ed.), *British Feminism in the Twentieth Century*.

50 E. Rathbone, *Milestones*, p. 4.

51 E. Rathbone, 'The remuneration of women's services', pp. 304–5.

52 *The Times*, 17 Oct. 1927, p. 16.

53 J. Lewis, *Politics of Motherhood*, pp. 181–6.

54 C.W. Armstrong, *The Only Way. A Suggestion to the True Solution of the Problems of Population*, London, Dunstan, 1921, p. 11.

55 E. Rathbone, op. cit., p. 247.

56 W. McDougall, *National Welfare and National Decay*, London, Methuen, 1921, pp. 196–7.

57 PP 1938, Cmd. 5752, 'The Report of the UAB for the year ending 31.12.37', p. 82.

58 *The Times*, 6 Jan. 1940, p. 4.

59 E. Rathbone, *Memo of Evidence on Belfast of the FES to the Royal Commission on the Coal Industry, 1925*, London, Family Endowment Society, 1925, p. 4.

60 J. Macnicol, *Family Allowances*, pp. 164 ff.

61 Public Record Office, T161/1116, *Memo on Wages and the Cost of Living*, 30 Nov. 1939.

62 PP (Hansard, Lords) 115 (1940), cols. 648–9.

63 PP 1943, Cmd. 6404, 'Report on social insurance and allied services', 1942.

64 J. Macnicol, *Family Allowances*, pp. 185–9.

65 J. A. Cecil Wright to *The Times*, 15.5.42, p. 5.

66 H. Land, 'The child benefit fiasco', in K. Jones (ed.), *The Yearbook on Social Policy*, London, Routledge & Kegan Paul, 1976.

67 H. Land, *Women Won't Benefit*, London, National Council for Civil Liberties, 1986.

68 M. Henwood and M. Wicks, *Benefit or Burden? The Objectives and Impact of Child Support*, Family Policy Studies Centre, Occasional Paper no. 3, London, 1986.

69 I. Breugel, 'Women's employment, legislation and the labour market,' in J. Lewis, *Women's Welfare, Women's Rights*, London, Croom Helm, 1983, p. 158.

Chapter 5

Visions of gender in the making of the British welfare state: the case of women in the British Labour Party and social policy, 1906–1945

Pat Thane

To a very large extent the social welfare actions of the British state, as of others, over the past century have been about women. Throughout the period, as for long before, females have had a higher propensity than males to suffer deprivation. Welfare provision has also to a great extent been administered, and welfare policies to some degree made, by women, voluntary and paid, trained and untrained, though they have been most prominent at the lower levels. We have come to learn how social policies (of official or unofficial agencies) are often shaped by, among many other influences, normative assumptions about gender roles, in particular about the sexual division of labour and of social responsibility, with its primary assumption of female dependency on male earning power. Also about how, reciprocally, sometimes explicitly and intentionally, sometimes not, social welfare policies shape, reinforce and perpetuate such roles.[1] We know much less about how the women's movements of the past century, whether defining themselves as feminist or not, have related to, been influenced by and tried to influence these social processes.

This chapter seeks to explore the relationship between feminism, women's movements and social policy by examining one organization of women in twentieth-century Britain: the women of the Labour Party and their approaches to policies directly related to women's lives. This has been chosen because, first, it formed a very large group within a party which during the period in question acquired major significance in British politics. Furthermore, the Labour Party was responsible for introducing the key legislation in the development of the British 'welfare state' during its first period of majority government from 1945 to 1951. The role of women in bringing about Labour's commitment to a welfare state has been underestimated. The women of the Labour Party gave especial attention to issues of social and economic policy concerning women, including women as mothers. They discussed and investigated them fully, were active in formulating and promoting policies, and they participated in their implementation, especially at the important local government level. They acted within a coherent set

of ideas which related feminism to an analysis of society, politics and the
economy.

THE POLITICS OF THE LABOUR WOMEN

Female support for the Labour Party was first organized in the form of the
Women's Labour League (WLL) in 1906.[2] Women were formally integrated
into the party in 1918, in women's sections of local party branches. This
was shortly after a majority of women aged 30 and above obtained the vote
in national elections. Women immediately joined the party in significant
numbers.[3] The pre-war membership of the WLL was probably no more
than 5,000; between 1927 and 1939 female party membership fluctuated
between 250,000 and 300,000. Women were at least half of the total individual
membership of the party in the inter-war years.[4] Their influence on national
party policy was, however, smaller than this might suggest due to the
power of the male trade union membership at the party policymaking
level.

Labour women came from a cross-section of occupations, paid and
unpaid, including housewives, manual workers, paid or voluntary employees
in a range of social services, including doctors, nurses, health visitors,
housing managers, from other professions, as well as from recipients of
welfare services. Perhaps a majority of members identified themselves as
primarily workers in the home; indeed the women's sections often described
themselves as 'the housewives trade union'. Many members experienced
severe poverty at some point in their lives and continued to do so due to
the effects of the Depression and of the miners' lockout of 1926. They came
from all regions of the country and the organization sought consciously to
draw in very poor women. They were conscious and proud of the social mix
and viewed as a positive asset the variety of experience and expertise in their
ranks for assessing, analysing, proposing, implementing and administering
remedies for social problems. They felt that their varied membership made
them uniquely capable of doing all these things in a way that was informed
whilst also sympathetic to the needs of women.

They were well aware of the difficulties and opposition they faced within
a party of mixed sex and of the tensions between class and gender loyalties.
There was criticism of their leaders and of the majority of members from
some feminists, including some within the party, for not taking a more
openly oppositional stance towards the men of the party on issues of especial
concern to women. Most of the Labour women, however, had chosen to be
active in a mixed sex political party because they believed that the changes
necessary to improve society, including women's position in it, required
political action. They believed that only the state had the power and the
resources to bring about necessary change. This, they believed, would only

result from organized political pressure, and the Labour Party, in view of its somewhat stronger record of support for women's rights, was more likely than its rivals to apply it on women's behalf. This did not mean that they were optimistic about their power strongly to influence the party or prepared to be subservient to males within it. They recognized that an historic change in gender roles would not be easily achieved, that it would take time and much persuasion to shift age-old structures of male power. Meanwhile, they believed, women required training and group support from other women if they were to learn to wield public power. One of their conscious roles was to provide such support along with political and administrative education for inexperienced women.[5]

Most of the Labour women aimed in the long run for a convergence of male and female influence and priorities within the party, but felt that in the shorter run women must emphasize issues of especial relevance to women, which men through ignorance or discrimination neglected. Many, however, believed that there was likely to remain a permanent difference between male and female perspectives and hence a need for a distinctive women's group within the party. Views differed on this point, as they always have done within feminism.

Labour women complained, time and again, that male professionals and politicians lacked the understanding of the social conditions with which they presumed to deal, which women possessed either from personal experience or through engagement in social or political work.[6] Men needed to learn from women's experience. Certainly the women had a different body of experience and a different style of working from most Labour men. Social deprivation was more central to their concerns; the problems associated with paid labour were at the core of the men's interests, though neither group focused solely upon these areas. The women based their policy proposals generally upon asking poor women what they felt their needs to be, and they worked to get such women elected to central or local government or appointed to administrative bodies, where their experience could guide their actions and, it was hoped, influence those of their colleagues.[7]

THE FEMINISM OF THE LABOUR WOMEN

They acted within a clear though contested and evolving framework of ideas. To summarize the mainstream view as expressed at their conferences and in their publications: the salient feature was their recognition that the multiple deprivation suffered by homebased women could not be dissociated from the sexual division, and the relative deprivation of females, within the economy as a whole. They developed a coherent critique of what would now be called the gender division in society and of the role both of state action and of the operation of the labour market in constructing and reinforcing it. No more than Labour men did Labour women believe that considerations of 'welfare' should be dissociated from such labour market questions as the determination of wages and allocation of employment, since the latter were the primary determinants of living standards.[8]

They assumed that most women were, and would continue to wish to be, wives and mothers. Like other feminists of the inter-war years they noted the currently prevailing differences between the sexes (without seeing them as total, necessarily 'natural' or immutable), and sought a feminism which valued rather than devalued the home and maternal experience of women without simultaneously devaluing women's paid labour. They saw the home, indeed, as potentially a base for the empowerment of women rather than as necessarily the source of their inescapable bondage, though plainly much change was needed before it could become so. They assumed that in the present the primary responsibility for children lay with the mothers who bore them, but did not see it as desirable that this should survive for all time. They were, for example, advocates of day nurseries, not only for the children of mothers active in the paid labour market, but for women working at home, to leave them space free from child care and domestic responsibilities to devote to their own leisure, education, political or voluntary action, and for self-development.

They were convinced that paid work in the formal labour market was not women's only escape route from the private to the public sphere, in particular in view of the double burden which it almost invariably entailed. They sought to ensure that work in the home was valued by enabling the largest occupational group in the country, the housewives, to assert themselves publicly, to contribute their voice to politics, and hence to advancement of their own status and causes, proportionately to their total numbers in society.[9] They believed that power could be achieved by women by means of political action.

More broadly they were concerned about the appropriate roles of women in civil society once most of them had attained the formal symbol of full citizen rights, the vote; and about the type of society and state which women as citizens should seek to shape. The debates among the Labour women, and among other women's groups, on these issues should be seen as part of a wider discourse in Britain and elsewhere during this period. This was a time when throughout Europe the roles of states and their formal and informal relations with their citizens, even the definition of who was a full citizen, were changing and widening in unprecedented ways and at unprecedented speed. In Britain the dominant theme among those women and men who were concerned with social and political questions, from the 1870s to the Second World War, was the nature of the social, political and legal rights and obligations which bound citizen, state and society together. The various strands of feminism did not inhabit an enclosed intellectual world but occupied a space within this broader field of discourse. The demand for the vote before 1918 in Britain was very rarely aimed at the vote as an end in itself but at achieving for women the range of rights, statuses and obligations of full citizens (which different groups defined in different ways).[10]

The state and the society which the Labour women sought to shape was one in which the marriage relationship and support from male earnings need not necessarily subordinate and silence women. They recognized, however, that women needed other forms of emotional and institutional support and some independent financial resources if they were to escape domestic subordination. State social and economic policy had an essential part to play in providing this. It was also important to strengthen the role of fathers in relation to children. The Labour women were not explicit about the content of paternal responsibility, other than financial, though there were suggestions that fathers should play a larger part in the education and leisure of their children. They did not explicitly challenge the division of labour between the sexes in the home. Such a challenge lay outside the conceptual framework readily available to contemporary thinking. The implicit challenge to orthodoxy, however, was immense in its long-term implications for gender relations.

They did not believe that mothers *ought* to remain in the home. It was occasionally asserted by members of the organization during the Depression that married women should vacate the paid labour market, to liberate jobs for men, but this was always heavily outvoted at the Labour women's conferences.[11] The central aim, rather, was to give women, including mothers of young children, an effective choice as to their place of work. They emphasized strongly that both domestic labour and activity in the paid labour market were acceptable goals for women, provided that either was freely chosen rather than imposed either by male authority or by poverty. Equally importantly women's work opportunities, conditions and rewards in the paid labour market should be equivalent to those of men.

This was the Labour women's formulation of what equality meant for women. In the language of today, it sought the difficult task of achieving compatibility between gender equality and gender difference in a flexible manner suited to the variety of female and male needs and choices. A central aim was to make women's choices a new reality by means of a range of strategies. One was support for trade unionism, including vigorous support for strikers,[12] to enable men or women to become effective household breadwinners where necessary or when they chose. They recognized that the male breadwinner norm was fictional in many, perhaps most, working-class families because of the low pay, unemployment, disability or absence of an adult male. This was certainly true of most working-class families before World War I; even the most skilled workers experienced irregular incomes that were due to seasonality or slackness of trade. This pattern continued through the inter-war years for many families, though others suffered more severely than before because of the length of the Depression in some occupations and regions, and many gained in level and regularity of income in those sectors of the economy which were expanding in the 1930s.[13]

The Labour women gave great emphasis to strategies to bring women's wages and work opportunities to the level of men's and to promote economic independence for those who chose or needed it: female trade unionism, legislative improvement in women's pay and working conditions, improved social services to provide greater support and freedom for all working mothers, paid and unpaid, were seen as complementary. They argued that state action was necessary to reduce the double burden on women engaged in paid labour, recognizing that however desirable it might be, there were few signs of men sharing the domestic burden (though it was not unknown)[14] and there were no known means of forcing them to do so. Their consistent demand was not simply for equal pay, which, they were very early to recognize, could be restricted to the very few areas of precisely equal work between men and women, but that women's wage rates in all occupations, *especially* those defined as exclusively female, which were notably low-paid, should be raised to comparable levels to those of men[15] and women's access to training and promotion should similarly be equalized. Equally actively they opposed the 'marriage bar' which in the inter-war years excluded women on marriage from a growing range of occupations, both professional and manual. These included the Civil Service and teaching, though in the latter it was often successfully resisted. These exclusions had little to do with pronatalism and much to do with male fears of unemployment and prejudice against women in positions of status and authority, in this first historical period in which significant numbers of women entered occupations which theoretically opened such opportunities to them. It was also due, in the growing 'white blouse' tertiary sector, to the policy of management of maintaining a high turnover of cheap labour as the need for clerical and secretarial workers grew.[16]

They insisted, however, that work in the home was in no way different – except in often being harder and the hours longer – from work in the paid labour market and was certainly as vital to the economy as a whole. In 1911 Margaret MacDonald, the wife of the Labour Party leader, complained that according to the new National Insurance Act

> All women who are not wage-earners working for employers are 'non-workers' . . . this sets up a quite erroneous standard of useful 'work', for the woman who looks after her house and family usually works quite as hard and contributes quite as much to the family wealth as her wage-earning husband.[17]

They were impressively careful in conference speeches and publications in their use of language to avoid the equation of 'work' exclusively with paid work in the formal labour market.

Their monthly journal *The Labour Woman* was early to espouse the notion of the companionate, sexually fulfilling marriage,[18] but it did not perceive a woman's world as bounded by marriage. To enable women to escape from unsupportive marriages they pressed vigorously and with some success for improved divorce, separation, maintenance and custody laws.[19] They demanded equal treatment for the unmarried and the married mother and her child, and also for women to have maximum control over reproduction and conditions for safe childbirth, to maximize their control over their own lives.

Strikingly, Labour women did not treat 'welfare' as wholly distinct from 'work' or as unrelated to the fundamental gender division in society. Similarly, their thinking transcended the dichotomies of work inside and outside the home, paid and unpaid, between public and private, equality and difference, class and gender, because such distinctions made little sense of most women's, especially working-class women's lives. Rather they sought more effective ways than had previously been available of enabling women to integrate the variety of experiences, needs and demands which made up their lives.

SOCIAL POLICY BEFORE 1914

A central place among the social services which the Labour women believed would enhance the capacity of women to reconcile personal fulfilment and public power with marriage was given to more and better housing at rents which working people could afford. Well laid out and equipped, these would transform women's lives by minimizing the drudgery of work in the home. They developed imaginative plans, especially during and after the two world wars, for improved housing, based upon the proposals of their members arising from responses to questionnaires; these were presented to government committees and to the party, with some effect. They had real influence upon the work of some city housing authorities e.g. Manchester, which was noted for its pioneering role in working-class housing.[20] The aim was to give workers in the home working conditions at least equivalent to those of members of the paid labour force.[21] These demands were at their peak around the time of World War I. It is not fanciful to see a parallel between these demands for shorter hours and better conditions for women working in the home with the demands of male workers for an eight-hour day – 'eight hours' work, eight hours' leisure, eight hours' sleep' in each day – which were then also at a peak.

The Labour women were equally committed to the expansion of maternity and child welfare services. Concern to improve the survival rates, health and education of children grew in all political quarters from at least the 1860s as the need to build a healthier race of workers, soldiers and future mothers became a major preoccupation in Britain, as in other leading industrial and imperial states. In all such states there was anxiety about the declining birth-rate, the physical unfitness of much of the population, and demands for state and voluntary action to improve health care, advice to mothers, feeding and education for children. These were an integral component of the intensified sense of nationalism, racism and international conflict – as much economic and imperial as military – visible in the last quarter of the nineteenth century, and culminating in the First World War.[22]

Strictly pronatalist pressure was weak in Britain. The emphasis was rather upon reducing infant mortality, for which there was much scope, upon saving the lives of the thousands who did not survive infancy, and improving the physical quality of surviving children,[23] rather than increasing the birth-rate. Although eugenicist thinking was discernible, its influence was limited and ambiguous.[24] More influential, and with a strong tradition in nineteenth-century thought and action especially in the field of public health, were environmentalist ideas which stressed the capacity of even the poorest 'stock' for improvement through medical care, better food, housing, education and a cleaner environment. The desire to increase births was somewhat stronger in the 1930s when the birth-rate fell to an unprecedentedly low level. The number of births per 1,000 population in England and Wales was 14.4 in 1933, having been 25.5 in 1920.[25] Gloomy projections were published of a coming serious decline in Britain's population size. But even then there was scepticism in influential circles as to whether any means existed to persuade mothers to have babies if they did not wish to and there were no vigorous attempts to promote childbearing.[26]

Labour women shared these demographic concerns, though with some different emphases. Whilst generally, if reservedly, patriotic they grasped the opportunity to improve conditions of childbirth and child rearing presented by the preoccupation with infant mortality of influential people whose motivations were quite different from their own. As they acquired a stronger voice they sought to redress the imbalance in the public debate on health and environmental issues, which had given more prominence to the needs of children than to those of mothers, by giving greater weight to the personal needs of mothers, indeed of all women. They could, however, still best guarantee a hearing when they associated the health of women with pregnancy and childbearing. They demanded improved health care before, during and after pregnancy, and also for illness not associated with pregnancy, access to birth-control advice and devices, and paid maternity leave for those in paid work.[27]

Labour women were critical of National Health Insurance when it was first introduced in 1911 because it made no provision for the general health care of women other than the minority employed in a limited sector of paid work. This continued to be the case until the introduction of the National Health Service in 1948. The only provision for such women under the 1911 Act was a maternity benefit of 30 shillings, payable for the wives of insured men. This scheme covered manual workers only, but in practice excluded many of the poorest families who had no member in regular employment and hence able to make the obligatory regular contributions. Initially the benefit was to be payable only to the man, but after a battle led by women was paid directly to the mother from 1913. This struggle was waged most fiercely by the Women's Co-operative Guild. The Women's Labour League, though not unsympathetic, held aloof. In principle they favoured such an independent cash resource for wives, but pointed out that a husband brutal enough to withhold maternity benefit from his wife might well withhold an equivalent amount from his wage-packet if she received the benefit directly and might even feel a resentful incentive to do so.[28] The central problem afflicting poor families, they argued, was low pay and underemployment rather than pervasive male selfishness. They recognized that poverty was a major cause of conflict within the household. They did not deny that, within the household, resources might be unequally distributed, but, in effect, though not in the language of the 1980s, they were insisting that the 'class' issue of the material deprivation of working people could not in any simple way be separated from issues of gender. They did not put class before gender but saw the two as inseparably linked.

In 1913 the Labour women established a mother and baby clinic in a poor district of London. They believed that poor mothers needed and wanted advice and material help when bearing and rearing children and that this should be supplied by the state with funds redistributed from the better-off, but until this could be effected voluntary effort was necessary, provided that it was done in no patronizing manner, that

> it was not a question of superior people trying to go in and teach the mother her job, she had the right to every kind of knowledge and the working mothers were asking for teaching in all the subjects which affect them in the life of their children.[29]

They were well aware that such actions could be interpreted as 'the imposition of middle class notions upon the working class and as part of the increasing invasion of the private domain by representatives of the public domain',[30] and they were determined to subvert such impositions. They recognized that voluntary action, if sensitively provided, could be as supportive as that of state agencies. However, they believed that the state could provide services more systematically than the voluntary sector and, even more importantly, could provide benefits and services as rights, as the voluntary sector could not. In addition, it was important to try to ensure that state services did not become excessively bureaucratized and intrusive, by striving for maximum decentralization through elective local authorities who should be responsible and accountable to local communities. Hence their determination to encourage women to stand for local election and to scrutinize, criticize and fight to improve local services. When the Labour women looked to the state it was very often to an ideal of a democratic, decentralized, accountable state which it was widely hoped in these early days that Labour would bring to fruition when in government.[31] In this respect also their thinking must be located within a wider social and political discourse.

Despite the anxiety expressed in influential circles about demographic and health questions, the central state was slow to act in response. The initiative in seeking to provide for the needs of mothers and children came from voluntary action which was gradually supplemented by the work of local authorities. This was consistent with the guiding liberal theory of the British state before 1914 that local communities should take responsibility for the needs of their members through either voluntary or local government action, calling upon the support of the central state only as a last resort.[32] From the 1850s female philanthropic organizations trained selected working-class women to give instruction on health care and treatment, and instruction in the Bible, to needy mothers. From the 1890s local authorities gradually adopted this model of of trained 'health visitors' advising mothers (but no longer giving religious instruction) in their homes.[33]

The 1900s saw the foundation in urban areas of maternity and child welfare centres whose activities concentrated upon providing advice to mothers about child care, plus a variable range of additional services including medical treatment, free or subsidized meals for mothers and young children and sometimes for pregnant women, and lessons in cookery, sewing and housewifery. Some centres were initiated by men, including local health officials, many by women, some by local authorities, more by voluntary action in which women were especially prominent. All made great use of mainly female, voluntary labour. At least 400 such centres existed by 1914.[34]

It is, then, to the level of combined local authority and voluntary action that we must look for the first sustained social policy measures concerning mothers and young children. These initiatives show women as innovators of a range of influential policy ideas, such as health visiting (which remains an important part of the British health service) and 'home helps' (free domestic service for mothers after childbirth and others in need), which remain part of local authority social service provision, and many of the activities of welfare centres. Such activities developed from the long experience of women in voluntary work with the poor. This experience drew a certain number of them to suffragism. They came to believe that state involvement in social welfare was essential if the worst deprivation was to be removed. They argued that a male-dominated state had ignored grave social problems, and therefore the state needed the experience and values of women at its centre if it was to respond to the needs of all of its citizenry. It was an argument for the vote not in terms of equality but of difference. The experience of women in philanthropic organizations of the conditions of poor women created an early link between the women's movement and welfare.[35]

The activities of welfare centres and of health visitors have been criticized as socially conservative, first for placing the blame for infant mortality and morbidity upon the incompetence of mothers and ignoring the role played by poverty, and second for reinforcing conventional gender roles. It would have been surprising if such individuals and institutions had been overtly critical of conventional gender roles and there must certainly have been occasions when health visitors and other professionals treated poor women insensitively. Yet there is also much evidence that men and women in voluntary and official positions understood that poverty and environmental hazards were the outstanding problems and recognized the terrible task of women battling to bear and raise children in appalling conditions.[36] They were also aware of how little could be done in the short run significantly to improve these conditions and that many babies would die and women suffer whilst the big solutions were awaited. On the other hand they could share with poor women advances in knowledge, especially about prevention, which could at least palliate their problems. This was a period in which knowledge about the connections between nutrition, hygiene and health were advancing and there was genuinely valuable and feasible advice to be made available to all mothers and not only poorer ones. Many middle-class mothers regretted that they had no access to the advice on infant care available to poorer women.[37]

Poor women expressed their gratitude for what seem in retrospect minor pieces of information, but which could make the difference between the survival of a child or not or between good or poor health for the mother: not knowing, even when they had (just) adequate incomes, the importance of eating regularly in pregnancy and what to eat; that even a short rest each day was desirable and often possible; that although no poor women could avoid regular housework, some of it heavy, when they were pregnant, it was better, and possible, to avoid unnecessary heavy labour; walls could go unwhitewashed and floors uncleaned for the period of a pregnancy.[38] At very low levels of knowledge, health and living standards, even small accretions of knowledge could have major effects.

Of course women resented inappropriate or 'patronizing' advice, and ignored it, as *Labour Woman* pointed out:

> The mother of a healthy baby of some six months old told the present writer that she had studied with great care the latest book of advice for the bringing up of babies and she had come to the conclusion that she did a number of things that were wrong according to the book and yet definitely helped in the general well-being of her household. She felt that no doctor or nurse knew the whole story and she began to wonder how many mothers with three or four children, all of them healthy, actually kept to the rules to which they listened so politely.[39]

But the learning process had two sides and some professionals and volunteers learned to understand the needs of poor women, to give sensible advice and to handle their relations with them some sensitivity.[40]

By 1914 health visitors had been appointed in 154 towns in England and Wales. Consultations about infant welfare, under either voluntary or official auspices were available in 45 towns. Meals for pregnant and nursing mothers were provided in at least 27 towns. It is highly probable that the extent of voluntary activity is underestimated.[41] The infant mortality rate fell dramatically from *c*. 150 per 1,000 live births in the 1890s to 110 in 1910–12 to 80 in 1920–2, 70 in 1926, 50 in 1939. However, it is wholly unclear, and controversial, what contribution was made to this fall by the work of health visitors and welfare centres in relation to the effects of rising living standards and public health improvements (such as improved water supplies).[42]

Action by the central state in relation to maternal and infant welfare was relatively slight before 1914. The Midwives Act, 1902, established a system of training and certification of midwives, which was to be compulsory for all new practitioners. It was an attempt to reduce that part of infant mortality attributable to incompetent delivery. In a limited way, initially, it improved standards of midwifery, though at the cost of a higher degree of male medical control of midwife training than female supporters of the Act thought desirable.[43] The provision of maternity benefit in 1911 has already been discussed.

In other respects before the First World War, the central state turned its attention to the health of older children and fully employed members of the manual labour force, male and female rather than to the needs of mothers and infants. From 1906 free school meals were provided for needy schoolchildren and from 1907 children in state schools underwent regular health inspections. It was the intention of the male civil servants who devised this legislation that conditions of ill-health thus revealed should be treated. They knew well that poor families could not easily obtain treatment, and free treatment for all was their ultimate aim, but they faced opposition from the medical profession to such threatened intrusion upon their territory. Nevertheless, treatment was encouraged and in many places provided and from 1912 it was financed by central government.[44]

In 1909 a new and lasting principle was introduced into the income-tax system: a £10 per annum abatement of tax for the lowest band of taxpayers, earning below £500 and above the tax threshold of £150. The motivation for this has not been adequately researched. Also in 1909, the Trade Boards Act provided for a minimum wage for women in some of the lowest paid occupations, after pressure from women's groups, in particular the Fabian Women's Group, which laid especial stress upon the effects upon health of their low pay and appalling conditions of work.

SOCIAL POLICY 1914–45

With other women's organizations, the Labour women carried on the fight for improved maternity services through the First World War. Politicians were receptive as a result of their anxiety to replace the men dead in the trenches and to ensure that recruits for future wars were physically stronger than many of the volunteers and conscripts to military service had proved to be on this occasion.[45] The Labour women demanded the involvement of working-class women in the administration of the new services, ideally incorporated within a comprehensive state maternity service staffed by women.[46] Such a service, but minus the feminist clause, became official Labour Party policy. By 1922 this included free medical services for the entire population, 'home helps' for mothers, free or low-cost food and milk for expectant and nursing mothers and for children at and below school age. These items of policy owed most to pressure from the women.

The combination of female with distinctly non-feminist war-related pressures encouraged the central government in July 1914 to give matching grants to local authorities to establish child and maternal welfare services. These were permissive but were increasingly taken up by local authorities, due in part to determined pressure from women at the local level, notably those of the Women's Co-operative Guild and the WLL. They took every opportunity to turn to women's advantage the widespread anxiety about the physical condition of the population. The Co-operative Guild's publication *Maternity*, a volume of letters from working women about the pain of childbirth and child rearing in poverty, published in 1915, was part of this campaign. Government expenditure on maternity and child welfare expanded during the war and central government civil servants worked to encourage improved services at local level, for reasons expressed by a member of the government:

> In the competition and conflict of civilizations it is the mass of the nations that tells. Again and again in history a lofty and brilliant civilization embodied in a small state has been borne under by the weight of a larger state of a lower type. The ideals for which Britain stands can only prevail as long as they are backed by a sufficient mass of numbers. It is not enough to make our civilization good. It must also be made strong . . . under existing conditions we waste before birth and in infancy a large part of our possible population.[47]

From 1917 central government provided increased funding for midwifery, doctors and ante-natal care, especially in the poorer regions of the country. From 1915 it also subsidized classes to train women in maternal skills and from 1916 midwifery training was made longer and more rigorous. The outcome, so far as it can be estimated, was that in 1914 there were 600 full-time health visitors in England and Wales, in 1918 1,355. By 1918 the number of welfare centres had grown to well over 1,525, over half of them voluntarily supported.[48]

These initiatives were consolidated and reinforced in the Maternity and Child Welfare Act, 1918. This enabled local authorities to establish Maternity and Child Welfare committees, which were required to include at least two women. These would receive central government subsidy for a range of activities, though none was obligatory. It was for local government to decide to implement them and to provide a substantial portion of the finance through local taxes. The services they might provide were: provision of hospital services for children under five, maternity hospitals, 'home helps' (i.e. domestic workers to take over the housework of the mother after childbirth, free of charge for necessitous women), food for expectant and nursing mothers and for children under five, crèches and day nurseries, homes for the children of widowed and deserted mothers and for illegitimate children and 'experimental work for the health of expectant and nursing mothers and of infants and children under five years of age'. From 1919 the government also subsidized voluntary agencies providing similar services.

Labour Woman welcomed the Act but reminded members that 'it will be of little value unless through the energy of working men and working women the Local Authorities are compelled to put into force the powers they have now been granted' and that

> The appointment of working women on the Maternity Committees is of pressing importance. No Medical Officer of Health and no Health Visitor can supply the knowledge which the working woman has gained from her daily experience. Both Health Visitor and Doctor are apt to think in terms of the sick baby rather than the healthy baby because their experience is so much founded upon the treatment of those who are ailing in hospitals or elsewhere. They must rub their scientific knowledge up against the everyday knowledge that the working woman has acquired.[49]

Labour and other women directed much of their effort in the inter-war years towards pressing for full implementation of this legislation in their localities, for maximum involvement of working women in policymaking and administration, for the staffing of services by women, and against attempts by central government in the Depression to cut services back to the minimum. They had increasing influence as Labour achieved local electoral success, especially in persuading Labour-controlled local authorities to improve medical, maternity and child welfare, housing, education and such services as public baths.[50] In 1924 all members of women's sections were asked to report on maternity hospital provision in their neighbourhood and the women regularly made child and maternal welfare an issue in local elections.

In general maternal and child welfare services, despite falling very seriously short of any ideal and despite local variations due to differing local economic conditions as well as differing political priorities, were significantly improved by 1939 compared to 1918. By the later 1930s there were 5,350 health visitors, all of them women, employed by voluntary bodies and local authorities in England;[51] all 409 welfare authorities in the country supplied milk to expectant and nursing mothers, either free or at less than cost price. Some also provided cheap meals and about 50 provided home helps. About 97 per cent of babies received at least one visit from a health visitor. About half of all mothers received ante-natal care; rather more than half of all babies attended welfare centres. There were 3,462 such centres by the end of 1937 which saw about 63 per cent of all babies. Conditions in the centres varied considerably but they were normally staffed by a health visitor and a doctor. They treated only minor ailments but were dispensers of free or subsidized food and/or milk. However, doctors did not always have the relevant expertise, the centres were often overcrowded and the health visitor too harassed to give individual attention. Yet for many women they were the only available source of individual advice.[52]

A survey of the health of 1,250 working-class women undertaken on behalf of women's organizations in 1933 found that 404 of them claimed to have had no instruction in health care, 591 had learned all they knew from welfare centres and antenatal clinics, 245 from a health visitor or district nurse, 67 from their own doctor. The report was devastating in its criticism of the inadequacy of health care for women and its description of terrible ill-health, which was attributed above all to poverty. But it was positive about the role of welfare centres and health visitors in all but their numbers. It pointed out how women always put the needs of their husbands and families first and were more anxious to learn how to care for the health of their children than of themselves. The introduction of the National Health Service in 1948 was of the greatest benefit to such women.[53]

The Second World War, like the First, saw enhanced government enthusiasm for maternal and child welfare services. By 1943 cheap or free milk was universally available. Provision of other services remained at the discretion of local authorities, but 1,389 free ante-natal clinics were provided by local authorities, which also provided the services of a midwife or a hospital bed if needed, free of charge to the 'necessitous'.[54]

Such services were greatly extended by the post-war Labour government and women also benefited from the expansion and reconstruction of health, education and housing services. The Labour women were not the sole influence upon the growth of services before during or after the war; indeed their relative importance is hard to assess in the current state of research. But they were an important source of pressure for the formulation and implementation of policies and especially of a number of innovative policy ideas (such as 'home helps').

FAMILY ALLOWANCES

Provision for the health of women before, during and after childbirth dealt with only part of women's needs. For women to be able to reconcile choice, independence and maximum control over their lives with marriage and motherhood they also needed to have some income independent of their husbands. Labour women differed among themselves as to the priority they gave to this.

Their conference of 1907 passed unanimously a resolution,

> whereby necessitous mothers shall receive monetary assistance at the time of the birth of children and whereby mothers with children dependent upon them shall receive continued adequate support to enable them to attend to the children without having to work for wages.

In 1909 a meeting of their Central London branch discussed, inconclusively, the 'endowment of motherhood'. The debate revealed much uncertainty about the meaning of the term and a variety of views and fears which were to re-emerge as the discussion continued over the following thirty-six years. One argument for 'endowment' was that it gave mothers choice as to whether to enter the paid labour market, another that it could reinforce woman's 'highest duty' of home-making. A majority, including Margaret McMillan, the pioneering campaigner for child welfare, and Mary Macarthur, a leading member of the women's trade union movement, vigorously opposed the latter view. Margaret MacDonald supported maintenance before and after childbirth, and added that the wife without children also deserved endowment 'for the work she performed in the home'. She went on: 'Public opinion should be changed in the direction of recognizing the wife's full share of her husband's earnings, and whatever reforms are proposed should be in the direction of increasing the responsibility of both parents for their children'.[55]

This issue was hotly debated among the Labour women. The working-class trade unionist Ada Neild Chew argued against it that the central problem was the inadequacy of wages, male and female. To guarantee wives a fixed proportion of the miserable sums entering working-class homes would not increase household incomes though it might increase tension between husband and wife in already difficult circumstances.[56] In her view the gender conflict over household resources had to be solved simultaneously with the class conflict over the distribution of national resources.

In 1913 the further argument was expressed that 'childhood pensions' would assist the achievement of equal pay by undermining the conventional argument that the family responsibilities of men justified their higher pay. The Labour women were divided in their response. Overwhelmingly, they opposed this justification for higher male wages, not least because it overlooked the substantial financial responsibilities of many women for kin. But many of them feared that 'childhood pension' proposals would unintentionally reinforce the social perception of parenting as the sole responsibility of the mother and would encourage fathers to neglect their responsibilities.[57]

The various proposals for family allowances acquired wider currency and support during World War I. The Labour women were convinced that the experience of the war, when many women had been left to cope alone with their families, had increased the sense of independence and fighting spirit of women. State action during wartime, such as the introduction of state dependants' allowances and pensions for the wives and children of servicemen and to those thrown out of work by the transition from war to peace, were widely seen as evidence of the need of families for regular state support and of the capacity of the state to supply it – and of the disciplinary controls that might accompany it.[58]

In 1918 Margaret Llewelyn Davies, general secretary of the Women's Co-operative Guild argued persuasively the case which was supported by a majority of Labour women: 'state endowment of motherhood' should be combined with the extension of health, welfare, housing and educational services to provide for children what poor parents could not, on any income realistically likely to become available to them. She argued that state payments would give women more freedom and independence. They would also redistribute wealth, boost the economy by increasing purchasing power, and strengthen workers in strikes: male workers were well aware that worry over the starvation of wives and children often forced a strike to a premature end and that employers knew this.[59] These arguments remained the heart of the case of the labour movement supporters of family allowances until they were implemented in 1945.

The Labour women differed from Eleanor Rathbone, the leading campaigner for family allowances[60] – although her precise proposals varied over time – in insisting that payments must be provided by the state and financed from national taxation and not at all, as she was sometimes prepared to accept, provided by employers. Labour sought to emancipate workers from the control of employers. Evidence from France suggested that this means of paying family allowances increased employer control.[61] Allowances could, for example, be withdrawn from workers on strike. Labour also opposed her readiness to advocate contributory allowances, on a national insurance model, arguing that this would be insufficiently redistributive and also likely to exclude many of the poorest; and they resisted her belief that the economy could only support such payments if, in compensation, the wages, especially of unmarried males, were reduced or not increased. At a time when employers were seeking to cut wages, often successfully, Labour had every reason to be disinclined to offer them one more means to do so.

However, Labour politicians and supporters differed among themselves about the most effective means to increase state assistance to poor women in the foreseeable future. The debate was conducted against the background of an economy in serious trouble, with consistently high levels of unemployment from 1920 until World War II, and high levels of concern about it and its effects on health and welfare. From 1921 to 1940 there were never less than 1 million people – one-tenth of the insured population – out of work;

from 1931 to 1935 the figure was never below 2 million and in 1931–2 it reached almost 3 million. The proportions unemployed in some industries and regions were much higher, e.g. 48.5 per cent of steelworkers in 1932, 24.8 per cent in 1938, 27.7 per cent of the insured population of Scotland in 1932.[62] Inter-war politics was dominated by Conservative governments, except for two brief periods of weak minority Labour government (1924, 1929–31). The Conservatives were inclined wherever possible to hold back social expenditure and the Labour Party, as we will see, was deeply divided on the question of family allowances. In these difficult circumstances, the leaders of the Labour women embarked on a policy designed to make gains for women piece by piece, but their caution sometimes provoked criticism among their members.

In 1917 the executive of the Women's Labour League passed a resolution in favour of 'pensions for mothers', 'urging that widows with children or women whose breadwinners are incapacitated should receive pensions for their children sufficient to ensure their upbringing in a suitable and comfortable fashion'. This they sent to ministers, hoping for sympathy for a moderate first step towards family allowances at a time of heightened consciousness of the plight of war widows. Mothers' pensions of this type were official Labour Party policy from 1918. Unsuccessful parliamentary bills for their introduction were several times put to the House of Commons by male Labour MPs from 1919. The Labour women strongly favoured extending such 'pensions' to unmarried mothers.[63] This did not become party policy.

The debate in the labour movement about family allowances in the inter-war years has been described elsewhere.[64] The Labour women remained committed to allowances as their ultimate goal, on the grounds of the need of women for an independent income. The party as a whole could agree to support a package of state funded *services* as the means to provide for the needs of all poor people, whether or not they had children. These included universal free education and health services, free or cheap milk for expectant and nursing mothers and children up to age five, free and subsidized school meals and clothing for schoolchildren, higher pensions and improved services for the elderly, and adequate housing at low rents for all in need. It was argued that the establishment of such a welfare infrastructure was Labour's primary task, given the low level of existing public provision, enormous and expensive as it would be. Labour at both local and national level, when it had the power, did its best to introduce and to improve such services.

There was also general support in the party for 'mothers' pensions' for those who had borne children respectably within marriage. The first Labour government in 1924 attempted to take the first step by drafting a bill introducing widows' and orphans' pensions. They lost office before this could be implemented. A similar measure was passed by the Conservative government in the following year. It followed pressure from women in all parties and it was one of the six immediate reforms for which the leading feminist organization at the time, the National Union of Societies for Equal Citizenship, was campaigning at this time (family allowances was not among them).[65] Awareness that women were now voters had done much to make it attractive to politicians. There was immediate benefit for 163,000 women and 262,000 children, the widows receiving 10s. per week, children 5s. The legislation was further extended in 1929 and by 1933 725,000 widows and 340,000 children received pensions funded through National Insurance contributions. These were very large numbers of needy women receiving a larger sum each week than the first family allowances were to provide.

Any further move towards family allowances, however, faced powerful, though not unanimous, opposition by trade unions. It was feared that payment of family allowances would encourage employers to refuse higher wages, on the grounds that family needs were being met by other means. If their needs were met by the state, the mass of non-unionized workers would see no reason to join a union – and this, it was argued, with some justice, was a reason why some Conservatives supported state welfare. There was also the problem of the very high total cost of Labour's social proposals, in a flagging economy. Trade unionists and others argued that if Labour was to be an effective political force it had to make practicable proposals. The extension of social services rather than payment of family allowances would make the most effective use of such funds as were realistically likely to be available in the foreseeable future. There was much political sense in these arguments.

However, many trade unionists had additional reasons for opposing family allowances and indeed for fearing the capacity of state welfare to undermine the trade union movement and the condition of the working class more generally at a time of high unemployment, wage cuts and falling union membership. One of the largest, most depressed and most contentious sectors of industry was coal-mining. In 1926 the Royal Commission on the Coal Industry had recommended a combined package of wage cuts and family allowances, to be paid by the employers to fathers, so that single workers but not families would suffer reductions. Eleanor Rathbone and other prominent members of the Family Endowment Society (notably William Beveridge) had supported this recommendation.[66] This goes far to explain the bitterness between Rathbone and the Labour women who had been active supporters of the miners in their prolonged struggle with the coal-owners, including in the long lock-out of 1926–7. The influential Macmillan Committee on Finance and Industry, set up to investigate the failings of British industry, had commented in 1929 that welfare payments and services were a more economical and desirable means of meeting need than wage increases, since the older industries were believed to be crippled in particular by excessive wage costs. In 1930 a struggle was in progress involving workers, employers and politicians over different perceptions of the causes and effects of the economic crisis. At its heart was the question of the relationship between wage levels, levels of employment and welfare. When male trade unionists opposed family allowances at this juncture, it was not just because they threatened wage bargaining on the basis of a man's right to a family wage but also because they feared that, in the form in which they were proposed, they would be linked with real wage cuts, which would benefit neither men nor women.[67] Again, the issues relating to class or gender cannot be separated in any simple fashion.

Trade union opposition was not, however, unanimous. A majority of a male-dominated Labour Party/ TUC committee in 1930 reported in favour of state-funded, non-contributory family allowances. At the annual conference of the TUC they were defended strongly, especially by the miners' representatives. They argued that state – as distinct from employer – provided family allowances would not incorporate the same potential threat to family living standards, indeed could strengthen workers against employers in their current weak bargaining position, in part by assisting them to hold out in strikes. In a strike the employer might withdraw the allowance along with the wage. A state family allowance would be a right which could not be so withdrawn. On balance, the miners had come to feel that in the current state of industrial relations working people had more to gain than to lose from the introduction of state family allowances. In a situation of high unemployment, trade unions were not strong enough to secure adequate wage rates; many of their supporters had come to recognize that they needed support from the state to secure living standards. They also believed strongly that in principle the rich should support the poor through tax-financed allowances.[68]

This debate in the labour movement was not only about gender relations. Once more, it must be located within a wider discourse about the relations between the trade unions and the Labour Party, and of both with socialism, and about the role of the state in relation to the labour market. Historically the liberal influence in the trade union movement was strong. A strand within British radical liberalism was sceptical about even the moderate socialism of the Labour Party and especially of its faith in the capacity of the state to remedy the inequalities produced by the market. Its influence had weakened with the growth of the Labour Party, but it remained powerful. Liberal trade unionists put their faith in voluntary institutions, such as trade unions, as the desirable mechanism for furthering individual and collective welfare and independence. They feared any tendency to undermine such institutions and feared the controls, inflexibility and intrusions they thought indissociable from state bureaucracies. Hence the opposition of some of them to such state welfare measures as family allowances. The family allowance debate was in part about the debate between liberalism and socialism in the Labour Party and trade union movement. In 1930 the Trades Union Congress refused to endorse family allowances by 1,740,000 votes to 495,000.[69] During the 1930s more trade unionists moved towards support for family allowances, for similar reasons to those which had swayed the miners, though substantial numbers continued to oppose them.[70]

The discussion in the trade union movement indicates how complex were the issues surrounding family allowances as a policy proposal. In other circles other themes had greater prominence, such as concern about population decline,[71] and opposition to family allowances did not come only from men defending what Eleanor Rathbone called their 'Turk complex', their right to provide for their children and wives, though this was an important dimension of the debate. In a severely troubled economy, in a society in which the provision of all social services was still very limited indeed, it was, and is, not easy to judge what could be afforded. It was not obvious, when choices had to be made, which of many competing claims should take priority.

It is important to note that during their long period in office the Conservatives did not seek to implement family allowances in any form, despite the possible advantages to themselves and their supporters among employers, so much feared by Labour. The reasons for this have been much less explored than those for Labour's restraint on the issue. They are highly unlikely to have been deterred by trade union opposition, to which the historiography has paid perhaps disproportionate attention.[72]

In minor ways, in difficult circumstances, the Labour government elected in 1929 sought to subsidize larger families by means other than family allowances. The Housing Act, 1930 enabled local authorities to charge lower rents to larger families, and an Education Bill, which would have raised the school-leaving age from 14 to 15, would also have allowed maintenance grants of 5s. per week to all schoolchildren in this additional year of schooling, in families below a certain income level. The government fell in 1931 before this Bill was passed, and severe cuts in social expenditure followed.[73]

The Labour women continued to support family allowances, together with improved services, through the 1930s and, when legislation was at last imminent in 1945, supported the fight to ensure that the allowances were paid to mothers and not, as originally proposed, to their husbands.[74] Although pressure from women was by no means decisive in bringing about the legislation, in its absence it is almost unimaginable that family allowances would have entered the political agenda.

The Labour women played an important part in keeping family allowances prominent in Labour Party discussion and in pushing for improvements in other services. They were equally vital in keeping another major issue, birth control, politically alive, as has been well recounted elsewhere.[75] The reluctance of the party leadership in the 1920s officially to support the provision of free birth-control advice in local authority clinics had much to do with the importance of the Roman Catholic vote for the growing party and the determined hostility of the Church to birth control. Labour women, male Labour councillors and non-Catholic church leaders were among the groups who by 1930 pressured the Labour government into giving limited and highly qualified sanction for such advice to be made available. Limited though this sanction was, the dying down of the birth-control agitation in the 1930s suggests that in practice it must, at least on occasion, have been flexibly interpreted[76] and brought some real benefit to women overburdened with childbearing.

CONCLUSION

British social policy as expressed in official action at central and local government level up to the end of World War II broadly took for granted that a woman's place was in the home, supported by a male breadwinner. Policymakers were, however, divided as to how realistic this assumption was, and indeed can never be considered as a monolithic group. Had such a view been universal, no legislation could have materialized to assist divorced and separated wives or women within marriage.

Immediately after the war the dominant assumption changed. As a result of labour shortage, women who no longer had small children to care for were encouraged by the government to re-enter the labour force. Their full-time commitment to home and maternity has since been assumed to occupy only part of their lives, though the assumption remains that they continue to take primary responsibility for domestic work, and they have not conspicuously been encouraged to compete with men in the labour market for higher paid and high status occupations.[77]

Organized women played an important role in modifying dominant normative assumptions about gender roles in the period before 1945, though in the current state of research the importance of their influence in relation to that of others is difficult to assess. Some women became part of the policymaking process on behalf of women; others entered new careers created by social legislation – caring careers defined as suitable for women.

The experience of the Labour women suggests what women could and could not achieve. Despite their large numbers, they could make only a limited impact on a male-dominated party, and very little where their proposals conflicted with the political, ideological or material interests of powerful sections of the party. They did, however, contest these interests as women – a new experience for any British political party – and they forced on the party serious consideration of all issues concerning women's lives, including maternity. They did so with notable independence of mind and within a coherent vision of gender relations within society as a whole. If, like most political groups, they achieved less than their full goals, it was not because they lacked ideas or vision or because they were subservient to the males of the party, but because they were fighting, with little experience, against long entrenched structures of power. Seen in this light, their achievements should not be underestimated. They could most effectively wield influence at the local, community level, least at national level.

Nevertheless, they played an important part in the construction of the social policies which made up the post-Second World War 'welfare state', most of which had their origins in these pre-war discussions. A study of this kind helps us to explore the degree to which women were objects of male power and also the limits to women's power, without denying the importance of their agency in effecting change.[78]

NOTES

1 G. Pascal, *Social Policy. A Feminist Analysis*, London, 1986; A. Showstack Sassoon (ed.), *Women and the State: The Shifting Boundaries of Public and Private* London, Hutchinson, 1987; J. Lewis (ed.), *Women's Welfare, Women's Rights*, London, Croom Helm, 1983.

2 C. Collette, *For Labour and for Women. The Women's Labour League, 1906–18*, Manchester, Manchester University Press, 1989.

3 P. Thane, 'The women of the British Labour Party and feminism, 1906–45', in H.L. Smith (ed.), *British Feminism in the Twentieth Century*, Aldershot, Edward Elgar, 1990.

4 ibid.; R. McKibbin, *The Evolution of the Labour Party, 1910–1924*, Oxford, Oxford University Press, 1974.

5 National Conference of the Women's Labour League (hereafter NC) 1907. *Report*.

6 ibid. For similar comments see NC 1910, 1913, 1943. *Labour Woman*, Aug. 1928, Feb. 1945.

7 P. Hollis, *Ladies Elect. Women in English Local Government, 1865–1914*, Oxford, Oxford University Press, 1987.

8 P. Thane, 'The working class and state "welfare" in Britain, 1880–1914', *Historical Journal*, 1984, vol. 27, no. 4, pp. 877–900; N. Whiteside, 'Welfare legislation and the unions during the First World War', *Historical Journal*, 1980, vol. 23, pp. 857–74; N. Whiteside, 'Social Welfare and industrial relations, 1918–1939, in C.J. Wrigley (ed.), *A History of British Industrial Relations Vol. 11, 1914–1939*, Brighton, Harvester 1987.

9 *Labour Woman*, Feb. 1945.

10 S. S. Holton, *Feminism and Democracy. Women's Suffrage and Reform Politics in Britain, 1900–1918*, Cambridge, Cambridge University Press, 1986; S. K. Kent, *Sex and Suffrage in Britain, 1860–1914*, London, Routledge, 1990.

11 e.g. at the Conference of 1932.

12 P. Thane, 'Women of the British Labour Party'.

13 For a summary of inter-war conditions see J. Stevenson, *British Society, 1914–1945*, Harmondsworth, Pelican, 1984.

14 E. Roberts, *A Woman's Place. An Oral History of Working Class Women, 1890–1940*, Oxford, Blackwell, 1984, pp. 110–21.

15 NC *Report* 1930, 1945, though this was discussed on many other occasions.

16 *Labour Woman*, November 1930; NC *1935*; S. Cohn, *The Process of Occupational Sex-typing. The Feminization of Clerical Labour in Great Britain*, Philadelphia, Temple University Press, 1985.

17 *The League Leaflet*, June 1911.

18 E.g. in the very favourable review given to Marie Stopes, *Married Love*, in *Labour Woman*, May 1918.

19 *Labour Woman*, July 1924, July 1925.

20 Manchester Women's History Group, 'Ideology in bricks and mortar – women's housing in Manchester between the Wars', *North West Labour History*, 1987,

no. 12, pp. 24–26; A.D.S. Furniss and M. Phillips, *The Working Woman's House*, London, Swarthmore Press, 1920.

21 *Labour Woman*, Sept. 1917; Feb., Mar. 1918; Jan. 1920, among others.

22 J. Lewis, *The Politics of Motherhood*, London, Croom Helm, 1980; D. Dwork, *War is Good for Babies and Other Young Children. A History of the Infant and Child Welfare Movement in England, 1898–1918*, London, Routledge, 1987; A. Davin, 'Imperialism and the cult of motherhood,' *History Workshop Journal*, Spring 1978, pp. 9–35.

23 S. Szreter, 'The importance of sanitary intervention in Britain's mortality decline *c.* 1850–1914: a re-interpretation of the role of public health', *Social History of Medicine*, vol. 1, no. 1, pp. 1–38.

24 G.R. Searle, *Eugenics and Politics in Britain, 1900–1914*, Leyden, Noordhoff International Publishing, 1976; J. Macnicol, 'Eugenics and the campaign for voluntary sterilization in Britain between the Wars', *Social History of Medicine*, August 1989, vol. 2, no. 2.

25 B.R. Mitchell, *European Historical Statistics*, London, Macmillan, 1978, pp. 27–32.

26 P. Thane, 'The debate on the declining birth-rate: the "menace" of an ageing population in Britain, 1920s–1950s', *Continuity and Change*, 1990, vol. 5, pp. 283–305; D.V. Glass, *The Struggle for Population*, London, Oxford University Press, 1936.

27 See M. Llewelyn Davies (ed.), *Maternity. Letters from Working Women*, (1915) repr. London, Virago, 1978.

28 *Labour Woman*, Dec. 1913.

29 *Labour Woman*, July 1925.

30 M. Stacey and M. Price, *Women, Power and Politics*, London, Tavistock, 1981, p. 83.

31 For further discussion of this strand of Labour Party thinking see Pat Thane, 'Labour and local politics: radicalism, democracy and social reform, 1880–1914', in E. Biagini and A. Reid (eds), *Currents of Radicalism: Popular Radicalism, Organized Labour and Party Politics in Britain, 1850–1914*, Cambridge, Cambridge University Press, 1991.

32 P. Thane, 'Government and society, 1750–1914', in F.M.L. Thompson (ed.), *The Cambridge Social History of Britain, 1750–1950*, vol. 3, ch. 1, Cambridge, Cambridge University Press, 1990.

33 D. Dwork, *War is Good for Babies*, pp. 125–6; F. Prochaska, *Women and Philanthropy in Victorian England*, Oxford, Oxford University Press, 1980; F. Prochaska, 'Body and soul: Bible nurses and the poor in Victorian London', *Historical Research*, Oct. 1987, vol. 60, pp. 336–48; C. Davies, 'The health visitor as mother's friend', *Social History of Medicine*, April 1988, vol. 1, pp. 39–60.

34 D. Dwork, *War is Good for Babies*, *passim*; Davin, 'Imperialism'; L. V. Marks, 'Irish and Jewish women's experience of childbirth in East London 1870–1939: the responses of the host society and immigrant communities to medical welfare needs', D.Phil. thesis, Oxford University, 1990.

35 P. Hollis, *Women in Public, 1850–1900*, London, Allen & Unwin, 1979–228 ff.

36 D. Dwork, *War is Good for Babies*, pp. 126ff; Marks, 'Irish and Jewish women's experience', 35.

37 J. Lewis, *Politics of Motherhood*, pp. 101–2.

38 M. Llewelyn-Davies (ed.), *Maternity*, pp. 7, 64–5, 112, 114–15.

39 *Labour Woman*, Sept. 1918, p. 43.

40 E. Peretz, 'The professionalization of child care: the health visitor', *Oral History Journal*, Spring 1989, pp. 22–8.

41 J. Lewis, *Politics of Motherhood*, pp. 90–1.
42 S. Szreter, 'The importance of sanitary intervention'.
43 J. Donnison, *Midwives and Medical Men*, New York, Schocken, 1977; Lewis, *Politics of Motherhood*, pp. 120ff.
44 B.B. Gilbert, *The Evolution of National Insurance*, London, Michael Joseph, 1966, ch.3; P. Thane, *The Foundations of the Welfare State*, London, Longmans, 1982, pp. 77–8; B. Harris, 'Medical Inspection and the Health of Schoolchildren, 1905–1939', Ph. D. thesis, University of London, 1987.
45 J.M. Winter, *The Great War and the British People*, London, Macmillan, 1985; J. M. Winter and R. Wall (eds), *The Upheaval of War*, Cambridge, Cambridge University Press, 1988.
46 *Labour Woman*, Sept. 1918.
47 M. Llewelyn-Davies (ed.), *Maternity*, 'Preface', no page number.
48 A. Davin, 'Imperialism', p. 42; J. M. Winter, *The Great War*, pp. 193–204.
49 *Labour Woman*, Sept. 1918.
50 *Labour Woman*, Dec. 1934; June 1935; March 1936; Jan. 1937; M. Savage, *The Dynamics of Working Class Politics. The Labour Movement in Preston 1880–1940*, Cambridge, Cambridge University Press, 1987; J. Mark-Lawson *et al.*, 'Gender and local politics: struggles over welfare 1918–1939', in L. Murgatroyd *et al.*, *Localities, Class and Gender*, London, Pion, 1985; J. Mark-Lawson, 'Gender segregation and women's politics', in S. Walby (ed.), *Gender Segregation at Work*, Milton Keynes, Open University Press, 1988; J. Lewis, *Politics of Motherhood*.
51 E. Peretz, 'The professionalization of child care', p. 22.
52 S. M. Herbert, *Britain's Health*, Harmondsworth, Penguin, 1939, pp. 132–9; L. V. Marks, 'Irish and Jewish women's experience'; E. Peretz, 'Local authority maternity care in the interwar period in Oxfordshire and Tottenham', in J. Garcia *et al.*, *The Politics of Maternity Care*, Oxford, Oxford University Press, 1990.
53 M. Spring-Rice, *Working Class Wives*, 1939, repr. London, Virago, 1981.
54 *Labour Woman*, July 1943.
55 NC 1909, pp. 28–30.
56 *Labour Woman*, Nov. 1913
57 *The League Leaflet*, Dec. 1913.
58 See Lewis in this volume; S. Pedersen, 'Social policy and the reconstruction of the family in Britain and France, 1900–1945', Ph.D. dissertation, Harvard University, 1989, pp. 89–130; G. Thomas, 'State maintainance for women during the First World War: the case of separation allowances and pensions', D. Phil. thesis, University of Sussex, 1988; Lewis, *Politics of Motherhood*, pp. 165ff.
59 M. Llewelyn Davies, 'The claims of mothers and children', in M. Phillips (ed.), *Women and the Labour Party*, Headley Bros., London, 1918.
60 She was a Liberal in politics and sat as an Independent Member of Parliament from 1927 to 1946. E. Rathbone, *The Disinherited Family*, (intr. S. Fleming), repr. Bristol, Falling Wall Press, 1986; H. Land, 'Eleanor Rathbone and the economy of the family', in H. L. Smith (ed.), *British Feminism in the Twentieth Century*, pp. 104–23.
61 S. Pedersen, *Social Policy and the Reconstruction of the Family*, pp. 285–390.
62 J. Stevenson, *British Society*, pp. 266–70.
63 *Labour Woman*, Feb. 1920.
64 J. Macnicol, *Family Allowances*; H. Land, 'The introduction of family allowances: an act of historic justice', in P. Hall *et al.*, *Change, Choice and Conflict in Social Policy*, London, Heinemann, 1975, pp. 157–230.
65 NUSEC, *Object and Programme*, London, 1919.
66 J. Macnicol, *Family Allowances*, pp. 150–1.

67 TUC *Report of Annual Conference* 1930. This is the conference at which the issue was most thoroughly discussed.
68 TUC *Report of Annual Conference* 1930, pp. 10–12, 19, 32–3.
69 J. Macnicol, *Family Allowances*, p. 149.
70 J. Macnicol, *Family Allowances*, pp. 172–6.
71 P. Thane, 'The debate on the declining birth-rate'.
72 J. Macnicol's chapter, 'Attitudes of political parties', devotes a single page to the Conservative Party, which was effectively in office for most of the inter-war period and 11 pages to Labour, which was never a majority government in that period: *Family Allowances*, pp. 138–68.
73 *Labour Woman*, Feb. 1931.
74 See J. Macnicol, *Family Allowances*; J. Lewis, *Politics of Motherhood*; H. Land, 'Introduction of family allowances', for details.
75 A. Leathard, *The Fight for Family Planning*, London, Macmillan, 1980, pp. 28ff.; R. Soloway, *Birth Control and the Population Question in England, 1877–1930*, Chapel Hill, University of North Carolina Press, 1982, pp. 280–318.
76 R. Soloway, *Birth Control*, pp. 304–18; Lewis, *The Politics of Motherhood*, pp. 197–8 offers a different interpretation.
77 P. Thane, 'Towards equal opportunities? Women in Britain since 1945', in T. Gourvish and A. O'Day (eds), *Britain Since 1945*, London, Macmillan, 1991.
78 For a discussion of these issues see S. Walby, *Theorizing Patriarchy*, Oxford, Blackwell, 1990.

Chapter 6

French feminism and maternity: theories and policies 1890–1918

Anne Cova

From the end of the nineteenth century until the end of the First World War, maternity was a fundamental element in the discourse of the French feminist movement. Different and contrasting views on motherhood were discussed; their diversity depended largely on different assumptions of how women's emancipation was to be achieved, and they reflect the varieties of French feminism.[1] The debates on motherhood were particularly prominent in the feminist efforts and arguments to influence the government to legislate for the protection of maternity – a difficult task, because women could not vote or be elected. This chapter attempts to identify several trends in this debate, which was carried on in a large number of women's journals and congresses. Here, feminists grappled with the views of other and non-feminist social forces on maternity and paternity, and their discourse focused on mothers' rights and responsibilities and on the relation between the public and the private sphere.

FEMINIST VIEWS ON MATERNITY AT THE EVE OF THE TWENTIETH CENTURY

Earlier than in other countries, the decline of the French birth-rate aroused widespread debate. Whereas, around 1800, France had been the most densely populated country in Europe, by 1914 it ranked fifth in population; not until 1920 would the birth-rate equalize itself with that in other countries, and it declined from 26 per thousand in 1870 to 22 in 1890, 19 in 1911, 10 in 1916/17 and 12 in 1918. The situation haunted the public authorities from 1870, because they feared that Germany would invade France. *Dépopulation* and *dénatalité* were considered to be a 'social plague' and maternity became an object of many and contradictory comments. To the Members of Parliament, support to mothers through appropriate laws seemed to be the only way to stop the decline in fertility. Many 'repopulators' accused the feminists of being responsible for the declining birth-rate, and the feminists, on the defensive, took exception to these propositions, ascribing the reason to the lack of support for mothers. The strategy of the feminist movement as a whole was to utilize the apparent demographic danger and the glorification of motherhood as a weapon in the struggle for the rights of mothers; in the words of Maria Martin, editor of *Journal des femmes*, in 1896: 'If you want children, learn to honour the mothers.' The majority in the feminist movement demanded women's rights by means of insisting on maternity and maternalism as a distinctive and common feature of the female sex, expressed in the doctrine of 'equality in difference'.[2]

A contrasting and influential position was developed by the demographer Jacques Bertillon and his followers, for whom the decline in the birth-rate was due to masculine egotism which feared the dissipation of inheritance and preferred celibacy. In 1896 he founded the National Alliance for French Population Growth, which became the most powerful among similar organizations and was officially recognized to be of 'public utility'. Yet to Maria Deraismes, leading feminist of the late nineteenth century, 'the desire to leave a considerable fortune to one or two children' did not sufficiently explain the declining birth-rate.[3] Whereas she emphasized the struggle for women's suffrage and civil rights, she believed that the prohibition on investigating paternity in the case of out-of-wedlock children was one of the major causes of depopulation. She called for the repeal of article 340 of the Napoleonic Civil Code of 1804 (*recherche de la paternité*) and thus employed the depopulation fears to claim a fundamental right of mothers.

The abrogation of article 340 was the prevailing theme in all feminist conferences, such as in 1892 the General Congress of Feminist Societies in Paris, organized by the French Federation of Feminist Societies and the Universal Women's Union and directed by Eugénie Potonié-Pierre, secretary of the Federation and of *La Solidarité des Femmes*. Here for the first time, a congress designated itself as 'feminist'. Maria Deraismes participated and saw the principle of the pursuit of paternity adopted. Léon Richer, present as a delegate of the French League for Women's Rights (LFDF), founded in 1882, proposed that 'the investigation of paternity be permitted just as the investigation of maternity is permitted'.[4]

Criticism of article 340 posed the problem of equality of responsibility of parents towards children, of the behaviour of the father, the rights of the mother, and more particularly of that maternity which was called 'illegitimate'. Unmarried mothers, particularly young ones – according to a Member of Parliament 'the least interesting of all mothers'[5] – bore a double oppression: moral opprobrium and victimization through law. A number of women had attempted to improve their deplorable situation through philanthropic activities and institutions. The 1892 congress advocated an increase in such initiatives and Madame Léon Béquet de Vienne, president of the 'Shelter for Nursing Mothers and Pregnant Women', called for the creation of such shelters in all larger cities. She was supported by Blanche Edwards-Pilliet, a doctor, who denounced abortion as a crime 'against humanity' equal to that of infanticide (only in 1911 was the legal death penalty for infanticide abolished).[6] This position did not achieve unanimity among all the participants at the congress; many refused to increase the sanctions against women.

Louise Koppe, founder and editor of the journal *La Femme de France*, changed into *La Femme dans la famille et dans la société* in 1880 and into *La Femme et l'enfant* in 1882, recommended that individual initiative and public powers should combine to establish maternity homes. When in 1891 Louise Koppe founded the first 'Maison Maternelle' in Paris, she was supported by the politician and ex-minister Léon Bourgeois, who had developed a philosophy of solidarity which became widespread in the early 1880s, as well as by Victor Hugo, ex-minister Paul Bert and the philanthropist Théophile Roussel. Through the teaching of the psychologist Louis Marion and Emile Durkheim's *De la division du travail social* (1893), the term 'solidarity' gained currency in the political and scholarly language, and through the work of Léon Bourgeois, theoretician of radicalism, this 'solidarism' became the official social philosophy of the Third Republic. There were obvious links between this social theory, philanthropy and French feminism. In 1891, Eugénie Potonié-Pierre and Maria Martin founded the vanguard group *Solidarité des Femmes*, and Louise Koppe's maternity home, conceived as a weapon against what she called 'forced child abandonment', was inspired by similar ideas.[7] Although initially its main purpose was to take in children whose parents were unable to support them, it increasingly emphasized the bonds between children and their parents, obliging the latter to make regular visits to their children. More than half of the 60–70 children in the home had only their mother left, and Koppe's was mainly concerned about single mothers. In 1899, the maternity home was recognized to be of 'public utility'.

The dignity of motherhood was at the centre of Koppe's thinking and she presented it as the highest fulfilment of women's existence: 'To raise motherhood is to raise woman.'[8] Her maternal feminism, for which she was well known at the time, valued sexual difference to the same degree as it valued maternity; in her view, women and men had different and complementary tasks, and she claimed 'harmony' between the sexes and their equality in difference. From this perspective she advocated legislation to protect women workers. Maternity protection was closely linked to the issue of women's employment and the feminist movement was tormented by the question as to whether specific laws on the protection of women's employment were to be favoured or rejected. Koppe approved without reservation the 1892 law which banned night-working for women in several trades. In the debates preceding the enactment of this law, the issue of obligatory maternity leave for factory workers (for four weeks after parturition) was raised by Albert de Mun but soon suppressed, one of the reasons given being that Parliament should not interfere too much with women's private or 'intimate life'.[9] Koppe disagreed, asking for state intervention in favour of mothers and – drawing a parallel to the Ministry of War – for a child welfare ministry which instead would prepare for life.

Like many other feminists, she argued for the rights of children in order to emphasize the rights of mothers.

In 1896 the Fifth International Feminist Congress took place in Paris, under the direction of Maria Pognon, president of the LFDF from 1893, and of Marie Popelin, doctor of law. In her opening address, Pognon demanded that the mother be placed on an equal footing with the father, and the congress appealed to Parliament for a law that would provide for maternity welfare during two months before and two months after parturition. Léonie Rouzade, socialist militant of *La Solidarité des femmes*, declared that maternity ought to be recognized as work, be considered as a 'social function' and be subsidized by the state. She demanded the creation of a state budget for maternity ('there are budgets for the rich, budgets for horse races, but no budget for maternity') and a petition of the congress to Parliament to this purpose.[10] Although the neo-Malthusian antinatalist and feminist Marie Huot refused to listen any longer and threatened to leave ('We women! To serve to manufacture cannon-fodder! For shame!'),[11] the majority of the congress tended to agree with Rouzade, and her proposal was adopted by *La Solidarité des femmes*. But the notion of 'maternity as a social function', on which the majority of feminists agreed, did not have the same meaning for all of them, and it ranged from state recognition of the maternal function to that of an actual mothers' wage.

Paul Robin, founder and leader of the French neo-Malthusian movement and advocate of birth control and free heterosexual love, provoked a general outcry at the congress when he affirmed that the indispensable condition for freedom of love was freedom of maternity.[12] Outraged by his proposals, Claire Galichon, an adherent of 'spiritual feminism' as well as of a state budget for needy mothers, left the congress, even though she shared some ideas with the neo-Malthusian feminists and advocated a woman's free choice to be a mother and her right to dispose of her body as she wished. Only the socialist Paule Minck, known for her defence of women who had abortions, supported Paul Robin.

Various other strands joined the debate on maternity. Christian feminism was represented by Marie Maugeret, founder of the journal *Le Féminisme chrétien*, in which she attempted to show that religion was compatible with feminism and that feminism was first of all the struggle for 'the right to have rights'.[13] She wished to rally all Catholics (the majority of the French population) to her cause, but her ideas were too radical for the male Catholic hierarchy. Her interpretation of the papal encyclical *Rerum Novarum* of 1891, which proclaimed motherhood and domestic work as women's 'natural' destiny, was to present women's rights as the most important social issue, the absence of such rights prohibiting them from fulfilling their 'natural' vocation as Christian mothers. The abrogation of article 340 was a leitmotiv of Maugeret's journal. Augusta Moll Weiss pursued a practical educational approach. In 1897 she founded a school for mothers at Bordeaux, which aimed at educating young women for their obligations as mothers and homemakers. Her school had immediate success and in 1903 it implanted itself also in Paris. Medical doctors such as Adolphe Pinard and Pierre Budin argued for educating young women for their future as mothers. Maternal and infant health courses and maternity guides multiplied; the feminist journals were eager to advertise them in order to combat 'maternal ignorance', to organize high-quality maternal instruction and to claim women's right to education in general.

The most important public forum for the feminist debate of these years was La Fronde, founded by Marguerite Durand, published as a daily journal from 1897 to 1903 and nicknamed 'Le Temps in petticoats'. It valued maternity most highly, preached the necessity of 'puériculture', and Durand herself advocated special protection for women in childbed, maternity insurance, equal pay for equal work, the payment of housework and the revision of laws that rendered married women inferior to their husbands.[14] Aline Valette, a militant socialist and collaborator on La Fronde, wrote a column 'Women's Work' and founded the weekly L'Harmonie sociale which promoted 'female rights and interests'. She praised maternal values and employed the terminology of maternity as a 'social function', deploring that this function did not imply any rights of mothers over their children. An expert in female workers' rights, she denounced their double exploitation in domestic as well as in extra-domestic work. But she believed that only through the latter could emancipation be reached,[15] and Valette was consequently faced with the dilemma between maternity as women's most noble task and employment, which caused the loss of their identity, yet permitted them to become independent. Clotilde Dissard, director of La Revue féministe and collaborator in La Fronde, extolled a 'familial feminism' which stressed women's maternal role and the complementarity and solidarity of the sexes.[16]

Hubertine Auclert, ardent suffragette and internationalist, editor of La Citoyenne, later collaborator in Le Radical (she wrote the weekly column 'Feminism' from 1896 to 1909) and the first woman who openly claimed the word 'feminist' as a label, called as early as 1885 for setting up 'the mother state' which would replace the 'minotaur state'. The new kind of state would, among other things, secure assistance to children.[17] In 1899 she advocated maternity endowment, to be financed by a paternal tax deducted from the men and to serve as a remedy for depopulation. On the model of a superannuation scheme introduced for the former senators in 1905, she advertised a superannuation fund for mothers. During the parliamentary elections of 1910, she put forward her (extra-legal) candidacy, along with other feminists such as Marguerite Durand, and their electoral programme described maternity as the greatest of all 'social functions': the state would have to meet the needs of mothers no less than those of soldiers. This argument had by now become quite common, and was often used in response to the argument of populationists and opponents of women's rights in general, i.e. that only men do military service. Feminists argued that women accomplished another, and more noble service for society, that of maternity which was, moreover, at least as laborious as military service.

The multiplicity of French feminist views on maternity was marked. Nonetheless, in all their demands emerged the preoccupation with improving the situation of mothers, with public recognition of female and motherly values and work, with a new relation between rights, responsibilities and protection, between the public and the private and between maternity and the state. Even though the proposed means differed, they were guided by a common interest in protecting mothers and children and in questioning the exclusive parental power of fathers. The transition to the twentieth century for the French feminist movement was accompanied by the loss of outstanding leaders. Maria Deraismes died in 1894, Eugénie Potonié-Pierre in 1898, Aline Valette in 1899, Louise Koppe in 1900, and Paule Minck in the following year; but other personalities appeared to take up the torch for the rights of mothers.

MOTHERHOOD, LEGISLATION AND POLITICS, 1900–14

From the turn of the century to the outbreak of the First World War, the feminist movement engaged in, and gained publicity by, organizing conferences, demonstrations, sending delegations to nearby public meetings, presenting petitions and legislative proposals, particularly for maternity protection. After the consciousness-raising of the preceding period, a somewhat more pragmatic approach came to prevail, for example through supporting the few key politicians who supported feminist demands – a method of influencing legislation to which feminists had to turn in the absence of female suffrage. In addition, the leaders of the republican women's movement seemed to make a concerted effort to identify feminism with the national community; 'les françaises repeatedly asserted their claims to equal standing with les français'.[18] In 1901 the Conseil National des Femmes Françaises (CNFF) was founded (with 75,000 members in 1909), in 1906 the feminist newspaper La Française, and in 1909 the Union Française pour le Suffrage des Femmes (UFSF). The pre-war period was also the time when pathbreaking laws concerning motherhood were enacted. It is difficult to evaluate the impact of the feminist demands and efforts on the legislation of those years, which marked a break with the earlier indifference to maternity; on the other hand, it is equally difficult to imagine that this legislation would have come about without the continuous pressure feminists put on Parliament even without the benefit of the vote.

The World Exhibition of 1900 in Paris was an occasion for feminists to reach a larger public, and three congresses in Paris were dedicated to women. For the first time, members of the government participated in two of them,[19] and their presence marked the achievement of some official recognition and made the women's movement appear serious and respectable. The first congress (*Congrès International des Oeuvres et Institutions Féminines*), directed by the Protestant philanthropist Sarah Monod, dealt with a wide variety of social and legal issues, especially the family in its relationship to employment, legislation and charity, and it propounded a moderate policy of 'small steps'. The legislative section demanded civil rights, notably for the mother of the family – in line with the common argument that women's responsibility as mothers entitled them to a recognition of their rights.

The second congress (*Congrès International de la Condition et des Droits des Femmes*), directed by Maria Pognon and with Marguerite Durand as general secretary, took a more offensive stance. In her opening speech, Pognon emphasized that it had 'the sole objective of demanding the economic, civil and political rights of women'. France should make up for its backwardness in what concerned the liberation of women; once again, the Civil Code was the target of heavy attacks. Of course, article 340 was on the agenda again, as was the demand that the term 'paternal power' be replaced by 'paternal protection'. Pognon intervened in this lively debate with the argument that a man who does not wish to support his child should not be forced to do so; instead, a state-sponsored fund for child-support should be created, accessible to all women, married or not, to render them independent of the father's support and replace him with support from the state. It was resolved that women had the right to initiate paternity suits, supplemented by the demand for a *caisse de la maternité* to be created in all civilized countries for any woman who claimed what was due to her child. A related subject was the evaluation of household work, and the debate revealed different conceptions of women's role within the family. Here, the delegates were not able to reach an agreement and solved the problem by setting up a special commission. The disagreements concerned the significant cleavage between radical feminists and socialists. The radicals underlined the economic importance of female housework, considering the issue as a social and public one and demanding rights for women on these grounds, whereas the socialists were exclusively interested in women who worked for pay and considered housework as a private issue.

On both sides, among the feminists and in the trade unions, few female workers were represented. In 1906 women represented nearly 38 per cent of the French labour force, and 20 per cent of married women worked – one of the highest proportions in western Europe; over half of the non-agricultural women workers were domestics or home workers, 25 per cent of factory workers, and 8 per cent of clerical workers. At the congress of 1900, Blanche Edwards-Pilliet reported on the health of the female worker who fulfilled 'her physiological function: the maternal function'. This was, in her view, a social function, understood as women's right to necessary care before and after childbirth. She defined the pregnant woman as a 'social functionary' and claimed that in exchange for 'the enormous effort of maternity', society must fully subsidize her with 'food, housing, and essential rest'.[20] Edwards-Pilliet put her ideas into practice when in 1901 she created, together with Augusta Moll Weiss, the *Ligue des Mères de Famille*. It was to assist and advise working-class women in maternal matters and permit them to give birth in their own homes; it lasted until 1940.

In respect of working-class mothers, one proposal at the congress led to lively controversy: 'A stay of at least one month in a special hospital or in convalescent homes should be imposed on the mother who after childbirth does not have the means of subsistence for herself and her child'. Many of the delegates protested at the difficulty for female workers who would be separated from their family for such a long time. The controversy centred on the term 'impose', some wishing to replace it with an option. Marguerite Durand explained that the idea was to protect the infant at birth and that the use of the term was deliberate. After a long discussion the resolution was adopted, and when a further proposal suggested that the welfare allocations should be deducted from the church budget, Maria Pognon retorted that the task of the congress was to formulate the demands and that it was up to the government to find the funding. This principle was also upheld in the debate on the resolution that

> in all governmental and other enterprises, women shall have the option of taking fifteen days' rest before the expected time of birth; that the employers shall be required to give them four weeks leave after childbirth; that during this whole period women have a right to a daily living stipend.[21]

This resolution was adopted and prefigured the law of 1909. In early twentieth-century France, there was no specific law to protect maternity, except for one of 1893 that granted free medical assistance to necessitous women, classifying them in the category of the sick. Feminists criticized the inadequacy of its implementation and particularly the assimilation of pregnancy to sickness. The 1909 maternity protection law (Engerand Act) guaranteed their jobs to women who stayed away from work for up to eight weeks before and after giving birth, thus being the first maternity protection measure that was independent of poor relief and universal at least for employed women. However, the maternity leave was not obligatory, and – to the distress of the feminists – no benefits were paid during this period. The two Members of Parliament who most supported the provision, Strauss of the Senate and Bonnevay of the Chamber, saw the law as a first step, and 'the second indispensable phase will be obligatory and paid maternity leave'.[22] It took another four years before, against strong resistance and with much agitation on the part of the feminists, this second step was taken. For female civil servants it took less time: a 1910 law granted to the school teachers a two-month maternity leave with wage replacement; in 1911, it was extended to the postal, telegraph and telephone operators, but only in 1928 to all government employees.

On the initiative of the delegates to the two 1900 congresses, the CNFF was founded as the French section of the International Council of Women (founded in Washington in 1888). It intended to gather together all those who shared an interest in women's 'social and material interests' and particularly in the lot of woman and child. Its first president was Sarah Monod (until her death in 1912), Maria Pognon and Julie Siegfried were vice-presidents, and by 1915 it had 100,000 members. Among its leaders, Protestants dominated who, imbued with Protestant philanthropy, ardently defended the family and maternity as a social obligation of women. As in all western women's movements, there was also a conspicuous number of Jewish women and women of Jewish origin, a fact which later led the radical feminist Madeleine Pelletier to complain of the CNFF as a 'Judaeo-Protestant conspiracy'.[23] Among its five sections, it was that on welfare, but particularly that on legislative reform, where maternity protection was of special concern. Marie d'Abbadie d'Arrast was the first chairwoman of the latter section, and her principal preoccupation was with mothers' custody rights, against exclusive 'paternal power', and in particular with the admission of paternity suits.[24] It was not until 1912 that the *recherche de la paternité* was finally permitted, even though the law authorized investigation only in certain cases and in most of them written proof or testimony against the father of the child was required which was usually difficult to obtain for single mothers.

Maternity was also at the centre of the interests of the neo-Malthusian feminists who were a small minority among the women's, as well as the male-dominated, neo-Malthusian movement which advocated antinatalism; nonetheless, they were very vocal in the pre-war period when neo-Malthusianism reached its apogee. Nelly Roussel, a lecturer and journalist for women's journals such as *La Fronde, La Mère éducatrice, La Voix des femmes, La Femme affranchie*, and for antinatalist journals such as *Génération consciente, Régéneration, Le Néo-Malthusien, Action*, achieved celebrity by the lectures she gave through all France and abroad, in which she defended woman's right to voluntary motherhood and to her body.[25] She used neo-Malthusianism as a springboard for these views which were shared by other followers of neo-Malthusianism such as Gabrielle Petit, founder in 1904 of the review *La Femme affranchie*, a tribune for voluntary motherhood, where she gave advice on how to avoid it. Nelly Roussel pronounced herself in favour of contraception, but against abortion except as a last resort. She publicly denounced the pain of childbirth, insisting upon her own experience (as mother of three children, one of whom had died), which had rendered her so full of pity for the plight of mothers.[26] Like other feminists, she protested – particularly in 1904 when the centenary of the Civil Code was celebrated – against the prohibition of paternity suits. But she considered them as a very inadequate means to improve the condition of mothers generally. It was more important to be able to do without the father of the child, particularly through the creation of an actual 'mother's wage'. In this respect, she differed from the male neo-Malthusians who diagnosed women's oppression only in the limited context of sexual behaviour. In Roussel's view, mothers should be recognized as workers who performed 'maternal labour' and who therefore had a right to go on strike. She proclaimed a 'strike of the womb', understood as a struggle to obtain rights and payment for mothers; such a 'just wage for the noble work of maternity'[27] would allow those women who so desired to dedicate themselves to their motherly tasks.

A different approach was followed by another neo-Malthusian feminist, Madeleine Pelletier, a psychiatrist, anthropologist, freemason and socialist who was the first woman to be admitted, in 1903, to the permanent staff of the psychiatric hospital in Paris. She criticized the feminist focus on what she saw as minor reforms of the Civil Code and disagreed with radical feminists, whom she believed to be motivated by hatred of men. She praised 'virilization', understood as emulation of male values such as ambition and independence, and advocated a type of emancipation that was based on reason rather than sentiment and for which the franchise, equal employment for both sexes and 'social rationalization' (replacement of the private by collective households) would be the *conditio sine qua non*. Her positions were unusual and marginal for her time. In her memoirs she deplored the major focus of the feminist meetings: 'One spoke only of the noble role of the spouse and mother.'[28] It was against this noble role that Pelletier stood up, demanding the dissolution of the family, which in her view was detrimental 'to both the one and the other sex' because it meant 'slavery, immobility and boredom'. She denounced maternity because 'it makes of life a true foolery for woman' who 'ceases to be an individual conscious of its dignity'.[29] She proclaimed voluntary motherhood and for this purpose the 'Right to abortion' – the title of her 1911 pamphlet which was soon criminalized by the authorities on the grounds of article 317 of the Penal Code. At this time, when abortion was extremely widespread, to speak out against its criminalization was more a question of principle than of numbers of convictions (between 1881 and 1910, of the cases brought to trial, verdicts were given in fewer than thirty cases per year and under 37 per cent were actually sentenced, often mildly and allowing for extenuating circumstances).[30] Pelletier's advocacy of abortion as a 'right' – if only during the first three months of a pregnancy – was an isolated voice in the feminist context in France as well as internationally; in fact, in 1909 the CNFF created a league against the crime of abortion. In 1939 Pelletier was accused of performing abortions, and the judge ordered a psychiatric examination, following which she was placed in an asylum where she soon died – most tragically in view of her early efforts to have female professionals accepted in such asylums.

In 1913 the CNFF organized the tenth international women's congress on the 'activities, institutions and rights of women' in Paris, where some of the major unfulfilled demands of the earlier congresses were taken up. Officially recognized, the organizing committee was even received by the President of the Republic, Raymond Poincaré. Julie Siegfried, now president of the CNFF, recommended placing women's duties in the foreground, with the understanding that women who claimed their rights must insist on their responsibilities as spouses and mothers. This approach proved to be conservative in many respects, but more open in others to the radical claims of feminists such as Maria Pognon, and the CNFF congress oscillated between a terminology of rights and of duties. Among the issues concerning maternity, a resolution was revived which had occurred frequently in the CNFF's welfare section, requiring that the term *fille-mère* (girl-mother) be replaced by that of *femme-seule* (single woman). In several instances, the CNFF had resolved that Parliament enact a law establishing the right of employed women to paid maternity leave. The matter presented itself with particular urgency at the 1913 congress, because Parliament was soon to decide on such a bill. Cécile Brunschvicg, secretary of the CNFF section on women's employment since 1911, particularly demanded that this bill be declared one of utmost urgency; in addition she claimed the right of 'all waged or unwaged women' to a maternity allowance and demanded that a further bill be elaborated to this avail.[31] A first step came to be adopted twelve days later.

The law of 17 June 1913 (Strauss Act) prescribed a mandatory maternity leave of four weeks after childbirth and two weeks later, a special financial law granted a daily allowance of between 0.5 and 1.5 francs, plus another half-franc for those who nursed the baby themselves. The provision covered all wage-earning women, including domestic workers. It had been a long way since the Engerand Act of 1909, and the situation in 1913, which was more favourable to women, was marked by an increasing and grandiloquent patriotism: the outbreak of war was approaching. The tactics of Paul Strauss, who had initiated the bill in Parliament, was not to demand too much from the state, even though he declared that he was far from abandoning the idea of a universal allowance for all mothers, including the non-employed ones, that the feminists had so often demanded; but the time was not yet ripe for such an extension. In general, the feminist movement agreed with this position, since it seemed to be a time for pragmatism. However, Strauss, as well as the feminists, was well aware of the fact that the law was incomplete: maternity leave before parturition was optional and thus could be circumvented easily, the allowance was insufficient and was not always granted at the time when it was most needed. In July of the same year, allowances were granted to necessitous families with four or more children and in December, they were granted to certain categories of civil servants. In both cases, they were paid to fathers (except for the cases where the mother was widowed and where the father was not the husband). Often, feminists objected heavily to such a focus on fathers.[32] The three 1913 laws paved the way for the French welfare state and particularly for universal child allowances.

Whilst Paul Strauss had been initiating the bill, he was in contact with Cécile Brunschvicg, who had also taken up contacts with parliamentary supporters of the women's cause such as Ferdinand Buisson and Louis Marin; it was part of her and her friends' strategy not only to demand rights but to get 'precise results through serious and well-organized parliamentary activity'.[33] It was also Cécile Brunschvicg who contributed actively to the success of the feminist group that was second in terms of number of adherents: the UFSF, founded by Jeanne Schmahl and affiliated with the International Alliance for Women's Suffrage. It owed its rapid growth throughout France, reaching 15,000 members in 1915, to Cécile Brunschvicg. The philosophy of the UFSF was that women's enfranchisement and political citizenship should be not only a goal in itself, but most of all a means whereby they could achieve their social rights. Among these figured prominently the rights of mothers.

Cécile Brunschvicg, a Jewish woman – this was held against her when she became, in the Blum popular front government of 1936, one of the first female secretaries of state – had since long engaged herself, among other things, in seeking more effective protection for mothers; she pursued the same goal within the framework of the UFSF and in *La Française*, journal of the UFSF, which she directed from 1924 to 1939. In her essay 'Is maternity a family function or a social function?' she responded to two opposing views: that the state should not interfere with maternity by covering its costs, and that it should grant an endowment of motherhood. The question she raised rephrased the older debate around the 'private vs. public' character of maternity, and her answer was a compromise: as a rule, child support was an obligation of the parents, but it was an obligation of the state in cases of distress, especially in the case of single mothers. Whereas the *fonction maternelle* merited certain rights which she set herself to have adopted by her parliamentary friends and in this sense was a 'social' issue, it nonetheless was in the first place a *fonction familiale*, a private matter in the context of which she praised the mother who fulfilled her maternal vocation. This view, expressed in the formula 'obligations and rights', was that of the UFSF, which unceasingly affirmed that it was women's responsibility to bring children into the world to struggle against depopulation. Even during the war, at its 1917 congress, the UFSF continued to demand that the state recognize maternity as a social service.[34]

MOTHERHOOD AT WAR

When on 7 August 1914 René Viviani, Prime Minister and a feminist of long standing, appealed to peasant women to bring in the harvest fast in order to replace the men who had gone to the battle-field, he was widely heard. On 12 August Marguerite de Witt Schlumberger, UFSF president since 1913, invited her militants to join the organizations for war service and to fulfil their duty by keeping the country functioning during the men's absence. She was echoed by *La Fronde*, which came out in September, 'not for claiming the political rights of women but for assisting them to fulfil their social duties'. In an atmosphere of exacerbated patriotism, women gave priority to the war effort and rallied around the 'sacred union' of all French people. In late 1914 *La Française* carried a telling title on its front page which was regularly taken up: 'French Women During War. What they do. What is being done for them.' The latter phrase indicated that the measures taken in favour of mothers now had priority because of the necessity to reconcile employment and maternity. In wartime fertility decreased, and the annual figures for live births in the 77 *départements* which had not been invaded by the German army, declined from 600,000 before the war to 386,000 in 1915, 313,000 in 1916 and 400,000 in 1918.[35]

The depopulation issue was powerfully revived. Schlumberger declared in 1916 at a UFSF meeting on the subject 'Moral and social action in favour of maternity': 'Women have to take a moral attitude. The revival of the country depends on their understanding of this necessity.' Such moral action meant, first of all, sacrifice, and she concluded that 'all those households of good health who refuse to give a child to the fatherland in the first year after the war shall be regarded as deserters.' Another speaker at the meeting was Paul Bureau, who had founded in 1916, in co-operation with Brunschwicg and Schlumberger, the *Ligue Pour la Vie* (pro-life league), which emphasized the need for moral action in favour of motherhood, even outside the law.[36]

'Moral action' was also at the core of the violent debate on the *indésirés* (undesired ones), children born by women who had been raped by German soldiers. The debate divided the feminists and the press participated enthusiastically. 'Must the child of the barbarian come to life?' asked the title page of *Le Journal* on 17 December 1914. The answers to this question varied, but many expressed an extreme nationalism that was illustrated with the testimony of one of the women who wished to keep the child: 'We will make of it a good French person, that will be our revenge.'

The different viewpoints were reported in *La Française* and commented on by its founder Jane Misme. She argued against abortion: 'It is true that sexual violence leaves marks on the woman. But a pregnancy is not a pollution, it is a manifestation of life. . . . The act that produces life, voluntarily or by force, cannot be in itself polluting.'[37] Socialist-feminist and pacifist Marcelle Capy did not share this view and demanded abortion; Camille Bélilon, president of *Le Suffrage des Femmes* and known for her intransigent feminism and nationalism, claimed 'the right and even the duty to eradicate this sinister virus'. It was a debate in which every point of view was taken into consideration. The writer Maurice Barrès asked for a law to permit the infant to be declared born of unknown father and mother. Catholics recommended that it should first be baptized. Victor Margueritte (author of the famous novel *La Garçonne*, 1922) demanded the right to abort – in order to 'suppress these monstrous beings in their embryonic form' – or, if such beings are born, the duty to assure them a normal existence.[38] In the Senate, Louis Martin presented a proposal to cancel penalties for abortion in the invaded territory, but it was rejected. Finally, it was resolved that victims of rape might refer back to the 1893 law which provided free medical assistance and to the 1913 Strauss Act, but applying directly to the national instead of to the city government. Special arrangements were made for the abandonment of the children to public welfare.

In this climate of nationalism and moralizing, the feminists were strongly accused of being responsible for the continuing *dénatalité*. Astutely as before, they responded untiringly that it was not their fault but due to the absence of support for maternity, and they demanded new legislation as the remedy. Combining maternity and employment was the issue now. For this reason in 1916 Albert Thomas, under-secretary of state in the Armament Ministry, established the *Comité du Travail Féminin* and Marguerite Durand initiated a similar committee. Feminists, child specialists and doctors declaimed that 'the mother is the one who nurses her baby', and a law of 1917 provided that mothers working in industry should get time off for this purpose: one hour a day during working hours in the course of the first year after childbirth. Employers of more than one hundred women aged fifteen and older were to install nursing rooms in their factories and businesses or close by. Even though the law was inadequately implemented and few nursing rooms were established, the overall war measures seem to have enabled women better to combine employment and motherhood. Most of them were clearly motivated by pronatalist aspirations but, as before, they had potential positive effects on a different level: the rights of mothers. What appeared as pronatalism to Members of Parliament could appear as social feminism[39] to mothers who profited from it.

Whereas the majority of feminists dedicated their efforts to war, there was a minority which was, or remained, pacifist. For their goals, they generally referred to motherhood, contrasting maternal and female values to masculinity as the symbol of destruction. The teacher Hélène Brion, known for her labour militancy but above all a feminist (like so many other teachers), fought for peace during the war and was therefore court-martialled in March 1918, being charged with defeatist propaganda for distributing tracts and brochures. Her trial aroused the women's movement and numerous feminists such as Nelly Roussel and Marguerite Durand supported her. Nevertheless, she was removed from her position as teacher and condemned to three years in prison, with time off for good behaviour. She had deliberately chosen motherhood outside marriage, and she had blamed men for imposing on women the depressing choice between 'multiple and exhausting births or abortions (that your laws condemn!) or sterility, which for her reduces the universe to one single person'.[40] Hélène Brion's view was original. Rather than advocating voluntary motherhood, she spoke about enforced motherhood, about women as objects of male sexuality.

Madeleine Vernet also rejected, in the name of the dignity of women, the notion of maternity as obligatory. She believed that there could be no true 'moral progress' as long as women, married or single, were dishonoured by their maternity. She founded the review *La Mère éducatrice* in 1917, in which Hélène Brion collaborated. A convinced pacifist, she fought for peace in the name of motherhood. She launched an appeal to found the League of Women Against War and spread tracts and pacifist poems which glorified motherhood, 'the apogee of feminine individuality', and came close to Ellen Key's views.[41] But she differed from the latter who demanded that motherhood be paid for; Vernet considered this immoral.

CONCLUSION

The variety of views on maternity in the feminist movement demonstrates its dynamism. The CNFF at the beginning of the twentieth century illustrates this tendency and permitted a regrouping of forces for the defence of the rights of mothers in particular and within a moderate discourse on 'duties and rights'. Reform-oriented feminists, moderate feminists and radical feminists struggled for maternity protection and for the rights of mothers. Even though their notions of motherhood, their visions of gender and their solutions to specific problems differed greatly at times, the efforts of each group had its impact on the movement as a whole. Feminists were among the first to deplore the *dénatalité*, and they focused on motherhood as a common bond among all women and as a strategy for claiming political, social and economic rights of mothers and of women generally. The philosophy of 'equality in difference' was a dominant feature of French feminism and, more generally, of 'relational feminism' or 'social feminism' in western women's movements; it differed, although with many overlaps and ways of interacting, from 'individual feminism' or 'equity feminism' which tended to minimize sexual difference.[42]

But what was the impact of French feminists on legislation and the world of male politics at large? It is difficult to evaluate. On the one hand, the absence of women's suffrage made it difficult to get the men in power interested in feminist claims and it restricted women's space for manoeuvre; on the other hand they incontestably had an influence due to their public activities and links with some Members of Parliament and other politicians. The issue of *dénatalité* mobilized the energies of a large number of social forces, of parliamentarians, medical doctors, demographers, repopulators of all sorts, and they conjured up the need for remedies in the context of a patriotic and even nationalist discourse. The laws that were enacted in favour of maternity were often motivated by pronatalist concerns, but they were also the result of humanitarian social policies and even of a policy of women's rights; they laid the ground for the rise of the future French welfare state. Yet their effect was modest in terms of the improvement of women's lot, and the important measures enacted just before and during the war did not satisfy the ambitions of the feminists; many of their congress resolutions remained a dead letter. On the side of the legislators, obstacles and resistances prevailed: budgetary constraints, the slowness of procedures, awareness of the limits of the power of law, but most of all a reluctance to venture into what was considered to be the private sphere, the family with the mother at its centre. Measured against their pronatalist hopes, the continuous decline in the birth-rate – despite the measures taken – proved their reluctance to be justified.

NOTES

1   L. Klejman and F. Rochefort, *L'Egalité en marche. Le féminisme sous la Troisième République*, Paris, Fondation Nationale des Sciences Politiques/Éditions des Femmes, 1989.
2   M. Martin, 'Dépopulation', *Le Journal des femmes*, June 1896; K. Offen, 'Depopulation, nationalism and feminism in fin-de-siècle France', *American Historical Review*, 1984, vol. 89, pp. 648–76; K. Offen, 'Defining feminism: a comparative historical approach', *Signs*, 1988, vol. 14, pp. 119–57; J. Dupâquier (ed.), *Histoire de la population française*, Paris, PUF, 1988, vol. 3, p. 125; vol. 4, p. 75, and p. 17 above.
3   Deraismes, quoted in M. Martin, 'Dépopulation', *Le Journal des femmes*, Jan. 1893; M. Deraismes, *Eve dans l'humanité* (1868), ed. L. Klejman, Paris, Côté-femmes, 1990; Françoise Thébaud, 'Le Mouvement nataliste dans la France de l'entre-deux-guerres: L'Alliance Nationale pour l'Accroissement de la Population Française', *Revue d'histoire moderne et contemporaine*, 1985, vol. 32, p. 277.
4   *Le Journal des femmes*, July 1892; further reports on the congress in the issues of May through September 1892, and in the file 'Congrès 1892' at the Bibliothèque Marguerite Durand (BMD); K. Offen, 'Sur l'origine des mots "féminisme" et "féministe"', *Revue d'histoire moderne et contemporaine*, 1987, vol. 36, pp. 492–6.
5   *Journal officiel*, Documents Parlementaires, Chambre des Députés, session of 7 March 1899, suppl. no. 789, p. 863.
6   *Le Journal des femmes*, June 1892; F. Leguay and C. Barbizet, *Blanche Edwards-Pilliet. Femme et médecin 1858–1941*, Le Mans, Cénomane, 1988.
7   Quoted in *La Maison Maternelle: historique. But de l'oeuvre. Extraits des discours prononcés par M. Léon Bourgeois aux assemblées générales des 16 décembre 1894, 7 novembre 1897, 29 janvier 1899 et 17 décembre 1899*, Levallois–Perret, Schneider, 1900, p. 6; see also L. Koppe, 'La Question féminine: la femme mère', *La Femme dans la famille et dans la société*, 25 July/1 Aug. 1880, no. 15; A. Cova, 'Louise Koppe (1846–1900) et sa maison maternelle', in *Actes du 155e Congrès National des Sociétés Savantes*, Paris, Ass. pour l'étude de l'histoire de la Sécurité Sociale, 1991, pp. 49–78.
8   L. Koppe, 'Prisons et berceaux', *La Femme et l'enfant*, 1 August 1886, no. 15; see also her 'La Question féminine: la femme épouse', *La Femme dans la famille et dans la société*, 27 June/4 July 1880, no. 11; and her 'Les Revendications

féminines', *La Femme et l'enfant*, 5 Jan. 1886, no. 1.

9 *Journal officiel*, Débats Parlementaires, Chambre des Députés, session of 5 February 1891, p. 231; M. L. Stewart, *Women, Work, and the French State: Labour Protection and Social Patriarchy, 1879–1919*, Kingston, Montreal, McGill–Queen's University Press, 1989; N. Chambelland-Liébault, 'La Durée et l'aménagement du temps de travail des femmes de 1892 à l'aube des conventions collectives', Ph. D. dissertation, University of Nantes, 1989.

10 *Le Journal des femmes*, May 1896 (quote); for the congress resolutions see the BMD file 'Congrès 1896' and the file 'Congrès' at the Archives M.-L. Bouglé of the Bibliothèque Historique de la Ville de Paris (BHVP); the congress report in *Le Journal des femmes*, May 1896; and W. H. Wilkins, 'The Paris International Feminist Congress of 1896 and its French antecedents', *North Dakota Quarterly*, 1975, vol. 43, pp. 5–28.

11 Quoted in Wilkins, 'The Paris International Feminist Congress of 1896', p. 23.

12 For Robin see F. Ronsin, *La Grève des ventres. Propagande néo-malthusienne et baisse de la natalité en France 19e–20e siècles*, Paris, Aubier, 1980; R.-H. Guerrand, *La Libre Maternité 1896–1969*, Tournai, Casterman, 1971; A. McLaren, *Sexuality and Social Order: The Debate over the Fertility of Women and Workers in France, 1770–1920*, New York, Holmes & Meir, 1983.

13 Quoted in R.-H. Guerrand and M.-A. Rupp, *Brève histoire du service social en France, 1896–1976*, Toulouse, Privat, 1978, p. 17; see M. Maugeret, 'Le Féminisme chrétien de France au congrès de Bruxelles', *Le Féminisme chrétien*, 25 Aug. 1897; S. C. Hause and A. R. Kenney, 'The development of the Catholic women's suffrage movement in France 1896–1922', *The Catholic Historical Review*, 1981, vol. 67, pp. 11–30; S. Fayet-Scribe, *Associations féminines et Catholicisme. De la charité à l'action sociale, XIXe–XXe siècles*, Paris Editions ouvrières, 1990.

14 K. Offen 'Depopulation', p. 661, 673; S. Goliber Helder, 'The life and times of Marguerite Durand: a study in French feminism', Ph.D. dissertation, Kent State University, 1975.

15 A. Valette, 'A nos lecteurs', *L'Harmonie sociale*, 15 Oct. 1892; E. Diebolt and M.-H. Zylberberg-Hocquard (eds), *Aline Valette, Marcelle Capy. Femmes et travail au XIXe siècle*, Paris, Syros 1984.

16 C. Dissard, 'Impressions sur le Congrès féministe', *La Revue féministe*, 1896, p. 245; Offen, 'Depopulation', p. 658.

17 H. Auclert, 'Programme électoral des femmes', *La Citoyenne*, Aug. 1885; Offen, 'Sur l'origine des mots "féminisme" et "féministe"', p. 494; E. Taïeb (ed.), *Hubertine Auclert: La Citoyenne, 1848–1914*, Paris, Syros, 1982; C. G. Moses, *French Feminism in the 19th Century*, Albany, State University of New York Press, 1984, p. 278, note 10; S. C. Hause, *Hubertine Auclert, the French Suffragette*, New Haven, Yale University Press, 1987.

18 K. Offen, 'Exploring the sexual politics of French Republican nationalism', in R. Tombs (ed.), *Aspects of French Nationalism*, London, Unwin Hyman (forthcoming). I want to thank the author for making available to me this article.

19 In the congresses which are documented in the following proceedings: *Deuxième congrès international des oeuvres et institutions féminines, Paris, 18–27 juin 1900*, ed. Mme Pégard, 4 vols., Paris, Blot, 1902; *Congrès international de la condition et des droits des femmes, 5–8 septembre 1900*, Paris, Imprimerie des Arts manufactures, 1901.

20 *Congrès international, 5–8 septembre*, pp. 66–8; see also Offen, 'Depopulation', p. 661; for the figures see M. Perrot, 'The new Eve and the old Adam: French women's condition at the turn of the century', in M.R. Higonnet et al. (eds),

Behind the Lines, Gender and the Two World Wars, New Haven, Yale University Press, 1987, pp. 52–3; S. C. Hause, 'More Minerva than Mars: the French women's rights campaign and the First World War', in M.R. Higonnet *et al.* (eds), *Behind the Lines*, p. 106; M. Guilbert, *Les Femmes et l'organisation syndicale avant 1914*, Paris, Centre National de la Recherche Scientifique, 1966, pp. 13–14.

21 Quotes from *Congrès international, 5–8 septembre*, pp. 92, 85–6.

22 *Journal officiel*, Débats Parlementaires, Chambre des Députés, session of 7 April 1908, p. 933.

23 Quoted in L. Klejman and F. Rochefort, *L'Egalité*, p. 153; M. Kaplan, *The Jewish Feminist Movement in Germany*, Westport, CT., Greenwood Press, 1979.

24 Mme Oddo-Deflou (ed.), *Congrès national des droits civils et du suffrage des femmes, 26–28 juin 1908*, Paris, Imprimerie spéciale du Congrès, 1910; see also S. C. Hause and A. R. Kenney, *Women's Suffrage and Social Politics in the French Third Republic*, Princeton, Princeton University Press, 1984.

25 N. Roussel, 'La Liberté de la maternité' (1907), *Trois conférences de Nelly Roussel*, Paris, Marcel Giard, 1930, pp. 17–51; see also her *Quelques lances rompues pour nos libertés*, Paris, Giard & Brière, 1910; A. Cova, 'Féminisme et natalité: Nelly Roussel (1878–1922)', paper presented at the conference on Comparative History of European Nationalism of the International Society for the Study of European Ideas, Leuven, 3–8 Sept. 1990; D. Armogathe and M. Albistur (eds), *Nelly Roussel, l'éternelle sacrifiée*, Paris, Syros, 1979.

26 N. Roussel, 'Liberté', p. 34.

27 N. Roussel, 'La "Journée des Mères de familles nombreuses"', *La Voix des femmes*, 6 May 1920; N. Roussell, 'Protestation féministe contre la célébration du centenaire du Code Civil', *La Fronde*, 1 Nov. 1904.

28 M. Pelletier, 'Mémoires d'une féministe' (manuscript), BHVP, Fonds M.–L. Bouglé, file Pelletier; M. Pelletier, *L'Education féministe des filles et autres textes*, ed. C. Maignien, Paris, Syros, 1978, p. 168; see also her article 'Les Suffragettes anglaises se virilisent', *La Suffragiste*, Oct. 1912, no. 31; F. Gordon, *The Integral Feminist: Madeleine Pelletier, 1874–1939. Feminism, Socialism and Medicine*, Cambridge, Polity Press, 1990; A. Cova, 'Féminisme et Maternité: la doctoresse Madeleine Pelletier, 1874–1939', forthcoming in *Actes du VIe Colloque d'Historie au Présent.* .

29 M. Pelletier, *L'Emancipation sexuelle de la femme*, Paris, La brochure mensuelle, 1926, pp. 20 ('Le Féminisme et la famille'), 41 ('La Maternité doit être libre'); M. Pelletier, 'Le Droit à l'avortement' (1911), in her *L'education féministe*, p. 126.

30 D. V. Glass, *Population Policies and Movements in Europe*, (first edn 1940) repr. London, Frank Cass, 1967, p. 158.

31 *Dixième congrès international des femmes: oeuvres et institutions féminines, droits des femmes, 2–7 Juin 1913*, ed. A. de Sainte-Croix, Paris, Giard et Brière, 1914, pp. 20, 443, 567.

32 K. Offen, 'Depopulation', pp. 669–70, and her contribution to this volume; R. Talmy, *Histoire du movement familial en France (1896–1939)*, Paris, Union Nationale des Caisses d'Allocations Familiales, 1962, vol. 1, pp. 159–63; J. H. Weiss, 'Origins of the French welfare state: poor relief in the Third Republic, 1871–1914', *French Historical Studies*, 1983, vol. 13, pp. 47–78; M.L. Stewart, *Women, Work, and the French State*, ch. 8.

33 C. Brunschvicg, 'Le Suffrage des femmes en France', *Documents du progrès*, Dec. 1913, pp. 297–301.

34 C. Brunschvicg, 'La Maternité, fonction familiale ou sociale?', *La Française*, 3 May 1930; A. Cova, 'Cécile Brunschvicg (1877–1946) et la protection de la maternité', *Actes du 113e congrès national des Sociétés Savantes*, Paris, Association

pour l'Etude de L'Histoire de la Sécurité Sociale, 1989, pp. 75–104. The UFSF resolution: *UFSF Bulletin*, 1917, p. 25.

35 F. Thébaud, *La Femme au temps de la guerre de 14*, Paris, Stock/ Pernoud, 1986, p. 266; F. Thébaud, *Quand nos grand-mères donnaient la vie. La Maternité en France dans l'entre-deux-guerres*, Lyon, Presses Universitaires de Lyon, 1986; M. Perrot 'The New Eve', pp. 52–5, 57; S.C. Hause, 'More Minerva', pp. 103–7, 111–13.

36 M.P., 'L'action Sociale et Morale en faveur de la Maternité', *La Française*, 25 March 1916 (quote); S.C. Hause and A.R. Kenney, *Women's Suffrage*, p. 195.

37 J. Misme, 'L'Intégrité féminine', *La Française*, 17 April 1915.

38 Quotes from the contemporary press, file 'L'Enfant du barbare', Archives Bouglé (BHVP), Arria Ly papers.

39 For this concept see N. Black, 'Social feminism in France: a case study', in N. Black and A. B. Cottrell (eds), *Women and World Change: Equity Issues in Development*, Beverly Hills, Sage, 1981, pp. 217–38; N. Black, *Social Feminism*, Ithaca, Cornell University Press, 1989; A. Buttafuoco's contribution to this volume; J. S. Lemons, *The Woman Citizen: Social Feminism in the 1920s*, Urbana, University of Illinois Press, 1973.

40 Quoted from H. Bouchardeau (ed.), *Hélène Brion. La Voie féministe*, Paris, Syros, 1978, p. 71.

41 C. Register, 'Motherhood at center: Ellen Key's social vision', *Women's Studies International Forum*, 1982, vol. 5, pp. 599–610.

42 K. Offen, 'Defining feminism', and note 39 above.

Chapter 7

Body politics: women, work and the politics of motherhood in France, 1920–1950*

Karen Offen

In May 1920 the government of the victorious but badly battered French Third Republic, led by premier Alexandre Millerand, celebrated Mother's Day by establishing medals to honour mothers of large families. These medals – bronze for mothers of five living children, silver for mothers of eight, and gold for mothers of ten – were intended to encourage French *natalité* by publicly rewarding those women who had demonstrated, in the oft-quoted words of Alexandre Dumas *fils* (in his 1889 play *Françillon*), that 'maternity was women's brand of patriotism'.[1] In July, at the behest of the newly instituted *Conseil Supérieur de Natalité*, the government outlawed antinatalist propaganda (*contre la natalité*), i.e. propaganda likely to influence and provide information to women. In 1923, it changed the juridical status of abortion, 'decriminalizing' it by transferring jurisdiction from lenient juries to stern judges, and replaced the previous harsh penalties by imprisonment for convicted abortionists as well as for their clients; both measures were intended to assure certainty of punishment.[2] In the meantime, the French General Maitrot complained in the *Echo de Paris* that 'there are too many women typists and civil servants here and not enough *mères de famille*. With respect to natality, the German mothers have beaten the French mothers; this is Germany's first revenge against France.'[3]

In the decade that followed the Allied victory in World War I, politicians and public spokesmen hammered home the pronatalist message. Public awareness of the continuing drop in the French birth-rate (see graph) became sufficiently pronounced that the term *crise de natalité* could become a metaphor for other national deficits, as, for example, in 1931, that of an insufficiency of ships for the merchant marine.[4] The government's restrictions on women's reproductive choice were followed by repeated defeats in the French Senate of woman suffrage measures passed by heavy majorities in the Chamber of Deputies (one of the reasons being that anticlerical men feared that as electors women would support *en bloc* the dictates of the Catholic church).[5] Following the failure of the short-lived Popular Front, the 1939 *Code de la famille* strengthened the penalties against abortion even as it significantly reshaped French marriage law. In

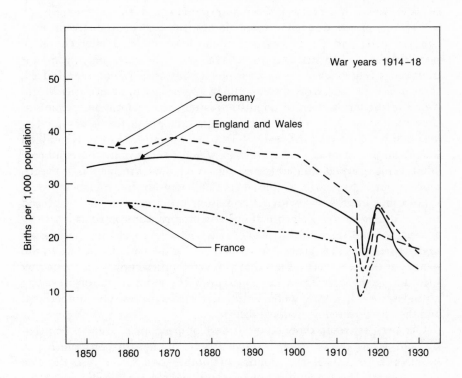

Figure 7.1 Crude birth-rates for France, Germany, England and Wales, 1850–1930

Source: B.R. Mitchell, *European Historical Statistics 1750–1950*, abridged edition,
London, Macmillan, 1978, pp. 21–32

1940 Maréchal Pétain, echoing his old colleague Maitrot, blamed France's capitulation to the Germans not only on a lack of weapons and allies but on 'too few children'. A Vichy law (the '300 Law' of 15 February 1942) declared the performing of abortion a crime against society, the state and the race – an act of treason punishable by death.[6]

Such measures and messages may seem shocking from the standpoint of late twentieth-century individualist feminism, with its emphasis on self-realization, its diffidence about domesticity and dependence on male breadwinners, and its ambivalence about governmental intervention in people's personal affairs. Yet to look at these measures only from this perspective is to misread or misconstrue their historical significance. Indeed, these measures underscore the continuing importance in France after World War I of the intersection of population issues, nationalism, and feminism; they attest eloquently to the enormous significance of gender issues in inter-war politics, following the severe losses of French men (some 1.3 million killed) during the war – a context in which adult women outnumbered adult men by several million. Issues concerning the emancipation of French women, including their employment and reproductive practices, were inextricably intertwined with an impassioned debate over the shape and future strength of the French national community, confronted as it was by a resurgent and resentful Germany.[7] The debate surrounding these issues underscores the felt urgency and desperation of the period, offering a grim picture of the needs and desires that motivated official policy elaborated by men during the later Third Republic and Vichy regimes and of prevailing attitudes towards women whom critics perceived to be resisting motherhood and thereby threatening national security.

Our perspective on these ominous developments must also be tempered by considering certain other positive aspects of the situation, which will be referred to here as the 'politics of motherhood'.[8] It is also the case that, even as Third Republic governments enacted sex-specific protective and restrictive legislation,[9] and promoted a certain vision of sex-specific male and female roles through public education, they continued – unlike some other European governments – to defend women's right to paid employment. Moreover, in response to the perceived demographic crisis and problems of poverty, the governments fostered the gradual development and extension of mandated paid maternity leaves (1928), state-sponsored family allowances in support of dependent children (1932), payments to mothers who nursed their own infants (1935), and first-birth premiums (1939). Even as ministries initiated an additional subsidy to mothers who opted to stay at home with children (in 1939, at the behest of social Catholics), they also made substantive progress in realizing the reform of the Civil Code to alleviate women's legal subordination in marriage, long demanded by secular feminists. These important yet piecemeal measures (e.g. in 1927 mothers were given the legal right to express their consent on the marriage of a child, in

1935 they were associated to the *puissance paternelle* in educational decisions concerning children, in 1942 their advice was equalized with that of the father in all matters concerning children), too long subsumed by policymakers under the politics of the family and ignored by earlier historians of women, were ultimately embedded in the foundation of the French welfare state in the years following World War II, from which time they made a distinctive contribution to the emancipation of French women.[10]

As the genesis and growth of the welfare state has begun to attract scholarly attention, these and other gender-specific measures have attracted the attention of historians of women as well as feminist analysts from other scholarly disciplines. It is indeed essential to re-evaluate the welfare state and its formation from a feminist standpoint.[11] In the course of such a re-evaluation, however, it is equally essential to pay close attention to the specific historical shape women's issues took in France during the inter-war period, to disentagle them both from 'family' issues as defined by the male-dominated pronatalist/family movements, and from late twentieth-century concerns, to return to the primary sources with an attentive ear to women's voices and to socio-political and economic context of the times, for this was not a period in which women were silent, on these or other subjects. And indeed, no comprehensive history of the French welfare state (or, for that matter, of French women's lives or of French feminism) can be written without measuring both populationist and feminist demands against what various women (and men) believed their respective interests to be and what they thought French society was capable of providing. Without arguing that all women thought alike, it is nevertheless possible to demonstrate a significant convergence between a broad range of politically outspoken women on several fundamental points: their insistence on bodily sexual difference and needs as a basis for women's civil, economic and political equality, and their overall agreement on the socio-political importance of motherhood and of women's economic independence.[12] Where they disagreed was on the form and scope of possible political solutions.

PRONATALISM AND THE ISSUE OF WOMEN'S EMPLOYMENT

French history in the inter-war period offers an exemplary case study of how central the politics of gender and women's issues could become to national politics in a time of demographic crisis, at both the national and international levels.[13] The political and ideological challenges of bolshevism, fascism and National Socialism, coupled with memories of the war and compounded by world economic instability, ensured that political solutions would not be swiftly or easily reached.

Women in inter-war France increasingly experienced the convergence of these issues as the world-wide economic depression began to affect France in the early 1930s, with the mounting onslaught made on women's (especially married women's) employment by the so-called family movement. According to official statistics, of all economically developed countries France had the highest percentage of women in the labour force, including the very high proportion who worked in agriculture (Table 7.2). Yet perhaps in no country except England had male prescriptive rhetoric insisted so adamantly yet so futilely, on the necessity of realizing an idealized sexual division of labour, with the husband as breadwinner and the wife as *maîtresse de maison* and mother-educator, raising the citizens, workers and soldiers of the future.[14] This neo-traditionalist prescriptive vision, shared by French Catholics, secular republicans (of a LePlayist or Comtean orientation), socialists (often Proudhonist), and communists alike, had even become a staple ingredient in the Third Republic's pre-war educational curriculum, especially in the primary schools.[15]

Earlier, during World War I, those who objected to women's participation in the labour force had strained to rationalize the necessity of women's war-time employment, in face of the need for more men at the front and the continuing demographic crisis.[16] Once again in 1916–17 the Academy of Medicine sounded the alarm about women's industrial work and the falling birth-rate, and meanwhile, under the aegis of the War Ministry, government armaments plants had begun to institute on-site nursing rooms and crèches to accommodate the infants and young children of women employees.[17] When the war ended and hundreds of thousands of women were released from the French labour force to make room for returning men, attention shifted to countering the still-falling birth-rate; the pronatalists and familial movement men focused obsessively on the 'problem' of the working wife,

Table 7.2   Economically active women as a percentage of the total economically active population in France, 1856–1961

Year	Total economically active population (in thousands)	% women
1856	14.123	31.2
1861	14.786	30.6
1871 [1872]	14.686	29.6
1881	16.629	32.2
1891	16.343	31.4
1901	19.736	34.6
1911	20.931	36.9
1921	21.718	39.6
1931	21.615	36.6
1946	20.792	37.9
1954	19.602	34.0
1961 [1962]	19.711	33.4

Source: Calculated from figures given in P. Bairoch, *The Working Population and its Structure*, ed. T. Deldycke, H. Gelders, J.-M. Limbor et al. *International Historical Statistics*, vol. 1, Brussels, Free University of Brussels, 1968.

and on the hope of returning these women to the *foyer* to make more babies, without which France's future industrial and military strength could not be guaranteed. Economics, demographics, nationalist and solidarist ideologies and politics – and considerable wishful thinking – thus combined to dictate the shape of proposed reforms in the situation of French women.[18]

Issues concerning the protection of women workers as well as equal pay for equal work had also been debated at great length before the war. Both radical republican and socialist feminists had made their views on these subjects known well before 1919, when they had in fact influenced the drafting of the charter for the newly founded International Labour Organisation, based in Geneva.[19] But as the world economic situation deteriorated and the 1930s depression brought massive unemployment to Europe, the seeming incompatibility of working wives and motherhood once again drew the fire of pronatalists, coupled with their defence by women's movement leaders. After a short upsurge in natality in the early 1920s, the French birth-rate again fell off toward pre-war levels. Then, in the wake of the papal encyclicals, *Casti Connubi* (1930) and *Quadragesimo Anno* (1931), which spelled out the dependent role of wives and the fiscal responsibilities of men, and as unemployment was perceived to increase dramatically in France during 1931, secular pronatalists such as the venerable physician and Nobel laureate Charles Richet called for the forcible eviction of all women from the work-force as the solution to both the birth-rate crisis and male unemployment.[20]

Women of all political persuasions leaped to the defence of women's right to work. Women's groups from all points in the political spectrum quickly perceived the dangers in Richet's ostensible solution to the economic crisis and adamantly resisted becoming its scapegoats. Various organizations mobilized information and arguments to blunt the attack. Unions such as the Fédération des Transports and the Fédération des Tabacs took steps to protect the many women who were employed in economic sectors such as public transport and in the state-run tobacco shops.[21] Even Andrée Butillard, head of the social Catholic *Union Féminine Civique et Sociale* (UFCS), argued in 1933 – against highly placed male Catholic spokesmen – that in current economic circumstances, women married or single must retain the choice of employment.[22] Such an emphasis on choice stretched to its limits official Catholic doctrine on marital arrangements.

Academically trained Frenchwomen such as the economist Fernande Dauriac and the social historian Marguerite Thibert (then at the International Labour Office) countered claims that women had taken 'men's jobs' by publishing studies of women's employment in France, which showed that the level of women's employment had remained remarkably stable overall since 1906. There had, in fact, been a slight decline since the early 1920s in women's participation in the labour force; what had changed markedly was women's occupational distribution. Statistics also revealed that the number of women employed in industry had decreased, but that they had become more numerous in the tertiary sector, especially in teaching and white-collar jobs. To allay the spectre of women's economic competition with men, Thibert specified that women and men were not, in the vast majority of cases, competing for the same jobs; indeed, she observed that most employed women held jobs that no man would want.[23] An important exception, however, was in the civil service; here educated women had made significant inroads and felt vulnerable. Unlike other European countries such as Italy, where more severe measures were enacted, married women employees in the French civil service were never required to resign, even though entry to the service was closed to women for several years. Caution was obviously the watchword, however; a 1936 book on career advice recommended to young women a variety of career opportunities, especially in the social services, that would not place them in open competition for those jobs men considered their own.[24]

I will now examine briefly the arguments of women's rights advocates across a political spectrum ranging from religious to secular, from social Catholic to communist, as these arguments are revealed in 1930s publications and in the press. This survey shows that the strategies and tactics of virtually all sectors of the French women's movement during the inter-war period turned on certain assumptions that characterize what I have called elsewhere 'relational' feminism.[25] Briefly, advocates of this approach, influenced by decades of French solidarist and corporatist thinking, as well as Catholic doctrine, insisted on the family as the basic socio-political unit of the nation-state and stressed the rights of women *as women* – and as mothers – within a framework of male–female complementarity; a 'natural' sexual division of social labour predicated on physiological differences between the sexes remained central to its vision. This did not mean that women should confine their efforts exclusively to housekeeping and child care; they also argued that women's particular motherly qualities should be actively exercised to reform the society beyond the household. In short, they sought to explode the 'public/private' sex-role dichotomy that antifeminists sought to maintain.[26]

These relational feminists sought state intervention to improve women's situation as wives and mothers, even as they fought to defend women's right to work outside the home and attempted to obtain the vote. In the context of the 1930s, their actions and attitudes can best be understood as political responses by actors who held no formal political power, except in so far as they could sway public opinion, within a pervasive pronatalist, nationalist and anti-individualist climate of opinion, hostile to and apprehensive about the 'egotism' that seemed intrinsic to demands for enhanced legal, political and economic rights for women as individuals. This climate of opinion had already affected French political life well before the First World War, but it became even stronger and more pervasive – and, it appears, placed even more psychological constraints on women's options (and on those men who were in a position to grant women's demands) – following the disastrous bloodletting of the First World War. It should be clear that all factions of the French women's movement were in a defensive, indeed a beleaguered position throughout this period, though one could never guess this from Louise Weiss' caustic and self-aggrandizing comments about the ostensible timidity of certain other women's rights leaders in pressing for the vote.[27]

RESPONSES OF FRENCH WOMEN'S GROUPS: SECULAR FEMINISTS, SOCIAL CATHOLICS, SOCIALIST WOMEN AND COMMUNIST WOMEN

Let us begin by reviewing the positions taken on these linked issues of pronatalism and women's employment by secular women's rights groups, beginning with the *Union Française pour le Suffrage des Femmes* (UFSF), founded in 1909. At the height of World War I, in 1916, at the same time as they continued to press for the vote, UFSF leaders had underscored 'the duty of women in the struggle against depopulation'. In so doing, they pointed out that in countries where women had already gained the vote, women's rights leaders were the ones who were spearheading campaigns for measures to improve conditions for maternity.[28] At their 1917 congress, UFSF delegates called on the state to recognize maternity as a national service, and by 1920 Marguerite de Witt-Schlumberger, mother of six, ardent suffragist, pronatalist, and the only female member of the newly established *Conseil Supérieur de la Natalité*, questioned publicly whether Frenchwomen would become 'mothers of the fatherland or traitors to the fatherland'.[29] Such reproduction was not to be indiscriminate, but the conscious choice of the women, and as a conscientious eugenicist, Witt-Schlumberger also demanded women's right to refuse unhealthy or diseased men as fathers. The criticisms that there might be some dangers for women in such an unequivocally pronatalist position was not one UFSF leaders saw fit to confront during the war years.

La Française, the official publication of the *Conseil National des Femmes Français* (CNFF), which equally sought the vote for women, had celebrated the publication of Witt-Schlumberger's provocative tract with an editorial asserting that the fight against depopulation was indeed women's business: 'the entire feminist question', wrote the editorialist, 'is intimately connected with the population question'.[30] Both the attorney Maria Vérone and the young Andrée Lehmann, leading activists in the *Ligue Française pour le Droit des Femmes*, also expressed their concern over the French population plight; keeping their distance from pre-war neo-Malthusian feminists, they argued that the state had an obligation to provide mothers with substantive financial assistance.[31] Witt-Schlumberger's successor, Cécile Brunschvicg, a key figure in the inter-war feminist movement, similarly insisted on the importance of maternity for women, demanding the vote to enable them satisfactorily to accomplish their maternal duties, as well insisting on government financial assistance for working-class women who needed it.[32]

Indeed, when the Senate defeated women's suffrage in 1923, a seemingly paradoxical alliance had emerged between leaders of the secular French women's movement and the family and pronatalist movements in pursuit of a new approach to suffrage that, by providing multiple representation of families, would include the vote for married women. The terms of the bargain here appear to have included a tacit agreement by the spokeswomen for the secular republican women's movement not to challenge the government or the pronatalist lobby over the severe repression of abortion and contraception effected in the later months of 1920.[33]

What united the secular feminists and the secular pronatalists was their common accord on the necessity to fight for major improvements in women's situation as wives and mothers. A state-sponsored programme of family allowances, introduced in 1913 for certain categories of families, came to be elaborated in the inter-war years into a system that would ultimately provide maternity allowances, bonuses for babies, and subsidies for women who stayed at home to raise children. This latter issue is singularly interesting from the standpoint of women's history. Article 2 of the 1913 law had stipulated that a monthly allowance would be granted to needy families with many children under 13 years of age, to provide for the fourth and each additional child born into the family. The allowance would be paid to fathers or to single mothers (in the absence of a male head-of-household); additional aid was provided by a supplemental law enacted in June 1918.[34]

During the 1920s and 30s women's movement leaders, secular and Catholic alike, sought to amend this legislation so as formally to direct these payments to the mothers themselves, rather than to the wage-earner, usually taken to be the husband/father. When in 1939 the government introduced an allowance for mothers who stayed at home to raise their children, a feminist writing in *La Française* considered it a victory: 'It is natural that this sum, granted in view of the housework done, be paid to that person who actually performs this work'. The introduction of maternity and family benefits, which have been mentioned above and will be dealt with more fully later on, were due, in no small part, to the combined efforts of social Catholics and secular pronatalists. Of particular importance in social Catholicism were the efforts of Andrée Butillard and her co-workers on the *Union Féminine Civique et Sociale*, founded in 1925. In 1930 Butillard's group undertook a survey of 30,000 working mothers concerning the problems posed by their double burden: over 80 per cent said they were working for economic survival. As an alternative to proposals emanating from many countries to effect state intervention eliminating women from the labour force, as an ostensible solution to the vast unemployment problems posed by the world-wide Depression, in 1936 Butillard's group founded the *Ligue de la*

Mère au Foyer, which pressed for direct subsidies to married women who opted against extra-domestic employment to stay at home and care for their families.[35]

These efforts capped years of effort by social Catholics to propose their own solutions to the 'woman question' and to the population question. In 1921 French Catholics had received Rome's authorization to enter the French pronatalist movement (which was then dominated by secular republicans). In 1923 (during his Easter week address) Cardinal Archbishop Dubois of Paris took up the population topic; that year's *Semaine sociale* likewise addressed the subject. In 1927 the topic of women in society was addressed at the yearly *Semaine sociale*.[36] In accordance with Catholic doctrine as articulated in the late nineteenth century by Pius IX and Leo XIII, the proceedings reveal a clear insistence on a home-based, family-centred life for wives, and on their social role as the able auxiliaries of men, a position subsequently reconfirmed by the papal encyclicals of the early thirties. At that meeting Eugène Duthoit (who worked closely with Butillard) spelled out the relationship of social Catholicism to secular feminism in these terms:

> In the light of Catholic teaching we can clearly define our position with regard to feminism. To the partisans of feminism we say, if by this word you mean to affirm woman's personality and . . . her *feminine* personality, with all the rights and obligations that follow, then we are with you; we are not only permitted but commanded to be feminists. If, on the contrary, you lose sight of the fact that man and woman are two complementary beings, together called upon to multiply the human species, if you deny that this proportioned and reciprocal assistance ought to be deployed in the family, then we are not feminists; then we are not only permitted but commanded to combat you.

Duthoit went on to insist on the development and deployment of women's talents in the interest of both temporal and spiritual maternity, and to express regret about employment that took married women out of the home.[37]

To listen to partisans of the Catholic women's movement, one might believe that all secular feminists were of one mind in denying motherhood, destroying the French family, and with it, the foundation of all social morality. That this was far from being the case is attested by looking at the opinions expressed on the secular Left – by socialist and communist women – during this same period.

Among socialist women, especially after the French section of the Third International broke with the Communist Party in 1920, conflicting points of view on the woman question could be found. The long-standing feminist socialist commitment to the establishment of motherhood as a paid social function, originating in the 1880s (with Léonie Rouzade), found its contradictors, as did the sexual liberationist perspective espoused most eloquently by Madeleine Pelletier (though in the 1930s even she advocated motherhood as a social function, to be paid by the state).[38] Madeleine Vernet, the editor of a small socialist monthly review, devoted her efforts to spreading mother-educator ideology and advice on hygiene to the 'mères du peuple'. Vernet's collaborators included Nelly Roussel, Louise Bodin and Hélène Brion, all of whom were publicly known as women with a radical feminist (and even neo-Malthusian) perspective. Vernet early raised the question as to 'why woman's greatest contribution [i.e. motherhood] should also be the keystone of her servitude?' Capitalism, she argued, denied the grandeur of the maternal task; but in contrast to Ellen Key and the early German *Mutterschutz* radicals, who called for the endowment of motherhood (for the unmarried as well as the married) by the state, Vernet argued that to pay women specifically for being mothers was immoral. Separating the issue of men's financial support for the children they fathered from that of supporting the mothers, Vernet suggested that all women be 'endowed' by the state at the age of 20; she insisted, however, on the necessity of men continuing to work to support the children they created. 'Free love', she later argued in reply to Madeleine Pelletier (and no doubt also to the arguments of the Russian communist women's movement leader Alexandra Kollontai), 'is not liberating for women'.[39]

Within a decade after the split with the communists at Tours, women of the French socialist party had raised the problem of women's feeble participation in party activities. As before the war, they felt a need to mobilize working-class women in order to counter the appeal of 'bourgeois' feminism.[40] Suzanne Lacore, later one of Léon Blum's three women undersecretaries of state in the Popular Front ministry, repeatedly addressed the problem of 'socialism and the family'. According to her view – like that of a number of French socialist women, it was at variance with the long-standing international socialist commitment to women's employment as an essential condition of their liberation – capitalism had snatched women from their homes and children, abandoning babies to mercenary care, abandoning husbands to hearths where sweetness no longer prevailed, and generally breaking the bonds of the family. In her view, which bore a strong resemblance to the 'sexualisme' advocated by Aline Valette in the 1890s, socialism would restore woman to her rightful place in the *foyer*.[41]

At the 1933 congress of the *Parti socialiste*, French socialist women held their first national conference. They reaffirmed women's right to work, but also called for strict application of protective legislation. At the same time they urged the passage of measures designed to 'conciliate and facilitate for women their functions as mothers, salaried workers, and housekeepers [*ménagères*]'; they called for increases in the existing programmes of *primes d'allaitement* and the extension of these programmes to all mothers; they supported maternity leave programmes. And, like Léonie Rouzade and Paul Lafargue in the late nineteenth century, the women's delegates reiterated the party's long-standing demand that maternity be established (*pace* Madeleine

Vernet) as a paid social function.[42] This perspective doubtless informed the arguments of party head and Popular Front prime minister Léon Blum. In 1936 he argued, with a sympathetic but somewhat different emphasis, that work should not be a necessity for mothers, that the salary of the head of the family (i.e. the male breadwinner) should be adequate to support the entire family, and that more children should not be a financial burden.[43] It appears that Blum never endorsed maternity as a paid social function.

What, then, of the Communist Party women in France? The position of the French section of the Communist International on the woman question, which in the 1920s had followed the Soviet Russian line on women's liberation through extra-domestic work, switched abruptly in 1934 to a focus on 'bonheur familial et maternal'. This has been read by some as reactionary Stalinism, pure and simple. In view of the emerging communist alliance with the socialists and radicals that produced the Popular Front, coupled with the pronatalist concerns of the period, however, it can also be viewed as simply expedient or as an acknowledgement of the French population problems. In late 1935 L'Humanité began to publish a series of articles calling for a *salaire vital* that would enable wives to stay at home, and in 1936 one male party leader, Jacques Duclos, publicly chastized the militant party women for their reluctance to appeal to other women where the latter's 'real interests' lay.[44] However judged, it is clear that from that time forth, the French communist line on the woman question – like that of their erstwhile allies – stressed motherhood and advocated that it be given full government support.

THE POLITICS OF MOTHERHOOD AND THE EMERGENCE OF THE FRENCH WELFARE STATE

Throughout this chapter, I have emphasized women's arguments with respect to the politics of motherhood, setting them within the context of populationist and national welfare concerns prior to the establishment of the French welfare state. In what follows, the focus will shift somewhat to consider the rationale and implementation of the so-called 'family policies' developed by the Fourth Republic and to look at other important changes made concurrently in women's status. In retrospect we might now say that the problem feminists confronted was, as before, how such policies with their emphasis on natality and *la femme au foyer* could be configured to empower women as acting, autonomous subjects.[45] Clearly family policy alone, as conceptualized prior to 1938 in terms of (male) workers' benefits, would be insufficient to achieve this end.

The formal beginnings of state family policy in France are generally dated from 1938–9. However, the Family Allowance Act of 1932 obliged all employers to participate in, and contribute to, the existing, voluntary, employer-financed system of child allowances (paid out of equalization funds, the *caisses de compensation*) and extended their coverage. Businesses had initiated these for their own employees, for reasons which had to do with labour management rather than pronatalism; in 1930, only 7 per cent of the enterprises were affiliated to the *caisses de compensation*. The 1932 Act implied not only an extension of business-sponsored child allowances under state supervision, but also an extension of the state-financed scheme of allowances for needy families and for civil servants introduced in 1913. It was designed to ensure that allowances were provided for most families supported by workers in industry, commerce and liberal professions. It was stipulated (article 74b) that the allowance should be paid to 'the wage-earner who supports the child'; if both parents work for wages it would be due to the father; but in addition, the regional *caisses de compensation* could, in principle or in certain cases, pay the allowance to 'the mother or to the person who is actually in charge of the education of the child'. It appears that in most cases the payment did get to the mothers, though only a minority of the family allocations funds – the most important ones – distributed the money directly to them (e.g. in the regions of Paris and Tours, Amiens, Caen, Dijon, Lille).[46] In November 1938 the government went a step further and cut loose the family allowances from the business establishments, contributed to their finance and extended them to agricultural and other independent workers. In the course of this extension, allowances in support of mothers (*allocations de la mère au foyer*) were established and paid both to support women's presence as home-based child rearers and to waged women who had exclusive care of children. These allowances were deliberately paid out separately from wages and benefits, just as they were administered separately from the health, unemployment, and old age benefits institutionalized in *Sécurité sociale* following Liberation, even though the funding for both was consolidated through the latter. The changes of November 1938 were embodied or further extended in the *Code de la famille* of 29 July 1939. It introduced a one-time birth-premium of several thousand francs for a first child born within the first two years of marriage (and instead cancelled the regular child allowance for the first child); this bonus and the *mère au foyer* allowance were paid directly to the mother. The regular family allowances (amounting to 10 per cent of the wage for the second child, 20 per cent for the third and further ones) were to be paid to the father unless he was absent, incapable of work or without employment.[47]

These initial phases of state family policies did not seem auspicious for women's empowerment. Despite the continuing significance of women's employment in France, the *Code de la famille* clearly privileged a prescriptive family model, explicitly depicted in terms of a male breadwinner and stay-at-home wife with three or more children and a first child born within two years after marriage. In early June 1940, the last government of the Third Republic established a Ministry of the Family. In July the new Vichy government, with its *révolution nationale* incorporated family concerns into a secretariat, and subsequently into a *commissariat général*, which then embarked on a nominally apolitical pronatalist and profamily programme that insisted even more on an all-too-familiar 'traditional' vision of women's role, sequestered in 'private' life. In such a setting governmental directives went out to order the dismissal of women from their jobs, and abortion could be officially equated with high treason. Through radio broadcasts and propaganda films, the Vichy state advocated the further restriction of civil divorce and lyrically promoted the celebration of Mother's Day. This same regime reconceptualized family allowances in terms of supplements to a *salaire unique* ('single wage') of the household breadwinner, extending them to widows with dependent children even as it somewhat surprisingly defended the *allocation de salaire unique* for single mothers.[48]

Following the Liberation, Fourth Republic political leaders largely maintained and expanded this approach to family policy (1946–58). Familial concerns were merged into a new Ministry of Public Health and Population. 'Family benefits' continued to be administered separately from the new national social security system. The politics of motherhood assumed concrete characteristics. That women as mothers, whether married or single, should receive governmental assistance or encouragement seemed generally agreed, although the language of 'maternity as a social function' was still carefully avoided; indeed, in August 1946 a full-scale system of state-supported maternity allowances was enacted, again payable in cash to the mothers themselves, and the very important benefit of free maternity care, prenatal, delivery and post-partum, was included in the social security medical benefits package. Birth premiums were established for each child born; in addition prenatal allowances payable to the woman to cover her expenses during pregnancy were added, with the explicit intent of discouraging abortion.[49] The symbolic and economic importance for women, especially poor women, of these financial supports for maternity, added to the family allowances (renamed *prestations familiales*) in support of children should not be underestimated.

It would be too much to say, however, that these measures responded to all women's needs in a comprehensive fashion. Still unsettled was a range of controversial questions about women's and men's relationships to one another, to property, and to children in the male-headed institution of marriage (as embodied in the still incompletely reformed French Civil Code), and about women's right to control their own bodies and the legal situation of children born outside marriage.[50] No Fourth Republic government could have been expected, in the wake of the demoralizing defeat and German occupation, to undertake such a re-evaluation. With the extraordinary exception of Simone de Beauvoir's philosophical and wide-ranging study of women's existential dilemma as the 'second sex' (1949), such questions would not attract significant public attention until well into the Fifth Republic, when memories of the wars had faded and a new generation reached maturity.[51]

In the meantime, other aspects of women's situation began to change significantly, and not merely on paper. Women's contributions to the Resistance effort – their acts of *de facto* citizenship – were loudly touted in support of their full citizenship.[52] In 1944 General de Gaulle's counter-government gave French women the vote by decree, a landmark decision that was confirmed in law the following year with France's liberation. The 1946 *Préambule* to the Constitution of the Fourth Republic guaranteed equal rights for women, and it also proclaimed each individual's duty to work and their right to employment (an earlier draft of the Constitution had spelled out 'liberties' and 'social and economic rights' for women far more explicitly, but it was narrowly defeated in a national referendum half a year before the Constitution was enacted on 27 October 1946).[53] The principle of equal pay for equal employment for both sexes in the French civil service was guaranteed (5 October 1946). These various measures, it is important to insist, substantively satisfied many of the political, legal and economic demands made by the French women's movement since the early nineteenth century.

The cumulative impact of this ensemble of measures is striking, especially in international comparison and in contrast, for example, to Germany. Overall, the accumulation of reforms enacted on women's behalf between 1920 and 1950 represent the logical climax to a feminist movement that, for historic reasons, did not openly contest the familial base of the French socio-political structure but attempted to reorganize it radically, one piece at a time. These women (and men) emphasized women's role as mothers in the republican nation-state and sought state support for that role. At the same time, by defending women's right to work and by continuing to argue for 'equality in difference', they promoted women's rights as embodied women in the French body politic rather than as individuals irrespective of gender considerations. It was not 'equality' or 'difference' but 'equality in difference' that triumphed in France.

Even as we cast a critical eye on the familial politics of the pronatalists, and a sceptical eye on the shifting of women's dependency to a not always 'motherly' state, we must acknowledge that these women's insistent advocacy of substantive societal support for maternity, along with insistence on their rights, bore important fruit. In the inter-war period, virtually all factions of politically active women had endorsed the importance of motherhood for women, and had argued for some form of meaningful financial assistance to mothers, especially poor mothers, which would ensure that maternity did not represent an insurmountable handicap to economic survival, especially during the first six months of an infant's life. Social Catholic women, though imbued with the notion that the best place for women was in the home, nevertheless endorsed women's right to work and promoted the idea that any maternity payments should be directed to the mothers themselves. Most secular feminists, as well as socialist and communist women, continued to argue that maternity must be made a paid social function, though they disagreed over whether this should be limited to poor women or comprehensively extended (as the communists insisted) to all women, irrespective of class or social standing.

Indeed, one might argue that by 1950 French women found themselves on a road that seemed to promise them the best of both worlds. With the vote, also, they had acquired a potentially significant clout in democratic politics, a clout that began to make some difference. Between 1965 and 1985, 'every policy affecting women, from reproduction to retirement, was rewritten'.[54] These included the complete empowerment of married women with regard to property and personal decisions, rights over children, and, for all women, the legalization of contraception and abortion. In the 1980s the French state established a Ministry for Women's Rights, began to sponsor programmes for family planning, and even legalized the infamous abortion pill. 'Medals for motherhood' were still in place, but state support for motherhood as well as women's full civil and political rights had entered the law and customs of the French. Would it be too much to say that the 'état minotaure' had evolved into what Hubertine Auclert once called the 'état-mère-de-famille'? Could it even be said, as Elisabeth Badinter now claims,[55] that France has become a post-patriarchal society? Has the late twentieth-century French welfare state laid the foundation for 'the paradise of women'?

NOTES

*An initial version of this paper was presented at the Sixth Berkshire Conference on the History of Women, Smith College, June 1984, an elaborated version at the European University Institute in 1987 which was circulated as EUI Working Paper no. 87/293 (Florence, 1987). I am particularly grateful to the Rockefeller Foundation for a Humanities Fellowship in 1985–6, which greatly facilitated my investigation of the woman question in inter-war France, and to Agnes Peterson at the Hoover Institution, Stanford University, for assistance in obtaining a variety of sources. Thanks, too, to colleagues who have offered astute comments and criticism of earlier drafts, particularly Sondra Herman, Susan Pedersen, Gisela Bock and Anne Cova, and to Edie Gelles for her invariably wise suggestions and her willingness to read yet another draft on short notice. None of them can be held responsible for my interpretation.

1 Letter from Millerand's Minister of Hygiene, Jules-Louis Breton, to the President of the Republic, 26 May 1920, accompanying the decree establishing medals for mothers, in English translation in S. G. Bell and K. Offen, *Women, the Family, and Freedom: The Debate in Documents*, Stanford University Press, 1983, vol. 2, doc. 84, pp. 308–9.
2 The law of 31 July 1920 is translated in S.G. Bell and K. Offen, *Women*, doc. 85, pp. 309–10. See P. Paillat and J. Houdaille, 'Legislation directly or

indirectly influencing fertility in France', in M. Kirk, M. Livi-Bacci and E. Szabady (eds), *Law and Fertility in Europe*, Dolhain (Belgium), Ordina Editions, 1975, pp. 240–73; D. V. Glass, *Population Policies and Movements in Europe* (first edn 1940), repr. London, Frank Cass, 1967, pp. 158–9.

3 C.-A.-E.-X. Maitrot, 'La Grande Pitié des berceaux de France: le mal, ses conséquences', *L'Echo de Paris*, 1 May 1922. More generally, see F. Thébaud, 'Le Mouvement nataliste dans la France de l'entre-deux-guerres: l'Alliance nationale pour l'accroissement de la population française', *Revue d'histoire moderne et contemporaine*, 1985, vol. 32, pp. 276–301; R. Tomlinson, 'The politics of dénatalité during the French Third Republic, 1890–1940', Ph. D. dissertation, Cambridge University, 1983.

4 René LaBruyère, 'La Crise de natalité des navires', *Revue des deux mondes*, 1 Feb. 1931, pp. 686–94.

5 S. C. Hause and A. R. Kenney, *Women's Suffrage and Social Politics in the Third Republic*, Princeton, Princeton University Press, 1984; V. Cox, 'Le Mouvement pour le suffrage féminin pendant l'entre-deux-guerres', Mémoire de maîtrise, Université de Paris X (Nanterre), 1982.

6 C. Watson, 'Birth control and abortion in France since 1939', *Population Studies*, 1952, vol. 5, pp. 261–86; H. P. Pétain, 'Appel du 20 juin' (1940), in *Le Maréchal vous parle . . . : Recueil des discours et allocations prononcés par le Maréchal Pétain, chef de l'état du 16 juin au 31 décembre 1940*, Le Mans, Editions 'CEP', 1941, unpaginated (quote).

7 K. Offen, 'Depopulation, nationalism, and feminism in fin-de-siècle France', *The American Historical Review*, 1984, vol. 89, pp. 648–76; K. Offen, 'Exploring the sexual politics of French Republican nationalism', in Robert Tombs (ed.), *Aspects of French Nationalism*, London, Unwin Hyman (in press); K. Offen, *The Woman Question in Modern France* (forthcoming). See also A. Cova's article in this volume and her 'Féminisme et dépopulation: protéger la maternité ou promouvoir la natalité (fin XIXe siècle–1920)?', paper presented at the 3rd Table Ronde Franco-Allemande d'histoire sociale, Arc-et-Senans, Oct. 1989. Before the mid-1980s historians of women's issues in France during this period focused almost exclusively on reproductive freedom; e.g. R. Guerrand, *La Libre Maternité, 1896–1969*, Tournai, Casterman, 1971; A. McLaren, *Sexuality and Social Order: The Debate over the Fertility of Women and Workers in France, 1770–1930*, New York, Holmes & Meier, 1983, esp. ch. 10. The latter account virtually dismissed all family-oriented or maternal thinking as either 'conservative' or 'reactionary'. Yet such thinking is central to the history of the time and cannot so simply be dismissed and classified.

8 The graphic term is borrowed from J. Lewis, *The Politics of Motherhood: Child and Maternal Welfare in England, 1900–1939*, London, Croom Helm, 1980.

9 M. L. Stewart, *Women, Work, and the French State: Labour Protection and Social Patriarchy, 1879–1919*, Toronto, McGill-Queen's University Press, 1989.

10 None of these measures is mentioned in the first survey of the period, H. Bouchardeau, *Pas d'histoire, les femmes . . . 50 ans d'histoire des femmes: 1918–1968*, Paris, Syros, 1977, or in the concluding chapters of J. F. McMillan, *Housewife or Harlot: The Place of Women in French Society, 1870–1940*, New York, St Martin's Press, 1981. For an example of the interpretation of the history of French family law as a regrettable movement toward the disaggregation of the patriarchal, authoritarian family, see J. Derruppé, 'L'Evolution du droit français de la famille, de début du siècle à la guerre de 1939', in R. Prigent (ed.), *Renouveau des idées sur la famille*, Paris, Institut National d'Études Démographiques, 1954, pp. 149–60. An example of earlier interpretations more sympathetic to the

notion of affirming the rights of women is J. Bonnecase, *Mariage et régimes matrimoniaux: leur réforme récente*, Paris, Rousseau, 1938.

11 See J. Lewis, 'Dealing with dependency: state practices and social realities, 1870–1945', in J. Lewis (ed.), *Women's Welfare, Women's Rights*, London, Croom Helm, 1983, pp. 17–37.

12 See Y. Knibiehler and C. Fouquet, *L'Histoire des mères du moyen-âge à nos jours*, Paris, Montalba, 1980, esp. part III; F. Thébaud, *Quand nos grand-mères donnaient la vie: la maternité en France dans l'entre-deux-guerres*, Lyon, Presses Universitaires de Lyon, 1986; M. Martin, 'Ménagère: une profession? Les dilemmes de l'entre-deux-guerres', *Le Mouvement social*, 1987, no. 140, pp. 89–106; F. Werner, 'Du ménage à l'art ménager: l'évolution du travail ménager et son echo dans la presse féminine française de 1919 à 1939', *Le Mouvement social*, 1984, no. 129, pp. 61–87.

13 A. Sauvy, *Histoire économique de la France entre les deux guerres*, 3 vols, Paris, Fayard, 1965–1972; J. Jackson, *The Politics of Depression in France, 1932–1936*, Cambridge, Cambridge University Press, 1985.

14 For the British case, see Lewis's and Thane's articles in this volume. For France see C. Sowerwine, 'Workers and women in France before 1914: the debate over the Couriau affair', *Journal of Modern History*, 1983, vol. 55. pp. 411–41; J. W. Scott, '"L'Ouvrière! Mot impie, sordide . . .": women workers in the discourse of French political economy, 1840–1860', in P. Joyce (ed.), *The Historical Meaning of Work*, Cambridge, Cambridge University Press, 1987. For a different view see J. Jenson, 'Gender and reproduction: or, babies and the state', *Studies in Political Economy*, 1986, vol. 20, pp. 9–46, and J. Jenson, 'Paradigms and political discourse: protective legislation in France and the United States before 1914', *Canadian Journal of Political Science*, 1989, vol. 22, pp. 235–58, esp. p. 241.

15 L. L. Clark, *Schooling the Daughters of Marianne: Textbooks and the Socialization of Girls in Modern French Primary Schools*, Albany, State University of New York Press, 1984.

16 Y. Delatour, 'Les Effets de la guerre sur la situation de la Française d'après la presse féminine 1914–1918', diplôme d'études supérieures, Université de Paris, 1965; J. F. McMillan, *Housewife or Harlot*, esp. part II; F. Thébaud, *La Femme au temps de la guerre de 14*, Paris, Stock, 1986; S. C. Hause, 'More Minerva than Mars: the French women's rights campaign and the First World War', in M. R. Higonnet et al. (eds), *Behind the Lines: Gender and the Two World Wars*, New Haven, Yale University Press, 1987; Y. Knibiehler and C. Fouquet, *L'Histoire des mères*, pp. 302–10; M.-M. Huss, 'Pronatalism and the popular ideology of the child in wartime France: the evidence of the picture postcard', in R. Wall and J. M. Winter (eds), *The Upheaval of War: Family, Work, and Welfare in Europe, 1914–1918*, Cambridge, Cambridge University Press, 1989, pp. 329–67.

17 A. Pinard, 'Cri d'alarme, l'usine tueuse des enfants', *Le Matin*, 6 Dec. 1916, and the reply from Mme le Grille de Ferrer in *La Française*, 23 Dec. 1916, followed by further contributions to the debate over women's employment in factory labour in the *Bulletin de l'Académie de Médecine*, Jan. – March 1917. See also *Allaitement maternel au magasin et à l'atelier; Rapport de M. Abel Craissac, au nom de la Commission permanente. Procès-verbaux, enquête et documents*, Paris, Ministère du Travail et de la Prévoyance Sociale, Conseil supérieur du Travail, 1916; M. Martin, 'Le Travail féminin et la maternité (rapport au congrès de l'U.F.S.F., 5 Avril)', *La Française*, 5 May 1917, as well as the reports and documents from the *Comité du travail féminin* in the *Bulletin des usines de guerre*, published by the Armaments Ministry, 1916–18.

18 Two important post-war statements on the conundrum of maternity and women's

work are L. Ancelle, *L'Heure de la femme*, Paris, Sansot, 1919, and E. Herriot, *Créer*, Paris, Payot, 1919.

19 A. Lehmann, *De la réglementation légale du travail féminin (étude de législation comparée)*, Paris, H. d'Arthez, 1924, esp. pp. 177–97; Ki-Tcheng, *La Femme et la Société des Nations*, Paris, Les Presses modernes, 1928, ch. 5; M. Boy, *Les Associations internationales féminines*, Lyon, Paquet, 1936.

20 C. Richet, letter in *Le Matin*, 5 Nov. 1931, and subsequent letters. See also the ensuing discussion in *La Française*, 14, 21 and 28 Nov. 1931, and S. Grinberg, 'La Crise économique et le travail féminin', *L'Etat moderne*, 1932, vol. 5, pp. 82–5, 358–63.

21 E. Sullerot, 'Condition de la femme', in Sauvy, *Histoire économique*, vol. 3, p. 429. The formation of a 'Comité de liaison pour la défense du travail féminin' was announced in *La Française*, 28 Dec. 1935.

22 H. Rollet, *Andrée Butillard et le féminisme chrétien*, Paris, Spès, 1960, p. 107.

23 M. Thibert, 'The economic depression and the employment of women', *International Labour Review*, 1933, vol. 27, pp. 443–70, 620–30, esp. pp. 449, 621–5; see also F. Dauriac, 'Le Travail des femmes en France devant la statistique', *Revue d'économie politique*, 1933, vol. 47, pp. 91–109; Sullerot, 'Condition de la femme', pp. 422–3; A. Jack, 'Le Chômage et le travail des femmes', *Revue politique et parlementaire*, 1936, no. 501, pp. 272–89.

24 S.F. Cordelier, *Femmes au travail: étude pratique sur dix-sept carrières féminines*, Paris, Plon, 1935; M. Schulz, *La Femme dans les professions libérales et les carrières sociales*, Paris, Musée social, 1936.

25 K. Offen, 'Defining feminism: a comparative historical approach', *Signs*, 1988, vol. 14, pp. 119–57; see also N. Black, *Social Feminism*, Ithaca, Cornell University Press, 1989; A. T. Allen, *Feminism and Motherhood in Germany, 1800–1914*, New Brunswick, Rutgers University Press (in press).

26 For antifeminist objections see E. Angot, *Féminisme et natalité*, Paris, E. Paul, 1923; R. Teutsch, *Le Féminisme*, Paris, Malfère, 1934.

27 L. Weiss, *Mémoires d'une Européenne*, 2nd edn, Paris, Payot, 1970, vol. 3 (1934–1939).

28 Mlle Clement, 'Le Devoir des femmes dans la lutte contre la dépopulation', *UFSF Bulletin*, 1914–16, pp. 22–6.

29 M. de Witt-Schlumberger, *Mères de la patrie, ou traîtres à la patrie?*, Paris, CNFF & Pour la Vie, 1920; *UFSF Bulletin* 1917, p. 25.

30 A.B., in *La Française*, 15 May 1920.

31 M. Vérone, 'Natalité et mortalité infantile', *L'Oeuvre*, 1 May 1924; M. Vérone, 'Pas d'argent pour les mères', *L'Oeuvre*, 27 Feb. 1932; M. Vérone, 'Quand un pays veut des enfants', *L'Oeuvre*, 30 May 1934; Lehmann, *De la réglementation*, pp. 58–67; Y. Netter, *Le Travail de la femme mariée: son activité professionelle*, Paris, Presses Universitaires de la France, 1923.

32 C. Brunschvicg, 'Feminisme et natalité', *La Française*, 10 Jan. 1931; A. Cova, 'Cécile Brunschvicg (1877–1946) et la protection de la maternité', *Actes du 113e congrès national des Sociétés Savantes*, Paris, Association pour l'étude de l'histoire de la Sécurité sociale, 1989, pp. 75–104, and her article in this volume.

33 J. Bertillon, 'Le Vote des femmes', *La Femme et l'enfant*, 1 and 15 March 1919; A. Toulemon, *Le Suffrage familial, ou suffrage universel intégral: le vote des femmes*, Paris, Sirey, 1933.

34 P. Trisca, *Aperçu sur l'histoire de la protection de la maternité et de la première enfance*, Paris, Maloine, 1922; E. Gaujoux, *Essai critique sur la protection légale de la maternité en France*, Paris, L'Expansion scientifique française, 1923; F. I. Clark, *The Position of Women in Contemporary France*, London, P. S. King, 1937, p. 169;

C. Watson, 'Population policy in France: family allowances and other benefits', *Population Studies*, 1954, vol. 7, pp. 263–86, vol. 8, pp. 46–73; R. Talmy, *Histoire du mouvement familiale (1896–1939)*, 2 vols, Paris, Union Nationale des Caisses d'Allocations Familiales, 1962, vol. 1, pp. 159–63; R. Fuchs, *Abandoned Children: Foundlings and Child Welfare in 19th-Century France*, Albany, State University of New York Press, 1984.

35 Andrée Jack, 'La Mise en place de l'allocation de la "Mère au foyer"', *La Française*, 15–22 April 1939 (quote); H. Rollet, *Andrée Butillard*; among the UFCS publications see e.g. E. Baudouin, *Le Travail industriel de la mère et le foyer ouvrier. Documents d'études, extraits du Congrès international de juin 1933*, Paris, UFCS, 1934. Two contrasting interpretations are N. Black, *Social Feminism*, part III, and N. Black, 'Social feminism in France: a case study', in N. Black and A. B. Cottrell (eds), *Women and World Change: Equity Issues in Development*, Beverly Hills, Sage Publications, 1981, pp. 217–38; on the other hand S. Pedersen, 'Social policy and the reconstruction of the family in Britain and France, 1900–1945', Ph.D. dissertation, Harvard University, 1989, pp. 529–49.

36 F. Gibon, *La Crise de la natalité et la croisade pour la répopulation*, Paris, Montligeon, 1923, esp. pp. 110ff.; F. Gibon, 'Semaine sociale de France, 19e session, Nancy 1927', *La Femme dans la société: compte rendu in extenso des cours et conférences*, Lyon, Chronique social de France, 1928.

37 E. Duthoit, 'La Famille: donnée essentielle du problème de la femme', *La Femme dans la société*, pp. 31–66.

38 K. Offen, 'Minotaur or mother: the gendering of the state in early Third Republic France', Proceedings of the conference on 'Gender and the origins of the welfare state' (mimeo), Harvard University, 1988; M. J. Boxer, 'When radical and socialist feminism were joined: the extraordinary failure of Madeleine Pelletier', in J. Slaughter and R. Kern (eds), *European Women on the Left: Socialism, Feminism, and the Problems Faced by Political Women, 1880 to the Present*, Westport, Greenwood, 1981, pp. 51–73.

39 M. Vernet, 'Le mensonge social et la maternite', series of articles in *La Mère éducatrice*, Oct.–Dec. 1919, Jan.–August 1920. For the debate see *Bulletin des groupes féministes de l'enseignement*, Oct. 1925, p. 3 ('Nous voulons que la société comprenne enfin le rôle qui lui incombe: qu'au budget de la guerre elle substitue le budget de la mère; au budget de la mort le budget de la vie'); H. Alquier, 'La Maternité, fonction sociale', *Bulletin des Groupes féministes*, Feb. 1927, pp. 13–20.

40 See the series of articles by B. Fouchère, G. Picard-Moch and L. Saumoneau, in *La Nouvelle Revue socialiste*, 1929–30, vol. 27, 32, 33; S. D. Nicolich, *Le Socialisme et les femmes, conférence prononcée à Saint-Etienne, le 18 juin 1932 à l'occasion de la journée internationale des femmes socialistes*, Paris, Editions du Parti Socialiste, 1933; F. Picq, '"Bourgeois feminism" in France: a theory developed by socialist women before World War I', in J. Friedlander *et al.* (eds), *Women in Culture and Politics*, Bloomington, Indiana University Press, 1986, pp. 330–43.

41 S. Lacore, *Femmes socialistes*, Paris, Editions du Parti Socialiste, 1932, and 'La Femme et les fléaux sociaux', *Revue féministe du Sud-Ouest*, Oct. 1923, pp. 149–57; S. Lacore, 'Qui a arraché la femme au foyer? Capitalisme!', in L. Saumoneau (ed.), *Propagande et documentations*, 1932, no. 10.

42 'La Première Conférence des femmes socialistes en France', *La Voix des femmes*, 15 June 1933; M. Louis-Lévy, *L'Emancipation politique des femmes: rapport présenté à la première conférence nationale des femmes socialistes (4–5 Juin 1933)*, Paris, Editions du Parti Socialiste, 1934; S. Buisson, *Les Répercussions du travail féminin*, Paris, Editions du Parti Socialiste, 1934; F. I. Clark, *The Position of*

Women, pp. 234–5.
43 *L'Oeuvre de Léon Blum*, Paris, Albin Michel, 1964, vol. 4, pt. 1 (1934–7), pp. 318–19.
44 J. Duclos, *Pour l'Union des femmes de France, rapport prononcé le 11 juillet à la Conférence nationale du P.C.F.*, Paris, Editions du Comité Populaire de Propagande, 1936; P. Vaillant-Couturier, 'Au Secours de la famille', *L'Humanité*, late 1935 to early 1936; C. Vassart, in *Cahiers du Bolshevisme*, 1 Oct. 1936 and 1 Jan. 1937; J. Evans, 'The Communist Party of the Soviet Union and the women's question: the case of the 1936 decree "In Defence of Mother and Child"', *Journal of Contemporary History*, 1981, vol. 16, pp. 757–75.
45 See the excellent discussion of this dilemma in Knibiehler and Fouquet, *Histoire des mères*, esp. p. 357: 'La mère n'est presque jamais pensée comme sujet, mais comme objet pour l'enfant'.
46 F. I. Clark, *Position of Women*, p. 169: D. V. Glass, *Population Policies*, pp. 107, 436. See J. Doublet, 'Family allowances in France', *Population Studies*, 1948, vol. 2, pp. 219–39; A. Barjot, *L'Allocation de salaire unique et l'allocation de la mère au foyer en France*, Saint-André-Bruges (Belgium), Imprimerie Verbeke-Loys, 1967; N. Questiaux and J. Fournier, 'France', in S. B. Kamerman and A. J. Kahn (eds), *Family Policy: Governments and Families in Fourteen Countries*, New York, Columbia University Press, 1978, pp. 117–82; A. Prost, 'L'Evolution de la politique familiale en France de 1938 à 1981', *Le Mouvement social*, 1984, no. 129, pp. 7–28; C. Watson, 'Population policy'; R. Talmy, *Histoire*; P. Laroque *et al.*, *La Politique familiale en France depuis 1945*, Paris, La Documentation Française, 1985.
47 Articles 6, 11 and 23 of the 1938 law, in *Le Code de la famille: décret-loi du 29 juillet 1939, modifié et complété par les décrets-lois des 16 décembre et 24 avril 1940, les lois du 18 novembre 1940, du 15 février, du 29 mars, du 17 novembre 1941, et 3 février 1942. Précédé d'un commentaire détaillé et suivi des textes interprétatifs*, 5th edn, Lille, Martin-Mamy, 1942; Prost, 'L'Evolution', pp. 8–10, with note 3; J. Doublet, 'Family allowances'.
48 See Act of 11 Oct. 1940 on women's work; M. Bordeaux, 'Femme hors d'état français, 1940–1944', in R. Thalmann (ed.), *Femmes et fascismes*, Paris, Tierce, 1986, pp. 135–55. Family allowances to widows and single mothers: J. Cann, *Les Allocations familiales*, Loudéac, Traonouil-Anger, 1944. See also A. Coutrot, 'La Politique familiale', *Colloque sur le gouvernement de Vichy et la Révolution Nationale, 1940–1942*, Paris, A. Colin, 1972, pp. 245–63, esp. p. 254. See also Y. Knibiehler and C. Fouquet, *L'Histoire des mères*, pp. 333–55; S. Fishman, 'Waiting for the captive sons of France: prisoner of war wives, 1940–1945', in M. Higonnet *et al.* (eds), *Behind the Lines*, pp. 182–93. On lyric celebrations of motherhood see e.g. *La Mère au foyer, ouvrière de progrès*, Paris, Ligue de la Mère au Foyer, 1941.
49 J. Doublet, 'Family allowances', p. 228; Knibiehler and Fouquet, *L'Histoire des mères*, p. 340; Coutrot, 'La Politique familiale', p. 263 emphasizes the continuities; see also J. Jenson, 'The liberation and new rights for French women', in M. Higonnet *et al.* (eds), *Behind the Lines*, pp. 272–84.
50 N. Moreau-Bisseret, 'A scientific warranty for sexual politics: demographic discourse on "reproduction" (France 1945–1985)', *Feminist Issues*, 1986, vol. 6, pp. 67–85.
51 A. Michel and G. Texier, *La Condition de la française d'aujourd'hui*, 2 vols, Paris, Gonthier, 1964; M. A. L. Weill-Hallé, *La Grande Peur d'aimer: journal d'une femme médécin* (1960), Paris, Gonthier, 1964.
52 M. L. Rossiter, *Women in the Resistance*, New York, Praeger, 1986; P. Schwartz,

'Redefining resistance: women's activism in wartime France', in M. Higonnet *et al.* (eds), *Behind the Lines*, pp. 141–53.
53 Both documents in M. Duverger (ed.), *Constitutions et documents politiques*, Paris, Presses Universitaires de France, 1966, pp. 124–8, 138.
54 D. McBride Stetson, *Women's Rights in France*, Westport, CT, Greenwood Press, 1987.
55 E. Badinter, lecture at Stanford University, April 1990.

Chapter 8

Pronatalism and motherhood in Franco's Spain

Mary Nash

The early years of the Franco regime saw the articulation of a new moral order based on a hierarchical structuring of society, national tradition, National Syndicalism, and National Catholicism which acted as an ideological legitimizer and provided cultural cohesion to the 'New State.'[1] The 'National Revolution' initiated by Franco constructed a discourse which not only invoked 'Fatherland, Bread and Justice' but also the *grandeza*, the greatness of Spain based on imperial expansion, population increase and its recuperation as a world power. The overriding concern about depopulation led to the development of pronatalist policies which had a very wide range and specific gender connotations. Francoist pronatalist thought generated a view of women as basically mothers or potential mothers and one of the targets of the new regime was the promotion of motherhood. Women were politicized through the notion of a common female destiny based on their reproductive capacities. Female sexuality, work and education were regulated in accordance with this social function while motherhood was idealized and considered as a duty to the fatherland. Francoist ideology marked women off as a separate species and identified them exclusively as mothers whose offspring would check the tendency towards declining birth-rates and thus prevent the decadence of Spain. Women as potential breeders were accordingly the key to halting national degeneration through an expanded birth-rate and maximum development of their reproductive capacities.

Familialism was another key element in the development of pronatalism and motherhood. Both National Catholicism and the pronatalist drive coincided within the crusade for moral regeneration and the restoration of the family as the primary social unit of Spanish society. Francoist ideology upgraded the family as a key social institution designed to generate population increase. Thus the regime combined pronatalist policies with the family's consolidation and material support. Furthermore, familialism had specific gender connotations and reinforced the overall conception of woman as the *angel del hogar* (angel of the home) whose biological and social destiny was motherhood.[2]

POPULATION GROWTH AND THE CONSTRUCTION OF THE NEW STATE

The Franco regime abolished republican legislation and attempted to discredit the former democratic regime. Francoists made out that the Second Republic had been a repository of decadence by stressing the social upheaval, economic disorder and nationalist tensions of the thirties, and, of course, by altering their significance. Gender and cultural factors were also prominent in this defamatory account, by which they attributed the 'moral degeneracy' of the regime to changes in traditional cultural values, irreligiosity and most especially to the changing status of women and the degradation of the family. Feminism and egalitarian demands all characterized women's growing corruption and denial of their natural mandate as mothers. According to Francoist ideologues, the model woman, the *'Perfecta Casada'*, the dedicated and submissive spouse and mother, had been transformed when women were granted political rights. Declining birth-rates, birth control, civil matrimony, a relaxation of the norms of sexual conduct and female suffrage were all signs of the moral decadence of the republican regime.

Of course Franco's propaganda did not deal with social reality but rather evoked a myth of decadence and moral degeneracy. It is true that there had been considerable improvement in the situation of women since the establishment of the Second Republic in 1931. Women achieved suffrage, divorce, and the derogation of the most blatant discriminatory legislation in the areas of family jurisdiction, politics and work.[3] However, despite the achievement of equal rights, in practice inequality still characterized the social situation of Spanish women. Informal instances of social control still operated to maintain asymmetry between the sexes, few women acceded to public life and politics and, despite legislation to the contrary, wage discrimination and occupational segmentation characterized female wage work.[4] Even during the Civil War, despite greater female intervention in public affairs through their dedication to the war effort and a change in rhetoric on women's status, basic gender power relations and the restriction of female cultural and professional horizons continued.[5] Although birth control was practised and abortion was legalized in Catalonia, neither one nor the other had been assimilated into the norms of acceptable social conduct. With the exception of some members of the minority sex reform and eugenic movements, who advocated the practice of birth control, and an even smaller minority which condoned abortion,[6] both issues were still publicly unacceptable cultural values, although it is true that, by then, they had been clearly integrated into the dynamics of everyday experience.

Abortion had been legalized in Catalonia under the auspices of the autonomous local government, the *Generalitat*, in December 1936. This initiative can be attributed to a small group of anarchist sex reformers who addressed themselves to reproductive issues when they acquired access to political power in Catalonia in 1936 and were in a position to direct public health policies. This 'eugenics reform'[7] responded to a eugenic class rationale and was primarily a hygienic measure designed to regulate the current practice of clandestine abortion in Catalonia. The proclaimed goals of the new legislation were the eradication of the clandestine practice of abortion and of consequent illnesses and mortality. It admitted abortions under a wide variety of categories based on therapeutic, eugenic, neo-Malthusian and personal grounds. In the context of the politics of abortion, it was the first time that a woman's choice was considered legitimate. However, despite such innovative legislation, the regulation of abortion was a failure. Only one birth control clinic was established during the brief period of the decree and the records of the major hospitals in the network show that abortion services were practically negligible.[8] There had, in fact, not been such dramatic changes in the codes of moral behaviour as Franco claimed. The family was still a prominent social institution while the divorce law had been used basically to regulate the situation of marriages which had already broken up. However, Francoist rhetoric was not concerned with reality but with deploying a discourse which discredited the republican regime while constructing a mythic past more in consonance with the objectives of the new regime.

By the end of the Civil War pronatalist policy was integrated into mainstream politics in the construction of the New State. The racial hygienist, Vallejo Najéra, warned as early as 1938: 'The New State would weaken one of its most important foundations if it ignored natalist policy, intimately articulated with racial policy.'[9] In 1939 war deaths and population loss over the decades resulting from a decline in birth-rates became current themes of discussion in the aftermath of the war, when the spectre of population decline became obsessive. Such a climate, together with the growing preoccupation of the new regime with achieving a position in the international power structure, motivated new policies on population. The belief in the 'supreme reality of Spain and the will to empower, strengthen and magnify her' constituted the principal basis of the New State.[10] However, empowerment was associated with the numerical superiority of a growing population, whereas a declining birth-rate meant decadence. Spain thus confronted a dilemma: 'Either Spain increases her birth-rate or her ascension to the rank of the great powers will be halted.'[11] This point of view was sanctioned by one of the major ideologues of the early Franco dictatorship, Ramón Serrano Suñer, in a speech addressed to the *Sección Femenina*,[12] the female branch of the *Falange* and official women's organization of the Franco regime. He urged the adoption of a 'serious demographic policy' and claimed that Spain would be 'a powerful nation only if it had a numerous and vigorous people'. The task of promoting pronatalism among women became one of the major drives of the *Sección Femenina* and motherhood the key to their general ideological discourse on women, although they also emphasized the religious and fascist components of their political discourse.

Not only politicians but demographers and sociologists also identified with this line of argument. Severino Aznar, a prominent demographer, identified the defence of Spain from the 'leprosy of neo-Malthusianism'[13] as one of the primary targets of the New State. Vigorous familialism and pronatalism were the pillars on which national economy, political solvency and military power were based:

> Families with many children are the ones that carry Spain on their shoulders. Through these she is conserved and grows and can hold hope to be a world power of the first order. Without them, Spain will be reduced, she will shrink, the national economy will be without producers and consumers; the State, without soldiers; the Nation, without blood.[14]

Javier Ruiz Almansa, another demographer, emphasized that a thriving population would also permit Spain to carry out cultural imperialism:

> And every year may 50,000 Spanish families leave Spain, not to leave their lives and blood abroad in exchange for a wage, but in order to collaborate with native Hispano-American populations in the elaboration of a universal Hispanic culture; and in order to teach native North African populations to think in Spanish and to tutor them until they themselves can use this instrument . . . which is known as the culture and civilization of the West.[15]

It is clear that Francoist pronatalism constituted an ambitious programme which not only upheld national interests but was also part of a larger strategy in defence of western civilization. Hence Spanish population growth would also help prevent the decline of the white race and avoid the threat that the 'Mongol peril' represented for western civilization.[16]

DEPOPULATION, MOTHERHOOD AND THE 'LEPROSY' OF BIRTH CONTROL: EARLY DEMOGRAPHIC STUDIES

The pronatalist drive was pervasive. However, although most of these policies directly affected women, with the exception of the *Sección Femenina* leader, Pilar Primo de Rivera, women had no voice in designing policies. Under Franco, policymaking was an exclusively male business even when its chief concern was women's reproductive capacities. The role of demographers in the design of reproduction politics was highly significant. They provided the scientific arguments to the ideological assertions of pronatalist state policies. One of the foremost platforms for the elaboration of population policies was the research centre, the *Instituto Balmes de Sociología* (1944), created to assess state policy on population. The *Instituto* also published the very influential *Revista Internacional de Sociología* and offered the regime the data and scientific research on which to sustain its pronatalist policies.[17] Despite its apparent scientific approach this journal adopted a singularly combative tone in the projection of pronatalist doctrine and the criticism of declining birth-rates. In the early 1940s demographic studies coincided in the view that Spain was undergoing a major population crisis which could not be attributed exclusively to the consequences of the Civil War but rather to an ongoing trend of declining birth-rates over the former decades. The findings of these demographic studies pointed to an alarming fall in population which was seen as a structural trend.[18] In fact these studies were not far wrong in their overall evaluation of the pattern of Spanish demography. Recent research has shown that the most visible impact of the Civil War on Spanish demography was due more to a fall in birth-rates than to mortality rates[19] although war deaths and the absence of young men that resulted from repression were significant in the overall post-war period, causing a substantial drop in nuptiality and birth-rates. The fertility index steadily dropped in the first decades of the century throughout Spain, although the decrease was much steeper in Catalonia (Table 8.1). Low birth-rates had been a clear pattern in demographic structures since the early twentieth century. However, Franco supporters tended to situate this decline in the republican era and to stress moral degeneracy and republican reproductive policies as the main features in the reduction of birth-rates.

Predictably, efforts were immediately directed towards establishing the cause of such an alarming decline and discovering the means to overcome it. Studies by Francoist demographers pointed to the pervasiveness of the practice of birth control and voluntary abortion as crucial factors in determining the drop in population. Birth control and neo-Malthusianism were presented as grim signs of the moral decadence of the former regime[20]

Table 8.1 Synthetic index of fertility, Spain 1922–65

Year	Spain	Catalonia
1922	4.139	2.599
1925	3.893	2.524
1930	3.627	2.225
1935	3.217	1.912
1940	2.971	1.847
1945	2.848	1.732
1950	2.459	1.727
1955	2.501	1.920
1960	2.761	2.230
1965	2.957	2.535

Source: A. Cabré, I. Pujades, 'La fecundidad en Cataluña desde 1922: análisis y perspectivas', Primer Congrès Hispano-Luso-Italià de Demografía Històrica, Barcelona, April 1987.

and the fight against birth control and family planning became key issues in pronatalist policies. Birth control was rejected out of hand. It was inexcusable and depicted by Severino Aznar as the 'social cancer of our times, a strike against biological duties, a dagger which is assassinating our civilization; it develops in decadent societies like worms in decomposed bodies'.[21] Franco supporters agreed in considering birth control a deviation from natural functions and in so far as women were concerned, an inadmissible rejection of their social and biological destiny.

Demographers attributed the adoption of birth control to a variety of causes of different scope and influence: the loss of 'authentic racial values'; a decline in Christian resignation; the pervasiveness of rationalization and secular mores; a breakdown in western Catholic civilization; socio-economic factors; geographical differences and changes in marital trends. However, not all agreed on the relative weights of these specific factors. On the whole one gets the sense that economic causes were not held to be very crucial while psychological, religious and moral determinants were key issues. For example, Ros Jimeno was doubtful about the weight of economic factors and alleged that at the most they were influential once they were combined with other psychological and moral factors. This prominent demographer maintained that rationalism and irreligion were the key explanation to voluntary limitation of fertility. On the whole 'economistic' accounts tended to be rejected in favour of theories of moral decadence, religious decline and spiritual apathy.

What is surprising is that Franco supporters did not refer to the development of the sex reform and eugenics movements as a vital factor in the diffusion of birth control. In fact, these movements had been the only forums where birth control had, at times, been openly advocated. In early twentieth-century Spain birth control was considered to be an inappropriate topic for public discussion. Because of socio-cultural pressures attitudes towards this issue were not made public and its discussion was socially unacceptable. Most social sectors were silent on this issue, as were women, while the vast majority of public evaluations of birth control were negative and rejected the legitimacy of its practice. In this context, the anarchist sex reform movement and the reformist eugenics movement were important focus points for circulating views on birth control.

By the 1920s anarchist neo-Malthusianism was a minority branch of the Spanish libertarian movement, which incorporated issues such as birth control, eugenics, sex reform and women's emancipation to the global anarchist strategies of social transformation. Addressed preferably to a working-class audience, their programme aimed at the popular circulation of information on these issues, which they considered basic for the improvement of working-class living conditions, the development of a satisfactory sex life and the achievement of 'conscious maternity' by women workers. It was fundamentally a non-professional, self-help movement which circulated scientific information on these issues in journals and also stressed the need for revolutionary change in society. By the 1920s it openly advocated birth control although its attitude towards abortion was more ambivalent. In December 1936 there was an initiative to legalize abortion in Catalonia by a prominent member of the anarchist sex reform movement, Félix Martí Ibáñez, who considered that the new dynamics of social change in Catalonia should also provide eugenic reform through the regulation of abortion and the development of birth control centres.

The eugenics movement was, in contrast, a reformist movement promoted by professionals, primarily doctors and lawyers, who were concerned with hygiene, public health, social welfare and especially with the high rates of infant mortality and the spread of infectious diseases.[22] Although eugenics surfaced in the early twentieth century, the eugenics movement as such was not formed until the late 1920s. Medical and legal journals were the fundamental channels of debate on eugenics and they became the platform for most ethical, medical and social discussion on this issue. In 1928 the First Eugenics Course held in Madrid constituted the first public forum for a debate on eugenics and the second important venue was the First Spanish Eugenics Symposium held in Madrid in 1933 which was sanctioned by some of the major political figures of the Second Republic. Although a small number of its members advocated birth control, on the whole the movement adopted an ambivalent attitude towards birth control and even more so towards abortion.[23] Spanish eugenicists believed that the improvement of the race could be achieved through measures such as eugenic marriage, pre-marital medical certificates and a very small minority advocated sterilization in exceedingly extreme cases.

It is difficult to assess as yet the significance of these movements in the adoption of birth control and their role in fomenting changes in cultural values by rendering birth control a more socially admissible practice in highly traditional Spanish society. What is more difficult to understand is why Francoist demographers ignored these movements in their attempts to explain the decline in birth-rates in Spain. This may mean that these movements were not really effective social interlocutors on these issues. The fact that some significant Franco supporters had formed part of the eugenics movements in former years may also explain their reluctance to dwell on this movement while anything associated with anarchism was simply considered untenable by the regime.

Together with cultural and economic interpretations of depopulation, demographers, doctors and politicians also provided a gender-oriented explanation for the drop in birth-rates. They held that changes in the social condition of women were responsible and argued that the masculinization of women, female displacement from home to workplace, changes in female psychology linked with expectations of independence and emancipation, women's economic independence and a weakening of the family were key factors in the breakdown of women's role as prolific mothers. However, there was no general agreement on this point. For example, Ros Jimeno did not consider female emancipation, cultural expectations and wage work as significant causes of the population crisis, precisely because of the low level of integration of Spanish women in the work-force and in educational institutions. He claimed that the transformation of cultural values, together with an increasingly rationalist world view and a non-Christian conception of life, were more decisive than any emancipatory trend in the social condition of women.

Historical studies have still definitively to assess the factors involved in the decline in the Spanish birth-rates in the twenties and thirties. My understanding of the evidence endorses Ros Jimeno's viewpoint that women's emancipation and female wage work were not decisive factors in declining birth-rates. According to the 1930 census women represented only 12.65 per cent of the employed population; of course official statistics do not include the predominant presence of women in Spanish agriculture. Even during the Civil War the actual development of the Spanish economy and, more significantly, the tenacity of traditional male hostility with regard to women's wage work determined the slow development of women's paid work in the war years. The women's movement does not appear either to have been decisive in developing birth control. Spanish feminism had not been based on equality and political rights, and indeed, women's suffrage (1931) cannot be attributed so much to the pressure of a feminist movement, which did not always openly advocate suffrage, but rather to the political cohesion of a democratic regime which saw inequality on a gender basis as an inadmissible political tenet.[24] More important still, Spanish feminism tended to be based on the notion of difference and the social projection of motherhood and gender roles and it was silent on the issues of birth control and abortion. It did not see the adoption of birth control in terms of female emancipation. Family economy and health appear to have been more important issues than emancipatory trends in the situation of women and indeed evidence points to the fact that by the 1930s the acceptability of the use of contraceptives depended on material motivations of economic survival and also on cultural exigencies more related to a society that laid greater stress on welfare, where demands for improvement in the quality of life were an integral part of cultural values.

Under Franco the primary focus for women's social function was motherhood. Hence aspirations to work, education and self-improvement, social activity or emancipation were a threat to women's biological destiny as forgers of the nation's future generations. However, demographers and politicians felt that Spanish women had already been contaminated and their maternal instinct had degenerated during the former regime.[25] Women were no longer resigned to accepting the number of children 'God sent them'. Motherhood had not been questioned as such but rather limited through the growing demand for 'conscious maternity' – the adoption of family planning in accordance with the health, economic and work situation of the mother and family – during the thirties. According to the gloomy accounts of Francoist demographers, Spanish women were no longer disposed to pay their contribution to the fatherland with numerous children and it was quite clear even to pronatalist enthusiasts that uncontrolled maternity was no longer attractive to Spanish mothers, who no longer looked on constant maternity as inescapable.

STRATEGIES FOR THE DEVELOPMENT OF PRONATALISM

The criminalization of abortion and the use or advertising of contraceptives were a first step in the state pronatalist campaign. The Abortion Law of January 1941 established the link between population increase and abortion quite clearly: 'An efficient demographic policy cannot be conceived without dealing with the problem of the thousands and thousands of lives which are destroyed before being born, through criminal manoeuvre.' Despite the failure of the 'eugenic reform' of abortion, Francoist propaganda nevertheless insisted on the widespread use of abortion and made both clandestine and legal abortion synonymous. Furthermore, Francoist propaganda elevated voluntary abortion to the rank of 'a social crime . . . which prevents many thousands of Spaniards from being born annually'.[26] Anti-abortionism became crucial in the protection of births and population growth and thus a key element in the social policy of the New State. Hence abortion was no longer considered a crime against human life as had been the case in previous legislation,[27] but rather as a crime against the state, since it was considered an attack on the race. Abortion went against the social interests of the state, whose duty was to preserve and conserve the race and thus all potential members of the population. For the same reasons the Abortion Law also made it a crime to advertise or sell all contraceptives. Both abortion and the use of contraceptives were considered as crimes against the integrity of the race.[28]

The Franco Abortion Law was very comprehensive in its attack on those who either performed abortions or provided the means to achieve one. Abortionists were given very stiff prison sentences, fines or were disqualified from the practice of their profession, as were any pharmacists who sold abortifacients. Manufacturers or traders who made or commercialized any instruments which could facilitate an abortion were fined or had their business closed. Gender differentiation was present in the penalization of abortion: the women involved were given somewhat more lenient sentences, although they, too, were sentenced to imprisonment. The acceptance of the double standard in sexual behaviour was implicit in the law in so far as it contemplated greater leniency if the abortion had been performed in order to avoid the 'dishonour' of the woman. This extenuating circumstance was not a novelty, as it had been admitted in former penal codes. The greater admissibility of an abortion in the case of an unmarried woman is significant in the context of a rigid code which saw the legitimization of women's natural destiny exclusively within the institutions of the family and marriage. Sexual behaviour which deviated from the norm was not admitted and indeed many of the propagandists of the 'National Revolution' saw themselves as 'immaculately religious' moral regenerators engaged in the purification of public morality.[29]

Roman Catholic teaching on women, the family and procreation were decisive components of the regime's persuasive pronatalist propaganda, which invoked Roman Catholic policy on natalism and identified its multiple components with state policies: 'combat malthusianism and neo-Malthusianism; encourage births, struggle against child mortality, promote child protection, subsidize large families, facilitate prematrimonial education, campaign against clandestine abortion and struggle against sterility.'[30] In fact, doctors rejected birth control not only on medical but also on religious grounds: 'All restrictions to fertility are dangerous for the health of the woman; all women blacken their souls with the black crepe of mortal sin, and all [such restrictions] are, besides, unsure and hazardous.'[31] Women therefore were not only warned of grave dangers to their physical well-being but were also threatened with eternal condemnation should they freely decide to control their reproductive potential. The Church openly supported the Franco regime on the issues of procreation and motherhood while Franco supporters assimilated religious viewpoints to reinforce cultural values which absolutely rejected the use of contraceptives on a moral basis and reinforced women's social function with a view of women as primarily mothers. As was to be the case in other spheres, National Catholicism integrated Church teachings into pronatalist discourse and both sanctioned and legitimized Francoist population policies. However, Church support for natalism and familialism was not circumstantial to Francoist policies; rather it reflected ongoing Church support for traditional values, political conservatism and the conservation of the family. National Catholicism represented just the politicization of this vigorous trend within Spanish Roman Catholicism, which, traditionally, had encouraged natalism, familialism and female subordination.

Franco's racial hygiene programmes were overtly pronatalist. Nevertheless, they did not focus on a eugenic element which stressed the value of fit children nor did they promote racial policies that favoured specific social groups and attacked others. It is true that they stressed the need to develop the Spanish race. However, they did not develop racist policies as such to prevent the survival of non-Spanish children. The Franco model of the *Raza Española* was undoubtedly built on the traditional Castilian race, whose forefathers were the *conquistadores*. It was an integrating, centralist model which attempted to nullify regional differences which had developed during the Republic with the creation of autonomous governments in the national regions of Catalonia and the Basque Country. Franco resorted to a unitary model of Spain which would weaken such nationalist aspirations and provide a genuine Spanish culture and race. The centrality of the Church in formulating natalist policies, of course, prevented Franco from developing a clearly eugenic policy which could mark off some of the population as unfit for reproduction. The *españolización* of cultural identity was the basis of Franco's racial policies, which did not contemplate genocide or sterilization. Moreover, according to Franco, the unity of Spain had already been established from the eighth century on with the *Reconquista*, the reconquest of the Peninsula from the Muslims and the *limpieza de sangre*, the blood purity campaign, through the elimination and repression of the non-Christian population of Spain, the Moors and the Jews in the sixteenth century. Thus a unitary model based on common religious and cultural identity prevailed, which called on models of saints of the *Reconquista* and Baroque Imperialism to guide the path of Spain through the development of a unitary Spanish race which would annul any national differences and provide the *grandeza* of Spain.[32] Of course, this unitary scheme was grounded in a systematic repression of nationalist identity and culture in Catalonia and the Basque Country. However, this had a cultural and political basis and was not developed as race policy.

FAMILY AND HOME: PRIMARY UNITS OF THE NEW STATE

Franco's pronatalist policies also hinged on familialism. The state played a decisive role in the rehabilitation of the family and accorded it a central place in its social construction of a new Spain. The family was the primary unit of society, a basic cell in the body politic of the state and the community. The family, however, was more than a social institution. One of the major legal statements of the New State, the *Fuero de los Españoles* (1945), declared that it was a natural institution with specific prerogatives and rights which went beyond the boundaries of human law. The status of the family as the prime unit of social organization was complemented in the *Fuero* by a declaration of the indissolubility of marriage. As the family underpinned the whole social order, protective legislation was passed to revoke the Republican legislation on civil matrimony and divorce and encourage the revitalization of the Christian family, essential for population growth.

Pronatalism and familialism were intimately connected, as natalist policy was based in the final resort on the fertility of Spanish families. Thus pronatalist rhetoric permeated debates on family policy. Women were particularly affected by the new legislation on the family, for not only did it imply the advocacy of a stable Catholic family but also the reconsolidation of a patriarchal family unit where women held a subordinate position. Thus familial ideology was also accompanied by legislative restrictions on married women which derogated the more egalitarian status of married women under the Republic; Franco legislation retrieved the 1889 Civil Code which starkly confirmed male authority. Paradoxically, advocacy of familialism was also gender orientated, as women were destined to play a crucial role in maintenance of the family. The natural destiny of all women was matrimony and the upkeep of the home. Given the prevalence of the idea that it had been precisely women's aspirations to social advancement and economic independence that had been crucial in drawing women away from their natural mandate of reproduction, many propagandists advocated restrictions on female access to work outside the home.[33] More significant still for pronatalist race hygienists was the fact that female wage work created a predisposition to small families even among the working class. Persuasive methods were primarily used to counter women's expectations of work outside the home. However, the pronatalist orientation of the regime led to a distinct differentiation between single and married women and coercive measures were introduced obliging women to give up work upon marrying. In 1938 the *Fuero del Trabajo*, the major legal statement on work, declared that the state 'will free married women from the workshop and the factory'. This norm was strictly applied in state and para-state firms and somewhat less rigidly in other sectors, with the aim of excluding married women from the labour market. It was an obvious deterrent to married women's work, while marriage prizes such as a *dote* (dowry), a grant conceded to women workers on marrying as a compensation for giving up their job, became an additional inducement to marriage. Nuptiality prizes (1948) were also conceded to couples formed by a woman under 30 and a man under 35, and loans were granted, repayment of which was reduced by 25 per cent on the birth of up to four children.

The *Sección Femenina* also promoted familialism in its 'mission' with women. Both education and political propaganda oriented women towards the acceptance of motherhood as their primary social function.[34] The *Sección Femenina* undertook this task of indoctrination and indeed had a vast forum for propaganda with the establishment of obligatory social service for all Spanish women, which generally consisted of a six-month period of training for motherhood and political indoctrination.[35] Its reinforcement of familialism had also the specific goal of educating mothers to socialize their own children according to the ideological canons of the *Falange*.

Representations of the state also reinforced the imagery of motherhood. Spain was described as a 'good mother of a large family' who would help to provide for her flock with family incentives. Legislative measures provided for family allowances, *premios de natalidad*, and certain concessions for specially large families, the *familias numerosas*, which were offered specific protection in the *Fuero de los Españoles*. In 1943 large families were defined by two categories: from four to seven children in the first and from eight children on in the second, with an honorary category of twelve children or more. Members of large families were allowed numerous fringe benefits, graded according to their category. These ranged from transport and school grants to tax exemptions, credit facilities, access to housing, sanitary assistance, etc. The annual concession of prizes to the most numerous families in Spain (ranging usually from over fourteen children) came to form part of the propagandist ritual attached to the figure of Franco even when pronatalism was no longer a major official policy.

More important still was the introduction of family allowances, *subsidio familiar* (1938), and family bonuses, *plus de cargas familiares* (1945), which affected a much wider section of the population. Both family allowances and bonuses were compatible and both represented a clear support of paternity through income supplement. Family allowances were not considered an extra wage or part of the salary but rather as a supplement paid directly to the *jefe de familia*, the male breadwinner. Mothers were eligible to receive this allowance only under very exceptional circumstances. With the exception of workers engaged in home work or domestic service, precisely the sectors in which the female work-force was significant, all contract workers had a right to family allowances which were financed by the state, business firms and all workers through the payment of an obligatory quota. Married workers were paid a sliding rate according to the number of children (40 pesetas monthly for two children to 1,080 for twelve and an extra bonus of 200 pesetas for over twelve children in 1938). This policy was geared particularly to reinforcing male authority within the family and compensating male workers for paternity. Given the male definition of the *jefe de familia*, this measure rewarded fathers rather than mothers.

The *plus de cargas familiares* also rewarded fathers and represented a supplement to the breadwinner's wage. It was considered as an extra wage for the worker and represented approximately 10 per cent of the total wages in any specific firm and was distributed to the married workers according to the number of children they had. Again, it was a measure which favoured fathers as it was paid to the husband and only in very exceptional circumstances to the wife. Married couples were awarded 5 points on a sliding scale which went from 6 points for one child to 30 points for ten children and 5 points more for eleven children or over. Working mothers were penalized as the couple did not receive any monetary compensation for marriage.

The receipt of family allowances and bonuses was conditional on employment and in the case of the *plus de cargas familiares* it was included in the paycheck. It overtly favoured men and reinforced the figure of the *jefe de familia*, the male head of the family, the patriarchal figure which was to be linked with the authoritarian figure of the *jefe de Estado*, Franco. Of course these measures were applicable only to legitimate marriages and legitimate children. State-sponsored family and pronatalist policies applied only to married couples and children engendered within the canons of prescribed social codes; only legitimately constituted families were eligible for benefits. Pronatalism was always discussed within the framework of Roman Catholicism, so the pursuit of population growth through illegitimate children was not sanctioned under Franco.

Marriage was thus sponsored as a means to guarantee the family and parenthood. Other social policies were aimed at protecting pregnant women, mothers and young children in the drive to reduce infant and maternal mortality. In 1941 *Sanidad Maternal e Infantil* was created as an administrative service of the Health Service and in 1942 maternity insurance was incorporated into the *subsidio familiar*. However, in the early years of the Franco regime, in contrast to the predominant discourse on motherhood, specific social policies aimed at welfare of mother and child were less developed than those aimed at the male-headed family. Mother and child incentives were more in the nature of social reform and implemented former social provision policies geared towards the development of the welfare state.[36] Family incentives were more specific to the Franco regime and obeyed an economic rationale as hidden wages at a time of a steep drop in real wages; they also had a clear ideological function through the promotion of the family wage and the male breadwinner, thus reinforcing social control and male hierarchy within the family and the regime itself.

WOMEN AND THE RESULTS OF PRONATALISM

Pronatalism undoubtedly constituted an important dimension in the construction of Franco's Spain. However, neither normative ideology nor coercive legislation are a mirror of social reality. Pronatalist policies were undertaken in the social context of the hardship and privations of the harsh socio-economic situation of post-war repression. Despite the pervasiveness of Francoist pronatalist ideology and the development of a concerted drive to promote population growth in the context of a repressive totalitarian state, it did not achieve its objective. Unlike other immediate post-war periods, there was not a 'baby boom' in Spain in the early forties. Demographic data point to the maintenance of the previous rhythm of population growth. Birth-rates steadily declined in the first decade of the Franco regime; demographic patterns did not change until the mid-fifties when an upward fertility trend can be observed in the decade between 1955 and 1965. However, by then, the socio-political context was quite different and the regime had desisted in its pronatalist policies of the immediate post-war years.

Birth control and, more significantly given the harsh legislation, clandestine abortions were still practised in the forties and early fifties. In 1949, a long article in the *Revista Internacional de Sociología* denounced the number of voluntary abortions practised at the time.[37] The biography and oral testimony of a midwife who practised in Catalonia in the late forties indicates that it was common custom for midwives to be requested quite openly to perform abortions.[38] Oral testimony drew my attention to the fact that family planning constituted a much more vital issue during the post-war years despite the revocation of the more tolerant Republican laws.[39] Family survival in the harsh circumstances of rationing, unemployment, housing problems, deficient sanitary services, severe economic difficulties and relentless repression led women to resort to home remedies, quacks, doctors or midwives in order to abort. They paid little attention to the pronatalist ideology of the regime in their reproductive strategies for family survival. The *Sección Feminina* appears to have been unable to persuade women to be prolific mothers. In fact, many women refer to the unconvincing discrepancy between the ideal of motherhood presented as the sole goal of all women and the fact that all *Falange* women leaders had to be single.[40] Nor did repressive legislation dissuade women from practising 'conscious maternity'. There is no evidence that suggests that women unquestioningly accepted their biological destiny as mothers according to the norms of the regime or that they identified with the ideological implications of the pronatalist policies of the 'New State'. Of course fertility rates declined partly because of the demographic consequences of the Civil War. However, evidence also points to the fact that married couples were no longer willing to accommodate themselves to unrestricted maternity and thus used every means at their disposal, from abstinence to birth control or abortion, to limit the number of children. Birth-rates did not increase until there was a decisive change in the Spanish economy and overall socio-political situation in the late fifties and sixties. Then increased fertility rates coincided with the economic revival and general improvement in the living conditions of Spanish families.

Such evidence generates the problem of interpreting women's failure to subscribe to Francoist pronatalism. Can such behaviour be interpreted in terms of an overall political resistance strategy to the regime by defying its population policy, as argued by Luisa Passerini in the case of Turin?[41] It is true that one of my interviewees did express women's resistance to having children in political terms:

> People refused to have children, because they considered that there wasn't an adequate environment to have a child and educate one, and so they refused to have them, ... it was like an act of protest against all that was happening in Spain and having a child for what ... , giving a child to Spain seemed to them to be an absurdity, because Spain did not merit that women should give her their children, and then, abortions were practised ... by the dozen.[42]

However, I get the sense that this particular interpretation owes a great deal to the marked politicization of this informant, a militant member of the Communist Party who had been active in the resistance. Her reading undoubtedly reflects her own personal political commitment but would appear to be unrepresentative of the general tenor of non-politicized women, who did not see their adoption of the decision to restrict the number of their children in this light. Rather than an identification with a strategy of political resistance, most of the women interviewed placed their decision in the socio-economic context of the harsh difficulties of survival[43] in the immediate post-war years. Despite affirmative measures motherhood and parenthood were far from being attractive to most families and were seen as an economic liability and even a health risk for the mother. Thus the rejection of pronatalist policies appears to have been based on what could be termed a socio-economic survival strategy of Spanish families, who did not necessarily consider such a decision in terms of a political resistance to the regime. The practice of family planning did not signify a rejection of Roman Catholic doctrine either. Indeed, well before the Franco regime many clearly religious couples and practising Roman Catholic women had perfectly reconciled contradictory personal decisions in their intimate life concerning birth control and their religious practice and identity. Codes of individual conduct did not necessarily coincide with established cultural and religious norms. Public adherence to religious and cultural values did not necessarily mean private ascription to them. In the same way, during the early Franco regime, intimate family criteria based on health, household economy and existing living conditions appear to have prevailed in determining personal conduct in natalist or anti-natalist behaviour, which had little to do with open political or ideological convictions but rather with everyday family survival. Despite the means at his disposal, Franco's pronatalist discourse and legislative policies were unsuccessful in enforcing pronatalist practice among Spanish women.

NOTES

1 A version of this chapter was presented at the symposium 'Women in dark times: private life and public policy under five nationalist dictatorships in Europe and Asia, 1930–1950', Rockefeller Foundation, Bellagio, August 1987. I should like to thank Claudia Koonz and the participants at this symposium for their discussion of this paper. I also wish to express my thanks to Geraldine Nichols, Susana Tavera and especially to Gisela Bock for their stimulating reading of this paper and constant support.

2 This ideology was not original to Francoism. See M. Nash, 'Control social y trayectoria histórica de la mujer en España', in R. Bergalli and E.M. Mari (eds), *Historia ideologica del control social (Un análisis comparado: España–Argentina)*, Barcelona, Promociones y Publicaciones Universitarias, 1989.

3 R.M. Capel, *El sufragio femenino en la Segunda República*, Granada, Universidad de Granada, 1975; G.M. Scanlon, *La polémica feminista en la España contemporánea*, Madrid, Siglo XXI, 1976.

4 M.G. Nuñez Perez, *Trabajadoras en la Segunda República. Un estudio sobre la actividad económica extra-domestica (1931–1936)*, Madrid, Ministerio de Trabajo y Seguridad Social, 1989.

5 M. Nash, *Las mujeres en la Guerra Civil*, Madrid, Ministerio de Cultura, 1989; M. Nash, '*Milicianas* and home front heroines: images of women in Revolutionary Spain (1936–1939)', *History of European Ideas*, 1989, vol. 11 pp. 235–44.

6 P. Folguera Crespo, 'Política natalista y control de natalidad en España durante la década de los veinte: el caso de Madrid', *Ordenamiento jurídico y realidad social de las mujeres*, Madrid, Universidad Autonoma de Madrid, 1986; M. Nash, 'Género, cambio social y la problemática del aborto', *Historia Social*, Autumn 1988, no. 2.

7 F. Martí Ibañez, *Diez meses de labor en sanidad y asistencia social*, Barcelona, Ed. Tierra y Libertad, 1937.

8 M. Nash, 'L'avortement legal a Catalunya: una experiència fracassada', *L'Avenç*, March 1983, no. 58, pp. 20–6.

9 A. Vallejo Najera, *Política racial del Nuevo Estado*, San Sebastian, Editorial Española, 1938, p. 40 and A. Vallejo Najera, *Eugenesia de la Hispanidad y regeneracíon de la raza*, Burgos, Editorial Española, 1937.

10 J. Ros Jimeno, 'La natalidad y el futuro desarrollo de la población de España'. *Revista Internacional de Sociología*, Jan.–March 1943, no. 1, p. 60.

11 J. Ros Jimeno, 'El decrecimiento de la natalidad y sus causas', *Estudios Demográficos* (Madrid, Instituto 'Balmes' de Sociología) 1945, vol. 1, p. 39.

12 *Discurso pronunciado por el Excelentísimo Sr. Ministro de Asuntos Exteriores y Presidente de la Junta Política, D. Ramón Serrano Suñer en el V Congreso Nacional de la Sección Femenina, inaugurado en Barcelona el día 11 de enero de 1941*, Madrid, Editora Nacional, 1941.

13 S. Aznar, 'El fromedio (sic; i.e. promedio) de la natalidad diferencial en las clases sociales de Madrid y Barcelona', *Revista Internacional de Sociología*, Oct.–Dec. 1947, no. 20, p. 374.

14 S. Aznar, 'El regimen de subsidios familiares, la fraternidad cristiana y las consignas del Nuevo Estado', *Revista Internacional de Sociología*, April–Sept. 1943, nos. 2–3, pp. 97–110.

15 J. Ruiz Almansa, 'Crecimiento y reparticición de la población de España', *Revista Internacional de Sociología*, Jan.–March 1944, no. 5, pp. 165–96.

16 Fear of Asiatic influence was also expressed in cultural contexts. *Bibliografía Hispánica*, Dec. 1945, vol. 4, no. 12.

17 The *Revista* was co-directed by Severino Aznar and the Italian demographer Corrado Gini.

18 See Ros Jimeno, 'La natalidad en España después de la guerra, y la población futura', *Estudios Demográficos* (Madrid, Instituto 'Balmes' de Sociología), 1946, vol. 11; J. Ruiz Almansa, 'Crecimiento y repartición'.

19 J.M. Solé Sabaté, 'El cost humà de la guerra civil: metodología per a la recerca', *L'Avenç*, March 1985, no. 80, pp. 26-30; T. Vidal and J. Recaño, 'Demografía y Guerra Civil', *La Guerra Civil. Historia 16* 1987, no. 14, pp. 52–69.

20 It is true that the practise of birth control developed during that period. See M. Nash, 'El neomaltusianismo anarquista y los conocimientos populares sobre el control de la natalidad', in M. Nash (ed.), *Presencia y protagonismo: aspectos de la historia de la mujer*, Barcelona, Serbal, 1984, pp. 307–40.

21 Quoted in 'La vida y la obra de Severino Aznar', *Revista Internacional de Sociología*, Oct.–Dec. 1959, no. 68, pp. 525–93.

22 M. Nash, 'Aproximación al movimiento eugénico español: el primer curso eugénico español y la aportación del Dr. Sebastián Recasens', *Gimbernat, Revista Catalana 'Història de la Medicina i de la Ciència'*, 1985, vol. 4, pp. 193–202.

23 M. Nash, 'Birth control and contraceptive methods: the debate in the Spanish eugenics movements', *I Congrés Hispano-Luso-Italià de Demografía Històrica*, Barcelona, April 1987, forthcoming.

24 C. Fagoaga, *La voz y el voto de las mujeres. El sufragismo en España 1877–1931*, Barcelona, Ed. Icaria, 1985.

25 Arbelo Curbelo, 'Contribución al estudio del problema de la denatalidad', *Revista Internacional de Sociología*, April–June 1944, no. 6, pp. 103–39.
26 Preámbulo Ley de Aborto, 24 January 1941.
27 M. Nash, 'Ordenamiento jurídico y realidad social del aborto: Una aproximación histórica', in *Ordenamiento jurídico*.
28 Analysts of the time pointed out the similarity between the Italian Penal Code and the Spanish Abortion Law: J. González Llana, 'El aborto provocado y la ley de 24 de enero de 1941', *Revista General de Legislación y Jurisprudencia*, Jan.–Feb. 1941, pp. 238–41.
29 'La moralidad publica en España', *Revista Internacional de Sociología*, April–September 1943, no. 2–3, pp. 344-47.
30 A. Vallejo Nágera, 'Fecundidad de los enfermos psíquicos', *Revista Internacional, de Sociología*, April–Sept. 1949, nos. 26–7, pp. 115–23.
31 Vital Aza, *Diez lecciones de higiene femenina*, Madrid, M. Marin y G. Campo Editores, 1941, p. 47.
32 G. di Febo, *La santa de la raza. Un culto barroco en la España franquista*, Barcelona, Icaria, 1987.
33 J. Bosch Marín, *Problemas de maternología y puericultura*, Valladolid, Artes Gráficas Afrodisio Aguado, 1938.
34 A. Alted Vigil, 'La mujer en las coordenadas educativas del regimen franquista', *Ordenamiento jurídico*.
35 See D. Gallego, *Mujer, falange y franquismo*, Madrid, Taurus, 1983.
36 M. Samaniego Boneu, *La unificación de los seguros sociales a debate. La Segunda República*, Madríd, Ministerio de Trabajo y Seguridad Social, 1988.
37 D. Gallego, 'Influencia del infanticidio y del aborto volontario sobre el crecimiento de la población', *Revista Internacional de Sociología*, April–September 1949, nos. 26–7, pp. 126–77.
38 R. Via, *Com neixen els catalans*, Barcelona, Club Editor, 1972. Interview with Ramona Via, El Prat de Llobregat, 20 September 1983.
39 Fifty-four women of different social extraction were interviewed in my oral history project: *La familia a la Catalunya autonoma*.
40 C. Martín Gaite, *Usos amorosos de la postguerra española*, Barcelona, Anagrama, 1987.
41 L. Passerini, 'Donne operaie e aborto nella Torino fascista', *Italia contemporanea*, September 1983, pp. 83–109.
42 Interview with Petra Cuevas, Madrid, 4 October 1981.
43 C. Molinero and P. Ysâs, *'Patria, Justicia y Pan'. Nivell de vida i condicions de treball a Catalunya 1939–1951*, Barcelona, La Magrana, 1985.

Chapter 9

Motherhood as a political strategy: the role of the Italian women's movement in the creation of the *Cassa Nazionale di Maternità*

Annarita Buttafuoco

'A NEW FEMALE ETHIC'

By the time the Italian Parliament, on 17 July 1910, passed the law creating the *Cassa Nazionale di Maternità* (National Maternity Fund) for women factory workers obliged to stop working during the first month after childbirth, the women's political movement in its various ramifications had thirty years of practical and theoretical engagement in the issue of the relationship between motherhood, the state and women's citizenship. It was thus thoroughly equipped to judge how far the law met the needs of women, and how far it corresponded with the demands of the various women's organizations when pressing for the state to introduce legislation regarding working mothers.

The request for legislation in this field was part of a larger pattern of claims. Provision for working women – whether factory workers, peasants, employees in the service sector, servants, or home workers – was considered by women active in the emancipation movement as an integral part of a broader platform of demands. Through these it is possible, especially from the 1890s, to trace the outlines of the political strategy of the women's movement in Italy and of the theory behind it.

The campaign for labour laws was linked in feminist thinking – even when there was division as to the suitability and nature of state intervention in this sphere – with agitation on behalf of women's parental rights, recognition of the dignity of unmarried mothers, provision for dealing with the problem of abandoned and maltreated children, and reform of those articles of the penal code dealing with incest and rape. This platform was closely related to the request for full legal equality and for the right both to vote and to be elected. This would enable women to achieve legislation through their representatives, on issues that directly concerned them – issues either ignored or mishandled by a Parliament composed of men.

Until the 1890s the struggle for female emancipation in Italy did not take the form of an organized movement. The first association tending in this direction, the *Lega per la Promozione degli Interessi Femminili* (League for the Promotion of Women's Interests), was founded only in 1881 by Anna Maria Mozzoni. Previously the emancipation struggle had been carried on by groups engaged either in political discussion and propaganda activities or in concrete undertakings on behalf of poorer women and working women. These two kinds of activity corresponded roughly to two different ways of thinking about the definition of gender identity and the nature of social relations between the sexes. Briefly, we might say that one was based on the concept of *equality* between men and women and interpreted the rights of citizens as 'neuter' – that is, not connoted by gender.

The other tendency also sought to obtain complete legal and social parity, but argued rather for the *equivalence* of men and women, positing a fundamental difference between the sexes and stressing the distinctive values of female experience and identity. This second line of thought, which was numerically preponderant, developed into 'social feminism' or 'practical feminism', aspiring to foster what Sibilla Aleramo called 'the autonomous female spirit',[1] creating a new female ethic. Through painstaking work with factory workers, servants, schoolmistresses and housewives it sought to provide them with practical tools and concepts for the battle for women's rights which did not entail renouncing 'female' values but exalted femininity against the threat of assimilation to the masculine model.

In other words, this movement wanted to create female citizens, not citizens who happened to be women. Since the difference and equivalence between the sexes was identified mainly with motherhood, both as reproductive capacity in the physical sense and as a value-creating power, it was predominantly in 'social feminism' that the most systematic attempt was made to build both a strategy for emancipation through the 'culture of the maternal' and a policy of intervention to safeguard and educate mothers, especially the most needy.

What has been called the 'culture of the maternal' or 'maternalism' or the 'cult of motherhood' particularly characterizes the period from the 1890s to the advent of fascism. These are the years in which concrete initiatives for assisting and educating mothers, undertaken by the feminist organizations, flourish and multiply. But from the first women based their claim to citizenship on their role as bearers and educators of future citizens. The first petition addressed by a group of women of Lombardy, who proudly signed themselves 'Cittadine Italiane', to the Parliament which had just installed itself after the proclamation of a united Italy, reminded members that 'the chief foundation [of the liberty of the nation] must be the broadest possible affirmation of the emancipation of woman', since 'the first eight years of the upbringing of a human being are the almost exclusive responsibility of the mother'.[2]

In the years following unification, the image of woman that emerged was essentially that of the 'mother of the nation'. Hence, in discussions of the emancipation question, the emphasis was laid above all on women's responsibility to society and their fulfilment of the regenerating function of motherhood. As Malvina Frank wrote in the journal *La donna*, 'being a good wife and an excellent mother constitutes for most women their entire destiny, even for those who are neither mothers nor wives',[3] since the latter could take on a role of vicarious motherhood with regard to society – for example as teachers, or as agents of moral improvement and social regeneration.

It is not enough, however, to explore the literal meaning of these appeals to motherhood. They have to be seen in the broader perspective in which nineteenth-century feminists placed them, and which persisted, with changing emphasis, into the early twentieth century. In some respects, of course, stressing the maternal role was a defensive response to the many attacks by those who accused women who professed ideas of emancipation of wanting to renounce femininity and create a kind of 'third sex'.[4] More centrally, however, the feminists' appeal to the dignity of motherhood and the emphasis laid on its vital importance for society were in no way aimed at leading women back to their traditional destiny. On the contrary, they were part of a cultural, social and political project for female emancipation. They tended, above all, to assert the *right* to motherhood as against the *duty* of being mothers. They laid bare the ambiguity and hypocrisy of the rhetoric of the 'mission of motherhood' which, in Italy as in other western countries in the later nineteenth century, saw mothers as stereotyped objects of a male fantasy of female 'nature'. Furthermore, arguing for the centrality of the maternal role in society meant foregrounding the responsibility of the state towards mothers and children as integral, essential elements of the nation itself.

The symbolic value and power of motherhood had no counterpart in the material conditions of existence of mothers. Thousands of women had to submit to maternity when they were not psychologically, culturally or materially prepared for it, and political and medical propaganda, together with popular opinion, laid the blame at their door for the high rate of infant mortality in later nineteenth-century Italy. The feminists pointed out the cultural backwardness of the great majority of women and the effects this could have on future generations. However, at the same time they vigorously condemned the faults of society in general and of the state in particular, criticizing the latter for failing to take action, whether through campaigns of information and education, through labour legislation, or the creation of social services essential for safeguarding working mothers as well as women and children in general.

The women engaged in the emancipation movement were not content simply to make accusations, nor did they expect the institutions to be able to measure up to a 'culture of motherhood'. This was an extremely delicate, complex issue which the feminists were endeavouring to define and give substance to in various ways. A number of different experiments can be traced back to this underlying purpose: the women workers' mutual aid society; the creation and 'political control' of obstetric first-aid stations; the various departments for assisting needy mothers operated by the organizations of the women's movement; the independent maternity funds.

These initiatives on behalf, mainly, of working women were not mere acts of philanthropy. They were a mode of political action: the feminist associations were putting into practice forms of assistance which originated in their thinking about the question of the relationship between motherhood and work, and about the social value of motherhood.[5]

The shape of the assistance programmes set up by the Italian women and the way these were related to their users derived from a careful study of similar feminist and socialist institutions abroad. Italian feminists (many of whom were Jewish intellectuals with strong international connections) knew best German and French institutions, but also English and American ones from personal observation, through publications, or especially from direct contact with their promoters. Large numbers of English, French, German and Scandinavian exponents of women's movements spent long periods in Italy giving lectures and visiting the organizations that had been set up in the main towns and cities, and their works were translated. The promoters of assistance programmes for women thus took the experiences of other countries into account, adopting those aspects best suited to Italian culture and social structure, and also introducing entirely original features.

At the political level, many aspects of these undertakings corresponded to the promoters' conception of their work as paving the way for that of the state which, they believed, should have tackled maternity assistance as a central issue of its social policy. 'Feminist claims' were seen, as Ersilia Majno emphasized, as 'demands for the welfare of society'.[6]

Italian feminism, like that of other European countries, might have been divided in its estimation of the advantages and drawbacks for women of a protectionist role for the state as regards female labour, but there was no such disagreement over the widely held idea that 'the work of motherhood', as the gynaecologist Bertha Novich phrased it, was 'a real social labour' and as such should be supported in every respect by the state. On the other hand, Teresa Labriola's awareness that the problem of the woman/work and woman/motherhood relation (involving as it does extremely complex aspects of female identity) could not be solved by formal provision was widely shared.[7] But so was the demand of the women's movement that it become, if not the central issue, at least a significant one in national politics.

THE PROJECT FOR THE MATERNITY FUNDS

During the International Congress on Industrial Accidents held in 1894, Paolina Schiff, the initiator and best-known propagandist for maternity funds, presented a project for a maternity insurance fund on behalf of the *Lega per la Tutela degli Interessi Femminili* (League for the Defence of Women's Interests) of Milan, a feminist-socialist organization of which she was a member.[8] This project was partly based on the practice, widespread among women-workers' societies for mutual aid, whereby a special fund, separate from the sickness fund, was set up to subsidize members during confinement. This practice was introduced in the latter half of the nineteenth century by the *Associazione Generale di Mutuo Soccorso e di Istruzione fra le Operaie* (General Association for Mutual Aid and Education among Working Women of Milan). Its founder, Laura Solera Mantegazza, had previously created in 1850 'homes for breast-fed and weaned children', seen as the first phase of an overall project aiming at the organization of a fully-fledged 'maternity institute'. This, among other things, was to provide assistance at home for women in childbirth and for mothers who breast-fed their own children without putting them out to nurse, thereby saving the children from almost certain death.

Similarly, the original practice of the *Associazione Generale* of providing a subsidy for members during confinement, a layette, and a further allowance to cover the expenses of childbirth, aimed to 'halt the abandoning of legitimate children' which was common among working-class families.[9] A few years later, however, when women members seemed sufficiently experienced to provide themselves with a form of maternal insurance, a maternity fund was created, three-quarters of which came from payments from all members, together with a 'minimal monthly fee' from all married members until the age of fifty. The remainder was provided by the Association from donations by the richer members. However, the inadequacy of this system was becoming apparent by the 1890s.

It was in the environment of the Milanese women-workers' society that most of the leaders of the emancipation movement of the 'moral capital' of Italy had their political apprenticeship. It was here, too, that the project for the *Unione Femminile Nazionale* (National Women's Union) came into being. This was one of the largest and best-structured organizations of the women's political movement in the first two decades of the twentieth century, and was the one which best expressed the model of 'social feminism', promoting the social value of motherhood and the protection of children.

In 1895, its most representative figure, Ersilia Majno, when she was still part of the *Associazione Generale*, had presented a paper at a national conference on industrial accidents on behalf of the *Associazone* dealing with female labour; she concluded with an outline draft for a bill regulating working hours and conditions of female labour. In addition to equal wages for the same work as done by males, it proposed leave from work for at least the four weeks after childbirth.[10]

Paolina Schiff on the other hand was against any form of legislative protection, which she considered a serious attack on the 'freedom and individual initiative of women'.[11] Nevertheless, she claimed the right for women workers to receive paid leave before and after childbirth from a maternity fund. This proposed fund was not to be financed by the women workers themselves, as were the existing funds, but partly from a small contribution by worker parents of daughters (who would presumably also become workers), and partly by workers' organizations, especially the trades unions. A large share would be paid by rich women, whom the speaker urged to aid this institution as they had to some extent aided women-workers' societies. Lastly, the state was to contribute a 40 per cent quota to the fund, as well as overseeing its administration and ensuring it was well managed.[12]

The important innovation of this proposal was the role given to male workers and their organizations, and to the state, as the bodies most concerned with the welfare of working mothers and children. No attempt was ever made to oblige *all* workers to contribute to the support of working mothers. The state's role in Schiff's project was that of financer and supervisor. The details of this role were not clearly defined, however, in her proposal, which was rather roughly drafted.

Her suggestion that the working family also should contribute a nominal share was important. It meant that both practically and symbolically the responsibility and burden of motherhood was shifted from the individual woman to the original family unit of the working woman who would benefit from the insurance. This was a serious flaw in the proposal since it failed to take into account the realities of the working-class family and the precariousness of female labour. It was still very difficult for women to identify with the role of paid worker outside the home and to accept this as a permanent condition. It was not easy for parents of a three-year-old daughter to look ahead to when she might become a worker, since women rarely worked on a regular basis. This was due, obviously, both to the state of the labour market and to a deep-rooted mental resistance. Moreover, it was not easy to instil in the working class as a whole the kind of work ethic necessary for the success of a form of insurance whose benefits would be reaped in a very distant, uncertain future.

The debate that subsequently developed over the project for a maternity fund went hand in hand with the discussion about labour regulations, especially after a bill drafted by Anna Kuliscioff and signed by the Milan women's socialist group began to circulate in 1897. Meanwhile, in some towns Paolina Schiff's proposals began to be tried in practice.

THE LOCAL MATERNITY FUNDS

In 1895 she had spoken both for her own League and the Turin *Lega per la Tutela degli Interessi Femminili*; each of these in their 'urgent minimal programme' planned to create a fund for working mothers.[13] In 1898, the Turin *Lega*, after the 1896 Piedmont Workers' Congress had voted in favour and after a series of disagreements over principles and practical details, founded the first maternity assistance fund in Italy, basing it in part on the French model of the *Mutualités maternelles*.

Rather than the principle of providence upheld by Paolina Schiff in her project, the principle of assistance seemed to prevail in the Turin institution. Women members were required to participate both by co-operating in various ways in the work of the institution, according to their capacities and by paying a quota of 50 centesimi per month for at least nine months.[14] The bulk of the finance – nine-tenths – was provided by benefactors. Only working women, however, were allowed on the board of directors, and the Turin *Lega* succeeded in maintaining complete control of the fund. In addition, the *Lega* also created the *Pro Maternitate*, a financial and educational organization that assisted mothers by providing lessons on hygiene and the correct rearing of newborn children.

The statutes of the Turin Fund gave special prominence to the contribution of richer women, listing among the purposes of this institution that of 'cooperating in uniting the hearts of those of diverse social conditions, bringing together well-to-do mothers and needy mothers whom nature has made equal in the joys and sufferings of motherhood'.[15] The more socially privileged women thus did voluntary work as visitors to members receiving assistance, as well as paying higher membership fees and raising funds in their own social circles.

Despite the energy put into it, the Turin Fund got off to a difficult start. Even to inform the large numbers of Turin women workers adequately about its activities was not easy, in spite of the fact that other working-women's associations and above all the local section of the *Unione Femminile* had joined the organization. In 1906 the latter reported that many working women who came to the union for assistance had not heard of the fund's existence. Those in charge of the union also pointed out that although they were doing everything they could to publicize the fund, 'unfortunately women's wages . . . are not high enough for us to insist, as we would like to do, on their making the small sacrifice necessary for them to be able to take advantage of such a wise and provident institution'.[16] The poverty of female workers was even more distressing than this suggests, for not only were they unable to pay even a minimal fee, they could not afford a single day off work. To qualify for a confinement allowance, members were obliged to abstain from working, which meant a considerable loss in comparison with their regular wage as well as with what they earned from extra work, since many did domestic jobs such as washing and cleaning in addition to their normal work-day in the factory.

The wages earned by women factory workers were a pittance, forcing them to eke them out by doing other regular or occasional jobs. A 1902 inquiry carried out by the Labour Department found that 12.3 per cent of women workers over 15 earned a maximum daily wage of 75 centesimi for an average of 10–12 hours' work; 28 per cent earned between 76 centesimi and 1 lira; 40.7 per cent earned between 1 and 1.5 liras; 13.4 per cent earned 1.5 to 2 liras, while only 5.6 per cent earned over 2 liras.[17] There were also other kinds of work, such as workshop trades, employing extremely young female workers who did not even manage to earn 25 centesimi a day.

The Milan *Lega per la Tutela degli Interessi Femminili* did not succeed in founding its own fund as its women members had hoped. This fund, which was launched towards the end of 1905, was not the outcome of women's initiative alone, as Paolina Schiff and Ersilia Majno had advocated. But the political contribution of the *Unione Femminile* was essential in laying its foundations. The *Unione* succeeded in extending the stated aims of the fund mainly to assist mothers in childbirth, to include those of 'giving backing to and coordinating institutions for the assistance of mothers and children' and 'exalting and propagating the concept of the social function of motherhood in the interests of both offspring and society'.[18]

The *Unione* co-operated with the *Federazione Lombarda delle Opere Femminili* to bring the fund into being, setting aside their mutual suspicions for this purpose.[19] Nonetheless, the Milan Fund was less under the control of women than that in Turin. For organizational and financial reasons, it came into existence as an autonomous section of the Benevolent Society for Insurance and Relief of Industrial Accidents, with the participation of the *Società Umanitaria*, a body concerned with the education and welfare of the proletariat founded by members of the progressive middle class close to or enrolled in the Socialist Party. These bodies seem mainly to have had a token function. However, they did provide the Milanese fund with political backing in the main city of Lombardy and in Italy as a whole which independent funds did not enjoy.

The statute of the Milan Fund, unlike that of Turin, required only ten board members to be full members of the fund (i.e. working women). The others were contributing members (i.e. benefactors) and the Chairman of the Benevolent Society for Industrial Accidents, who was a member as of right. On the 1911 board, however, there were only four female members, together with Fanny Pisa, the chairwoman.[20]

The annual subscription of 9 liras 60 centesimi that women-worker members were officially supposed to pay was judged by the board itself to be 'high, and above the means of working women'.[21] The decision to set a high contribution level (unlike the other independent funds) derived from the necessity of retaining the voluntary savings character of the fund, thus avoiding reducing it to a charitable institution. In 1907 the government granted it the legal status of Provident Institution as opposed to *Opera Pia* (Charitable Institution). In practice, however, half the income was paid by the fund itself, thanks to the contributions of benefactors, who must have been numerous judging from a remark in the board's five-year report: 'it has been easier to find benefactors than members'.[22]

The low membership of working women, here as in other cases, seems to have been partly due to unfamiliarity with, as well as resistance to, insurance precautions on the part of the working classes, and partly to the fact that there was a considerable risk that the premiums might be paid without the benefits being reaped, due to instability of employment. Moreover, as the law of 19 June 1902 permitting a month's maternity leave applied only to factory workers, others who were domestic workers, washerwomen or even workers in small factories not included in the law, risked dismissal if they did not turn up for work immediately following childbirth. In 1911, of 491 members of the Milan Fund, 25.86 per cent were artisans (self-employed dressmakers, embroiderers, etc.); 21.38 per cent were housewives (probably spouses of working men and craftsmen); 15.29 per cent were employed in the state-owned tobacco company, the most secure category of women workers both in terms of wage levels and job stability; only 9.16 per cent were silk-workers and weavers. The remainder were minors not yet employed, schoolmistresses, shop-assistants, and maidservants.[23]

The majority of members, 304 in all, were from one of the bodies that promoted the fund, the *Associazione Generale delle Operaie*. This had reduced its individual commitment to the maternity fund in order to join forces with other bodies whose aims it shared. A hundred and twenty-five belonged to other working-women's societies in Milan and its province, which had enrolled its members of childbearing age *en bloc*.

In Rome, the Maternity Assistance and Provident Fund was founded by the *Consiglio Nazionale delle Donne Italiane* (National Council of Italian Women), on the initiative of the Countess Ferraris, who had visited the Milan Fund and been much impressed by it. The Rome institution was promoted by rich middle-class and aristocratic women who shared feminist ideals. It enjoyed the patronage of the Queen Mother and Queen Elena and thus almost immediately obtained a (non-recurrent) donation from the government. Working-women members had to pay a monthly fee of 25 centesimi for at least ten months to acquire the right to a subsidy of 1 lira 50 centesimi a day for the fortnight preceding and following childbirth. The report of the Roman board members seems more optimistic than that of their northern counterparts, though the records are incomplete for this body. This, however, was still active in 1920 as a section of the National Alliance for the Protection of Motherhood and Infancy.[24]

Over the next few years independent funds were created in other Italian towns and cities (Bergamo, Brescia, Florence, Naples, Palermo, Voghera), mostly modelled on the Milanese Fund, although the criteria and the contributions varied according to local conditions. We know little about how these funds came to be established apart from the fact that the impetus came from societies of women workers. Some of the latter converted their traditional dowry funds into subscriptions for maternity insurance. The funds of Biella, a town with a big woollen industry, and of Vercelli, an agricultural town, whose main produce was rice – which employed a large number of seasonal, female workers – were municipal funds,[25] that is to say financed by public money: the first instance of 'state' participation in this sector.

Almost all the maternity funds launched by women's groups or, like that in Milan, inspired by them, sought and obtained legal recognition from the state. Acquiring the legal status of Provident Institution meant that they received some guarantees of stability and public financing. Although the funding provided by provincial or municipal administrations was often minimal and took the form of charitable donations which officially were not regular contributions, it was usually reliable. While this was a long-standing practice followed for charitable institutions, it now marked the first state involvement with maternity funds, although it was indirect and with no guarantee of permanence.

Private initiatives were not necessarily seen as the only way forward. Indeed it was precisely from the independent or so-called 'free' funds that the strongest pressures came for creating a central state fund or a number of state-run local funds.

THE ESTABLISHMENT OF THE NATIONAL MATERNITY FUND

During the First National Congress of Women's Practical Activities convened by the *Unione Femminile* in 1908, Nina Sierra and Bianca Arbib placed the issue in a broader framework. The former argued that a single month's rest after childbirth was quite insufficient for carrying out a mother's tasks. She proposed forms of insurance that would enable women to devote themselves entirely to their families during the years of 'active motherhood', and be paid for this.[26] Bianca Arbib, after giving an outline of the history of maternity assistance in modern and contemporary Europe, concluded with the following remarks:

> We know how hard it is to transform even the best and most necessary idea into law: the apathy of the law-makers with respect to what concerns us can only be shaken by the unanimous voice of women themselves, united by a single feeling of gentle pity and sisterhood . . . We must demand that for all matters regarding motherhood and infancy, before a bill be brought before parliament, women have the opportunity of discussing them, as well as women's associations involved in issues of this kind. This is necessary until women obtain the right to vote, at least in this vital area. We are not asking this out of ambition but because only women have the right to decide on matters that so intimately affect their essential functions.[27]

It took over ten years for the bill founding the National Maternity Fund to go through the legislative machinery. During that time it was widely discussed at all levels.[28] Above and beyond the slow pace of parliamentary discussion, a serious problem facing Giolitti's Italy was that social reform projects, which were generated in large numbers in the period and were supported by a wide range of people with differing political views, were not backed by a clear reform policy on the part of the government. Even reforms with apparent widespread support underwent in Parliament a process of 'sterilization' through major amendments of the original bills and long periods of 'hibernation' in the offices of the Chamber of Deputies.

Linked as it was to the law regulating female labour, the fund project shared this fate, though a number of members of the Socialist Party fought tirelessly to force Parliament to draft and pass insurance provisions for working mothers, no matter how provisional or incomplete.

The 1902 law regulating female and child labour was a pallid compromise between the socialist project and various government bills, careful not to encroach on the interests of industrialists. It was thus full of loopholes, designed to meet the requirements of employers rather than of women, and quite inadequate for the purposes for which it was originally drafted. Those who were most dissatisfied with it were the very women who had fought to set a limit on the exploitation of women and minors.

The activities of the *Unione Femminile* among women workers enabled it to show how the shortcomings of the law drove women to make agreements with their employers to circumvent it. At their assemblies they protested: 'make us stay at home for a month after giving birth? They should have asked us for permission to make this law; we'd have answered: pay us and we'll stay at home. It's *our* bread that's at stake.'[29]

The obligation to abstain from work during the period of childbirth was the most contentious issue concerning labour regulations. The parliamentary committee itself which had been appointed to examine the various proposals spent a long time discussing a form of insurance, but was unable to decide whether this should be a single national fund, or a number of regional or provincial bodies, or indeed, 'whether they should be compulsory or optional, independent or state-run, or linked to existing bodies'.[30]

An inquiry among women workers carried out by the Labour Office on behalf of the government between 1 December 1902 and 30 November 1903 showed that the fertility rate of women workers in industry was 'far below the average fertility rate of the female population as a whole'. This was because factory owners preferred to take on young unmarried girls who stayed in the factory until they got married or had their first child; they would then return there if their husbands became unemployed, if widowed, or when their children had grown up. Given the rate of childbirth, which was 4.5 per cent (compared with 12 per cent for the entire female population between 15 and 54 years, inclusive), it was calculated that in order to provide a daily allowance equivalent to four-fifths of the average salary for four weeks, maternity subsidies would amount to about 710,000 lire, an expenditure not considered excessive by the Labour Department.[31]

However, the most serious obstacle to a state fund was the refusal of the government to contribute to it. Ministers claimed that the state could not afford any expenditure for maternity insurance, insisting that only women workers and employers should contribute. The state would simply finance its setting up and management. The employers campaigned vigorously against the possibility that the fund might be supported by themselves and women workers alone – the more so as they already considered themselves penalized by having to do without a woman's work for a month of compulsory maternity leave. They argued that the fund could be created through a health insurance scheme. This was firmly rejected by the women, who would not countenance the idea that pregnancy and childbirth be equated with sickness. Should the fund be established, the employers urged the state to take its share of the costs, a point with which the General Confederation of Labour fully agreed.[32]

The law which was finally passed by Parliament[33] required the government to integrate into the fund the payment to childbearing mothers, raising it from the calculated 30 liras to 40 liras. The essential principle that the state should participate in financing the fund alongside women workers and employers was thus accepted. The employers were required to contribute, according to the age of the workers, 50 centesimi per annum for women aged 15 to 20 and 1 lira for those over 20, the same contributions as paid by the women. Both married and unmarried women had the right to the allowance, which covered both childbirth and miscarriages occurring after the third month of pregnancy. In the latter case, however, the subsidy would be granted only after a doctor had ascertained that it was an actual miscarriage, and not a voluntary, or, as it was usually phrased, a 'criminal' abortion.

The board which was to administer the national fund (which was conceived as an independent division of the National Providence and Invalidity Fund) was made up of three groups, each with one-third of the board members: representatives of the employers, of women workers (not necessarily women, although the law was ambiguous on this point) chosen from those elected to the arbitration boards of industries employing mainly women, and members of the Board of Directors of the National Providence Fund.

As noted earlier, the provisions applied to those women workers who were subject to the 1902 labour law, which extended in 1907 to rice-pickers the prohibition against working in the thirty days after childbirth. Nevertheless, the vast majority of women workers were still excluded.

THE FUND IN OPERATION

The law establishing the National Maternity Fund did not come into force until 6 May 1912. From the outset its shortcomings were obvious. Employers were responsible for collecting the women-workers' contributions. This had a number of serious practical as well as psychological drawbacks. There were also few safeguards for women who had paid the contribution for the minimum period allowed but who then left their job: they lost their money while being unable to benefit from the insurance.[34] All of this increased the discontent of women with the law as a whole.

As many had foreseen, strikes against the law soon followed, especially in areas with a high proportion of female labour. In the province of Como, where the largest silk factories were concentrated, there were numerous demonstrations against the scheme. A report from the Prefect of Como told the Minister of the Interior how groups of working women had presented him with 'a protest bearing a large number of signatures'.

> In Maggianico the women refused to accept the fund membership cards . . . in Civate the female workers of the Ponti factory refused to pay the contributions. . . . In Bellano, in the works of the [Gavazzi] company, the women insisted on refusing to take their pay-packets from which the prescribed fees had been deducted. Since trouble seemed to be increasing I sent a police official there to maintain order and ensure the freedom to work, as well as to explain the importance and utility of the new law to the women.

It took the police force to explain the meaning of the law, and, on that occasion, it was the employers who took it upon themselves to defend the law by closing their factories for two or three days until the women had 'bowed to the new ordinances'.[35]

The trades unions and the Socialist Party, both of whom had fought for the law and had played a major role in getting it through Parliament, had failed to wage a satisfactory propaganda campaign. Moreover, even if it was possible to defend the law, in principle it was hard to convince women that the procedure laid down could work. Delays in payment, or non-payment, by employers, left women defenceless.

During the first year in which the fund was in force, only one-sixth of industrialists made the required payments, 'so that' – as Francesco Saverio Nitti, Minister of Industry, observed – 'the receipts for the first six months of the law's application are sufficient to cover only one third of the estimated number of workers who should benefit from it.'[36] In some cases the employers had not defrauded the women but had made an agreement with them to avoid making the payment: the women would receive their full wage while the employers would save their share of the contributions. The risk of fines was hardly sufficient to dissuade them, given the almost complete lack of enforcement; on balance, they would stand to gain in any event.

The women's strikes were sharply criticized by the women of the Socialist Party, above all in the columns of their recently founded journal *La difesa delle lavoratrici* (The Working Women's Defence). Giselda Brebbia, a socialist-feminist until a short time before, accused the protesting women workers of giving more weight to the words of the priests than to feelings of solidarity with female fellow-workers. Apparently the strikers were arguing that 'spinsters don't want to have to *spoon-feed* married women; good girls don't want to encourage *wretches* (i.e. unmarried mothers)'. On the other hand, Giselda Brebbia also saw the strikes as 'an unconscious vendetta against a State that . . . has always neglected female workers, against the governments that have always betrayed their interests'.[37]

Socialist women also attacked the independent maternity funds, however. There were now nine of these in the whole of Italy, and they had recently formed a confederation to co-ordinate their activities more effectively. These attacks were unjustified; indeed, they had more to do with conflicts between the socialist and 'bourgeois' women's movements than with the conduct of the private funds. These funds had pressed for the extension of state insurance legislation to include all women in need and had devised a plan whereby the state could make use both of their experience and their administrative structures to improve the coverage of the fund. They had, indeed, become more philanthropic and less political over time, but they had played a vital role both before and after the introduction of the law, especially in supporting those women workers who were not protected by it. The introduction of state-managed insurance had not reduced the work of the local funds. That in Milan, for instance, expanded considerably, providing, in addition to the unusual subsidies for the period of childbirth, supportive and educational services for mothers in counselling centres situated in various working-class areas of the city.[38]

A number of other funds run by feminist organizations, like that in Rome, showed some expansion, though remaining limited and staffed by volunteers, and despite the serious crisis besetting the women's movement at that time. This was the period, when, first, the Christian feminists broke away, obliged to cease co-operating with the socialist and other non-religious groups by the church authorities, on account of their different positions on compulsory religious instruction in elementary schools. They were followed three years later by the socialist women, who were obliged by their parties to leave feminist associations. But above all the crisis was due to a gradual impoverishment of ideas and enterprise in the movement as a whole.

WAR AND FASCISM

With the First World War and the employment of large numbers of women in industry, the number of workers coming under the law increased, but not to the maximum possible. Of 1,397,607 women potentially covered by this insurance scheme only 476,722 were registered with the National Fund, a further proof of inadequate implementation of the law. Home workers, agricultural workers and employees were still excluded from the scheme.

A 1917 decree introduced important changes: it extended the benefits to women in the telephone services, allowed women to sit on the Board of Administration, and increased and standardized the contributions (1 lira for all women workers; 1.25 lire for employers), whereas the allowance remained at 40 lire. There were further increases over the next three years: by 1920 fees for the workers were 1.50 lire, the employers' quota was 2 lire, and the allowance, to which the state now contributed 20 lire, had been raised to 100 lire.[39]

The period immediately after the war saw a marked revival of agitation in favour of women's suffrage. At the same time there was a renewed involvement in welfare activities by the feminist associations, once again aimed above all at helping mothers. 'The spirit of motherhood', wrote Laura Casartelli Cabrini in 1919, 'is at the core of women's associations' interests'. The Women's Association tried to resuscitate an old issue, of a form of payment for housework, to be financed by the state: 'a proposal is being drawn up', continued Laura Casartelli, 'for State renumeration of "maternal labour": there is a growing tendency to seek to give a financial value to those useful services rendered by women as manager of the household, housewife, spouse and mother.'[40] The project died, however, partly due to the overall social and political situation of Italy on the eve of a twenty-year dictatorship.

Some of the feminist organizations still active were shut down by the new regime half-way through the 1920s; others, like the *Unione Femminile Nazionale*, now mainly engaged in charitable assistance work with women, were allowed to continue for a few years more. The founding of the *Opera Nazionale Maternità e Infanzia* (National Institution for Maternity and Infancy) did not at first affect the maternity fund or the broad range of support for mothers now set up by the *Unione*. This was despite the fact that the independence, which the association defended by various techniques – from simply ignoring warnings to rarely attending meetings or taking virtually no part in them – was a considerably nuisance to the authorities. The *Unione* was finally banned in 1938, the reason given being that there was no further need for independent social assistance since the state was now capable of fulfilling all the requirements of social security.[41] In fact, both the *Unione Femminile* and other female associations were dissolved as a result of the race laws. They had always been animated by a substantial proportion of Jewish women, and in recent years they had become practically the only point of reference for antifascists. Non-practising Jewish women, who could no longer turn to their community, could not take part in the *Azione Cattolica* (Catholic Action Association) – which, thanks to the 1929 Concordat, had a degree of autonomy from the regime – and, of course, could not become members of fascist socio-cultural bodies.

There was, however, a grain of truth in the official explanation given for the closing of the *Unione*. The regime had based its policy towards mothers on a 'biological formulation of the maternal function' and upheld 'a particular structure and conception of the family',[42] one based even more than in the past on the primacy of the father. It could thus not tolerate the survival, however marginal they had become, of bodies which presented mothers and women in general as the leading protagonists of change, as the vital, though still repressed, force for the transformation of the whole of society.

NOTES

1 S. Aleramo, *La donna e il femminismo. Scritti 1896–1910*, ed. B. Conti, Rome, Editori Riuniti, 1978. On the Italian women's movement in this period: F. Pieroni Bortolotti, *Alle origini del movimento femminile in Italia, 1848–1892*, Turin, Einaudi, 1963; F. Pieroni Bortolotti, *Socialismo e questione femminile in Italia, 1892–1922*, Milan, Mazzotta, 1974; A. Buttafuoco, *Cronache femminili. Temi e momenti della stampa emancipazionista in Italia dall'Unità al fascismo*, Arezzo–Siena, Dipartimento di studi storico-sociali e filosofici, 1988.

2 'Alla Camera dei Deputati' (printed handbill), Milan, Tipografia Ciminago, 1861, Archive of the Museo del Risorgimento, Milan, Bertarelli Collection, b. 212, n. 4.

3 M. Frank, 'Lettori e lettrici', *La Donna*, 25 July 1873.

4 See, among many, C. Serono, *Femminismo e maternità*, Rome, Centenari, 1912.

5 A. Buttafuoco, 'La filantropia come politica. Esperienze dell'emancipazionismo italiano nel Novecento', in L. Ferrante, M. Palazzi and G. Pomata (eds), *Ragnatele di rapporti. Patronage e reti di relazioni nella storia delle donne*, Turin, Rosenberg & Sellier, 1988, pp. 166–87; A. Buttafuoco, *Le Mariuccine. Storia di un'istituzione laica*, Milan, Angeli, 1985.

6 E. Majno Bronzini, 'Vie pratiche del femminismo', November 1902, Majno Archive, Milan.

7 B. Novich, *Maternità e lavoro*, Milan–Palermo, Remo Sandron, 1907, p. 148; Teresa Labriola, 'Pro maternitate', *Infantia*, 20 June 1910, pp. 53–4.

8 P. Schiff, *Istituzione di una Cassa d'Assicurazione per la Maternità*, Milan, A. Colombo, 1895.

9 *Associazione Generale di M.S. ed Istruzione delle Operaie di Milano, 1862–1911. Cinquantennio di fondazione*, Milano, n.d. [1912]. On child abandonment: V. Hunecke, *Die Findelkinder von Mailand. Kindsaussetzung und aussetzende Eltern vom 17. bis zum 19. Jahrhundert*, Stuttgart, Klett-Cotta, 1987 (Ital. transl., *I trovatelli di Milano*, Bologna, Il Mulino, 1989).

10 E. Majno Bronzini, 'Norme per regolare il lavoro delle donne', in *Congresso sugli infortuni del lavoro indetto dalla Camera del Lavoro di Milano, marzo 1895*, Milan, Tipografia Nazionale Ramperti, 1901.

11 P. Schiff, *La pace gioverà alla donna? Conferenza tenuta a Milano al Ridotto della Scala*, Milan, Galli, 1890, p. 24.

12 P. Schiff, *Istituzione*.

13 'Lega per la Tutela degli Interessi Femminili in Milano', in S. Merli, *Proletariato di fabbrica e capitalismo industriale. Il caso italiano: 1880–1900*, Florence, La Nuova Italia, 1973, vol. 2, pp. 404–5.

14 P. Schiff, E. Scodnik, 'Les Caisses de prévoyance et d'assistance pour la maternité en Italie', in *Congrès international des accidents du travail et des assurances sociales, Paris 1900*, Paris, Béranger éditeur, 1901 vol. 1, pp. 679–80.

15 M. Borsanelli Tommasina, 'Per le madri', *Cronache femminili*, 17 Jan. 1904.

16 Unione Femminile Nazionale, *Relazione 1906*, Milan, Tipografia Nazionale Ramperti, n.d. [1907], p. 26.
17 Ministero Agricoltura Industria e Commercio [MAIC], Ufficio del Lavoro, *La donna nell'industria italiana*, Rome, Bertero,1905, pp. 44–5; MAIC, Ufficio del Lavoro, *Operai e orari negli opifici soggetti alla legge sul lavoro delle donne e dei fanciulli (anno 1907)*, Rome, Bertero, 1908.
18 Unione Femminile Nazionale, *Relazione 1906*, p. 5.
19 The Unione considered the Federazione extremely 'moderate' since it consisted of aristocratic and upper-class women; the Federazione on the other hand saw the Unione as a den of subversives on account of its ties with the Socialist Party.
20 Cassa di Maternità, *Relazione del Consiglio Direttivo sulle condizioni e sull'opera della Cassa nel suo primo quinquennio, 1906–1910*, Milan, A. Bertarelli e C., 1911, pp. 32, 37.
21 Cassa di Maternità, Sezione autonoma del Patronato Infortuni publicity leaflet, s. 1., n.d., Majno Archive, Milan.
22 Cassa di Maternità, *Relazione*, p. 12.
23 ibid., pp. 18–21.
24 Consiglio Nazionale delle Donne Italiane [CNDI], *Resoconto pel 1907*, Rome, n.d., p. 22; Laura Casartelli Cabrini, 'Rassegna del movimento femminile italiano', in *Almanacco della donna italiana*, 1921.
25 G. Casalini, 'A difesa delle madri operaie. Progetto sommario per la creazione di una Cassa libera di Maternità nel circondario di Biella', in *Critica sociale*, 16 March 1903; L. Rava, 'Le Casse di Maternità. Discorso pronunciato alla Camera dei Deputati nella 2a tornata del 14 dicembre 1903', *Bollettino ufficiale*, 18 February 1904, p. 5.
26 N. Sierra, 'La protezione sociale della donna salariata', in Unione Femminile Nazionale, *Atti del I Congresso Nazionale di attività pratica femminile, Milano 24–28 maggio 1908*, Milan, Società Editrice di Cultura Popolare, 1909, pp. 92–3 and 100.
27 B. Arbib, 'Protezione della maternità', *Unione Femminile Nazionale, Atti del I Congresso*, p. 112.
28 See, besides the Parliamentary Proceedings, A. Cherubini, 'Introduzione storica alle assicurazioni sociali. La tutela della maternità (1900–1922)', in *Rivista degli infortuni e delle malattie professionali*, 1973, no. 1.
29 Una donna [E. Majno], 'A proposito della legge sue lavoro delle donne e dei fanciulli', *Unione Femminile*, 1903, no. 10.
30 MAIC, Ufficio del Lavoro, *Basi tecniche di una cassa di maternità*. Rome, Bertero, 1904, p. 5.
31 ibid., pp. 5 and 2. There is criticism as to the reliability of the inquiry in C. Ficola, 'Legislazione sociale e tutela della maternità nell'età giolittiana', in M. Luisa Betri, and A. Gigli Marchetti (eds), *Salute e classi lavoratrici in Italia dall'Unità al fascismo*, Milan, Angeli, 1982, pp. 699–712.
32 Federazione Industriale Piemontese–Confederazione Generale del Lavoro, *Sul disegno di legge per la Cassa di Maternità*, Turin, Celanza, 1909, pp. 5–6.
33 Legge 17 luglio per la Instituzione di una Cassa di Maternità, *Leggi e decreti del Regno d'Italia*, 1910.
34 E. Reina, 'Lotte e difesa del lavoro. Per le operaie madri o. . . che lo diverranno', in *La difesa delle lavoratrici*, 4 Feb. 1912; E. Reina, 'Casse di maternità', ibid. 2 June 1912.
35 Archivo Centrale dell Stato (ACS), Rome, *Ministero dell' Interno, Direzione Generale di P.S.*, b. 232, Prefetto di Como al Ministero dell'Interno, 20 May 1912.
36 ibid., Il Ministro dell'Agricoltura, Industria e Commercio al Presidente del

Consiglio dei Ministri, Rome, 13 Oct. 1912.
37 G. Brebbia, 'La donna . . . contro la madre', in *La difesa delle lavoratrici*, 19 May 1912.
38 Unione Femminile Nazionale, *Relazione morale 1919–1920*, Varese, Varesina, 1920; *Relazione morale 1926–1927*, Milan, Ramperti, 1927; id., *Relazione morale 1933–1934*, Milan, Ramperti, 1934.
39 A. Cherubini and A. Coluccia, *La previdenza sociale nell'epoca giolittiana*, Rome, Istituto Nazionale per la previdenza sociale, 1986, pp. 154–5.
40 L. Casartelli Cabrini, 'Rassegna del movimento femminile italiano', in *Almanacco della donna italiana*, 1920, p. 139; B. Novich, *Maternità e lavoro*; T. Labriola, 'Il salario della moglie', in *La Vita*, 21 Dec. 1908.
41 ACS, *Ministero dell'Interno, Direzione Generale di P.S.*, b. 30, fasc. 345.
42 See Saraceno's contribution to this volume.

Chapter 10

Redefining maternity and paternity: gender, pronatalism and social policies in fascist Italy

Chiara Saraceno

PRONATALISM, FAMILY AND GENDER RELATIONS

The fascist regime subjected the family to specific interventions relating to both of its main pivots: relations between the sexes, and thus the gender structure, and relations between the generations. Though it is true that the explicit aim of these measures was population increase, the immediate target of the various forms of intervention was the structure of family relationships and the distribution of power and authority within the family: between man and woman and between parents and children.[1] The family was not only encouraged to be prolific but also organically linked with the state, of which it was meant to become a full component and instrument. Fourteen years after the coming to power of Mussolini, this idea was put forward by Loffredo in 1936[2] and made explicit in the 1930 Penal Code and then the 1942 Civil Code, whose compiler, Rocco, defined the family as a 'social and political institution'.[3] This is why, though it is true that most of the family policies of the regime were in reality pronatalist policies aiming not so much at the welfare of families, however understood, as at population growth, their actual effect was not to increase the number of births, but to support a particular structure and concept of the family. In fact, fertility in marriage, which had fallen dramatically between 1871 and 1901 in the big northern and central cities (being 30 per cent lower than in rural areas or southern cities) and had involved mainly the upper and upper-middle classes, followed by white-collar workers and, well behind, blue-collar workers, continued in the fascist period to fall at the same rate and among the same strata, even though the regime's measures focused on towns and on those very strata.

According to some scholars,[4] the various legislative and social policy measures introduced by the regime from 1926 until the eve of the Second World War constituted a coherent, structured whole, and their relative failure should be attributed not to their intrinsic weakness or inconsistency, but to their timing. The trend of fertility decline which, by arousing the regime's concern (solemnly expressed in Mussolini's well-known 'Ascension Day Speech' of 1927), had led to these measures could not be stopped at the time, for it was a long-term process with deep roots. Moreover, the possibility of verifying their long-term effects was ruled out due first to the war, then to the fall of the regime. This interpretation, though largely convincing as far as the question of timing goes, leaves aside the fact that the fertility decline implied changes in family culture and in the relationship between the generations. It was not a simple outcome of economic calculation, but part of a process of transformation in the position of children within the family and in investment in the family, just as was happening, or had happened, in other European countries. From this point of view, no fertility bonus could make up for the investment in terms of time and affection that was now thought necessary for each child, nor even be financially sufficient for the investments regarded as necessary to guarantee the children a good life.

However, this interpretation underestimates the overall social and economic context in which these measures were set and which defined the conditions of paternity and maternity: growing unemployment for the urban working classes and sections of the lower-middle class, reductions in real wages, health care guaranteed only for restricted groups of workers and their families, restriction of some traditional channels of family and individual survival such as internal and external migration, the acceleration of such processes as urbanization (despite the constraints imposed by the regime) and industrialization, leading to changes in social stratification. Maternity and infant care offered by such services as the ONMI (*Opera Nazionale Maternità e Infanzia*, created in 1925), which will be discussed more fully later, taxes on bachelors (introduced in 1927) and tax exemptions according to family size (1933), child allowances (1936) and fertility bonuses (1939) were all operating in a context where, on the one hand, the position of children in the symbolic and material economy of families was changing (this change had begun several decades earlier, Italy being a 'latecomer' by comparison with other countries). On the other hand, the economic and political situation was bringing about changes in the conditions of life of a broad section of the population, even if it was still a minority, namely the urbanized, who were taking the lead in reducing their birth-rate. While for some there was significant deterioration in living standards, as indicated by wage and consumption figures for the period,[5] in general there were changes in opportunity structures which in turn affected the way individuals, couples and families thought about their own future and defined goals and hopes. Some aspects of the regime's intervention in areas other than the population question, such as those concerning the expansion of leisure facilities (*dopolavoro*), holidays, mass consumption goods (such as radio sets) in practice contributed to building up new models of normality, even though they did not touch the majority of the population.[6]

Hence the individuals exposed to the regime's pronatalist measures interpreted them in the light of these complex material and symbolic conditions, which not only had nothing to do with those measures, but sometimes were even in contradiction with them. Furthermore, it is perfectly possible that some of the regime's measures took on unforeseen meanings and outcomes among people, derived precisely from that larger and older context. Thus, the increased value put on child welfare by the offer of health care and maternity education may not have strengthened the desire for many pregnancies so much as enhancing the value and rights of the individual child, thereby further justifying the limitation of their numbers.

Rather than going into a further assessment of the actual or potential effectiveness of the regime's pronatalist measures, I want to argue that, despite the regime's defeat in the 'demographic battle', its policy promoted, in a still largely rural Italy, the emergence of a particular family type as a culturally dominant model: the new patriarchate of the urban middle classes. It did not centre so much around a socially authoritative and powerful male figure, as in the bourgeoisie, nor around the more or less idealized patriarch of the rural extended families. Rather it centred around the salary or wage of the employed worker whose fragile self-sufficiency was held together and complemented, on the one hand, by provision from a state which was simultaneously benevolent and controlling, and on the other by the good housewife's work in the home. During the fascist regime the nightmare of the middle class – an irresponsible, spendthrift wife, well described in such turn-of-the-century novels as Emilio de Marchi's *Demetrio Pianelli* – came to blend with the other, entirely fascist, nightmare of the infecund wife: the woman who 'just buys perfume and gewgaws for herself' (as one song went), not only throwing the family (the husband's) money out of the window but neglecting the family and even being incapable – psychologically, but also physically – of bearing children. It was not a totally new image, to be sure, nor the last to be developed. In the rural culture the beautiful woman was perceived as a risk when she became a wife, since she was thought of as frail and unsuitable for the work of either production or reproduction. And in the eighties, once again, the reduced fertility is imputed, by Catholics as well as by lay demographers, to consumerist egotism, particularly by women. 'Female egotism' continues to bear the blame for the perceived disintegration of both family and society, right at the foundations of demographic continuity.

With regard to this cultural *topos*, fascism constituted not so much a radical innovation as a pointed expression of a trend, laying down the legislative, social and symbolic foundations for the pattern of the family and of the welfare state that were to last far longer than fascism itself. For instance, the family legislation of the Rocco Code was not changed until 1975, the year when the ban on distributing contraceptive knowledge and devices was also removed. And while abortion ceased to be a crime 'against the race' only in the 1970s, rape and sexual violence continue to be crimes not against the person, the woman raped, but against morality, thus indicating woman's potential as a prey and the gap in rights between women and men.

Similarly, incest is still regarded a minor offence and as differing from sexual violence as long as it does not give rise to public scandal, pointing to the continued existence on the legal level of a proprietorial, hierarchical view of family relationships, in particular between males (fathers, brothers) and females (wives, mothers, sisters).

From this viewpoint, it is only partly possible to share De Grand's conclusion[7] that fascism was successful where it asserted not so much innovative, totalitarian principles, but conservative principles much like those prevailing in other non-totalitarian countries in the 1920s and 1930s. Or rather, the question is what we mean by the term 'conservative'. While it is indeed true that fascism, like other non-totalitarian cultures, maintained a strong asymmetry in gender relations (an attitude shared by many contemporary cultures too), it updated it by placing at its centre a model of paternity and maternity that was only partly 'old'. Procreation as a social duty is a not insignificant cultural innovation, with manifold implications, by comparison with procreation as a more or less unavoidable fact of nature or at most as a family duty. It is an innovation which, though certainly not only in fascism, as De Grand rightly points out, marks the emergence of the state as a strong and demanding partner of the family with regard to the responsibilities and purposes of reproduction, and by no means only biological reproduction.

It is equally true that the strong presence of an organized Catholic culture and of the Vatican encouraged, from the Concordat of 1929 onwards, the development and continuation of the pattern of asymmetrical division of labour and of power between the sexes. This was also the case on the level of legislation, as shown, up to the present, by the legislative developments concerning the family, the relations between the sexes and sexuality. However, the formulation of this model derived from the culture and objectives of fascism.

Both the apparent biological formulation of the maternal function, reducing women to producers of the race, and its linking with the interests of the nation are characteristic of fascism. Any experience that might even minimally take women away from this task was looked at with suspicion: from work outside the home to higher education. Nonetheless, a blind eye was turned to the heavy work done by women in the fields, in factories, or at home under the pressure of economic necessity and family needs, or it was seen as a necessary evil, to be contained through restrictive measures and compensated for through supports to employed mothers. Access to higher education by the daughters of the middle classes and their entry to the professions were hindered in every way, even if with only partial success. This was done through propaganda ridiculing female intellectuals, bars on the exercise of certain professions by women, including high-school teaching, exclusion from public-service competitions.[8]

Even the associationism, more or less obligatory in fascism, met resistance in respect of female participation, not only from women, too caught up in their own duties to add another one, or too accustomed to seclusion to join mass meetings, but also from the Party itself. It was in a sense in contradiction with itself here: if it wanted women to marry early and have lots of children they ought not to be 'distracted', i.e. not offered opportunities, however temporary, for other desires and activities.[9] Women's *fasci* grew to any extent only in the 1930s, when they were given a role in the pronatalist campaign and then in the struggle against the economic sanctions imposed by the League of Nations (because of the Ethiopian war).[10] The fascist activist woman, the female *squadrista* of the early days, never constituted a role model for the regime. Indeed, she could be regarded as a troublesome, embarrassing presence, to be kept under control precisely because of the message of deviance from a feminine normality of homemaking, obedience, fertility and seclusion. It recalled the futurist, emancipationist cultural origins of fascism, the traces of which were erased under the regime but which still resounded feebly in the ambivalent positions put forward by an association, albeit pro-fascist, of intellectual women like the *Alleanza Muliebre Culturale Italiana* and in its journal *Attività muliebre*, which sometimes claimed the right of women to education and to employment in the civil service.[11] Apart from these exceptions, which were in any case low-profile (though middle-class women were going to high school in increasing numbers) and increasingly less explicit as time went on, the presence of fascist women in the regime's agencies, including ONMI, came progressively to be defined within the traditional limits of home visitors, ladies of charity, school teachers. The image was never that of the leader or head of an agency or one of initiative.

The pomposity, and indeed coarseness imposed on the fascist male, who with uniforms, parades, goose-stepping and acrobatic feats gave a pantomime of sexual and racial superiority which was hard to achieve for the puffed-up petty bourgeoisie, required a complement. The proper one was not an equally pompous and coarse woman, nor one in positions of responsibility, but the modest, subdued wife, who at least in social behaviour confirmed that fragile superiority. The slogan '*le donne a casa* (women back to the home)' had the same symbolic function. Applied officially only in the public service where the female presence had been low, it had a function mainly as a message: it constructed women – who were 'stealing jobs from breadwinners' – as guilty of the endemic, growing unemployment in Italy and also of the birth decline, while it affirmed the priority assigned by the regime to male workers as breadwinners, a priority which, as we shall see, was underlined also by many measures with purely pronatalist intent. At the same time, it drew collective awareness away from the costs for women, but also for families, of the lesser legitimation for female labour power that it underlined: the need to live within the narrow limits of an inadequate salary in families of middle-class employees, engaged in safeguarding their own social respectability, where work in the home by the wife and mother often had to go as far as 'inventing' essential items of consumption which they lacked or which were inadequate

– from remaking hand-me-down clothes to the time-consuming preparation of poor foods;[12] the abandonment of female labour to the blackmail and exploitation of employers, with additional costs over and above those borne by the whole working class under fascism; the work burden on women working at home was rendered invisible, especially in the case of the rural housewives so often cited as examples of compatibility between family responsibilities and work needs (and also of fertility). It was because of this need to teach women to keep to their place and to devote themselves to their families, accepting any sacrifice in their name, that Catholic women's associations enjoyed more respect or more indifference from the regime than their male counterparts, which were instead seen as potential competition for fascist membership and culture as well as for its image of aggressive virility. Everyday Catholic religiosity, in particular its pastoral version *vis-à-vis* women, was not only regarded as 'naturally' feminine (and hence unvirile), but also as an effective means for inculcating those features of resignation, spirit of sacrifice and humility that formed part of the ideal female model. For this reason, the Catholic mediation and reformulation of the place of woman and of the centrality of the family, at least richer symbolically than the pronatalist – and since 1938 racist – messages of the regime, were far from opposing the latter and rather strengthened them in the popular mind, guaranteeing them much longer duration than the regime itself.

MATERNITY, PATERNITY AND SOCIAL WELFARE

As already mentioned, the fascist policies concerning the family and its gender structure were not confined to more strictly pronatalist policies. Family life was also interfered with, to differing extents and in differing ways for the various social classes, by the (restrictive) policies on work and wages, by policies on compliance with compulsory schooling, various measures aimed at organizing daily life including the sponsoring of the first mass leisure activities, the *Opera Nazionale Dopolavoro*, and even by the effects of such dramatic initiatives as the Ethiopian War, autarchy as a response to sanctions and entry into the Second World War. All these initiatives and events in turn interacted with an economic framework in which fascism, after having reacted to the workers' struggles following the First World War (the 'Two Red Years'), found itself having to deal with the effects of the 1929 world economic crisis. The latter's effects and the regime's became mixed inextricably in the conditions of life of urban working-class and lower middle-class families (as well as enriching a new class of speculators of various types).

A pointer to this intermingling, in which political circumstances (the weakening of workers' powers of negotiation and self-defence) and economic circumstances overlapped and strengthened each other, is the fact that at the outbreak of war real wages were at lower levels than in 1921, with the consequent deterioration of consumption.[13] Another indicator is the course of female unemployment: in 1921–2 it was below male unemployment, but in 1926–32 above it, indicating progressive expulsion of female labour to the point of discouraging women from going on to the labour market. In 1933–5, despite low real wages and the deterioration in consumption, the female rates of both employment and unemployment fell, signalling that women were leaving the workforce – at least the official one (though 'moonlighting' could not manage to absorb all of them, since low male wages in the official economy did not make the labour offered by female moonlighters greatly attractive or competitive).[14]

Furthermore, some social policy and social support initiatives taken by the regime – from family allowances to the *Opera Nazionale Dopolavoro*, to summer camps for workers' children – were aimed at controlling the urban working classes by replacing with projects controlled by the regime the associations and institutions of solidarity developed in previous decades by the labour movement. This intervention by the state in the living conditions of urban industrial workers – admittedly a minority in the Italian population at the time[15] – was, moreover, supported by the fascist trade unionists most concerned with workers' living conditions, who pressed for compensation for the wage restrictions promoted by the regime through expansion of public intervention to support standards of living (thereby *de facto* supplying employers with a double subsidy).[16] Even the ONMI, though in principle addressed to all the population in modest or poor conditions, *de facto* had a mainly urban distribution. Paradoxically, we might say, though fascism's ideal model of the family was the multiple, prolific family of rural Lombardy and Emilia-Romagna (which the regime sought to reproduce even in situations of agricultural wage labour, through share-cropping and tied-herding contracts), it was the relatively smaller and politically less trustworthy families of urban industrial workers that were the main beneficiaries of the regime's pronatalist measures.

These measures were either 'positive', i.e. aimed at giving bonuses and support, or 'negative', aimed at discouraging or even punishing behaviour regarded as undesirable. Some of those measures, moreover, were aimed at women as mothers (real and potential) and at children, but others were aimed at men as fathers (actual and potential). Thus, not only maternity but also paternity were objects of redefinition by fascism and by its pronatalist policy: in this sense too the policy of the regime was more than mere pronatalism.

Some of the 'positive' measures were in reality nothing but continuations of measures begun under pre-fascist governments, impelled by demands from the workers' movement. The *Cassa Nazionale di Maternità* had been set up in 1911, financed by contributions from both female workers and employers. It paid a birth grant of 40 lire to women working in the lowest-paid industries; they had to stay away from work for a month before and a month after the birth. The fascist reform of the *Cassa* in 1923 confined itself to raising both the female workers' contribution (making it three-sevenths of the total) and the grant (to 100 lire). The categories of women covered were not extended, so that among those still excluded were not only the higher-paid clerical women and teachers, but also the great mass of female workers, petty clerks, retail workers and especially agricultural workers, and domestic servants, i.e. the two most numerous categories of female workers. There was not even any provision for recognition of the medical costs of pregnancy and childbirth within the sickness insurance schemes. Extension to further categories and partial cover of medical expenses came only after 1935, when administration of the contributions and the maternity grant was handed over to the *Istituto Nazionale di Previdenza Sociale*, which also handled contributions for pensions, accidents, disability, unemployment allowance and sickness insurance for most employed workers.[17] Not only non-contract workers, but also many agricultural female workers, all home workers and housewives continued to be excluded. In other words, even whilst remaining within a strictly pronatalist perspective, the regime did little to guarantee conditions of work and health which were to improve or at least maintain the physical well-being of pregnant female workers. On the contrary, the short period of compulsory rest before birth for women working in industry, the absence of any protection for broad categories of female workers and working conditions that frequently produced diseases of the reproductive organs continued to cause thousands of miscarriages every year (while fury raged against illegal abortions), as even some fascist female commentators recognized.[18]

Faced with this indifference to the actual conditions in which many women became pregnant, endured their pregnancies and gave birth, the introduction of fertility bonuses in 1939 seems not only partial but even to some extent paradoxical. They replaced the maternity grant for working mothers with an amount that increased with the number of births, which was paid to 'any worker male or female' to whom a child was born.[19] Contrary to appearances, this did not mean extending an income supplement to all mothers, but supporting paternity. Given the prevalence of male workers over female workers, this measure rewarded fathers rather than mothers. Moreover, since the amount was paid only when the child was born and alive, a birth that went wrong, however much loss of pay it might have meant to the working woman, was not compensated for in any way.

In general, this substitution and the very term *premio di natalità* indicate a shift in attention from support (however partial) to working women and their health conditions during pregnancy and childbirth, from a recognition of her rights as a working mother, to support for large families through a supplement to the breadwinner's wage. This policy had already begun with the introduction in 1936 of family allowances (*assegni familiari*), the amount of which increased with the growing number of children, which was payable to the breadwinner and hence again mainly to fathers, in partial compensation for their wage cuts. The same direction of support for large families and for paternity was pursued with tax exemptions granted for dependent children, which again increased with the number of children. Since the person receiving the family income, and in general a taxable income, was in the main the husband and father, it was he who was entitled to the exemptions. Little money reached women directly which they could control, in exchange for their fertility, despite the encouragements and even financial investments by the regime. On the contrary, the discouragement of women's employment, along with growing female unemployment, increasingly excluded them from direct access to such benefits. Moreover, it cannot automatically be assumed that the money reached the family and was redistributed there. The evidence of oral history tells us how little say peasant women had in the administration of the family money, and even middle-class women often did not know how much their husbands earned. As for working-class women, they often had more control over family resources, but only because they were assigned the task of making scarce resources suffice, and husbands often kept extras for themselves.[20]

The favouring not only of the regular, or legitimate, family but also of the paternal figure as the subject both of social responsibilities and of benefits is indicated by other measures:[21] a marriage bonus given to male workers who married before the age of 26, and the marriage loans introduced in 1937, repayment of which was gradually cancelled with the birth of up to four children. In the public service, married men were preferred to bachelors both on recruitment and in promotion. After 1938 one of the requirements to become a headmaster, university professor or *podestà* was to be married, while women were excluded from science teaching in secondary schools, and even from elementary teaching of male classes. The condition whereby women were excluded from higher employment – being married and a parent – was a title of merit for men. This can of course be read as compensation for the reduced possibility of family earnings, faced with increased costs. Nevertheless, the direction of the recognition and of the exclusion both symbolically and practically marks the different value and the different responsibilities assigned to each sex in procreation.

The punitive measures too differed in the burden and cost they imposed upon the two sexes. The tax on bachelors, introduced in 1927 and subsequently modified through progressive extension of the exemptions, payable by bachelors aged between 25 and 65 (except for the clergy, invalids and the poor) and coupled with a number of disadvantages in public-service careers, was certainly annoying and oppressive. In 1939 it was paid by over 1 million bachelors, for a total amount of 230 million lire (compared with some 260 million paid out in fertility and marriage bonuses, loans and tax exemptions, which it accordingly almost completely financed, as a means of redistribution between bachelors and married fathers).[22] But it operated in a situation where marriage rates were high and had been constant for several decades, whilst there was an economic crisis that encouraged later rather than earlier marriage. The long-term cost for the individual but also for the family (often in need of a son's wages) of a marriage could not be balanced out by the burden of the tax. Nor could the cost of the tax affect the decision of an upper-class youth or his family to finish his studies and start a career before marrying.[23] It is, however, interesting to note that it was males who were taxed, implicitly suggesting that it was up to them to marry, something that could not be expected of young women, who were presumably subject to the authority of parents and subordinated to male initiative.

But women faced severe punishment should they deliberately reject a pregnancy. While miscarriages that were due to hard or unhealthy working conditions aroused no public response, a woman's deliberate rejection of a pregnancy was punished as a severe crime, with up to three years' imprisonment (and along with her any accomplices, including the husband if he was proved to have known which hardly ever happened). What was already regarded as a crime in previous legislation as well as by Catholic morality was made through the race laws into a crime against the race, and therefore against the nation. Those most exposed to this risk, and to the risk of death or disability resulting from dangerous practices in abortion, were working-class women and women of the lowest middle class, too poor to pay for the discretion and security of clinics and doctors, as confirmed by the 'Report on procured abortion offences brought to justice in 1941'.[24] On the one hand, judges appeared particularly reluctant to apply the full rigour of the law even when the offence was proven, justifying their indulgence by the poverty of the women having recourse to abortion and thereby implicitly denying the validity of the regime's pronatalist policy. On the other hand, women were always exposed to the arbitrariness of judges and of informers, fear of which often prevented timely resort to a doctor when something went wrong.

MOTHERS' WELFARE AND THE *OPERA NAZIONALE MATERNITÀ E INFANZIA*

The regime's most ambitious action, and also the one most directly aimed at the welfare of mother and child, was undoubtedly the ONMI, introduced by a law of 10 December 1925, amended in 1933 and 1934, and intended to 'promote, by acting to integrate the welfare tasks and the activities of other public and private institutions, the defence and physical and moral improvement of the race'.[25] A semi-governmental body, with a complex structure of central and peripheral agencies and offices in every province, it was to co-ordinate and supervise the whole range of activities and measures aimed at mothers and the young – from the running of *casse di maternità* (as long as they continued to exist), to the establishment of the paternity of illegitimate children, to the placing of minors in institutions and in jobs when they left them, up to supervision of juvenile delinquents. Much of this activity pre-dated the ONMI and in fact went on operating independently of it. But apart from its work of supervision and control, the novelty and the primary activity of the ONMI was assistance of pregnant women, women in childbed and the newborn up to the age of three. Indeed it lasted until the 1970s, when the ONMI crèches were converted into municipal crèches, and consultant obstetricians and paediatricians incorporated into the USSL (local health centres).

It should be noted that ONMI's health work had preventive and educative rather than curative aims. In this sense it was the first, and for long the only, preventive health initiative, acting on the three levels of adequate nutrition, hygiene and preventive checks (or prophylaxis, in the term used then, relating particularly to the risks of tuberculosis, alcoholism and syphilis, which were regarded as particularly widespread among the poorest urban strata). The ONMI's work was flanked by the work of the so-called circulating maternity classes, sort of itinerant rural schools, teaching the rudiments of child rearing and infant hygiene. Though they were less widespread than ONMI offices, and, on the admission of those in charge themselves, insufficient,[26] especially since they were aimed at the rural population, which was not only more numerous than the urban one but also more prolific, these maternity classes were the first indication of an interest in the actual conditions of rural families and their children. Paradoxically, they thereby continued, in bureaucratic and centralized fashion and for motives quite other than those of emancipation, the tradition of the rural literacy classes begun at the turn of the century by progressive and socialist intellectuals.

Women and children without adequate resources were entitled to assistance. This circumstance was ascertained not from some sort of certificate (for instance the certificate of poverty), but was decided at the discretion of the lady visitors. While this broadened the range of those potentially entitled to cover, in practice many working and working-class mothers and women of the lowest middle class, as well as single mothers who agreed to bring up their own children, it exposed the women to arbitrary assessment by women who, with no specific qualification apart from being selected by the provincial committees on the basis of their own morality, support for fascism and their 'predisposition for mother-and-child care', were entitled to go into their houses and judge their needs and their favourable attitude to the ONMI's role. Moreover, the fact that the ONMI was linked with the Party at both local and provincial level (party leaders were patrons by right, along with other institutional leaders – all men, except for the female secretary of the women's *fascio*) made its function of social and political control explicit, over and above the intentions, and perhaps also actions, of individual committees or individual members of them. The lady visitors themselves, who were not members as of right, were chosen not only among *fascio* members, but among upper- and middle-class women *fascio* members. This meant that women in the poorest strata wishing to benefit from ONMI services, or who came under its control, were subject to twofold scrutiny by other women (albeit by authority of the men in the medical, legal and party institutions): on a class and a party basis.

In every case, once the material, moral and political right to assistance had been ascertained, the pregnant women and then those who had given birth, with their children, were followed up from a hygienic and health viewpoint and also as regards nutrition, through travelling instructors who had the twofold aim of verifying the regularity of the pregnancy and growth of the children and of teaching the mothers the rules of hygiene and nutrition. As is evident from publications, in particular the organization's magazine *Maternità e infanzia*, hygienic rules and moral standards were often inextricably linked: not that this is a characteristic peculiar to fascism.

Where it was found necessary, mothers were also given food supplements through canteens for pregnant women from the sixth month on and for nursing mothers up to seven months. The obligation to go to the canteen, though aimed at guaranteeing that it was the mother who benefited from the food offered and not other members of the family and that the money was not spent for other reasons, had the further object of keeping under observation women who were otherwise regarded as not entirely capable of looking after themselves. Moreover, the centralization of the service made access difficult for those who, because they lived far away, could neither pay the transport nor afford to waste too many hours procuring the food, especially if they had other small children or had to go out for work.

Powdered milk or wet nurses were also supplied for mothers who could not nurse their babies themselves. Conversely, mothers who refused to breast-feed without medical justification received no assistance, so that their children were also excluded from all services (with a risk of having the child taken away should moral or material inadequacy be found). The same applied to single mothers who refused to keep their child (thereby leaving it to public assistance or the foundling home) or, though keeping it, did not want to breast-feed. There was an obligation to breast-feed on mothers who kept their children. This rule was not just meant to guarantee health in situations where it was hard to sterilize water and cows' milk and in which powdered milk was still uncommon. It also, if not primarily, expressed an image of a mother who is good because she breast-feeds, i.e. devotes everything to her child, and through breast-feeding develops, especially in the case of single mothers, a strong attachment to and sense of responsibility for the child.

Breast-feeding single mothers received not only assistance but also help in finding the father and convincing him that he should marry (through dowry bonuses), or at any rate secure economic support. The ONMI had the further duty of assisting separated women to secure payment of alimony. The legitimate family with a clear allocation of roles to each of the parents was affirmed, even if it was motherhood, accepted and performed in accordance with the prescribed hygienic and moral roles, that was directly being rewarded and supported. In this sense, unmarried mothers were not discriminated against, but received the same assistance as married mothers, which sometimes resulted in hostility from the latter, who saw this as 'rewarding' socially deviant and 'immoral' behaviour.[27]

The maternal and family pattern, combined with the model of the productive rural family and a specific authority structure as the ideal pattern for the growth and development of children, was also underlined by the preference given, at least in principle, to fostering, where possible in the countryside, over 'institutionalization', or else to the creation of small agricultural colonies with family-type educational arrangements. This was more an ideal than a reality, since institutionalization of children continued not only throughout the fascist period but well beyond it. The inertia, and also the power of the existing structures, mostly belonging to religious orders, proved stronger than the regime's intentions; in any case, the latter did not make much financial investment in this direction, apart from having little time to achieve anything. Concern for good child rearing soon took second place to sending their fathers and brothers to war in the 1930s, whilst their own conditions of daily survival, nutrition and even physical safety deteriorated. Imperial expansion was the aim of the concern for mothers and children, and war was its paradoxical conclusion.

Activities directed at children who stayed with their mothers in the family also remained well below the potential number of users, contrary to intentions. According to the figures published at the time and clearly intended as a defence of the system, in 1934 children under three who received some form of assistance numbered some 475,000 over the whole nation, amounting to some 50 per cent of all those receiving ONMI assistance (pregnant women, nursing mothers, infants). Of these, 326,000 had attended the consulting-rooms for at least one paediatric visit. The others were presumably cases of institutionalization, fostering or home visits. In the same year, only 17,779 children under three were received into ONMI crèches. These were mainly children of working mothers. Even with this restriction, given the rates of female employment at the time, the figure appears very low. Finally, the ONMI paid for meals for needy children aged between three and six in kindergartens: these numbered 155,000, again for 1934.[28]

The spread of activity seems numerically fairly uniform throughout the nation, but the distribution of individual services shows a concentration of crèches in the northern towns, where there were higher rates of female employment in industry. Children of female farm labourers, home workers, moonlighters or housemaids scarcely had access to this type of service. The same applies, as indeed for all ONMI services, to mothers and children who could not or would not prove need. The welfare function of the ONMI, in addition to its ideological function, excluded from preventive and support services a broad sector of mothers and children in the middle and lower classes, as well as almost all women living in the countryside, but also those in the more stable working class where economic conditions and desire for privacy and respectability did not permit display of visible need, and at the same time did not allow recourse to paid assistance. Assistance was a matter for their own resources or for family solidarity.

While the class exclusions were bound up with the ONMI's welfare character and the exclusions based on morality with its ideology, the introduction of the anti-Jewish race laws in 1938 brought one further type of possible exclusion or self-exclusion: that of Jewish mothers and children.[29] Along with the imperial, expansionist aims of the regime, this race demarcation undoubtedly constitutes one of the gravest and most dramatic paradoxes of the regime's activity, which, after all, in day-to-day matters had been based more or less on common sense and even on solidarity with the neediest and had sought to combine fascist mystique with modern pedagogy (which was visible in the sometimes disquieting patchwork of theoretical references in the writings of the time). For all the emphasis on procreation, even within the very measures taken to encourage it, what was being done was to state who was entitled to be rewarded as a mother and as a child, thereby defining them as having rights as well as needs.

The reduction of the woman as mother to a pregnant or nursing being – the only conditions that entitled her to preventive health advice, to possible treatment and to welfare – represented a severe limitation of her rights as a person. This limitation was to apply for much longer than fascism itself, since for long in Italy women were regarded as having rights only through recognition of their duties – actual or potential – as mothers. Accordingly, their rights often appeared simultaneously as protection and as constraint.

These were serious limitations, to which should be added the fact that the major part of the female population, including those eligible for welfare, had no easy access before, during, and after pregnancy, to the conditions of adequate hygiene and healthy nutrition taught by the lady visitors, obstetricians and social workers of the ONMI; still less to adequate health care, so that infant mortality rates continued high throughout the fascist period, even after the establishment of the ONMI, and began to fall only after the war.[30] Nevertheless, the ONMI cannot be reduced to a mere creature of the regime. It was not only in fascist Italy that women and children had access to recognition of their needs and rights only on the basis of the government's national and imperial interests. Moreover, this recognition of rights, despite its limits, not only constituted the first form of service and support aimed directly at women and their children, without the mediation of fathers. It also – though this was an unforeseen and unintended consequence – formed a basis from which, in the changed cultural, social and political context, women were able to begin to formulate their own needs and rights in terms of rights to health and services: as mothers, but not only as mothers.

NOTES

1 On this issue see also D. Detragiache, 'Un aspect de la politique démographique de l'Italie fasciste: la répression de l'avortement', in *Mélanges de l'Ecole Française de Rome. Moyen Age–Temps Modernes*, 1980, vol. 92, pp. 693–735, esp. p. 697.
2 F. Loffredo, *Politica della famiglia*, Milan, Bompiani, 1936. See also G. Rugiu, 'Teoria della popolazione e politica demografica', in C. Gini (ed.), *Trattato elementare di statistica*, vol. II, *Demografia*, Milan, 1933, pp. 21–3; B. W. Gorjux, *La responsabilità della donna italiana nel regime fascista*, Rome, Fasci Femminili 1936.
3 See the comments by post-war legal scholars, e.g. P. Ungari, *Il diritto di famiglia in Italia*, Bologna, Il Mulino, 1970, pp. 178–9; C. Cardia, *Il diritto di famiglia in Italia*, Rome, Editori Riuniti, 1975, pp. 204–5.
4 See, e.g., M. Livi Bacci, *Donna, fecondità e figli*, Bologna, Il Mulino, 1980, p. 342.
5 On working-class living conditions in particular during fascism, see my article 'La famiglia italiana sotto il fascismo', in *Annali della fondazione Giangiacomo Feltrinelli*, 1979/80, vol. 22, pp. 189–230.
6 On the *Opera Nazionale Dopolavoro* see E.R. Tannenbaum, *L'esperienza fascista. Cultura e società in Italia dal 1922 al 1945*, Milan, Mursia, 1974 (*The Fascist Experience. Italian Society and Culture*, New York, Basic Books, 1972); V. de Grazia, *Consenso e cultura di massa nell'Italia fascista*, Bari, Laterza, 1981 (*The Culture of Consent. Mass Organizations of Leisure in Fascist Italy*, New York, Cambridge University Press, 1981).
7 Cf. A. de Grand, 'Women under Italian fascism', *The Historical Journal*, 1976, vol. 19, no. 4, p. 968.
8 Cf. ibid., pp. 947–68; E. Scaramuzza, 'Professioni intellettuali e fascismo. L'ambivalenza dell'Alleanza Muliebre Culturale Italiana', *Italia contemporanea*, Sept. 1983, pp. 111–33; S. Franchini, 'L'istruzione femminile in Italia dopo l'unità: percorsi di una ricerca sugli educandati pubblici di elite', *Passato e presente*, 1986, vol. 10, pp. 53–94. For an overview of recent research on women and fascism see M. Fraddosio, 'Le donne e il fascismo. Ricerche e problemi di interpretazione', *Storia contemporanea*, 1986, vol. 17, no. 1, pp. 95–135.
9 See, e.g., P. Meldini, *Sposa e madre esemplare*, Bologna, Guaraldi, 1975, pp. 19–26.
10 De Grand, 'Women', p. 961.
11 See Scaramuzza, 'Professioni'. On the complex relations between feminism, or some strata that in the early years of the century had associated themselves with feminism as well as with fascism, see also, along with De Grand's article, F. Pieroni Bortolotti, *Socialismo e questione femminile in Italia, 1892–1922*, Milan, Mazzotta, 1974; E. Santarelli, 'Il fascismo e le ideologie antifemministe', *Problemi del socialismo*, 1976, vol. 8, no. 4, pp. 83–5.
12 This was to become obvious in the period of autarchy, when the various homekeeping books read by middle-class housewives, e.g. the *Consigli di Petronilla*, started to suggest ersatz tea or coffee, artificial wool clothes, etc., and became involuntarily comic during the war, when the ever-present Petronilla was telling how to make pasta and desserts without sugar, without eggs, without milk and even without flour. See M. Mafai, *Pane nero*, Milan, Feltrinelli, 1987.
13 See M. Matteotti, *La classe lavoratrice sotto la dominazione fascista. 1921–1943*,

Rome–Milan, Edizioni Avanti!, 1944; B. Buozzi, 'Le condizioni della classe lavoratrice in Italia, 1922–1943', (ed. A. Andreasi, in *Annali dell'Istituto Giangiacomo Feltrinelli*, 1972, vol. 14, pp. 423–76; M. Saibante, 'Il tenore di vita del popolo italiano prima dell'ultima guerra in confronto con quello degli altri popoli', in Commissione per la riconversione *Rapporto al Ministero dell'Industria e del commercio*, Rome, Ministero dell' Industria e del commercio, 1947, pp. 197–200; V. Zamagni, 'La dinamica dei salari nel settore industriale, 1921–1939', *Quaderni storici*, 1975, vol. x, no. 2–3, pp. 530–49.

14 The percentage of women in the total work-force fell from 26.9 per cent in 1921 to 24 per cent in 1936, though female employment rates continued to remain high if compared with later ones in the 1960s. See L. Fornaciari, 'Osservazioni sull'andamento del lavoro femminile in Italia', *Rivista internazionale di scienze sociali*, 1956, vol. 27, no. 4, pp. 222–5; N. Federici, 'Caratteristiche e problemi dell'occupazione e disoccupazione femminile', *Inchiesta parlamentare sulla disoccupazione*, book IV, vol. 5, 1953, pp. 88–93.

15 The 1931 census showed that approximately 22 per cent of families' breadwinners were blue-collar workers; white-collar workers 5.7 per cent, professionals 2.5 per cent, businessmen 3.6 per cent, traders and craftsmen 9.6 per cent. Breadwinners involved in agriculture in various ways were over 40 per cent.

16 See G. Napolitano, 'La politica demografica tra le classi lavoratrici', *Critica fascista*, 1935, vol. 10, pp. 197–8; R. Sarti, *Fascismo e grande industria. 1919–1940*, Milan, Moizzi, 1977, pp. 92–3.

17 For an analysis of the transformations of the *Casse di Maternità* see A. Buttafuoco's contribution to this volume and A. Cherubini, *Storia della previdenza sociale*, Rome, Editori Riuniti, 1967; I. Piva and G. Maddelena, 'La tutela delle lavoratrici madri nel periodo 1923–1943', in M. Petri and A. Gigli Marchetti (eds), *Salute e classi lavoratrici in Italia dall'unità al fascismo*, Milan, F. Angeli, 1982, pp. 835–56.

18 See the remarks by Fassio, cited by Meldini, *Sposa*, p. 103; and by M. Matteotti, *La classe*, pp. 99ff.; G. Sapelli, *Organizzazione, lavoro e innovazione industriale nell'Italia tra le due guerre*, Turin, Rosenberg & Sellier, 1978, pp. 368–96.

19 See A. Cherubini, *Storia* and I. Piva and G. Maddalena, 'La tutela'.

20 See chp. 9 of M. Barbagli, *Sotto lo stesso tetto*, Bologna, Il Mulino, 1986; C. Saraceno, 'Percorsi di vita femminile sotto il fascismo', *Memoria*, 1981, vol. 2, pp. 64–75.

21 For a full presentation of the regime's pronatalist measures and its financial investments see ISTAT (*Istituto Centrale di Statistica*), 'L'azione promossa dal governo nazionale a favore dell'incremento demografico', *Annali di statistica*, 1943, 7th series. A summary table taken from this text can be found in M. Livi Bacci, *Donna*, p. 343; see also the overview in the chapter on Italy by D. V. Glass, *Population Policies and Movements*, (first edn 1940) repr. London, Frank Cass, 1967.

22 Figures from the table in M. Livi Bacci, *Donna*.

23 The marriage rate remained constant throughout the period at around 7.3 per thousand, apart from a peak of 8.3 per thousand in 1937 after the end of the Ethiopian War (which presumably meant postponement of marriage by young soldiers sent to the fighting). As for the marriage age of males, from 1921 onwards there was a clear decline in marriage under the age of 25; while between 1921 and 1930 some 34.7 per cent of males were married by that age, in the period from 1931–1940, despite the tax on bachelorhood, the figure was only 24.7 per cent. The average age was 27. See S. Somogy, 'Nuzialità', in ISTAT, *Sviluppo della popolazione italiana dal 1861 al 1961*, Rome, 1981, pp. 321–96.

24 This report has been analysed by D. Detragiache, 'Un aspect', esp. pp. 701ff.
25 P. Corsi, *La tutela della maternità e dell'infanzia in Italia*, Rome, Società Editrice Novissima, 1936, p. 21. On the ONMI see also S. Fabbri, *L'Opera Nazionale per la protezione della maternità e dell'infanzia*, Milan, Mondadori, 1933; G. de Robilant, *L'assistenza obbligatoria agli illegittimi riconosciuti*, Turin, Tipografia Vincenzo Bona, 1937.
26 Cf. Lo Monaco Aprile, 'Il sistema fascista di difesa dell'infanzia illegittima', *Politica sociale*, March–April 1930, pp. 278–87.
27 L. Passerini, *Torino operaia e fascismo*, Bari, Laterza, 1984, pp. 185–220. This study presents interviews with women workers and shows the divisive effects of the regime's pronatalism not only between married and unmarried mothers but also between women with and without children. Sometimes the fact of not having children or having only a few is seen as a form of resistance to fascism; at other times hostility to prolific women was a hostility towards people seen as exploiting the community.
28 P. Corsi, *La tutela*, p. 45; S. Fabbri, *Direttive e chiarimenti intorno allo spirito informatore della legislazione riguardante l'ONMI e alle sue pratiche applicazione*, Rome, Failli, 1934.
29 The situation of Jewish women after 1938, when marriage between Jews and non-Jews was forbidden, following the German model of 1935, has not yet been studied. For the different population policies in National Socialist Germany which reached from antinatalism to physical elimination (the latter pursued also in the northern parts of Italy through the German occupation from 1943 on), see G. Bock, *Zwangssterilisation im Nationalsozialismus: Studien zur Rassenpolitik und Frauenpolitik*, Opladen, Westdeutscher Verlag, 1986, and her chapter in this volume.
30 The infant mortality rate was 120 per thousand born in the period 1921–1930, 102 for 1931–40, 90 for 1941–50, 52 for 1951–60.

Chapter 11

Housework and motherhood: debates and policies in the women's movement in Imperial Germany and the Weimar Republic

Irene Stoehr

From the late nineteenth century, the German women's movement discussed the issues of women's domestic work and of maternity, mothers' rights and mothers' protection, in the context of female emancipation. In 1905 Käthe Schirmacher, a prominent member of the *Verband Fortschrittlicher Frauenvereine* (VFF, League of Progressive Women's Associations), the umbrella organization of the left or radical wing of the *bürgerliche* (meaning civic as well bourgeois) women's movement, argued at a meeting of the VFF that women's domestic work was 'real work', 'value-creating work', 'productive work', even though 'it may look like nothing'; that it includes many different activities, and that 'there is no more "productive work" than that of the mother who, all by herself, creates the value of values, called a human being'. She protested against 'the exploitation of the housewife and mother' and asked for an economic, legal and social re-evaluation of this work, including its payment.[1] Later on and somewhat surprisingly, the issues of housework and of motherhood were discussed rather separately. This chapter presents the two strands of this debate. It will be argued that the heated debate on the value of women's domestic work was subdued by incorporating this value into the older concept of women's more general 'cultural contribution' (*Kulturleistung*), the social recognition of which became the main emancipatory goal; that physical mothers took second place to 'spiritual motherhood' and that, during the Weimar Republic, women's common efforts to raise the level of maternity welfare were conspicuous but their results remained limited, because of economic crises, lack of response on the part of the political world at large, but also because of the concept of 'spiritual motherhood' itself.

HOUSEWORK AND ITS VALUE: PAYING, UPGRADING OR ABOLISHING IT?

When Schirmacher in her lecture denied that the economic emancipation of housewives required them to work, in addition, outside the home, and instead called for payment of their domestic work, most of the housewives present agreed; most other speakers disagreed, above all because the claim for payment of housework was perceived as an expression of excessive 'individualism'. Schirmacher's remarks were meant as a counter-statement to Maria Lischnewska's lecture on 'the economic reform of marriage'. Lischnewska had impressed progressive women with the then very popular idea that the family economy was in the process of disintegration. She had linked this theory with the emerging ideas on communal living, such as those of Social Democrat Lily Braun who propagated, from 1901, collective houses or 'centralized households'. Lischnewska stressed the importance of the reorganization and reduction of individual housework, which was to result from these institutions, mainly as a precondition for the employment of wives and mothers. She was concerned not only with women's economic independence but with their value to the national economy, which in her view had replaced the family economy, and therefore saw the married female factory worker as the 'prototype of the New Woman'. This view included a markedly negative evaluation of the non-employed housewife, which was no doubt the immediate stimulus for Schirmacher's counter-statement. Lischnewska described the housewife as 'only consuming' and as 'supported', referring explicitly to the definition in the Imperial Statistical Office's classification for the occupational census of 1895.[2]

Yet four years earlier the VFF had itself protested against this definition. Its 'Memorandum to the Imperial Statistical Office' of 1901, signed by the first president, Minna Cauer, and the secretary, Maria Lischnewska herself, anticipated Schirmacher's argument of 1905: 'Let the Imperial Statistical Office adopt a classification for the next census that will give married women's work in the domestic economy the value it deserves in the occupational statistics, as the exercise of an occupation that is one of the most important to the national economy'. Four columns in *Die Frauenbewegung*, the VFF's official journal, argued that 'professional work' in the home is a 'productive occupation' even when performed by the wife or the domestic servant. The authors accused the Statistical Office of wrongly including wives and maids 'in the category of supported persons, i.e. of those of inferior economic value'. Instead they claimed for the housewife the title of 'supporter', in a twofold respect: she was active not only 'in the form of services', but additionally provided 'products of value to economic output'. According to the Statistical Office's definition, either would be enough in order to be counted in the category of 'supporter'. 'Husband and wife are . . . complementary supporters of equal economic value', the Memorandum states, in stark contrast to Lischnewska's later statement.[3]

Another prominent representative of the VFF, Helene Stöcker, in 1902 in her essay on 'Domestic economy as a profession', took the Memorandum as a cue to call for 'financial independence' for housewives and mothers, in view of the work they performed.[4] Whereas she took the prevailing theory of the shift of productive work out of the household fully into account, she nevertheless noted a transformation – rather than the oft-asserted disintegration – of family work into an 'administrative and organizational, even directly interventionist, activity'. It might not be productive, but it was valuable and 'measurable in figures'. Yet Stöcker avoided the terms 'payment' and 'wages' as well as any proposal as to where to address any such demands. She did propose that 'the state should guarantee to every mother a child raising allowance' as something quite fascinating, though with a 'very painful obverse': it might 'endanger the responsibility painfully arrived at over time in husbands'. In the last instance, she left the solution of the problem to those who 'wish to keep woman in family life and the "home"' and recommended that they should 'finally draw the consequences of their own views and transform the housewife's activity, which they see as the sole and "natural occupation" of woman, into a genuine "profession"'.

At the time of the women's meeting of 1905, with Schirmacher and Lischnewska as speakers, Helene Stöcker had ceased to interest herself in the issue. The co-founder and central figure of the new *Bund für Mutterschutz* (BfM, League for the Protection of Mothers) was now committed to the idea of gender reconciliation, which had also formed the background to her previous reflections on other issues. With regard to the question of the domestic economy, she had seen the fact that 'the man valued his activity too highly and the woman hers too low' as an important reason for the 'fateful gap between the sexes', which in her later activities she sought directly to overcome, namely by sexual reform. The BfM, in the way Stöcker as president shaped it, stood for 'a growing together of the sexes on a basis of mutual understanding', and it was not by accident that it was the first women's organization with about a third of active male members.[5]

In fact, radical demands on behalf of housewives and mothers at this time were if anything in conflict with the ideal of gender reconciliation. In this context, the original founder of the BfM, Ruth Bré, was early on excluded from the organization by Stöcker and her friends. Her plea for 'mothers' rights', instead of 'parents' rights' as called for by other members of the executive, isolated her from the beginning, as did her project to set up settlements for single mothers and their children in the countryside. These settlements were to be financed by government subsidies, which would render mothers independent of the fathers of their children. Likewise, Bré's view that 'the woman with her child already constitutes a fully complete family' met with opposition from the BfM.[6]

Even though Ruth Bré did not deal with housework as such, her writings nevertheless resemble those of Käthe Schirmacher above all in the rhetoric of the battle between the sexes. In 1905 Schirmacher had analysed the male wage as dependent on women's domestic work; the latter was the *'conditio sine qua non* for the husband's employment outside the home'. Accordingly, the husband owed the wife half of his earnings. His employer could secure the man's work only by making it possible for him to 'be replaced by a wife in the indispensable domestic work'. Therefore it might appear that the husband was working for two, 'whereas in fact he is only pocketing for two'. While Schirmacher had no scruples about directing wage demands to the husband, she also formulated a related problem which was later brought up against her: the wife's work load was in inverse ratio to her husband's wage. Hence her opinion that 'every housewife and mother who works without being paid incurs indebtedness of the whole society to her', and this debt included also the work of single mothers. She recognized state subsidies such as the widows' pension as a possible model for payment for housework, and she referred to a future 'social world' ('ours does not unfortunately deserve this name') in which 'the repayment of this debt would be organized on a large scale'.[7]

Schirmacher certainly did not share one of the scruples that many progressive proponents of women's rights felt at the idea of a wage demand against the husband: she had no fears about matrimonial peace. When, four years later, she discussed unequal pay for men's and women's employment, she once again fought for an economic upgrading of women's work, conceptualizing it as a gender struggle. Men's extra earnings amounted to a 'sex bonus'. In the case of married men, it was a 'family supplement' which was really due to the wife and ought to be paid to her directly. The 'sex bonus' was also given to unmarried men so that they could buy sexual intercourse. It meant that men could take with both hands: '*His* pay incorporates the earnings of the legitimate wife, and *his* wages are increased in order that he can buy an *illegitimate* wife: the "family supplement" is based on a twofold robbery of women.' Already in 1905, when she had answered the question as to why men had such a low estimate of women's domestic work, Schirmacher had not spared the other sex: 'We live in a "man's world", created by man in the first place for himself, after *his own* image, for *his* comfort. In this world, man has made himself the measure of all things and beings, and the measure of women too. Whoever wanted to be *his equal* had to be *equal to him*, to do what he did, in order to secure his respect. For him, *equal value* lay only in *sameness*; only assimilation could count for him as equality.'[8]

Käthe Schirmacher's 'counter-statement' of 1905 was not a sudden intervention by an outsider, but it radicalized earlier arguments for the symbolic and financial recognition of domestic work put forward by the radical wing of the women's movement since the turn of the century; moreover, she was strongly influenced by her familiarity with the French women's movement from the 1890s when she had first, and in French, formulated her reflections.[9] It is not so much the sharpness of Schirmacher's polemic as the rejection of her position by many speakers of the association that allows us to conclude that contrary approaches had emerged or were growing stronger. They included the establishment of a number of communal households and single-kitchen tenements, the development of the BfM with its focus on sexual reform, and a considerable number of voices that tended to criticize housewives.

The lawyer Anita Augspurg, a major figure of the 'radical wing' and editor of *Die Frauenbewegung*, is a case in point. On the occasion of the 1905 meat price increases, she attributed some of the fault to housewives: 'The economic blindness of the much-praised German housewife, whose intelligence is limited by the walls of her kitchen and pantry, whose political indifference and incomprehension is counted as a virtue, has largely contributed to this emergency.'[10] Interestingly enough, Augspurg herself had two years earlier engaged in the debate on maternity insurance, with the most far-reaching proposal to date. Following the Swedish feminist Ellen Key, she had called for an eighteen months' 'state maternity pension' as payment for 'mothers' contribution to the state', so that women could 'devote themselves to their maternal duties independently of their husbands and without worries about sustenance'. It was not by accident that her demand for payment of mother-work, including that of women without jobs and 'right up to the wives of ministers', coincided with the period when the VFF still endeavoured to raise the value of domestic work.[11]

From the start, in 1895, of women's debate over the new German Civil Code, which she led, Augspurg advocated the reform of matrimonial property law, but she did not link this issue to that of the valuation of housework, even though the VFF had argued against discrimination against non-employed wives as being 'supported persons' on the grounds not only of their labour power but also of their property.[12] In the struggle for property rights, the point was to prevent the acquisition of the wife's goods by the husband, just as the debate over the value of housework aimed at rendering visible the wife's economic contribution, concealed behind the husband's earnings. But this link faded into the background, as did that between housework and motherhood and that between housework and 'love'. The separation of these areas even became an outline of a programme: 'We must above all clearly separate marriage, homekeeping and child raising as three independent institutions, by showing that each of them exists separately without the others', wrote the Hungarian radical feminist Rosika Schwimmer in a pamphlet which propagated the idea of the centralized household in 1907.[13] Even Käthe Schirmacher no longer raised the issue of pay for housework when she spoke about 'facilitating housework through modern technology' at a meeting of the VFF in 1909, pointing instead to an 'intellectualization of women' as a consequence of industrialization. It was the president of the *Bund Deutscher Frauenvereine* (BDF, League of German Women's Associations), Marie Stritt, who raised the subject again at the same meeting. She decisively opposed 'statutory provision for paying the wife for her domestic activity according to the husband's income', since any such provision would 'only make marriages more difficult, whereas the wife's employment would make them easier'.[14]

Whereas on the left or radical wing of the women's movement the valuation of housework clearly declined, the argument was taken up by the moderate majority of the German women's movement and posed in permanent terms. 'The Women's Movement regards as the primary and immediate profession of the married woman the duties involved in marriage and family', runs the first sentence in the 1905 programme of the *Allgemeiner Deutscher Frauenverein* (ADF, General German Association of Women), characteristically under the title 'Professional activities', not under that of 'Marriage and family' (which was of course also part of the programme). 'The satisfying performance of this vocation', it continues, 'must be secured in the interest of society by all the means of education, economic reform and legal protection. Women's work in the performance of this vocation shall be valued, both economically and legally, as a fully valid cultural contribution'. In her explanation of the programme, ADF president Helene Lange underlined that this valuation did not yet constitute a demand for payment for this 'cultural contribution': 'An attempt to express it externally', indeed 'to seek to assess the husband's debt in figures' seemed to her to be 'premature today'. For the 'convictions that would make such proposals acceptable' were 'not yet a part of the general moral consciousness', not least because of the 'low estimate of the family tasks shown by women themselves', for instance when they called on every housewife to accept a job 'in addition'. Seven years later the time was ripe for official 'Principles and demands of the women's movement in the area of marriage and the family' issued by the BDF. It claimed that the work of the housewife 'also be counted as a fully valued task and that she be granted a solid claim to a sum from the husband's income for her personal needs'.[15]

In these years there had been a reorientation in the moderate women's movement, characterized by its increasing interest in housework and the family. The great exhibition 'Woman in home and employment' at Berlin in 1912 documented this turn. In her talk on 'Valuing housewives' work', Marianne Weber formulated the henceforth valid position on the question, which had, since Schirmacher's 1905 essay, 'no longer entirely disappeared from the debate'.[16] Weber, by defining the problem as married women's need for 'financial independence', significantly deviated from the implications of her title, the question of valuation, in order to reject the claim for a 're-evaluation of housework' and of its payment as 'only one of several possible solutions'. What disturbed Weber about Schirmacher's argument was the close connection between housewives' work and housewives' pay; in Weber's view, housewives' claims ought to be guided not by their work but by their family income. Her own proposal – 'introduction of property separation as the statutory property situation' and the 'right of the wife to agreed fixed housekeeping money and to certain special money' – appears as a modest answer to her question as to financial independence. In fact, economic independence of mothers did not seem to her at all desirable. Her main criticism of a 'motherhood endowment' high enough to provide modest sustenance for mothers and their children – for which funds were lacking anyway – was that this would mean a highly undesirable economic emancipation of husbands and fathers (from their maintenance obligations). Like many of her colleagues in the progressive women's association, Weber was so concerned with marital harmony as even to regard the proposal for a community of goods giving both marital partners equal access to their income as unacceptable to husbands.

However, by comparison with the 'Principles and demands of the women's movement', Weber's solution was an advance in two respects: in the first place, a claim on legislation was formulated for the first time, and second, the distinction between 'housekeeping money' and 'special money' made it clear that the wife's needs were not to be taken as identical with the needs of the household. For those who objected that her proposal meant no improvement for workers' wives because they had in any case to spend the total family income for the family's mere survival, Weber pointed to other experiences. At the 'First German Conference to Promote the Interests of Working Women' in 1907, an initiative set up by various women's organizations, working-class women had spoken in public. They complained of the heavy 'burden on the family income because of the husband's personal needs, above all his drinking'. The remedies proposed by progressive speakers, such as better conditions on the job, were opposed by the women workers with a call for higher wages for their husbands and for a higher share of them to be devoted to the family.[17]

Marianne Weber's statement to the 1912 Berlin Women's Congress made it clear that the moderate women's movement was not intending to question the sexual division of income through fair payment for housework. But the procedure to separate the question of pay from that of work had a further implication, namely the concept of women's 'cultural contribution' (*Kulturleistung*) with which this women's movement legitimized itself. Gertrud Bäumer in particular dealt with the relationship between women's cultural contribution and the money question. For instance, in 1906 she rejected with gentle mockery the assertion by her friend Friedrich Naumann that on one side, 'the production of human beings' made up women's 'economic value' but that, on the other side, it was 'work that could not be paid for'. In her own view, she informed this main representative of national social liberalism, 'the money economy is quite simply compelling us to express even these, the finest spiritual values, in money terms'. She did not therefore favour motherhood endowment. Whereas Naumann basically wanted, by his argument, to encourage employed women to have children too – and therefore called for a removal of the marriage bar and for the combination of motherhood and employment – Bäumer and most other moderate women advocated that combination only in such cases where mothers had to take a job because of economic need. Above all, she did not wish to throw doubt on the 'economic value' of the childless, employed woman.[18]

On another occasion Bäumer, reporting to a women's conference on the population question in the second winter of World War I, spoke against motherhood endowment. Representatives of the BDF had met to criticize the population policy proposals of the male *Verein für Volkswohlfahrt* (Association for the People's Welfare), because it treated 'the question of the birth-rate exclusively from the military viewpoint': 'A whole bribery system of insurances, recognitions and compensations, in order to conjure up life.' On behalf of the women's movement, Gertrud Bäumer stood out against 'an arms race by mothers' set going by representatives of the association. Yet the BDF did not reject pronatalist policies in principle. In 1915, for instance, it formulated the 'women's position' on this issue as the demand for reforms 'which guarantee mothers the possibility of a fully felt experience of motherhood'. Maternity and infant care could not go far enough. The state was called on directly to provide money for such reforms, and taxation on childless and unmarried people seemed one way; such proposals had become popular shortly before the war and were a controversial topic in the women's movement, particularly as to whether it was aimed not only at bachelors, but at single women too.[19]

The function of housework in increasing the value of wages was not questioned by the moderate women's movement. At the 'First German Conference to Promote the Interests of Working Women', Helene Simon proposed two measures 'whereby the purchasing power of wages could be increased' by making housework more efficient: consumers' co-operatives and domestic science education 'which would render the working woman able to use her or the family's income in more rational ways'. In this context, the German women's movement, often on a local level, set up cooking and household schools in the 1890s, propagated a work year for women, elaborated curricula for female social workers' schools and adult education and became involved in plans for rationalizing housework during the Weimar Republic.[20]

But the interest of the women's movement, which saw itself as a 'cultural movement', was not limited to the economic aspect of any women's work, and the attempt to incorporate women's home and family life into this cultural movement ultimately led it to focus on other issues than payment for such work. A pointer to this is the above-mentioned 1905 programme in which the ADF formulated not only the material value of housework, but also, and for the first time, its own overall political theory. Its starting point was 'the fact of a general physical and emotional difference between the sexes', resulting in the need for a 'cooperation of equal value between man and woman', so that 'all possibilities for cultural progress could be realized'. The moderate women's movement thus called for equal rights not on the basis of human rights but of women's rights and tasks; their objective was to 'permit the full inner development and free external efficacy of woman's cultural influence', and women should see this as their most worthy task.[21]

This formulation was the outcome of years of struggle for access to hitherto male professions, particularly academic ones, and to public positions. They concerned the emancipation of mostly childless, often unmarried women, and it was argued that women would bring a 'special cultural contribution', resulting from their maternal capacities, to a world which was shaped, one-sidedly, by men and male values. This was the emancipatory programme of 'expanded' or 'organized motherhood', applied to all areas of women's lives. The novelty here was not just the discovery of the value of women's domestic work, but above all the application of the concept of 'spiritual motherhood' to housework and mother-work, combined with the claim to transform this work too into a 'cultural contribution'.[22]

The immediate stimuli for this new orientation were the attempt of radical women to make the 'private' public, the response to the debate on housework in the VFF and to the foundation of the BfM and, finally, the fact that woman's domain, the home, was no longer unaffected by industrialization on the one hand, and by state intervention (e.g. through welfare legislation) on the other. The moderate women's movement saw the transformations in domestic economy less as a loss of function[23] than as a loss of women's power. To regain influence in their traditional private sphere, women had to emerge from it by rendering it public. Women's counter-strategy to the socialization of the 'private sphere' from above was, as it were, a politicization of housework 'from below'.

Many participants in the moderate women's movement were less interested in political suffrage (even though the demand was included in the 1905 ADF statement) than in this 'politicization' of housework. 'Politics' was understood here not as a consequence of the acquisition of civil rights, whereby a part of the person enters the political public sphere in order to act as a *zoon politikon* there, but as a concerted effort to render women's sphere public, especially their domestic work. Women should become aware of the economic and political importance of their daily work and carry over its importance into practical politics.[24] The strategy of upgrading housework and motherhood into a cultural contribution in the women's movement's sense came to incorporate the objective of economic re-evaluation, as well as the earlier ethos of fulfilment of duties. The cultural contribution was no longer only to serve the 'common good', but also to meet women's interest in shaping society according to their own views and needs. Yet this approach was not able to give precision to the exchange value of female cultural contributions. In fact, said Bäumer in 1906, it would be a materialist misunderstanding of the women's movement to view women's social valuation as dependent on the 'total value of the money that the totality of women receives in cash'. It depended instead much more 'on the total impact of the effects produced by them'.[25]

THE WOMEN'S MOVEMENT AND MOTHERS' PROTECTION

'How is it possible to educate girls to the profession of motherhood?' was Ruth Bré's indignant response to such a demand put forward by Helene Lange. 'What if the girl wants to become a mother, after completing this education to be a mother? She is not allowed to. She has to wait until a man wants to become a father and takes her on as a vehicle. How is it possible to expose a girl to such false images? Or does Miss Helene Lange's speech at the Women's Congress mean only education in "everyman's motherhood" (*Allerweltsmutterschaft*)?' This was Bré's mocking term for the moderate women's slogan of 'spiritual (or emotional, social, expanded, organized) motherhood'. In fact, for them spiritual motherhood counted more than physical motherhood. 'It is not simply a paean to physical motherhood that the women's movement sings', underlined Agnes von Zahn-Harnack in her account of the movement's history:

> It is only where physical motherhood purifies itself and breaks through into spiritual motherhood that we can speak of the highest fulfilment of life, which does not at all consist in the fact that a newborn child is lying in a cradle.[26]

The concept of *geistige Mütterlichkeit* had been coined in 1870 by Henriette Schrader-Breymann. Linked to the newly created profession of nursery-school teacher, the term expressed the view that motherhood in no way presupposed physical maternity.[27] The women's movement took it up later and made it refer to the demands for employment and participation by mostly childless women, arguing that maternity was in principle a quality of all women, and expressed not only in the family. Initially these politics of motherhood had not much to do with actual mothers. The BfM challenged the majority of the German movement not least because its valuation of unwed motherhood jeopardized the primacy of spiritual motherhood. The journal *Die Frau*, published by Helene Lange, warned against one of the 'most dangerous generalizations', namely of calling children 'the wealth of the nation in and for themselves' and therefore 'making the unmarried mother quite generally into a martyr of society'. To be sure, it was only Ruth Bré among the founding members of the BfM that had expressed herself in this hyperbolic way. She wanted to have the concept of 'mothers' protection' (*Mutterschutz*), which she had introduced, understood entirely in this sense. The concept very soon became popular, but for something quite different, namely for the public measures aimed, in the words of Alice Salomon, at 'removing a state of emergency brought about by the condition of motherhood – that is by pregnancy, accouchement and breast-feeding'.[28] The German women's movements – including the BfM and the Social Democratic women – were largely responsible for the general use of the term *Mutterschutz* in this limited sense. Although they often called for protection of all mothers, they nonetheless placed it in the tradition of female labour protection, since the major issue was to protect pregnant and nursing women against the harmful effects of factory work.

In 1898, four years after its foundation, the BDF set up a Committee on Protection of Women Workers, following its recent shift in priorities from the issue of education to the 'social question' whereby it had responded to the 'new era in social policy', i.e. the abrogation of the anti-socialist law, the rise of the Social Democratic Party (SPD) and of labour protection laws.[29] The far-reaching agreement between both wings of the independent women's movement (the moderate and the radical) and the Social Democratic women's organization in advocating protection for women workers was seen by its major proponents as a specifically German phenomenon; opposition to it was criticized by Helene Simon as the 'most desolate expression of outdated Manchesterism'. However, regardless of this significant consensus, hostility between the SPD women's organizations and the independent women's movement continued, mostly for ideological reasons, up to World War I.[30]

In Germany, a law of 1878 intended to protect mothers had introduced a mandatory maternity leave for factory workers of three weeks after birth (one year after the first such European law enacted in Switzerland). Social Democrat Lily Braun criticized the law for not including factory inspection, so that it was evaded by most women workers, with the silent connivance of employers and the government. Alice Salomon stressed that the women would understandably evade it as long as such protection meant a loss of earnings.[31] This position was characteristic for the motherhood protection policy of the entire women's movement. They underlined the importance of the money issue for effective protection of mothers. On the other hand, financial and other material benefits were called for exclusively in order to make the legal maternity leave effective.

Whereas male progressives, such as Alfons Fischer, praised the Bismarckian health insurance act of 1883, which included maternity benefits for women workers (but it was optional, the payment being at the discretion of the sickness funds), as being a pioneering achievement in and for Europe, Alice Salomon criticized the fact that only a fraction of employed women – those who were self-insured – received maternity benefits for three weeks after birth, amounting to half or three-quarters of their wage.[32] Little was changed in the subsequent years, before the reform of the industrial labour law in 1908 and the insurance law in 1911, except for an extension of the benefit period to six weeks and a minor raise of the benefits. Women of all political affiliations intervened in the debates preceding these reforms, with demands, petitions, resolutions and pamphlets; it was particularly prior to the second amendment of the insurance act in 1903 that the idea of a general maternity insurance emerged.

Lily Braun was the first German feminist to propose state maternity insurance in 1897 and again, with a stronger impact, in 1901 and 1906 when she referred to the Italian feminist Paolina Schiff's similar proposal and criticized the BfM because it focused only on sexual ethics and not on legislative financial reform. Such a maternity budget was to cover employed and particularly employed proletarian women. She called for benefits for four weeks before and eight weeks after birth to the full amount of the average wage, free doctors and drugs, free nursing care including care for the infant and for the household, homes for pregnant and nursing women and birth centres; beyond wage replacement, she also demanded benefits for all lower-class women, employed as well as non-employed, married or not. The costs were to be met from insurance contributions and perhaps also from a tax on single people, but mostly from a progressive income tax. Subsequently, many women from both wings of the women's movement and from the SPD called for state maternity insurance (agreeing on full wage compensation for at least six weeks after birth and for two to six before, and extending the insurance to domestic servants, agricultural and home workers), even though it seems that none, except for Anita Augspurg, went so far as Lily Braun, who saw her own proposal as a compromise between an ideal motherhood endowment for one and a half years, and job maintenance.[33] Their claims, debates and policies implied important assumptions as to the relationship between rights, duties and work, and as to that between motherhood, society, state and fatherhood.

By contrast with Lily Braun's initial advance, almost all her successors took the existing health insurance law as a starting point and advocated, for pragmatic reasons, incorporating maternity insurance into sickness insurance. The objection that maternity was not an illness and the related reference to the 'sacred function of motherhood' was rejected by Gertrud Bäumer as 'sentimentality unjustified from the viewpoint of social policy'. Else Lüders too, one of the few advocates of organizational autonomy for the maternity insurance scheme, adduced technical insurance reasons.[34]

The link made between motherhood protection and female labour protection implied the exclusion of non-employed mothers (including the wives or other women dependent on the insured person) from maternity insurance. However, the debate displayed noteworthy differences in this respect. Whereas Anita Augspurg had asked for a maternity pension for all women, regardless of their marital and occupational status, the BDF Committee on Protection of Women Workers, in its 1903 listing of groups of women to whom maternity benefits should be extended, did not mention male workers' wives or dependants. Else Lüders advocated the entitlement to benefits of women who did not lose earnings themselves, referring to Henriette Fürth, who supported universal compulsory family insurance. Maria Lischnewska, who believed in the gradual disappearance of domestic work, favoured maternity benefits for the 'overwhelming mass of working-class wives not yet in independent employment'. Alice Salomon proposed to limit the entitlement of non-employed housewives to services (midwife, medical treatment, home care) and not to provide any financial support 'since there are no lost wages to replace'.[35] Since, obviously, the issue was not the payment of mothers' work, it is of interest on what grounds and for what reasons maternity benefit was called for, the differences that emerged and who was to pay.

'Motherhood is a social function', wrote Lily Braun in 1901, and Alice Salomon in 1908 declared that the greatest interest in 'the birth of the largest possible number of healthy children able to become productive citizens' was not that of the family but that of 'society and state'. Social recognition of motherhood increased with the debate on infant mortality after the turn of the century. In 1904 some 20 per cent of legitimate and over 31 per cent of illegitimate children died before completing their first year. Scarcely any statement in favour of maternity protection failed to refer to this issue and to its connection with women's employment. The BfM in 1907 attributed infant mortality to poor perinatal care and short confinements of mothers, artificial feeding and inadequate care of infants, overwork and under-nutrition of pregnant women.[36]

The Social Democratic Women's Conference expressed the link between maternity protection and infant mortality in 1906 in a resolution on the period of maternity leave and maternity benefit; it distinguished between mothers of stillborn infants or those dead within six weeks (with a benefit period of six weeks) and mothers of infants still living after six weeks (eight weeks). Mothers 'able and willing to breast-feed their child themselves' were to be given maternity support for thirteen weeks. Many Social Democratic women, particularly Lily Braun, saw the protection of women workers primarily as a child-protection measure, including the proposals for a ban on night-working. From 1910, the BfM increasingly formulated its objectives in the emerging race-hygienic vocabulary and content. 'Our maternity protection would bring about unheard-of improvement of the race and guarantee Germany's worldwide power through a healthy and strong progeny', said Maria Lischnewska at the International Congress for Maternity Protection in 1911 in Dresden, arguing for a child allowance for families with an income of up to 5,000 marks per year, from the third child onwards.[37]

Most representatives of the moderate women's movement defined the function of motherhood and its protection for state and society less directly. Marianne Weber, Alice Salomon, Helene Lange, Gertrud Bäumer and others compared women's employment in manual jobs with motherhood from the point of view of its respective value. They asked where women could best assert their energies, both to the benefit of society and in the interest of their own self-development, and the unanimous answer was in favour of motherhood (as a 'cultural profession'). According to Salomon, factory work could only be advocated for reasons of economic need; in all other cases the cultural value of women's work would be greater where the mother devotes herself to home and children, where she creates ideal values not expressible in money terms, than where she contributes in a factory through mechanical operations to increasing the output of material goods.

This position implied a revision of the unconditional demand for a 'right to work', advanced by the ADF since its foundation in 1865, for working-class women also. By the 1890s, moderate women saw 'modern commodity production', particularly factory work, no longer as a medium for emancipation, and Helene Lange instead criticized industrial progress 'which mercilessly makes the individual a cog in an enormous machine, proves too inelastic to be able to incorporate women's labour as the labour of women', and where 'women can be employed only according to the criteria of male labour, or not at all'.[38] On the other hand, maternity protection for factory workers was sometimes advocated as an opening wedge for a female cultural contribution even in the industrial sphere.[39]

The female advocates of maternity protection also considered how it was to be financed. Their different views on this issue also concerned fatherhood, which was seen as a 'social duty', for instance by Salomon. His was not the duty to bring children into the world but that of taking on responsibility for those brought into the world: 'It is only right for the father to take the financial burden on his shoulders, if he is capable.' Men were jointly responsible for financing maternity insurance. But many male politicians rejected an obligatory contribution from men (particularly bachelors).[40] In her 1901 model Lily Braun proposed progressive taxation according to income and property, the proceeds of which should be devoted to governmental financing of maternity insurance. The BfM recommended state subsidies in 1907 (25 marks per birth), without any link to progressive taxation, whereas Salomon preferred contributions to a maternity insurance scheme to be paid by workers and employers, with state subsidies only for its administration.

Women's far-reaching hopes for the labour law of 1908 and the insurance reform of 1911 remained largely unfulfilled. The 1908 measure extended the maternity leave to eight weeks, and the 1911 law extended the obligatory insurance to domestic servants, agricultural and home workers, granting them, however, lower benefits than to factory workers. For the latter the wage compensation during maternity leave remained at the previous level (half to three-quarters of the wage), free services remained at the discretion of the sickness funds, and wives of insured husbands were not covered. The reason was 'the iron resistance of the majority in the parliament and government, which wanted at all costs to prevent any burden on employers going beyond the extent previously provided for'.[41]

After the introduction of female suffrage in 1918 and under the constitution of the Weimar Republic, which included provisions on equal rights for men and women as well as on the protection of motherhood, women parliamentarians saw themselves not only as representatives of their parties but also as women with common interests. All women in the Reichstag dedicated particular efforts to maternity and infant care. In the Parliament, long-standing proponents of maternity protection and women-centred policies from the BDF, most of whom now belonged to the left-liberal German Democratic Party (DDP), met representatives of the Social Democratic women's organization. The new generation of female SPD deputies had not shared in the distance from and outright hostility towards the 'bourgeois women's righters' of the pre-war period. Moreover, they had now themselves to exert a moderating influence on the radical left; for instance, in 1921 Louise Schröder opposed a demand by Lore Agnes, member of the Independent Social Democratic Party (USPD), arguing that 'if the sickness funds collapse, that hurts the working class the most'.[42] Against this background, the inter-party co-operation of women deputies was based fundamentally on a kind of division of labour in which the DDP members largely left the maternity issue to SPD women such as Louise Schröder.

In 1919 Marie Baum of the DDP proposed to draft a bill for state maternity benefit, giving a permanent basis to the previous war-time maternity allowance. Under the leadership of the Social Democrat Louise Schröder, women from all the seven parties drafted the bill. It was enacted in 1919, was repeatedly extended and amended in subsequent years and was considered one of the first laws on which women and their newly acquired civic status had left its marks. The women agreed on some important improvements, among them the extension of the benefits to the relatives of the insured (introduced in 1924), a breast-feeding allowance and a special benefit for non-insured necessitous women.

For the nature of this inter-party women's activity two examples are characteristic: the issue of breast-feeding money (*Stillgeld*) and the treatment of non-employed mothers. A far-reaching consensus on the entitlement to breast-feeding benefits and its legislative enactment could not yet emerge in the context of the debate on infant mortality at the turn of the century (some women had refused it then because it might push into breast-feeding women who were not really willing or able to, whereas the BfM favoured the allowance).[43] Consensus was reached only with the debate on the fertility decline, which spread after around 1911, and later on the human losses in the war. In 1921, Lore Agnes called for daily breast-feeding money amounting to the price of a litre of milk and therefore being 'flexible', i.e. adapted to the fast-increasing inflation. The proposal met with broad agreement among the women, with only two, Christine Teusch (Catholic Centre Party) and Margarethe Behm (German National People's Party) calling for a 'fixed' allowance, because it was easier to combine with insurance procedures. When it became clear that the 'flexible milk price' could not be put through, the female parliamentarians agreed – except for the Communist – very quickly on a fixed amount, and in this way were able to achieve a considerable rise (from 3 to 4.5 marks).

Obviously, pragmatism facilitated inter-party women's politics. Moreover, this example shows that early Weimar women's politics did not clearly fit into a left–right political spectrum. The 'flexible breast-feeding money' was the more 'radical' position, not only because it might ultimately have been higher than any fixed amount, but also in the quite unusual sense that all women could in principle agree on it. Inflation alone is not a sufficient explanation for this. Presumably the litre of milk also had a symbolic significance, expressing the value of breast-feeding. Furthermore, the allowance counteracted the tendency to relativize maternity assistance as a mere labour-protection measure. Its primary objective was not to replace women's loss of wages (such was Social Democrat Louise Schröder's criticism), but to contribute to the sustenance and health of the nursing mother.[44]

Agreement also prevailed as to the much-debated extension of maternity benefits to non-employed women. When in 1921 male conservatives objected to the coverage of non-employed dependants of the insured person other than the wives, the Centre Party deputy Helene Weber clearly set women's solidarity above party discipline; she did not share the 'severe reservations' of her party against granting maternity benefits to daughters, step-daughters and foster-daughters of the insured, and insisted that 'necessitous mothers – whether married or not – must be assisted under all circumstances'. Women's parliamentary rhetoric, such as Louise Schröder's, placed the mothers at the centre – different from the pre-war petition rhetoric which had focused on the value of housework, but also different from male parliamentary rhetoric which, when it supported mothers' welfare, did so with respect to the loss of 'human material' during the war. Schröder, however, based her call for major improvements in maternity care on different arguments: behind the high figures of stillbirths and infant deaths lay the 'unspeakable torments and pains of mothers'.[45]

From 1925 on, the parliamentary debate focused on the confinement allowance (in the context of the health insurance law), on maternity leave for women workers (in the context of the factory legislation), and particularly on the adoption of the 1919 Washington Convention of the International Labour Organisation, which most women favoured. It included provisions for leave from work, breast-feeding pauses, maternity benefits and, above all, a ban on dismissal for the period from six weeks before to six weeks after birth. With the 1927 Maternity Protection Act, one of the most important welfare laws of the Weimar Republic, Germany was the first major country to implement the Washington Convention. However, women parliamentarians had not succeeded in getting agricultural workers and domestic servants included in the provisions for maternity leave, and these workers constituted a large proportion of the female labour force. Whereas one reason for this defeat may have been disunity between conservative women parliamentarians on one side, and Bäumer (DDP) and Schröder (SPD) on the other, women's influence in Parliament also declined more generally from the mid-twenties, when they protested, in vain, against abolition of the breast-feeding allowances and the cancellation of federal state contributions to maternity benefits, which now depended on the budgets of individual cities. Thus, the state had, in Schröder's words, 'cleared its budget at the expense of our mothers and children and therefore at the expense of our people's health'.[46]

During the Weimar Republic, the German women's movement did not claim child allowances for mothers as did, for instance, the British National Union of Societies for Equal Citizenship from 1925 on. Family allowance, as an income supplement for workers, was granted in a few industries after World War I, upon the French model of equalization funds; it met the opposition of a strong section of the trade union movement and did not survive inflation and depressions. In the 1920s, family allowances of 10–30 marks from the first child on were gradually introduced for married employees of the central government (salaried employees, manual workers and civil servants). In 1933, when unemployment had reached an unprecedented peak and unemployment compensation was hotly debated (becoming a major factor in the collapse of the Weimar Republic), Gertrud Bäumer published a proposal to extend child allowances to private industry; they should cover the effective costs of children and be financed through equalization funds along the French and Belgian model. Her proposal did not aim at rewarding mothers for their labour, but at relieving unemployment among heads of household and preventing employers from preferring unmarried men;[47] she viewed child allowances as no more than a supplement to fathers' income. This view was probably not due to a sudden sympathy for men, but rather to an increasingly *realpolitisch* attitude of the BDF leaders, reinforced by the recurring economic crises of the Weimar Republic: the struggle for material improvements for mothers, minimal as they might have been was not to be jeopardized by more fundamental issues. But, in addition, the absence of any demand for motherhood endowment in the moderate women's movement of the 1920s illustrates once more the fact that this movement's fundamental principle, 'spiritual motherhood', had remained separated from the material interests of bodily mothers.

NOTES

1 K. Schirmacher, *Die Frauenarbeit im Hause, ihre ökonomische, rechtliche und soziale Wertung*, 2nd edn, Lipsia, Dietrich, 1912, pp. 3–8 (partially repr. in G. Brinker-Gabler (ed.), *Frauenarbeit und Beruf*, Frankfurt a.M., Fischer, 1979).

2 Report in *Die Frauenbewegung*, Oct. 1905, vol. 11, no. 20, pp. 153–5, esp. p. 154; M. Lischnewska, *Die wirtschaftliche Reform der Ehe*, Lipsia, 1907, p. 5 (repr. in G. Brinker-Gabler, *Frauenarbeit*); L. Braun, *Reform der Hauswirtschaft* (1901),

repr. in G. Brinker-Gabler, *Frauenarbeit*, pp. 275ff. For the larger context see esp. B. Greven-Aschoff, *Die bürgerliche Frauenbewegung in Deutschland 1894–1933*, Göttingen, Vandenhoeck & Ruprecht, 1981; U. Frevert, *Women in German History*, Oxford, Berg, 1989; A. Hackett, 'The politics of feminism in Wilhelmine Germany, 1890–1918', Ph. D. dissertation, Columbia University, 1976; K. Anthony, *Feminism in Germany and Scandinavia*, New York; Holt, 1915; T. Wobbe, *Gleichheit und Differenz. Politische Strategien von Frauenrechtlerinnen um die Jahrhundertwende*, Frankfurt a.M., Campus, 1989; J. Stoehr, *Emanzipation zum Staat? Der Allgemeine Deutsche Frauenverein-Deutscher Staatsbügerinnenverband, 1893–1933*, Pfaffenweiler, Centaurus, 1990.

3 'Memorandum', *Parlamentarische Angelegenheiten und Gesetzgebung. Beilage der Frauenbewegung*, 1 Feb. 1901, vol. 3.

4 H. Stöcker, 'Die Hauswirtschaft als Beruf', *Die Liebe und die Frauen*, Minden, Bruns, 1908, pp. 65–70; see also A. Hackett, 'Helene Stöcker: left-wing intellectual and sex reformer', in R. Bridenthal *et al.* (eds), *When Biology Became Destiny: Women in Weimar and Nazi Germany*, New York, Monthly Review Press, 1984, pp. 109–30; C. Wickert *et al.*, 'Helene Stöcker and the Bund für Mutterschutz', *Women's Studies International Forum*, 1982, vol. 5, pp. 611–18.

5 H. Stöcker, 'Hauswirtschaft', p. 69; H. Stöcker, *Zehn Jahre Mutterschutz*, Berlin, Verlag Bund für Mutterschutz, 1915, p. 4; in Stöcker's journal *Mutterschutz* (from 1908 on: *Die neue Generation*), housework was no longer discussed.

6 R. Bré, *Keine Alimentationsklage mehr! Schutz den Müttern!*, Lipsia, Dietrich, 1905; H. Stöcker, 'Zur Reform der sexuellen Ethik', *Mutterschutz*, Jan. 1905, vol. I, no. 1, p. 10; for the controversy around Bré see A. Schreiber, 'Die Ansätze neuer Sittlichkeitsbegriffe im Hinblick auf Mutterschaft', in A. Schreiber (ed.), *Mutterschaft*, Munich, Langen, 1912, pp. 163–85, 176ff.; H. Fürth, 'Die Lage der Mutter und die Entwicklung des Mutterschutzes in Deutschland', in A. Schreiber (ed.), *Mutterschaft*, pp. 278–98.

7 K. Schirmacher, *Frauenarbeit*, pp. 10–11.

8 K. Schirmacher, *Wie und in welchem Masse lässt sich die Wertung der Frauenarbeit steigern*, Leipzig, Dietrich, 1909, pp. 1, 10 (repr. in G. Brinker-Gabler, *Frauenarbeit*); K. Schirmacher, *Frauenarbeit*, p. 12.

9 Her activities and publications from 1897 are described in the introduction to her *Frauenarbeit*; she had studied at French universities.

10 'Wer nicht hören will muss fühlen', *Parlamentarische Angelegenheiten*, Jan. 1905.

11 Augspurg's proposal is described in K. Scheven, 'Vom Hamburger Frauentag', *Centralblatt des BDF*, 1903, vol. 5 no. 14, p. 109. In her later life, Augspurg turned against all legislation aimed only at women.

12 'Memorandum', p. 9.

13 R. Schwimmer, *Zentralhaushaltung*, Lipsia, Dietrich, 1907, p. 2.

14 Both points of view are described in the report on the VFF meeting of 1909 in Berlin, *Die Frauenbewegung*, Oct. 1909, vol. 15, no. 20, p. 157.

15 'Ziele und Aufgaben der Frauenbewegung' (ADF pamphlet), *Die Frau*, Nov. 1905, vol. 13 no. 2, pp. 65–8, esp. p. 66 (transl. in K. Anthony, *Feminism* pp. 20–6); H. Lange, 'Moderne Streitfragen in der Frauenbewegung', *Die Frau*, Nov. 1905, vol. 13, no. 2, pp. 69–80, 73; I. Freudenberg, 'Grundsätze und Forderungen der Frauenbewegung auf dem Gebiet der Ehe und Familie', *Grundsätze und Forderungen der Frauenbewegung* (BDF pamphlet), Berlin–Leipzig 1912, pp. 1–10.

16 M. Weber, 'Zur Frage der Bewertung der Hausfrauenarbeit' (1912), *Frauenfragen und Frauengedanken*, Tübingen, Mohr, 1919, p. 88; the following quotes are from

pp. 83–93.

17 G. Bäumer, 'Die erste deutsche Konferenz zur Förderung der Arbeiterin-neninteressen', *Die Frau*, 1907, vol. 14, no. 7, pp. 385–93.

18 G. Bäumer, 'Neudeutsche Wirtschaftspolitik und Frauenfrage', *Die Frau*, 1906, vol. 14, no. 3, pp. 166–72, esp. pp. 168 and 171; G. Bäumer, 'Materialistische Irrtümer in der Frauenbewegung', *Die Frau*, 1906, vol. 13 no. 7, pp. 414–22, esp. p. 416. The VFF agreed with most of Naumann's assumptions; cf. *Die Frauenbewegung*, 1906, vol. 12 nos 12–14.

19 G. Bäumer, 'Der seelische Hintergrund der Bevölkerungsfrage', *Die Frau*, 1915, vol. 23, no. 3, pp. 129–34. C. Usborne, '"Pregnancy is the woman's active service". Pronatalism in Germany during the First World War', in R. Wall and J. Winter (eds), *The Upheaval of War*, Cambridge, Cambridge University Press, 1988, esp. pp. 398–400.

20 G. Bäumer, 'Die erste deutsche Konferenz', p. 387; A. von Zahn-Harnack, *Die Frauenbewegung*, Berlin, Deutsche Buchgemeinschaft, 1928, pp. 65ff., 81ff., 219ff., 228ff.

21 See the ADF pamphlet quoted in note 15.

22 H. Lange, 'Das Endziel der Frauenbewegung', *Die Frau*, 1904, vol. 11, no. 12, pp. 705–14, esp. p. 713; cf. I. Stoehr, 'Organisierte Mütterlichkeit. Zur Politik der deutschen Frauenbewegung um 1900', in K. Hausen (ed.), *Frauen suchen ihre Geschichte*, (2nd edn), Munich, Beck, 1987, pp. 225–53.

23 See, e.g., E. Heuss-Knapp, 'Die Reform der Hauswirtschaft', in G. Bäumer (ed.), *Der deutsche Frauenkongress Berlin 1912*, Lipsia, Teubner, 1912, pp. 6–11.

24 H. Lange, '"Neuorientierung" in der Frauenbewegung', *Die Frau*, 1916, vol. 24, no. 1, pp. 1–4.

25 G. Bäumer, 'Materialistische Irrtümer', p. 418.

26 R. Bré, *Staatskinder oder Mutterrecht?*, Lipsia, Malende, 1904, pp. 29–44, esp. p. 31; A. von Zahn-Harnack, *Frauenbewegung*, pp. 76–7.

27 H. Breymann, quoted in M. Twellmann, *Die deutsche Frauenbewegung*. vol. II (*Quellen 1843–1889*), Meisenheim, Hain, 1972, p. 268; cf. A. T. Allen, 'Spiritual motherhood: German feminists and the kindergarten movement, 1848–1911', *History of Education Quarterly*, 1982, vol. 22, pp. 319–39.

28 'Mutterschutz', *Die Frau*, 1905, vol. 12, no. 7, p. 438; A. Salomon, 'Mutterschutz als Aufgabe der Sozialpolitik', in G. Bäumer (ed.), *Frauenbewegung and Sexualethik*, Heilbronn, Salzer, 1909, pp. 132–62, esp. p. 139; for the term *Mutterschutz* see A. Schreiber (ed.), *Mutterschaft*, p. 286; K. Anthony, *Feminism*, p. 7.

29 G. Bäumer, 'Die Geschichte der Frauenbewegung in Deutschland', in G. Bäumer and H. Lange (eds), *Handbuch der Frauenbewegung*, vol. I, Berlin, Moeser, 1901, p. 119.

30 H. Simon, 'Arbeiterinnenschutz und bürgerliche Frauenbewegung', *Soziale Praxis*, May 1901, pp. 817–23, esp. p. 822. For the contradiction between the consensus and the hostility between the socialist and the other women's movements see K. Anthony, *Feminism*, pp. 121, 194; for the assumption of German specificity in this field (but to which there were definite similarities in other countries in the early twentieth century, whereas in the early 1890s the socialist Clara Zetkin still had fervently opposed specific protection for women workers), see L. Braun, *Die Frauenfrage*, Lipsia, Hirzel, 1901, pp. 466f.; G. Bäumer, 'Geschichte', p. 139.

31 L. Braun, *Frauenfrage*, pp. 466–7; A. Salomon, *Mutterschutz und Mutterschafts-versicherung*, Lipsia, Duncker & Humblot, 1908, p. 9.

32 A. Fischer, *Die Mutterschaftsversicherung in den europäischen Ländern*, Lipsia,

1911, Dietrich, p. 22; A. Salomon, *Mutterschutz*, pp. 47–8.
33 L. Braun, *Frauenfrage*, p. 547; L. Braun, *Die Mutterschaftsversicherung*, Berlin, Vorwärts 1906, and her contribution in *Brauns Archiv für soziale Gesetzgebung und Statistik*, 1897, vol. 11, pp. 543ff.; A. G. Meyer, *The Feminism and Socialism of Lily Braun*, Bloomington, Indiana University Press, 1985, esp. chs 6, 9, 11; A. Pappritz, 'Die Errichtung von Wöchnerinnenheimen und Säuglingsasylen – eine soziale Notwendigkeit, eine nationale Pflicht', *Sozialer Fortschritt*, 1904, vol. 12, no. 13, pp. 5–6; A. Salomon, *Mutterschutz*, p. 51; H. Stöcker (ed.), *Petitionen des Deutschen Bundes für Mutterschutz 1905–1916*, Berlin, Bund für Mutterschutz, 1916, pp. 9–12.
34 G. Bäumer, 'Mutterschutz und Mutterschaftsversicherung', *Die Frau*, 1909, vol. 16, no. 4, p. 201; E. Lüders, 'Zur Frage der Mutterschaftsversicherung', *Die Frauenbewegung*, 1903, vol. 8, nos 13–14, p. 125.
35 Resolution of the Berlin group of the BDF Committee on Protection of Women Workers, in A. Pappritz, 'Die Errichtung', p. 6; E. Lüders, 'Zur Frage', p. 130; M. Lischnewska, *Die Mutterschaftsversicherung*, Berlin, Verlag Bund für Mutterschutz, 1908, p. 4; A. Salomon, *Mutterschutz*, p. 61.
36 L. Braun, *Frauenfrage*, p. 547; A. Salomon, 'Mutterschutz', p. 137; H. Stöcker (ed.), *Petitionen*, p. 10; see also Augspurg (note 11 above).
37 'Mutterschutz. Resolution der Sozialdemokratischen Frauenkonferenz 1906', in G. Brinker-Gabler, *Frauenarbeit*, p. 193; L. Braun, *Frauenfrage*, p. 537; M. Lischnewska, 'Leitsätze', in H. Stöcker (ed.), *Petitionen*, p. 36. For the larger context see A. T. Allen, 'German radical feminism and eugenics, 1900–1918', *German Studies Review*, 1989, vol. 11, pp. 31–56.
38 H. Lange, *Die Frauenbewegung in ihren modernen Problemen* (1914), Münster, Tende, 1980, pp. 26, 113; H. Lange, 'Was bedeutet in der deutschen Frauen-bewegung "jüngere" und "ältere" Richtung?', *Die Frau*, 1905, vol. 12 no. 6, pp. 323–4; M. Weber, *Frauenfragen*, p. 25; A. Salomon, 'Fabrikarbeit und Mutterschaft', *Die Frau*, 1906, vol. 13 no. 6, p. 369.
39 H. Simon, quoted in G. Bäumer, 'Die erste deutsche Konferenz', p. 387.
40 A. Salomon, *Mutterschutz* pp. 57–9.
41 A. Fischer, 'Staatliche Mutterschaftsversicherung', in A. Schreiber (ed.), *Mutter-schaft*, p. 308.
42 R. Deutsch, *Parlamentarische Frauenarbeit II*, Berlin, Herbig, 1928, pp. 34, 77.
43 G. Bäumer, 'Die erste deutsche Konferenz', p. 391.
44 R. Deutsch, *Parlamentarische*, p. 45.
45 R. Deutsch, *Die politische Tat der Frau. Aus der Nationalversammlung*. Gotha, Perthes, 1920, pp. 18, 35, 44–6; R. Deutsch, *Frauenarbeit II*, p. 41.
46 ibid., p. 39.
47 G. Bäumer, *Familienpolitik*, Berlin, Verlag für Standesamtswesen, 1933; cf. D. V. Glass, *Population Policies and Movements in Europe* (first edn 1940), repr. London, Frank Cass, 1967, pp. 292–4; A. Augspurg and L. G. Heymann (Hg.), *Die Frau im Staat. Eine Monatsschrift*, Munich, 1919–33; L. G. Heymann, 'Open Door International – Freie-Bahn-Internationale', *Die Genossin*, July/Aug. 1929, vol. 8, p. 333, argues against women-specific legislation but contains a brief though unspecified reference to maternity pensions for 'all mothers'. See also J. Lewis, *The Politics of Motherhood*, London, Croom Helm, 1980, pp. 172, 198.

Chapter 12

Antinatalism, maternity and paternity in National Socialist racism

Gisela Bock

Understanding the policy of the National Socialist regime towards women as mothers within a European perspective requires this issue to be placed in a context which allows the identification of similarities as well as differences between the National Socialist experience and that of other European countries. This can best be approached by examining three broad areas of research: first, those features of National Socialism which come close to, or are at least comparable with other countries' welfare reforms and which allow us to see Nazi Germany as a kind of welfare state (or as a society in the process of 'modernization');[1] yet studies of the emergence of the European welfare states usually do not include women- and family-related National Socialist policies such as the introduction of child allowances in 1935/36. Second, there is the extreme opposite of social reform, i.e. National Socialist racism. Its various forms – particularly anti-Jewish and anti-Gypsy policy, race hygiene or eugenics – illustrate that in this respect National Socialism was unique, despite the fact that racism was an international phenomenon. It was unique most of all because, from its rise to power in 1933, it began to institutionalize racism at the level of the state, through innumerable laws and decrees which discriminated against those considered to be 'racially inferior'. National Socialism transformed racism into a state-sponsored race policy, and put into practice all its forms to a degree unheard of before and after. In this field too, women-related policies are rarely considered, even though women were half of all victims. Third, there is a growing body of research on women under National Socialism and the regime's policy towards them. Its most salient common assumption is that National Socialism meant pronatalism and brought a cult of motherhood, that it used propaganda, incentives, and even force in order to have all women bear as many children as possible and to keep them out of employment for the sake of motherhood. Whereas research on National Socialist racism usually does not deal with women, research in women's history usually does not deal with National Socialist racism, and female victims of racism are mentioned marginally at best.

Yet, the number of such women – and the issue is, of course, not only one of numbers – is conspicuous. For the purpose of raising the population's 'quality', of 'race regeneration' or 'racial uplift' (*Aufartung*), the National Socialist state pursued a policy of birth-prevention or antinatalism: through compulsory mass sterilization from 1933 on, through non-voluntary abortion from 1935 on, through marriage restrictions from 1935 on, through mass murder and genocide after 1939. Between 1933 and 1945, almost 200,000 women, 1 per cent of those of childbearing age, were sterilized on eugenic grounds. About 200,000 German Jewish women were exiled and almost 100,000 killed. Probably over 80,000 female inmates of psychiatric institutions and several million non-German Jewish women were killed in the massacres during the Second World War, and in addition an unknown number of non-Jewish non-German women. During the war, there were over 2 million non-German women who had to perform forced labour in Germany and on whom, particularly on those from eastern Europe, hundreds of thousands of abortions and sterilizations were performed.

This chapter explores some of the features of National Socialist welfare policies, race policies and gender policies which focused on women as mothers and potential mothers. The first section deals with National Socialist racism in its form of antinatalism, of the prevention of 'inferior offspring' for the purpose of 'racial uplift'. It shows that compulsory sterilization, though it was performed on both sexes, had in many respects different social and cultural meanings for women and men. The second section deals with National Socialist welfare reforms concerning procreation and the family. It shows that the view of National Socialist gender policies as essentially consisting of 'pronatalism and a cult of motherhood' is largely a myth. Whereas Nazi antinatalism was revolutionary, unique and efficient, Nazi pronatalism used largely traditional means; where it was novel, it resembled comparable family-centred welfare reforms in other European countries. The third section deals with some aspects of motherhood – or rather, of its opposite – in the massacres of the 'race struggle' (*Rassenkampf*) during the second half of the regime.

In different ways, the three sections deal with a number of more general assumptions and results. First, just as National Socialist race policy was not gender-neutral, so National Socialist gender policy was not race-neutral. Second, the National Socialist welfare measures were comparable to those introduced in other countries around the same time, but they differed from them in important respects. They did not focus on mothers but on fathers, and most importantly, they were never universalized, because they had a definite limit in race policy which excluded the 'inferior' from their benefits. Third, this limit, the inner dynamics of National Socialism and the comparison with other countries show that race policies were more crucial to National Socialism than were welfare policies, and that just as racism was at the centre of Nazi policies in general, it was also at the centre of Nazi policies toward women.

STERILIZATION POLICY OR ANTINATALISM FOR 'RACE REGENERATION'

In June 1933, five months after Hitler came to power, his Minister of the Interior, Wilhelm Frick, gave a programmatic and frequently quoted speech on 'population and race policy'. It was intended to pave the way for the imminent sterilization law which had been prepared for by years of eugenic propaganda. Eugenic and compulsory sterilization had been advocated not only by National Socialists, but also – albeit for different reasons, though always in view of a perfect society – by many members of other political affiliations, including socialists and some radical feminists (not however by the Catholic Centre Party, because of the Pope's encyclical *Casti Connubi* of 1930 which spoke out against all artificial birth control, nor by moderate feminists such as Gertrud Bäumer, who in 1931 had taken a firm stand against eugenics, *Aufartung* and raising the population's 'quantity and quality').[2]

Frick unrolled a 'dismal picture'. He pointed to the 'cultural and ethnic decline', demonstrated by over a million people with 'hereditary physical and mental diseases', 'feeble-minded and inferior' people from whom 'progeny is no longer desired', especially not where they show 'above-average procreation'. He went on to estimate that 20 per cent of the German population, i.e. another 11 million, were undesirable as mothers or fathers. He concluded that 'in order to increase the number of hereditarily healthy progeny, we have first of all the duty to prevent the procreation of the hereditarily unfit'. This project of state-run birth control became law on 14 July 1933, introducing compulsory sterilization. The official commentary stressed that 'biologically inferior hereditary material' was to be 'eradicated (*ausgemerzt*)', specifically among the 'innumerable inferior and hereditarily tainted' people who 'procreate without inhibition (*hemmunglos*)'; sterilization 'should bring about a gradual cleansing of the people's body (*Volkskörper*)', and around 1.5 million people were to be sterilized, 400,000 in the short term. In fact, this was the number of those sterilized over the next decade, half men and half women, as well as an unknown but probably considerable number outside the law.[3]

All the sterilizations were compulsory; none came about by the free will of a sterilized person. Voluntary sterilization was forbidden by the same law (article 14), and frequently the police were employed, a possibility laid down in the law itself (article 12) and applied in 3–30 per cent of the cases, depending on regional variations. Almost all the sterilized were selected by doctors, psychiatrists, and other officials. Sterilization was decided by specially created courts, on which sat doctors, psychiatrists, anthropologist, experts in human genetics and jurists. Thus, birth control was not outlawed but introduced by law, for people considered to be of 'inferior value' (*minderwertig*). Article 1 specified the kinds of 'inferiority'. They were described essentially in psychiatric terms, as intellectual and emotional 'departures from the norm' which had been elaborated and declared as hereditary, since around 1900, by the science and policy of 'race hygiene', 'social hygiene', 'procreation hygiene', 'eugenics', 'human genetics' or *Erb- und Rassenpflege*. Ninety-six per cent of the sterilizations were based on (in order of frequency) real or alleged feeble-mindedness, schizophrenia, epilepsy and manic-depressive derangement; the others on real or alleged blindness, deafness, 'bodily malformation', St Vitus' dance and alcoholism. The sterilized were from all social classes and occupational groups, and their respective proportion corresponded to that in society at large. The quantitatively and strategically most important group were the 'feeble-minded'. They made up some two-thirds of all those sterilized, and almost two-thirds of them were women.[4]

The sterilization law did not provide for the sterilization exclusively of Jews, Gypsies, Blacks and other 'alien' races but they were, of course, included; moreover, particularly Gypsies and Black people were sterilized both within and outside the 1933 law. None the less, the sterilization policy – and race hygiene as a whole – was a form of racism and an integral component of National Socialist racism. For racism means not only discrimination of 'alien' races or peoples, but also the 'regeneration' of one's own people, in so far as that was aimed at through discrimination of the 'biologically inferior' among one's own people. For the theoreticians and practitioners of racism the 'master race' was not already there, but had to be produced. In *Mein Kampf* Hitler had summarized current race theory in the mid-twenties: just as 'one people is not equal to another', so 'one person is not equal to another within one *Volksgemeinschaft* (ethnic community)', and therefore 'the individuals within a *Volksgemeinschaft*' must be differently 'evaluated', especially as regards the right to have children. He recommended the sterilization of 'millions' of people. Later, a jurist in the Reich Ministry of the Interior summarized: 'The German race question consists primarily in the Jewish question. In the second place, yet not less important, there is the Gypsy question . . . But degenerative effects on the racial body may arise not only from outside, from members of alien races, but also from inside, through unrestricted procreation of inferior hereditary material.' Like all racism, eugenics or sterilization racism used social and cultural criteria to define the 'alien', 'different', 'sick', 'inferior': namely emotional, physical, moral and intellectual criteria. The common denominator of all forms of National Socialist racism was the definition and treatment of human beings according to a differing 'value' defined and ascribed by other human beings. The value criteria were declared to be 'biology', as was the social and cultural field in which they were embodied: descent and procreation. The common denominator not of all forms of Nazi racism but of its most dramatic forms was the attempt to 'solve' social and cultural problems with means that were also called 'biology': namely by intervening with body and life. Thus, in 1936 Himmler praised the sterilization law to the Hitler Youth: 'Germans

... have once again learned ... to recognize bodies and to bring up this godgiven body and our godgiven blood and race according to its value or lack of value.'[5]

The sterilization law was one of the first manifestations of National Socialist racism on a national and state level. Officials of the Reich Ministry of the Interior declared, referring to the sterilization law, that 'the private is political' and that the decision on the dividing line between the private and the political is itself a political decision. In one respect, the sterilization law went even further than the anti-Jewish laws of 1933, since it ordered compulsory bodily intervention and was thereby the first of the Nazi measures that sought to solve social and cultural problems by 'biological' means. The sterilization law, just as the anti-Jewish laws, made a political reality of the classical racist demand, proclaimed in Germany specifically by eugenicists: 'unequal value, unequal rights' (*ungleicher Wert, ungleiche Rechte*).[6] For the 'valuable' of both sexes sterilization was forbidden, and for the 'inferior' of both sexes it was obligatory. For National Socialism, modern antinatalism took precedence over old-fashioned pronatalism, in terms of chronology as well as in terms of principle.

The sterilization law was officially proclaimed as embodying the 'primacy of the state over the sphere of life, marriage and family'[7] and this primacy was particularly significant for women. All state intervention in the giving and maintaining of life, in begetting, bearing and rearing children, are important to women, and often more important than for men; their meaning for women may be different from that for men. In fact, sterilization racism, although it affected as many men as women, was nonetheless anything but gender-neutral. This is apparent above all from the three essential features of sterilization: bodily intervention, childlessness, and separation of sexuality and procreation. Other important gender differences included the criteria for selecting those who were not to have children and the propaganda for sterilization.

For women, by contrast with men, the intervention meant a major operation with full anaesthesia, abdominal incision and the concomitant risk. Shortly before the sterilization law was enacted, there was a debate as to whether such intervention on hundreds of thousands of women could be risked. But then the Propaganda Ministry announced that just as many women as men would have to be sterilized. The decision for mass compulsory sterilization of women meant violent intervention not only with the female body but also with female life. Probably about 5,000 people died as a result of sterilization, and whilst women made up only half of the sterilized, they were about 90 per cent of those who died of sterilization. A large number of them died because they resisted sterilization right up to the operating table and rejected what had happened even after operation. An unknown number of people, mainly women, committed suicide because of sterilization.[8] Hence, the first scientifically planned and bureaucratically executed massacre of the

National Socialist state was the result of antinatalism, and women were its chief victims.

Childlessness has a different meaning for women and for men, just as having children does. Therefore, their reactions and forms of resistance to sterilization differed in many respects. Women as well as men protested against their stigmatization as 'second-class human beings' – in thousands of letters to the sterilization courts that have been preserved – but women complained of the resulting childlessness far oftener than men, especially young women. Many tried to get pregnant before sterilization, and this resistance was important enough for the authorities to give the phenomenon a special name: *Trotzschwangerschaften* ('protest pregnancies'). For instance, one girl said that she had got pregnant in order 'to show the state that I won't go along with this'. The protest pregnancies were an important reason for extending the sterilization law, in 1935, into an abortion law: now abortions could also be performed for race hygiene reasons. In the case of such an abortion, sterilization also was compulsory.[9]

The separation of sexuality and procreation had a differing meaning for men and women. One doctor wrote about sterilized men in 1936: 'Happy that nothing can happen to them any more, that neither condoms nor douches are necessary, they fulfil their marital duties without restraint.' In relation to women it was another aspect of sexuality that was publicly discussed in the professional press. Tens of thousands of women who, as one of them asserted, did not 'care at all about men' and had never had sexual intercourse were sterilized because, according to the opinion of the (exclusively male) jurists and doctors, the possibility of pregnancy through rape had to be taken into account. Therefore, the commentary to the law explicitly laid it down that 'a different assessment of the danger of procreation is necessary for men and for women', and in sterilization verdicts the following principle regularly appeared, and was prescribed by government decree in 1936: 'In the case of the female hereditarily sick, the possibility of abuse against her will must be taken into account.' Frequently compulsory sterilization was propagated as a means of preventing the 'consequence' of a potential rape, namely pregnancy. The risk of 'inferior' women being raped seemed to male contemporaries to be so high as to be a ground for the sterilization of women. In fact, sterilized women became objects of sexual abuse, both in the countryside, where sterilization quickly became generally known, and in cities, where sometimes soldiers or factory workers asked each other 'on Mondays': 'Did you not find a sterilized woman for the weekend?'[10]

The psychiatric diagnoses were largely gender-based. Those for women measured their 'departure from the norm' against the norms for the female sex, and those for men against the norms for the male sex. To determine female 'inferiority', heterosexual behaviour was regularly investigated, and negatively evaluated when the women frequently changed their sexual partner or when they had more than one illegitimate child. Men were less investigated on this issue, and the findings had no particular weight in the sterilization verdict. Women, not men, were tested as to their capacity and inclination for housework, for childrearing (also in the case of childless women) as well as to their capacity and inclination for employment. Men were assessed mostly for their work behaviour. The decisive criterion came to be *Lebensbewährung* ('conduct of life'), again prescribed by a government decree.[11]

These were, of course, not genetic but social and cultural criteria, because the sexes are social and cultural entities (like race or ethnicity). These socio-cultural diagnoses were the reason why most of the women and more women than men, were sterilized for 'feeble-mindedness'. Thus, for instance, the sterilization verdict on Mrs Schmidt, mother of ten children, stated that while her 'feeble-mindedness' had not actually been proved, she nevertheless 'is to a quite unusual extent unclean and neglectful, and shockingly neglects her children and the household. Such uncleanness and neglect is however not conceivable with a more or less mentally normally disposed person.' About 10 per cent of the sterilization trials ended with acquittal: in the case of women, when they could prove that they did their work, inside and outside the home, to the satisfaction of the doctors and lawyers of the sterilization court (who often came to inspect the household during the trial). This could not be shown by Luise Müller: she was condemned to sterilization because, according to the court decision, 'her knowledge is confined to mechanically acquired information; she can indicate how to prepare various foodstuffs such as pudding, bread soup or rice soup, but only in the way usual at home'.[12]

The sterilization policy was not carried on secretly – as was the later extermination policy – but almost entirely in public view. The population was virtually bombarded with antinatalist propaganda in the 1930s, and this propaganda was often directed specifically at the female sex. It contrasted starkly with the earlier feminist view on motherhood and the female sex. One of the official Nazi brochures, distributed in millions of copies in 1934, explained to women that their task was not prolific propagation but 'regeneration'. The female characteristic of maternalism (*Mütterlichkeit*) became the object of racist polemic and was treated as contemptible 'sentimental humanitarianism' (*Gefühlsduselei*). Female gender difference, femininity and maternalism were to come to an end in National Socialist racism – even among 'valuable' women. The Berlin doctor Agnes Bluhm, one of the early race hygienicists, wrote in 1934 in the journal of the dissolved Federation of German Women's Associations, *Die Frau*, about the 'danger arising for women precisely from their *Mütterlichkeit*', since maternalism, 'like any egoism, acts against the race'. Like many male eugenicists, she polemicized against the 'female instinct to care for all those in need of help'. Of the fact that 'woman, because of her physical and mental characteristics, is particularly close to all living beings, and has a particular inclination towards all living beings', it was said that there was 'scarcely any worse sin against nature'. In one women's magazine[13] the objection that with sterilization 'the National Socialist state was going against the laws of nature' was stated to be a false conclusion, because

> Until National Socialist rule, the German people neglected the laws of nature ... It not only disregarded the laws of heredity, of selection and of eradication (*Auslese und Ausmerze*), but directly opposed them, by not only keeping the unfit alive at the cost of the healthy, but even guaranteeing their procreation ... Every hereditarily sick German woman will, once she realizes this, take this operation upon herself in order to keep her whole race healthy. 'But doesn't that mean she's sinning against life?' ... What does life mean then? Just go to a lunatic asylum ...

National Socialists by no means wanted children at any cost and it never propagated the slogan 'Kinder, Küche, Kirche' which has been so often, but wrongly, ascribed to them. The biblical 'Be fruitful and multiply' was often and explicitly rejected, as well as the assumption that 'the State allegedly wants children at all costs'. Indeed, this assumption was rejected in the propaganda and instructions from Goebbels' Ministry for Propaganda: 'The goal is not: "children at any cost", but: "racially worthy, physically and mentally unaffected children of German families".' An expert on large families stressed that 'childbearing in itself is, from the race viewpoint, far from being a merit'. Instead the point was 'whether the biological basis', namely the hereditary value, was there 'which alone makes many children into a value for the race'.[14] In fact, not just a small minority of (sterilized) women were undesired as mothers, but somewhere between 10 and 30 per cent depending on the author of the estimate. On the other hand, those women who were considered desirable mothers were not a majority, but also a minority of about 10 to 30 per cent. The blood-and-soil ideologue Darré in a well-known publication divided women into four classes: those in the first should be encouraged to marry and have children; children of the second group, though not to be encouraged, were not objectionable; the third group should be allowed to marry, but where possible be sterilized beforehand; the fourth group should not marry and be sterilized at any cost. The head of the Party Race Policy Office considered it as 'utopian' and 'overoptimistic' to think that 'almost all German women are worthy of procreation', and one of the most important sterilization promoters emphasized that even 'those who are not hereditarily sick within the meaning of the sterilization law need by no means be worthy of procreation'.[15] Never in history had there been a state which in theory, propaganda and practice pursued an antinatalist policy of such dimensions.

PRONATALISM, SOCIAL REFORM AND THE
NATIONAL SOCIALIST WELFARE STATE

What is then the substance of the view which identifies National Socialist birth and gender policy as essentially pronatalist, as encouragement, incentive, or even compulsion to bear children, as a cult of motherhood and as an attack on women's employment for the sake of motherhood? How did National Socialism conceive of gender relations in this area, and what are the links between these issues and its race policy?

Again, current assumptions need to be revised. In Nazi Germany, as in other countries that were hit by the deep economic depression of the 1930s, the early polemics of Nazis and non-Nazis against women's employment remained largely ineffective. There were no Nazi laws against it, nor compulsory or mass firing of women from their jobs. Women's employment increased after 1933 (even though somewhat less than men's), and before as well as during the Nazi regime it was higher than in most western countries. The number of officially registered employed women rose from 11.5 million in 1933, when it made up 36 per cent of all employed persons and 48 per cent of all women between the ages of 15 and 60 years, to 12.8 million in early 1939 (within the German territory of 1937, but if most annexed territories are included, the number is 14.6 million), with the corresponding figures of 37 per cent and 50 per cent. In 1944, 14.9 million German women were employed (including Austria), making up 53 per cent of the German civilian labour force and well over half of all German women between 15 and 60 years.[16]

Along with the development from low employment to full employment to labour scarcity, largely because of the expansion of war industry, the number of female industrial workers increased by 28.5 per cent between 1933 (1.2 million) and 1936 (1.55 million), and by further 19.2 per cent in the following two years. Not only did the number of employed single women rise, but even more that of married women and mothers. Between the Weimar period and the time before World War II, the number of married women in the labour force, and their proportion of all employed women, rose dramatically, and it almost doubled for married female workers in industry (21.4 per cent in 1925, 28.2 per cent in 1933 and 41.3 per cent in 1939; all married employed women: 31 per cent in 1925, 37 per cent in 1933, and 46 per cent in 1939). In 1939, more than 24 per cent of all employed women had children, and the married ones among them made up 51 per cent of all married employed women. As usual in the case of women, an unknown but considerable number must be taken into account as (more or less gainfully) employed outside official registration. During World War II, altogether about 2.5 million foreign women were brought to work, mostly by force, in German industry and agriculture to substitute – along with male foreign civilian workers and prisoners of war – for German men who were now at the battle lines. The lower their 'racial value', the higher was the proportion of women among these workers and the heavier their work: among the Russian civilian workers, 51 per cent were women, and 58 per cent of all Russians working in the munitions industries were women.

The prohibition of free abortion through the old section 218 of the Penal Code was tightened up in 1933, but the additional stringency (sections 219 and 220) had little effect; what was instead effective was the introduction of legal eugenic and medical indications for abortion in 1935. The number of women on whom eugenic abortions were performed for the sake of the *Volkskörper*, often against their will and without their consent or knowledge and always combined with compulsory sterilization, was about 30,000. Voluntary abortions continued to take place, despite difficult conditions, at hundreds of thousands per year. By contrast with what is frequently asserted, the number of convictions for free and illegal abortion under section 218 did not rise during National Socialism, but fell by about one-sixth by comparison with the Weimar Republic (from 1923–32: 47,487 to 1933–42: 39,902).[17] The number of women who were forced to abort against their will or without their consent and who were compulsorily sterilized is over ten times as high as the number of the women convicted under section 218. During this period, *Gebärzwang* (compulsory childbearing) did not go beyond what was usual before 1933, after 1945 or in other countries. National Socialist compulsion and terror was reserved for antinatalism, not for pronatalism. National Socialism did not nationalize the birth question, as often asserted, by compelling women into childbearing, but by preventing women from childbearing.

Instead, an increase in births was one of the goals of state welfare measures that were to assist those who wanted to have children, at a time when politicians still believed, or at least hoped, that economic support might influence men's and women's choice to have children. On the level of central government, they consisted mainly in three social reforms that were part of the much-publicized, largely tax-funded *Familienlastenausgleich* (relief of family burdens) which no longer conceived of family subsidies as poor relief but as independent state benefits. In 1933, marriage loans were introduced for husbands whose wife had been employed and gave up her job upon marriage (but from 1936 on, with full employment, she could keep it and was often pressed to do so). They were not paid in cash, but in the form of coupons to be used for the purchase of furniture and household equipment, and they were to be repaid at a modest interest and to be forgone by one-fourth per birth, i.e. up to the birth of four children (unless they were spaced with longer intervals, during which interest had to be paid). One of the main objectives of this loan was to lower the male marriage age and therefore men's need for prostitution. Second, in 1934 and 1939 the income tax was reformed to give heads of household increasing exemption amounts for spouse and children, and the income tax for the childless (couples as well as single men and women) was raised. Third, monthly state child allowances of 10 marks were introduced in 1936, payable from the fifth, three years later from the third child on. Initially, they were a form of poor relief, to be paid only to those below a certain income level; later on, the income limit was abolished. In international comparison,[18] such measures were not, or did not remain, unique: marriage loans were introduced in Italy, Sweden and Spain during the 1930s, and similar tax reforms and child allowances in most European countries between the late 1920s and the late 1940s. All national types of family allowances, including the German ones (but apparently with the exception of the French ones), shared one feature: they were not to cover the costs of childbearing and raising, and particularly National Socialists warned that this should 'not become a profitable business'. But it deserves to be underlined that in most other countries child allowances were paid from the first or second child on.

Nonetheless, National Socialist state subsidies differed from others in two major respects. One of them (although it resembled the model of the two other masculinist dictatorships, Italy and Spain) was their combination with sexism: they privileged fathers over mothers. The principle was laid down by a Nazi minister, Hans Frank, when he declared that 'the concept of fatherhood has been handed down through age-old processes of natural law' and 'the concept of father is unambiguous and must be placed at the centre of the financial measures'. Here it was fatherhood, not motherhood, that was glorified as 'nature': a nature, however, that did not exclude economic rewards – as in the case of women's nature – but included them. In Germany, this view may have been reinforced by current racial visions of 'nordic patriarchalism' (*vaterrechtlicher Geist der nordischen Rasse*). It was the prospective husband who was entitled to the marriage loan. Family allowances went not to mothers, but to fathers – different from Britain, Sweden, Norway and in part also from France. German single mothers received child allowances only if the father of their children was known to the authorities. The tax rebates for the head of household brought by far the most substantial benefits, particularly for husbands in the upper income brackets. The husband's tax exemption for children was less significant than that for his wife: it was he who was being paid by the state for her housework (Goebbels had momentarily polemicized against the high rate of the husband's wife rebate).[19]

The 'relief of family burdens' was meant to balance out, not the differing burdens of fathers and mothers, but the differing burdens of bachelors and fathers, so that – in the words of the State Secretary to the Ministry of Finance, praised by the head of the Party Race Policy Office – 'a man will no longer be materially or morally worse off in competition with the so-called clever bachelor, merely because he has done his duty to his nation.' The 'duty' of begetting was considered more valuable than that of bearing and rearing children, women's contribution to procreation inferior to men's. This was not an old-fashioned cult of motherhood, but a modern cult of fatherhood.

Fatherhood deserved economic rewards from the state, motherhood was seen as incompatible with them. Accordingly, the male leader of the party's welfare organization (*Nationalsozialistische Volkswohlfahrt*, NSV) and its section 'Mother and Child' condemned the 'reward motive' (*Lohnmotiv*) of 'selfish love' and stressed that

> there is no more beautiful image of selfless service than that of a mother with her children. She continues to care and to give, to show her child love upon love, never thinking whether she is going to get anything in return . . . In the very moment she began to calculate returns, she would cease to be a good mother.[20]

The cult of motherhood was to some extent propaganda and ritual, the cult of fatherhood was propaganda and tough state policy. Of course it was not the family subsidies as such that were anti-woman, but the fact that they were refused to mothers and houseworkers.

Nonetheless, it was the NSV section 'Mother and Child' that supported mothers with many children, pregnant women and unmarried mothers, helping them to find employment, establishing kindergartens and offering vacations from home – not, however, as a right, but as poor relief, not as a new civic recognition by the state as in the case of fathers (and as to some degree in the case of the state-run Italian ONMI), but as a traditional handout.[21] Nazi women's organizations also supported 'valuable' mothers, but since they had no funds to offer, they offered courses on baby care. Whereas the NSV's support focused on the poor among the 'valuable' and the women's organizations on women of all classes, and whereas single mothers with more than one child risked being taken to a sterilization court, in 1936 Himmler created the *Lebensborn* organization in order to assist those mothers who bore children by men who were thought to belong to the racial elite, mostly SS-men. The *Lebensborn* was not an institution for forced breeding nor an SS bordello. It established well-furnished maternity hospitals (six in Germany, later nine in Norway, one in Belgium and one in France), mostly in the countryside. In Germany, about 7,000–8,000 women gave birth in such homes over the nine years of the *Lebensborn*'s existence (plus, 6,000 in Norway during the war), and about 55 per cent of them were single mothers. Before being admitted to the maternity homes, they were carefully selected, often by Himmler himself, according to the ethnic and eugenic credentials of the father of their child and of their own. But from 1939 on, the *Lebensborn* homes in Germany were used for those 'valuable' children of the conquered territories in the East whose parents had been killed or who had been kidnapped in the course of Himmler's 'search for nordic blood'.[22]

For most women, there were only the cheap honours of Mother's Day and – for those with four children or more – the mother cross; the former was introduced in the 1920s (as in many other countries), the latter in 1939, years after the father-centred reforms, upon the French model of 1920 (in 1944 to be imitated in the Soviet Union). Even though the Nazi state enacted no law in favour of mothers as such, ten years after its beginnings, in 1942, it considerably improved the 1927 law for the protection of those pregnant women and young mothers who were employed – with the exception of Jewish, Polish and Russian women – in order to encourage them to combine employment and motherhood, particularly in war-work, but also in a long-term perspective. Maternity leave of six weeks before and six weeks after parturition remained as established in 1927 and was combined with a maternity benefit amounting to the full wage; agricultural and domestic workers were finally included, and the job continued to be protected against dismissal during pregnancy and four months after. The major innovation of the law was its provision for childcare services. However, maternity benefits were reserved to employed mothers only. Mothers were awarded state recognition and benefits only if they worked in addition outside their home. When in 1942 Robert Ley, the leader of the German Labour Front (the Nazi surrogate union) proposed to extend maternity benefits to non-employed women too, particularly the hard-working working-class mothers, Hitler rejected the proposal on the grounds that the state budget was needed for the 'difficult tasks' of the next years:[23] the costs of military and non-military massacres.

The effect of pronatalist propaganda and of those welfare measures which included pronatalist goals was limited. The figures for the birth-rate (in 1933 they were among the lowest in Europe, along with Britain and Austria) increased by about one-third until 1936 (from a net reproduction rate of 0.7 to one of 0.9); then they remained almost stagnant, reaching no more than the level of the late 1920s, which had long been deplored as an expression of 'birth-strike' and 'race suicide', and they dropped again during World War II. Most of the increase was due to couples who had not been able to have the children they wanted because of depression and epidemics in the early 1930s and who made up for it when employment and income increased. The proportion of married women with four or more children (viz. the number proposed by Nazi demographers as 'valuable' women's 'duty') among all married women declined from 25 per cent in 1933 to 21 per cent in 1939. Those who married and had children from 1933 on limited their number to one, two or three children and thus followed the trend which had characterized Germany, as well as other industrialized countries, before the Nazi regime. The family benefits contributed not to an increase in births (even less the mother cross) but, at least before the war, to a growing belief in the capacity of the Nazi regime to overcome the depression. Whereas Nazi politicians had hoped that state welfare for children would increase their number, most men and women perceived it simply as a social reform that compensated for their low income and helped them survive with the children they wanted. Some women, including some Nazi women, protested openly against the reinforcement of male dominance through father-centred benefits, but such voices were silent after 1934.[24]

The behaviour of three particular groups illustrates both the specificity and the limits of the Nazi type of pronatalism as well as some motives for having children which usually remain hidden behind demographic figures. The leading Party functionaries, i.e. those 'valuable' Germans who were the real objectives of pronatalism and who were closest to National Socialism, demonstrated that they believed in the pronatalist goals, if at all, only for others but not for themselves. Nazi demographers deplored that of those functionaries who had married between 1933 and 1937, 18 per cent were still childless in 1939, 42 per cent had one child and 29 per cent had two children. Among the all-male SS members, 61 per cent were unmarried in 1942, and the married ones had 1.1 children on average; the same was true for medical doctors, who were the professional group with the highest membership figures in the party and the SS. Obviously, there was an inverse relationship between adherence to National Socialism among the elite and the number of their children.[25] On the other side, one statistical group had a clearly above-average number of children: those whose claim for marriage loans and child allowances was rejected because of their 'disorderly' conduct and their classification as 'large asocial families'. In respect of such people, Nazi demographers also deplored that up to half of the families with above-average numbers of children were to be considered undesirable.[26] The third group are those who produced two minor, but conspicuous, baby booms during World War II, when the average figures were declining, which were often noted and explained by contemporaries. In 1939, employed women, particularly of the working class, were forbidden to quit their job because they were urgently needed for the war economy – unless they were pregnant. Pregnant women and young mothers were also exempted from the labour conscription introduced in 1943. On both occasions, many women preferred to have children instead of working for the war, and this was one major reason why between 1939 and 1941, the number of employed women decreased by 500,000. All three groups illustrate – in different ways and to different degrees – that in Nazi Germany, the refusal to procreate and the use of contraceptives and abortion was not, as has been argued for other countries, an indication of political opposition.[27]

The second group is a pointer to the second outstanding feature of National Socialist state family benefits: their combination with racism. Race policy distinguished them from those in all other countries. None of the Nazi benefits was meant to be universally applied (not even to men and despite the abolition of the upper income limit), since those classified as *minderwertig* were excluded: parents or children who were considered eugenically or ethnically 'unfit' – Jews (to whom even family-related tax rebates were denied), Gypsies, the physically, emotionally and mentally handicapped (particularly, but not only, the sterilized), 'asocials', political opponents, labourers from eastern Europe. For instance, whereas in other countries and in Germany before 1933, a handicapped child was a reason for extending child benefits beyond the usual age limit, in Nazi Germany it was a reason for excluding it, and its parents, entirely.[28] With respect to the 'inferior', National Socialism pursued a policy not of family welfare, but of family destruction.

Government subsidies for marriage and procreation were not in themselves part of sexism and racism. They were a component of the emerging modern welfare states which for the first time in history subsidised the family, the sphere of male reproduction and female housework. But National Socialism combined them with sexism and with racism by privileging men over women and 'valuable German' men over 'racially inferior' men. The combination of the *Familienlastenausgleich* with racism was specific and unique to National Socialism; its combination with sexism was specific to it, as well as to other European dictatorships, and it distinguished them from the European democracies. Hence National Socialist birth and family policy consisted not of 'pronatalism and a cult of motherhood', but of antinatalism and a cult of fatherhood and masculinity. Not a deterministic, but a historical continuity leads from there to the escalation of racism in the 1940s.

FROM ANTINATALISM TO GENOCIDE

During World War II, it was not maternity but its very opposite that came to play a significant role in the race policy of those years, including its murderous forms. The antinatalist 'primacy of the state in the sphere of life' was now extended to a number of women who were far from being a minority and, more importantly, it implied the primacy of the state in the sphere of death.

When war was declared in 1939, legal sterilization was curtailed, mainly in order to liberate work-forces for war and massacre. But antinatalism took on other forms, directed almost exclusively against women. Early in the war, Polish women were sent back east upon pregnancy, and it seems that many deliberately took advantage of this method to be relieved from forced labour: their gesture was, again, babies rather than war-work. But from 1941 on, Russian and Polish women had to stay despite pregnancy, were encouraged and often forced to undergo an abortion, sometimes also sterilization, and often their children were taken away from them, in a complex interplay between Himmler's race experts, labour offices, employers and the medical profession. Particularly Russian women were purposefully put to work at 'men's jobs' in the munitions industry so as to bring about miscarriages: a policy of war-work against babies. The plans for the conquered Eastern territories (particularly the *Generalplan Ost*) included a large number of carefully elaborated, voluntary and non-voluntary methods of decreasing the number of children born, which aimed almost exclusively at mothers and potential mothers.[29]

Around the same time, sterilization experiments were pursued in some of the concentration camps, under Himmler's command, particularly in Auschwitz and Ravensbrück, on Jews and Gypsies. Originally they were meant for sterilizing the Jewish 'half-breeds' (*Judenmischlinge*) who were exempted from extermination. After the failure of experiments with chemicals and X-rays on women as well as men, the experiments focused on women only, through injections in the uterus. They were performed by Clauberg, who since 1934 had gained experience in sterilizing women and was searching for a 'bloodless' method, i.e. without operations, complications, resistance and death. His method had advanced so far by 1943 that he considered he was able, with a team of ten men, to sterilize up to a thousand women per day. By now, the new procedure was aimed not only at female Jewish 'half-breeds', but also at mass sterilizations of other women, hopefully – in Clauberg's words – 'during the usual gynaecological investigation familiar to every doctor'.[30] Jewish and Gypsy women in the camps became the model for the fate that in future was to be earmarked for hundreds of thousands of ethnically and eugenically 'inferior' women.

National Socialist sterilization policy before 1939, called 'prevention of unworthy life', was also a 'forerunner'[31] of the 'annihilation of unworthy life' ('euthanasia' or 'action T4'). It started in 1939, and up to 1945 around 200,000 ill, old and handicapped people, mostly inmates of psychiatric clinics, women as well as men, were killed after having been selected as 'incurable' or unable to work. Moreover, all Jewish inmates were killed, even without such selection, and therefore T4 was also the first phase of the systematic massacre of the Jews. Special killing gas was used for the first time in T4. It was for various reasons that National Socialist antinatalism led to this policy of massacre. It grew out of a mentality which saw sterilization not as a private and free choice, but as a 'humane' alternative to killing for the sake of the *Volkskörper*, as an 'elimination without massacre',[32] as a political substitute for 'nature' which 'naturally' (i.e. without modern charity and medicine) would have prevented 'unfit' people from surviving. Second, it was in sterilization policy that medical and psychiatric experts had already become used to dealing with bodily intervention and death, mostly that of women. Third, the very first victims of the massacre were 5,000 handicapped children up to the age of three years, i.e. precisely those whose mothers (and fathers) could not be identified before birth, since 1937, by means of the abortion and sterilization policy. Finally, many of those who had been active in, or had advocated, the policy of compulsory sterilization, were also active in the massacre of the ill – mostly doctors and other medical personnel – and many of them also played an important role in the genocide of the Jews.

In late 1941, the T4 gas chambers and their male personnel were transferred from Germany to the newly constructed death camps in the occupied eastern territories where they served for the systematic and industrial killing of

millions of Jews and Gypsies, women as well as men. This transfer was
not only one of technology, but also one of mentality and strategy, and it
had significant gender dimensions which have by far not yet been sufficiently
explored. Hundreds of thousands of Jews had already been killed before gas
was used, mostly through mass shooting. The SS men involved seem to
have had considerable 'psychological difficulties', particularly with shooting
women and children, as was underlined, for instance, by the commandant
of the Auschwitz camp; even Himmler and Eichmann became sick while
watching executions which included women and children, and they asked
for new methods to be developed. Gas technology was introduced, from
late 1941, not only as a means to accelerate mass killing, but also because a
'"suitable" method', a 'humane' alternative to overt bloodshed, was required
which would relieve the SS-men of their largely gender-specific scruples.[33]
The first mobile gas vans were applied mainly, sometimes exclusively, for the
killing of women and children; 'men, women and children' is the frequent
description of the gas van victims. In the early phase of the massacre of
the Jewish ghetto population, the majority of the victims were women.[34]
When the stable gas chambers in Auschwitz were functioning, from late
1941, it was mostly Jewish women, and particularly those with children
who were selected for death right upon arrival – 'every Jewish child meant
automatically death to its mother' – whereas most able-bodied Jewish men
were sent to forced labour. Almost two-thirds of the German Jews deported
to and killed in the death camps were women, and 56 per cent among those
Gypsies who were sent into the Auschwitz gas chambers;[35] the precise
number of women among the other millions of dead will forever remain
unknown. A recent study of the Nazi doctors in the death camps found
that these men, who turned from healers into killers, were able to function
largely because of male bonding, heavy drinking and their adaption to an
'overall Nazi male ideal'.[36]

The leading massacre experts were by no means blind to such gender
dimensions of genocide, and in 1943 Himmler exhorted his SS men in a
speech which summed up earlier reflections:

> We came to the question: what about the women and children? I have
> decided to find a clear solution here too. In fact I did not regard myself
> as justified in exterminating the men – let us say killing them or have them
> killed – while letting avengers in the shape of children grow up.

Hence, Jewish women were killed as women, as childbearers and mothers of
the next generation of their people. But Himmler went even further, placing
the female victims at the centre of his own definition of genocide:

> When I was forced somewhere in some village to act against partisans and
> against Jewish commissars, . . . then as a principle I gave the order to
> kill the women and children of those partisans and commissars too . . .

Believe you me, that order was not so easy to give or so simple to carry out as it was logically thought out and can be stated in this hall. But we must constantly recognise that we are engaged in a primitive, primordial, natural race struggle.

Here, in the successful attempt to overcome male scruples towards a war of men against women, the National Socialist *Rassenkampf* in its most extreme form was defined as a deadly struggle of men not just against men – such as in a traditional military war – but also, and particularly, against women as mothers. The significance of this largely women-centred definition of 'race struggle' has been recognized by some historians as one element of the singularity of the National Socialist genocide of the Jewish people.[37]

Female activists in Nazi race policies were a minority among the perpetrators and a minority among women generally, though a remarkably tough and efficient one. The more active among them were usually unmarried and without children. They were from all social classes except for the highest ones, and their participation in racist policies was mostly, as in the case of many men, a function of their job or profession. Whereas the sterilization policy was entirely directed by men, some of the female social workers and medical doctors helped select the candidates. Nurses in the six T4 killing centres assisted the male doctors in selecting and killing. Some women academics co-operated with their male superiors in Gypsy studies and laid the groundwork for the selection and extermination of Gypsies; for this purpose they used their easier access, as women, to Gypsies and Gypsy culture. Female camp guards who supervised women in the concentration camps came mostly from a lower or working-class background and had volunteered for the job in expectation of some upward mobility. Among all women activists, they were closest to the centre of the killing operations and responsible for their functioning; it is misleading to believe that 'they did not affect the workings of the Nazi state'.[38] National Socialist racism was not only institutionalized as a state policy, but also professionalized.

Historians, including some feminist ones, have argued that German women's share of guilt and responsibility for Nazi evil was to have adjusted to Nazism by believing in motherhood and by being nothing else but mothers and wives, a view that has been common, particularly among the left, for a long time.[39] But those women who participated in it did not believe in maternalism as a feature of the female sex, were rarely mothers and did not act as mothers; instead they adjusted themselves to male-dominated political, professional and job strategies, to professionalized race policy. More importantly, neither was the image of women as mothers at the core of the Nazi view of the female sex as a whole, nor was that view, to the degree that it played some role, specific to National Socialism. Instead, from the beginnings of National Socialism modern eugenics (race hygiene) had taken precedence over traditional procreative ethics; within modern eugenics its 'negative' (antinatalist) strand had taken precedence over its 'positive' (pronatalist) strand, and within its 'positive' strand modern welfare policy had taken precedence over the earlier fantasies of 'genius-breeding'. What was left of the latter was the more realistic and successful attempt at curtailing the procreation of allegedly 'feeble-minded' people and of 'inferior' peoples and, finally, to prevent the latter from living. This race policy, in all its complexity, was at the core of National Socialism, was its novelty and specificity; it shaped National Socialism's multiple views of women. Most of all, it broke with the maternalist image of the female sex. Under National Socialism, the values of maternity and maternalism, like human values in general, had reached an historical and international nadir.

*

When German women and men were liberated from this murderous regime, they were also liberated from state antinatalism. But paradoxically enough, the Allied Control Commission, the American MIlitary Tribunal and later German jurisdiction maintained that on the one hand, the Nazi sterilization policy was neither a crime to be brought before a court nor part of the regime's racism (because sterilization laws existed also in the United States), and on the other hand, that child allowances (not, however, tax rebates) were part of the regime's racism and therefore payment had to be stopped. Thus in the late 1940s, when some European states, e.g. Britain and Norway, introduced child allowances as the first major reform of their fully developing welfare states, Germany was almost the only European country without child allowances.[40]

Both the East and West German constitutions included a clause on the equal rights of men and women, following the example of the Weimar constitution (which National Socialism had not bothered to abolish). In East Germany, which followed the model of the Soviet Union, equal rights were now interpreted as women's duty to perform extra-domestic work; domestic labour was downgraded (somewhat following Lenin's notorious scornful views on women's domestic work) and propaganda pressed housewives to take on a job and therebyhelp establish socialism and give precedence to the 'We' instead of the 'I', to the collectivity instead to selfishness.[41] This policy was reinforced by low wages and, in 1950, by maternity provisions for employed women (maternity leave with full wage replacement); necessitous mothers and widows received welfare grants only if they were incapable of performing extra-domestic work, often 'asocial' unmarried mothers had their children taken away, and whereas all mothers received a single grant at the birth of the third and further children, a universal monthly child allowance was paid only from the fourth child on. In reaction to an extreme fertility decline and with the development of a 'welfare socialism' in the 1970s, it was resolved that 'the services of bearing and rearing children in the family are to be recognized and valued':[42] by special female labour law (a forty-hour week for mothers who tended two or more children), temporary support for single mothers who wished to quit their job, and a paid 'baby year' for mothers at the birth of second and further children.

Nor was mother-work as such valued by the early West German state, which also guaranteed equal rights in its constitution. Confinement benefit for employed women was improved; when child allowances (*Kindergeld*) were reintroduced in 1954, they functioned upon the older French model of employers' equalization funds and were paid to employed fathers of third and subsequent children. Only in 1964 the federal government took over the responsibility, universalizing and gradually raising the allowance as well as the number of eligible children; even though the law provided for payment either to the father or to the mother, it was usually the father who requested it. Until 1975, the major tool continued to be (breadwinner-focused) tax deductions for wife and children.[43] In 1979, the Social Democratic government introduced a (modestly) paid maternity leave of half a year (beyond confinement benefits), and in 1987, the Christian Democratic/Liberal government replaced it by a universal 'childraising allowance' of up to 600 marks per month for a period of one and a half years. It differs from Lily Braun's similar ideal, suggested over eighty years before,[44] in two important features: it does not fully cover needs, and it is payable either to the mother or to the father, depending on who chooses child care instead of employment. Even though few feminists of the new women's movement have struggled for this reform, it would hardly have come about without the coincidence between the rise of the modern welfare state and the growth of women's movements in the twentieth century. It remains to be seen whether the difficult process of unifying Germany in a free welfare state will also recognize and respect the political and social rights of mothers and women generally.

NOTES

1 G. A. Ritter, *Der Sozialstaat. Entstehung und Entwicklung im internationalen Vergleich*, Munich, Oldenbourg, 1989, esp. pp. 130–8; P. Flora and A. J. Heidenheimer (eds), *The Development of Welfare States in Europe and America*, New Brunswick, Transaction, 1981, esp. p. 83; H. Kaelble, *Auf dem Weg zu einer europäischen Gesellschaft. Eine Sozialgeschichte Westeuropas 1880–1980*, Munich, Beck, 1987.

2 W. Frick, *Bevölkerungs- und Rassenpolitik*, Langensalza, Beyer, 1933; A. T. Allen, 'German radical feminism and eugencis, 1900–1918', *German Studies Review*, 1989, vol. 11, pp. 31–56, esp. pp. 45–6; G. Bäumer, *Die Frau im neuen Lebensraum*, Berlin, Herbig, 1931, esp. pp. 207–10, 229–30; G. Bock, *Zwangssterilisation im Nationalsozialismus: Studien zur Rassenpolitik und Frauenpolitik*, Opladen, Westdeutscher Verlag, 1986, ch. 1.

3 W. Frick, *Bevölkerungs- und Rassenpolitik*; A. Gütt, E. Rüdin and F. Ruttke, *Gesetz zur Verhütung erbkranken Nachwuchses vom 14. Juli 1933*, Munich, Lehmann, 1934 (hereafter GRR), p. 60; G. Bock, *Zwangssterilisation*, ch. IV.3.

4 G. Bock, *Zwangssterilisation*, esp. pp. 182ff., 281, 302ff., 400, 421ff.

5 Quotes from A. Hitler, *Mein Kampf*, vol. II, Munich, Eher, 1928, pp. 80–1; W. Feldscher, *Rassen- und Erbpflege im deutschen Recht*, Berlin, Deutscher Rechtsverlag, 1943, pp. 26, 118; B. F. Smith and A.F. Peterson (eds), *Heinrich Himmler: Geheimreden 1933–1945*, Frankfurt, Propyläen, 1974, p. 54–5. For the Nazi concept of the 'production' of the 'master race' see H. Arendt, *The Origins of Totalitarianism*, New York, Harcourt Brace Jovanovich, 1968, ch. 12 with note 54. For the sterilization of Gypsies, Blacks and Jews see G. Bock, *Zwangssterilisation*, pp. 353–63.

6 GRR, p. 176; H. Burkhardt, *Der rassenhygienische Gedanke und seine Grundlagen*, Munich, Reinhardt, 1930, p. 93.

7 GRR, p. 5.

8 L.G. Tirala (Ministry of Propaganda), 'Die wirtschaftlichen Folgen des Sterilisierungsgesetzes', *Volk und Rasse*, 1933, vol. 8, pp. 162–4; G. Bock, *Zwangssterilisation*, pp. 372–80.

9 G. Bock, *Zwangssterilisation*, pp. 280, 384 (quotes), 97–9, 386.

10 Quotes and documents in ibid., pp. 431, 396, 212, 398–9, 393.

11 Of 22 April and 22 August 1936: ibid., pp. 401–31, 322–5.

12 *Juristische Wochenschrift*, 1935, vol. 64, p. 2143; *Staatsarchiv Freiburg*, Gesundheitsamt Lörrach, no. 534.

13 E. von Barsewitsch, *Die Aufgaben der Frau für die Aufartung*, Berlin, Reichdruckerei, 1933, p. 14; she referred (like many others of the time and like earlier radical feminists such as Helene Stöcker) to Nietzsche's saying 'Thou shalt not propagate, but elevate, the race' (see K. Anthony, *Feminism in Germany and Scandinavia*, New York, Holt, 1915, p. 94). A. Bluhm, 'Das Gesetz zur Verhütung erbkranken Nachwuchses', *Die Frau*, 1934, vol. 41, pp. 529–38; J. Haarer, 'Die rassenpolitischen Aufgaben des Deutschen Frauenwerks', *Neues Volk*, 1938, vol. 6, no. 4, pp. 17–19; the following quote: M. Hess, 'Das Gesetz zur Verhütung erbkranken Nachwuchses', *N.S.-Frauenwarte*, 1935, vol. 4, no. 2, pp. 33–6. Among the women (and men) who actively opposed sterilization propaganda and activity, the Catholics were the most prominent and they referred to the papal encyclical *Casti Connubi* of 1930 which condemned eugenic sterilization.

14 'Richtlinien für eine bevölkerungspolitische Propaganda und Volksaufklärung', *Bundesarchiv Koblenz* (BAK), NS 18/712; *Partei-Archiv*, Nov. 1937, p. 19; W. Knorr, 'Kinderreichenauslese durch das Rassenpolitische Amt der NSDAP in Sachsen', *Volk und Rasse*, 1936, vol. 11, p. 270. Cf. G. Bock, *Zwangssterilisation*, pp. 122–3, 129–31.

15 R. W. Darré, *Neuadel aus Blut und Boden*, Munich, Lehmann, 1930, pp. 169–71; W. Gross, 'Denkschrift zur Frage des unehelichen Kindes als Problem der deutschen Bevölkerungspolitik' (1944), BAK, R 22/485; H. Linden, minutes of a meeting on population policy 1935, *Auswärtiges Amt, Politisches Archiv*, Inland I Partei 84/4.

16 D. Winkler, *Frauenarbeit im 'Dritten Reich'*, Hamburg, Hoffman & Campe, 1977, esp. chs 2 and 5, pp. 198, 201; S. Bajohr, *Die Hälfte der Fabrik*, Marburg, Arbeiterpolitik, 1979, ch. 4, esp. p. 252; A. Willms, 'Grundzüge der Entwicklung der Frauenarbeit von 1880 bis 1980', in W. Müller *et al.*, *Strukturwandel der Frauenarbeit 1880–1980*, Frankfurt a.M., Campus Verlag, 1983, p. 35. For the following figures see also R. Hachtmann, 'Industriearbeiterinnen in der

deutschen Kriegswirtschaft, 1935–1945' (forthcoming); C. Kirkpatrick, *Woman in Nazi Germany*, London, Jarrolds, 1939, ch. 7; U. Herbert, *Fremdarbeiter*, Bonn, Dietz, 1985.

17 Figures from *Statistisches Jahrbuch für das deutsche Reich*, 1926–1942, vols 45–59; G. Bock, *Zwangssterilisation*, pp. 160–3, 388. There were few convictions for sections 219 and 220. For a comparable situation in fascist Italy, see Detragiache, quoted in Saraceno's contribution to this volume, note 1.

18 The best overview is still D. V. Glass, *Population Policies and Movements in Europe*, (first edn 1940) repr. London, Frank Cass, 1967. For Nazi pronatalism and its impact see G. Bock, *Zwangssterilisation*, pp. 141–77.

19 Quotes from H. Frank, speech of 18 Nov. 1937 (BAK, R 61/130); H.F.K. Günther, *Rassenkunde des deutschen Volkes*, Munich, Lehmann, 1923, pp. 345f., 274ff.; Goebbels' criticism (1941): BAK, R2/31097.

20 F. Reinhard, quoted in W. Gross, 'Unsere Arbeit gilt der deutschen Familie', *Nationalsozialistische Monatshefte*, 1939, vol. 9, pp. 103–4; Hilgenfeldt reporting to Bormann about a conversation with Himmler, 16 September 1942 (BAK, NS 18/2427).

21 J. Stephenson, *The Nazi Organisation of Women*, London, Croom Helm, 1981, esp. p. 164; see Saraceno's article in this volume.

22 G. Lilienthal, *Der 'Lebensborn e.V.'*, Stuttgart, Gustav Fischer, 1985, esp. pp. 53, 66–7, 100, 113, 182–3, 242–4. Despite the *Lebensborn* children's privileges, they were not spared being killed if they were 'incurably ill'.

23 Documents in G. Bock, *Zwangssterilisation*, pp. 174–5.

24 C. Heinrichs, 'Besoldung der Mutterschaftsleistung', *Die Frau*, 1934, vol. 41, pp. 343–8; I. Reichenau (ed.), *Deutsche Frauen an Adolf Hitler*, Leipzig, Klein, sd (1933), pp. 7, 15, 37. For the demographic figures see G. Bock, *Zwangssterilisation*, pp. 143–6, 151–7, 168 and 173.

25 K. Astel and E. Weber, *Die Kinderzahl der 29.000 politischen Leiter des Gaues Thüringen der NSDAP*, Berlin, Metzner, 1943, pp. 87, 114ff., 157, 161; Koller, 'Haben Ärzte im Durchschnitt wirklich nur 1,1 Kinder?', *Deutsches Ärzteblatt*, 1942, vol. 72, p. 343.

26 F. Burgdörfer, *Geburtenschwund*, Heidelberg, Vowinckel, 1942, pp. 157, 184; W. Knorr, 'Praktische Rassenpolitik', *Volk und Rasse*, 1938, vol. 13, pp. 69–73.

27 See Nash's contribution to this volume (note 41) as well as Saraceno's (note 27). For the two baby booms see G. Bock, *Zwangssterilisation*, pp. 168–9.

28 D.V. Glass, *Population Policies*, pp. 106, 253, 293.

29 H. Heiber (ed.), 'Der Generalplan Ost', *Vierteljahrshefte für Zeitgeschichte*, 1958, vol. 6, pp. 317–8; G. Bock, *Zwangssterilisation*, pp. 442–51.

30 J. Sehn, 'Carl Claubergs verbrecherische Unfruchtbarmachungs-Versuche an Häftlings-Frauen in den Nazi-Konzentrationslagern', *Hefte von Auschwitz*, vol. 2, Oswiecim, 1959, pp. 3–32; R. Hilberg, *The Destruction of the European Jews*, New York, Holmes & Meir, 1985, vol. III, pp. 940–46, 1081.

31 R.J. Lifton, *The Nazi Doctors. Medical Killing and the Psychology of Genocide*, New York, Basic Books, 1986, p. 22.

32 H.-W. Schmuhl, *Rassenhygiene, Nationalsozialismus, Euthanasie*, Göttingen, Vandenhoeck & Ruprecht, 1987, p. 40. For the 1942 decree, mentioned below, see G. Bock, *Zwangssterilisation*, pp. 358–9.

33 R.J. Lifton, *The Nazi Doctors*, p. 159, also pp. 15, 147; M. Broszat (ed.), *Kommandant in Auschwitz*, Munich, DTV, 1963, p. 127; R. Hilberg, *Destruction*, vol. I, pp. 332–4.

34 R. Hilberg, *Destruction*, vol. II, pp. 690–1; vol. III, p. 871; J. Ringelheim, 'Deportations, deaths and survival: Nazi ghetto policies against women and men

in occupied Poland', in T. Wobbe (ed.), *Nach Osten : Verdeckte Spuren national-sozialistischer Verbrechen*, Frankfurt a.M., Neue Kritik, 1991; J. Ringelheim, 'Women and the Holocaust', *Signs*, 1985, vol. 10, pp. 741–61; E. Kogon *et al.* (eds.), *Nationalsozialistische Massentötungen durch Giftgas*, Frankfurt, Fischer, 1986, e.g. pp. 88, 91, 93–7, 105–8, 122, 131, 134, 158, 210–15.

35   L. Adelsberger, *Auschwitz*, Berlin, Lettner, 1953, pp. 126–8 (quote); M. Richarz, *Jüdisches Leben in Deutschland*, Stuttgart, Deutsche Verlags-Anstalt, 1982, vol. 3, p. 61; J. Ficowski, 'Die Vernichtung', in T. Zülch (ed.), *In Auschwitz vergast, bis heute verfolgt: Zur Situation der Roma (Zigeuner) in Deutschland und Europa*, Reinbek, Rowohlt, 1979, pp. 135–6.

36   R.J. Lifton, *The Nazi Doctors*, p. 462; see also pp. 193–6, 199, 231, 312–3, 317, 443.

37   By E. Jäckel, 'Die elende Praxis der Untersteller', in *'Historikerstreit'. Die Dokumentation der Kontroverse um die Einzigartigkeit der nationalsozialistischen Judenvernichtung*, Munich, Piper, 1987, p. 118. E. Nolte objected on the grounds that this massacre of women (and boys and old men) was self-evident; therefore it seemed to him superflous to mention it specifically (ibid., pp. 229–30). Himmler's speeches: F. Smith and A.F. Peterson (eds), *Heinrich Himmler*, pp. 169, 201.

38   C. Koonz, *Mothers in the Fatherland*, New York, St Martin's Press, 1987, p. 405. For women's professional and job strategies in the context of race policy see R. Gilsenbach, 'Wie Lolitschai zur Doktorwürde kam', in W. Ayass *et al.*, *Feinderklärung und Prävention*, Berlin, Rotbuch, 1988, pp. 101–34; H. Friedlander, in E. Katz and J. Ringelheim (eds), *Proceedings of the Conference 'Women Surviving the Holocaust'*, New York, Institute for Research in History, 1983, pp. 115–16; G. Bock, *Zwangssterilisation*, p. 208.

39   C. Koonz, *Mothers*, esp. chs 1 and 11. Some leftist writers assume that 'among the persecuted and incarcerated, by far the majority were men' (R. Kühnl, 'Der deutsche Faschismus in der neueren Forschung', *Neue politische Literatur*, 1983, vol. 28, p. 71). For an influential criticism of this view see A. Tröger, 'Die Dolchstoss legende der Linken: "Frauen haben Hitler an die Macht gebracht"', in Berliner Dozentinnengruppe (ed.), *Frauen und Wissenschaft*, Berlin, Courage, 1977, pp. 324–55.

40.   See V. Hentschel, *Geschichte der deutschen Sozialpolitik 1880–1980*, Frankfurt a.M., Suhrkamp, 1983, pp. 139, 202; G. Bock, *Zwangssterilisation*, pp. 115–16, 244–6.

41   'Das "Wir" steht vor dem "Ich"', *Frau von heute*, 1959, vol. 39, p. 2, quoted in G. Obertreis, *Familienpolitik in der DDR 1945–1980*, Opladen, Westdeutscher Verlag, 1985, p. 146; also pp. 51–73, 119, 136–8, 155, 292–3.

42   E. Honecker, 'Neue Massnahmen zur Verwirklichung des sozialpolitischen Programms des VIII. Parteitages' (1972), quoted in G. Obertreis, *Familienpolitik*, p. 292; also pp. 315–18.

43   U. Gerhard *et al.* (eds), *Auf Kosten der Frauen. Frauenrechte im Sozialstaat*, Weinheim and Basel, Beltz, 1988, pp. 83, 91–2, 195; P. Flora (ed.), *Growth to Limits. The Western European Welfare States Since World War II*, Berlin, De Gruyter, 1986–87, vol. II, pp. 278–81.

44   See Stoehr's contribution to this volume.

Index